The Metamorphoses by Ovid

Books I-VII

Literally Translated into English Prose by Henry Thomas Riley

Publius Ovidius Naso but better known to us as simply Ovid was born on 20th March 43 BC in Sulmo (modern day Sulmona) in Italy.

He was educated in rhetoric in Rome in preparation for the practice of Law. Accounts of his character say that he was emotional and not able to stay within the argumentative boundaries of rhetoric disclipine. After the early death of his brother, Ovid ceased his law studies and travelled to Athens, Asia Minor, and Sicily. He held a number of minor public posts but, around 29-25 BC began to pursue poetry, a decision that brought with it his father's disapproval.

Ovid's first recitation occurred when he was eighteen (around 25 BC). He was part of the circle centered on the patron Marcus Valerius Messalla Corvinus, and appears to have been a friend of poets in the circle of Maecenas.

He married three times and divorced twice by the time he was thirty years old. He fathered a daughter, who eventually bore him grandchildren. His last wife was connected to the influential gens Fabia (an ancient Roman patrician family) and would help him during his later exile.

The first decades of Ovid's literary career were mostly spent writing poetry with erotic themes. The chronology of these early works cannot, however, be relied upon.

His earliest extant work is thought to be the 'Heroides', letters of mythological heroines to absent lovers, which is believed to have been published in 19 BC.

The first five-book collection of the 'Amores', erotic poems addressed to a lover, Corinna, is believed to have been published in 16–15 BC. The surviving three book version appears to have been published c. 8–3 BC.

Between these two editions of the 'Amores' his tragedy 'Medea', which was much admired in antiquity but is no longer extant, was performed.

Ovid buoyed by his glowing reputation now increased the tempo of his writing. 'Medicamina Faciei', was followed by the 'Ars Amatoria, the Art of Love' and immediately followed by 'Remedia Amoris'. This body of elegiac, erotic poetry saw Ovid cited as the equal of the Roman elegists Gallus, Tibullus, and Propertius.

By AD 8, he had completed his most ambitious work, the 'Metamorphoses', a 15-book hexameter epic poem. It catalogued Greek and Roman mythology, from the emergence of the universe to the apotheosis of Julius Caesar.

Concurrent with this, he worked on the 'Fasti', planned as 12-books but only 6 volumes (January to June were completed) in elegiac couplets on the calendar of Roman festivals and astronomy were completed. The remaining six books were interrupted by Ovid's sentence to exile.

In AD 8, Ovid was banished to Tomis, on the Black Sea, by the Emperor Augustus. This event shadowed his life and shaped his remaining poetic output. Ovid wrote that his exile was for carmen et error – "a poem and a mistake", claiming his crime was worse than murder, more harmful than poetry.

Ovid was also a contemporary of the older Virgil and Horace, with whom he is often ranked as one of the three canonical poets of Latin literature. The Imperial scholar Quintilian considered him the last of the Latin love elegists.

His poetry was much imitated during Late Antiquity and the Middle Ages, and greatly influenced Western art and literature. The Metamorphoses remains one of the most important sources of classical mythology.

In exile, Ovid wrote 'Tristia' and 'Epistulae ex Ponto', pointedly focused on his sadness and desolation. He was far from Rome and his beloved third wife.

The five books of the elegiac Tristia, a series of poems expressing the poet's despair in exile and advocating his return to Rome, are dated to AD 9–12.

'The Ibis', an elegiac curse poem attacking an adversary at home is also dated to this period. 'The Epistulae ex Ponto', a series of letters to friends in Rome asking them to effect his return, are thought to be his last compositions.

Ovid died at Tomis in AD 17 or 18. It is thought that the Fasti, which he spent time revising, were published posthumously.

Index of Contents

INTRODUCTION

The Metamorphoses of Ovid are a compendium of the Mythological narratives of ancient Greece and Rome, so ingeniously framed, as to embrace a large amount of information upon almost every subject connected with the learning, traditions, manners, and customs of antiquity, and have afforded a fertile field of investigation to the learned of the civilized world. To present to the public a faithful translation of a work, universally esteemed, not only for its varied information, but as being the masterpiece of one of the greatest Poets of ancient Rome, is the object of the present volume.

To render the work, which, from its nature and design, must, of necessity, be replete with matter of obscure meaning, more inviting to the scholar, and more intelligible to those who are unversed in Classical literature, the translation is accompanied with Notes and Explanations, which, it is believed, will be found to throw considerable light upon the origin and meaning of some of the traditions of heathen Mythology.

In the translation, the text of the Delphin edition has been generally adopted; and no deviation has been made from it, except in a few instances, where the reason for such a step is stated in the notes; at the same time, the texts of Burmann and Gierig have throughout been carefully consulted. The several editions vary materially in respect to punctuation; the Translator has consequently used his own discretion in adopting that which seemed to him the most fully to convey in each passage the intended meaning of the writer.

The Metamorphoses of Ovid have been frequently translated into the English language. On referring to Mr. Bohn's excellent Catalogue of the Greek and Latin Classics and their Translations, we find that the whole of the work has been twice translated into English Prose, while five translations in Verse are there enumerated. A prose version of the Metamorphoses was published by Joseph Davidson, about the middle of the last century, which professes to be "as near the original as the different idioms of the Latin and English will allow;" and to be "printed for the use of schools, as well as of private gentlemen." A few moments' perusal of this work will satisfy the reader that it has not the slightest pretension to be considered a literal translation, while, by its departure from the strict letter of the author, it has gained nothing in elegance of diction. It is accompanied by "critical, historical, geographical, and classical notes in English, from the best Commentators, both ancient and modern, beside a great number of notes, entirely new;" but notwithstanding this announcement, these annotations will be found to be but few in number, and, with some exceptions in the early part of the volume, to throw very little light on the obscurities of the text. A fifth edition of this translation was published so recently as 1822, but without any improvement, beyond the furbishing up of the old-fashioned language of the original preface. A far more literal translation of the Metamorphoses is that by John Clarke, which was first published about the year 1735, and had attained to a seventh edition in 1779. Although this version may be pronounced very nearly to fulfil the promise set forth in its title page, of being "as literal as possible," still, from the singular inelegance of its style, and the fact of its being couched in the conversational language of the early part of the last century, and being unaccompanied by any attempt at explanation, it may safely be pronounced to be ill adapted to the requirements of the present age. Indeed, it would not, perhaps, be too much to assert, that, although the translator may, in his own words, "have done an acceptable service to such gentlemen as are desirous of regaining or improving the skill they acquired at school," he has, in many instances, burlesqued rather than translated his author. Some of the curiosities of his version will be found set forth in the notes; but, for the purpose of the more readily justifying this assertion, a few of them are adduced: the word "nitidus" is always rendered "neat," whether applied to a fish, a cow, a chariot, a laurel, the steps of a temple, or the art of wrestling. He renders "horridus," "in a rude pickle;" "virgo" is generally translated "the young lady;" "vir" is "a gentleman;" "senex" and "senior" are indifferently "the old blade," "the old fellow," or "the old gentleman;" while "summa arx" is "the very tip-top." "Misera" is "poor soul;" "exsilio" means "to bounce forth;" "pellex" is "a miss;" "lumina" are "the peepers;" "turbatum fugere" is "to scower off in a mighty bustle;" "confundor" is "to be jumbled;" and "squalidus" is "in a sorry pickle." "Importuna" is "a plaguy baggage;" "adulterium" is rendered "her pranks;" "ambages" becomes either "a long rabble of words," "a long-winded detail," or "a tale of a tub;" "miserabile carmen" is "a dismal ditty;" "increpare hos" is "to rattle these blades;" "penetralia" means "the parlour;" while "accingere," more literally than elegantly, is translated "buckle to." "Situs" is "nasty stuff;" "oscula jungere" is "to tip him a kiss;" "pingue ingenium" is a circumlocution for "a blockhead;" "anilia instrumenta" are "his old woman's accoutrements;" and "repetito munere Bacchi" is conveyed to the sense of the reader as, "they return again to their bottle, and take the other glass." These are but a specimen of the blemishes which disfigure the most literal of the English translations of the Metamorphoses.

In the year 1656, a little volume was published, by John Bulloker, entitled "Ovid's Metamorphosis, translated grammatically, and, according to the propriety of our English tongue, so far as grammar and the verse will bear, written chiefly for the use of schools, to be used according to the directions in the preface to the painfull schoolmaster, and more fully in the book called, 'Ludus Literarius, or the Grammar school, chap. 8.'" Notwithstanding a title so pretentious, it contains a translation of no more than the first 567 lines of the first Book, executed in a fanciful and pedantic manner; and its rarity is now the only merit of the volume. A literal interlinear translation of the first Book "on the plan recommended by Mr. Locke," was published in 1839, which had been already preceded by "a selection from the Metamorphoses of Ovid, adapted to the Hamiltonian system, by a literal and interlineal translation," published by James Hamilton, the author of the Hamiltonian system. This work contains selections only from the first six books, and consequently embraces but a very small portion of the entire work.

For the better elucidation of the different fabulous narratives and allusions, explanations have been added, which are principally derived from the writings of Herodotus, Apollodorus, Pausanias, Dio Cassius, Dionysius of Halicarnassus, Strabo, Hyginus, Nonnus, and others of the historians, philosophers, and mythologists of antiquity. A great number of these illustrations are collected in the elaborate edition of Ovid, published by the Abbé Banier, one of the most learned scholars of the last century; who has, therein, and in his "Explanations of the Fables of Antiquity," with indefatigable labour and research, culled from the works of ancient authors, all such information as he considered likely to throw any light upon the Mythology and history of Greece and Rome.

This course has been adopted, because it was considered that a statement of the opinions of contemporary authors would be the most likely to enable the reader to form his own ideas upon the various subjects presented to his notice. Indeed, except in two or three instances, space has been found too limited to allow of more than an occasional reference to the opinions of modern scholars. Such being the object of the explanations, the reader will not be surprised at the absence of critical and lengthened discussions on many of those moot points of Mythology and early history which have occupied, with no very positive result, the attention of Niebuhr, Lobeck, Müller, Buttmann, and many other scholars of profound learning.

A SYNOPTICAL VIEW OF THE PRINCIPAL TRANSOFRMATIONS MENTIONED IN THE METAMORPHOSES

BOOK I

Chaos is divided by the Deity into four Elements: to these their respective inhabitants are assigned, and man is created from earth and water. The four Ages follow, and in the last of these the Giants aspire to the sovereignty of the heavens; being slain by Jupiter, a new race of men springs up from their blood. These becoming noted for their impiety, Jupiter not only transforms Lycaon into a wolf, but destroys the whole race of men and animals by a Deluge, with the exception of Deucalion and Pyrrha, who, when the waters have abated, renew the human race, by throwing stones behind them. Other animated beings are produced by heat and moisture: and, among them, the serpent Python. Phœbus slays him, and institutes the Pythian games as a memorial of the event, in which the conquerors are crowned with beech; for as yet the laurel does not exist, into which Daphne is changed soon after, while flying from Phœbus. On this taking place, the other rivers repair to her father Peneus, either to congratulate or to console him; but Inachus is not there, as he is grieving for his daughter Io, whom Jupiter, having first ravished her, has changed into a cow. She is entrusted by Juno to the care of Argus; Mercury having first related to him the transformation of the Nymph Syrinx into reeds, slays him, on which his eyes are placed by Juno in the tail of the peacock. Io, having recovered human shape, becomes the mother of Epaphus.

BOOK II

Epaphus, having accused Phaëton of falsely asserting that Phœbus is his father, Phaëton requests Phœbus, as a proof of his affection towards his child, to allow him the guidance of the chariot of the Sun for one day. This being granted, the whole earth is set on fire by him, and the Æthiopians are turned black by the heat. Jupiter strikes Phaëton with a thunderbolt, and while his sisters and his kinsman Cyenus are lamenting him, the former are changed into trees, and Cyenus into a swan. On visiting the earth, that he may repair the damage caused by the conflagration, Jupiter sees Calisto, and, assuming the form of Diana, he debauches her. Juno, being enraged, changes Calisto into a bear; and her own son Arcas being about to pierce her with an arrow, Jupiter places them both among the Constellations. Juno having complained of this to Oceanus, is borne back to the heavens by her peacocks, who have so lately changed their colour; a thing which has also happened to the raven, which has been lately changed from white to black, he having refused to listen to the warnings of the crow (who relates the story of its own transformation, and of that of Nyctimene into an owl), and having persisted in informing Phœbus of the intrigues of Coronis. Her son Æsculapius being cut out of the womb of Coronis and carried to the cave of Chiron the Centaur, Ocyrrhoë, the daughter of Chiron, is changed into a mare, while she is prophesying. Her father in vain invokes the assistance of Apollo, for he, in the guise of a shepherd, is tending his oxen in the country of Elis. He neglecting his herd, Mercury takes the opportunity of stealing it; after which he changes Battus into a touchstone, for betraying him. Flying thence, Mercury beholds Herse, the daughter of Cecrops, and debauches her. Her sister Aglauros, being envious of her, is changed into a rock. Mercury returns to heaven, on which Jupiter orders him to drive the herds of Agenor towards the shore; and then, assuming the form of a bull, he carries Europa over the sea to the isle of Crete.

BOOK III

Agenor commands his son Cadmus to seek his sister Europa. While he is doing this, he slays a dragon in Bœotia; and having sowed its teeth in the earth, men are produced, with whose assistance he builds the walls of Thebes. His first cause of grief is the fate of his grandson Actæon, who, being changed into a stag, is torn to pieces by his own hounds. This, however, gives pleasure to Juno, who hates not only Semele, the daughter of Cadmus, and the favourite of Jupiter, but all the house of Agenor as well. Assuming the form of Beroë, she contrives the destruction of Semele by the lightnings of Jupiter; while Bacchus, being saved alive from his mother's womb, is brought up on the earth. Jupiter has a discussion with Juno on the relative pleasures of the sexes, and they agree to refer the question to Tiresias, who has been of both sexes. He gives his decision in favour of Jupiter, on which Juno deprives him of sight; and, by way of recompense, Jupiter bestows on him the gift of prophesy. His first prediction is fulfilled in the case of Narcissus, who, despising the advances of all females (in whose number is Echo, who has been transformed into a sound), at last pines away with love for himself, and is changed into a flower which bears his name. Pentheus, however, derides the prophet; who predicts his fate, and his predictions are soon verified; for, on the celebration of the orgies, Bacchus having assumed a disguise, is brought before him; and having related to Pentheus the story of the transformation of the Etrurian sailors into dolphins, he is thrown into prison. On this, Pentheus is torn in pieces by the Bacchanals, and great respect is afterwards paid to the rites of Bacchus.

BOOK IV

Still Alcithoë and her sisters, neglecting the rites, attend to their spinning, during the festivities, and pass the time in telling stories; and, among others, that of Pyramus and Thisbe, by whose blood the mulberry is turned from white to black, and that of the discovery of the intrigues of Mars and Venus, on the information of the Sun. They also tell how the Sun assumed the form of Eurynome, that he might enjoy her daughter Leucothoë; how Clytie, becoming jealous of her sister, was transformed into a sun-flower; and how Salmacis and Hermaphroditus had become united into one body. After this, through the agency of Bacchus, the sisters are transformed into bats, and their webs are changed into vines. Ino rejoicing at this, Juno, in her hatred and indignation, sends one of the Furies to her, who causes her to be struck with insanity, on which she leaps into the sea, with her son Melicerta in her arms; but by the intercession of Venus, they become sea Deities, and their Sidonian attendants, who are bewailing them as dead, are changed into rocks. Cadmus, afflicted at this fresh calamity, retires from Thebes, and flies to Illyria, together with his wife, where they are both transformed into serpents. Of those who despise Bacchus, Acrisius alone remains, the grandfather of Perseus, who, having cut off the head of the Gorgon Medusa, serpents are produced by her blood. Perseus turns Atlas into a mountain, and having liberated Andromeda, he changes sea-weed into coral, and afterwards marries her.

BOOK V

A tumult arising during the celebration of the nuptials, Phineus claims Andromeda, who has been betrothed to him; and together with Prœtus, he and Polydectes are turned into stone. Pallas, who has aided Perseus, now leaves him, and goes to Helicon, to see the fountain of Hippocrene. The Muses tell her the story of Pyreneus and the Pierides, who were transformed into magpies after they had repeated various songs on the subjects of the transformation of the Deities into various forms of animals; the rape of Proserpine, the wanderings of Ceres, the change of Cyane into a fountain, of a boy into a lizard, of Ascalaphus into an owl, of the Sirens into birds in part, of Arethusa into a spring, of Lyncus into a lynx, and of the invention of agriculture by Triptolemus.

BOOK VI

Influenced by the example of the Muses, Pallas determines on the destruction of Arachne. She enters with her into a contest for the superiority in the art of weaving. Each represents various transformations on her web, and then Arachne is changed into a spider. Niobe, however, is not deterred thereby from preferring her own lot to that of Latona; on account of which, all her children are slain by Apollo and Diana, and she is changed into a rock. On learning this, while one person relates the transformation by Latona of the Lycian rustics into frogs, another calls to mind how Marsyas was flayed by Apollo. Niobe is lamented by Pelops, whose shoulder is of ivory. To console the Thebans in their afflictions, ambassadors come from the adjacent cities. The Athenians alone are absent, as they are attacked by hordes of barbarians, who are routed by Tereus, who marries Progne, the daughter of Pandion. Tereus coming a second time to Athens, takes back with him to his kingdom Philomela, his wife's sister; and having committed violence on her, with other enormities, he is transformed into a hoopoe, while Philomela is changed into a nightingale, and Progne becomes a swallow. Pandion, hearing of these wondrous events dies of grief. Erectheus succeeds him, whose daughter, Orithyia, is ravished by Boreas, and by him is the mother of Calais and Zethes, who are of the number of the Argonauts on the following occasion.

BOOK VII

Jason, by the aid of Medea, having conquered the bulls that breathe forth flames, having sowed the teeth of a serpent, from which armed men are produced, and having lulled the dragon to sleep, recovers the Golden Fleece. Medea, accompanying Jason to Greece, restores Æson to youth by the aid of drugs; and promising the same to Pelias, having first, as a specimen, changed a ram into a lamb, by stratagem she kills him. Passing through many places made remarkable by various transformations, and having slain her children, she marries Ægeus, when Theseus returns home, and narrowly escapes being poisoned by her magic potions. Minos interrupts the joy of Ægeus on the return of his son, and wages war against him; having collected troops from all parts, even from Paros, where Arne has been changed into a jackdaw. Minos endeavours to gain the alliance of Æacus, who, however, refuses it, and sends the Myrmidons, (who have been changed into ants from men after a severe pestilence), under the command of Cephalus to assist Ægeus. Cephalus relates to Phocus, the son of Æacus, how, being carried off by Aurora and assuming another shape, he had induced his wife Procris to prove faithless; and how he had received from her a dog and a javelin, the former of which, together with a fox, was changed into stone; while the latter, by inadvertence, caused the death of his wife.

INTRODUCTION by EDWARD BROOKS JR.

P. Ovidius Naso—commonly known as Ovid—was born at Sulmo, about, ninety miles from Rome, in the year 43 B.C. His father belonged to an old equestrian family, and at an early age brought his son to Rome, where he was educated under the most distinguished masters. Very little is known of the poet's life, except that which is gathered from his own writings. After finishing his education at home he visited Athens, in company with the poet Macer, for the purpose of completing his studies, and before returning visited the magnificent cities of Asia Minor and spent nearly a year in Sicily.

Although as a young man Ovid showed a natural taste and inclination for poetical composition, he was by no means encouraged to indulge in this pursuit. His father thought that the profession of law was much more apt to lead to distinction and political eminence than the vocation of a poet. He therefore dissuaded his son from writing poetry and urged him to devote himself to the legal profession. Compliance with his father's wishes led him to spend much time in the forum, and for a while poetry was abandoned. Upon attaining his majority, he held several minor offices of state; but neither his health nor his inclinations would permit him to perform the duties of public life. Poetry was his love, and in spite of the strong objections of his father, he resolved to abandon the law courts and devote himself to a more congenial occupation. He sought the society of the most distinguished poets of the day, and his admiration for them amounted almost to reverence. He numbered among his intimate friends the poets Macer, Propertius, Ponticus and Bassus, while Æmilius Macer, Virgil's contemporary, used to read his compositions to him, and even the fastidious Horace, it is said, occasionally delighted the young man's ear with the charm of his verse.

Ovid was married three times. His first wife he married when little more than a boy, and the union does not seem to have been a happy one, though it was probably due to no fault of the wife. His second wife seems also to have been of blameless character, but his love for her was of short duration. His third wife was a lady of the great Fabian house and a friend of the Empress Livia. She appears to have been a woman in every way worthy of the great and lasting love which the poet lavished upon her to the day of his death.

Up to the age of fifty Ovid had lived a life of prosperity and happiness. Though not a wealthy man, his means were such as to permit him to indulge in the luxuries of refined life, and his attainments as a poet had surrounded him with a circle of most desirable friends and admirers. He had even obtained the favor and patronage of the royal family. About the year 8 A.D. he, however, incurred the great displeasure of Augustus, and was ordered by him to withdraw from Rome and dwell in the colony of Tomi, on the shore of the Euxine sea. Leaving behind him a wife to whom he was devotedly attached he obeyed the edict of his emperor and entered upon an exile from which he was destined never to return. He died in banishment at Tomi in the year 18 A.D.

The exact reason for Ovid's banishment has never been clear, though there have been many conjectures as to the cause. About two years previous to his exile Ovid had published a composition which had greatly displeased Augustus, on account of its immoral tendency. Almost coincident with this publication was the discovery of the scandal relating to Julia, daughter of the emperor. It is probable that the proximity of these two events tended to intensify the imperial displeasure, and when some time later there was made public the intrigue of the emperor's granddaughter, the indignation of Augustus gave itself vent in the banishment of Ovid.

The writings of Ovid consist of the Amores in three books; the Heroic Epistles, twenty-one in number; the Ars Amatoria; the Remedia Amoris; the Metamorphoses, in fifteen books; the Fasti, in six books; the Tristia, in five books; the Epistles, in four books, and a few minor poems. In the following pages will be found a translation of the Metamorphoses.

THE METAMORPHOSES

BOOK THE FIRST

THE ARGUMENT [I.1-4]

My design leads me to speak of forms changed into new bodies.[1] Ye Gods, (for you it was who changed them,) favor my attempts,[2] and bring down the lengthened narrative from the very beginning of the world, even to my own times.[3]

[Footnote 1: Forms changed into new bodies.—Ver. 1. Some commentators cite these words as an instance of Hypallage as being used for 'corpora mutata in novas formas,' 'bodies changed into new forms;' and they fancy that there is a certain beauty in the circumstance that the proposition of a subject which treats of the changes and variations of bodies should be framed with a transposition of words. This supposition is perhaps based rather on the exuberance of a fanciful imagination than on solid grounds, as if it is an instance of Hypallage, it is most probably quite accidental; while the passage may be explained without any reference to Hypallage, as the word 'forma' is sometimes used to signify the thing itself; thus the words 'formæ deorum' and 'ferarum' are used to signify 'the Gods,' or 'the wild beasts' themselves.]

[Footnote 2: Favor my attempts.—Ver. 3. This use of the word 'adspirate' is a metaphor taken from the winds, which, while they fill the ship's sails, were properly said 'adspirare.' It has been remarked, with some justice, that this invocation is not sufficiently long or elaborate for a work of so grave and dignified a nature as the Metamorphoses.]

[Footnote 3: To my own times.—Ver. 4. That is, to the days of Augustus Cæsar.]

FABLE I [I.5-31]

God reduces Chaos into order. He separates the four elements, and disposes the several bodies, of which the universe is formed, into their proper situations.

At first, the sea, the earth, and the heaven, which covers all things, were the only face of nature throughout the whole universe, which men have named Chaos; a rude and undigested mass,[4] and nothing more than an inert weight, and the discordant atoms of things not harmonizing, heaped together in the same spot. No Sun[5] as yet gave light to the world; nor did the Moon,[6] by increasing, recover her horns anew. The Earth did not as yet hang in the surrounding air, balanced by its own weight, nor had Amphitrite[7] stretched out her arms along the lengthened margin of the coasts. Wherever, too, was the land, there also was the sea and the air; and thus was the earth without firmness, the sea unnavigable, the air void of light; in no one of them did its present form exist. And one was ever obstructing the other; because in the same body the cold was striving with the hot, the moist with the dry, the soft with the hard, things having weight with those devoid of weight.

To this discord God and bounteous Nature[8] put an end; for he separated the earth from the heavens, and the waters from the earth, and distinguished the clear heavens from the gross atmosphere. And after he had unravelled these elements, and released them from that confused heap, he combined them, thus disjoined, in harmonious unison, each in its proper place. The element of the vaulted heaven,[9] fiery and without weight, shone forth, and selected a place for itself in the highest region; next after it, both in lightness and in place, was the air; the Earth was more weighty than these, and drew with it the more ponderous atoms, and was pressed together by its own gravity. The encircling waters sank to the lowermost place,[10] and surrounded the solid globe.

[Footnote 4: A rude and undigested mass.—Ver. 7. This is very similar to the words of the Scriptures, 'And the earth was without form and void,' Genesis, ch. i. ver. 2.]

[Footnote 5: No Sun.—Ver. 10. Titan. The Sun is so called, on account of his supposed father, Hyperion, who was one of the Titans. Hyperion is thought to have been the first who, by assiduous observation, discovered the course of the Sun, Moon, and other luminaries. By them he regulated the time for the seasons, and imparted this knowledge to others. Being thus, as it were, the father of astronomy, he has been feigned by the poets to have been the father of the Sun and the Moon.]

[Footnote 6: The Moon.—Ver. 11. Phœbe. The Moon is so called from the Greek φοῖβος, 'shining,' and as being the sister of Phœbus, Apollo, or the Sun.]

[Footnote 7: Amphitrite.—Ver. 14. She was the daughter of Oceanus and Doris, and the wife of Neptune, God of the Sea. Being the Goddess of the Ocean, her name is here used to signify the ocean itself.]

[Footnote 8: Nature.—Ver. 21. 'Natura' is a word often used by the Poet without any determinate signification, and to its operations are ascribed all those phenomena which it is found difficult or impossible to explain upon known and established principles. In the present instance it may be considered to mean the invisible agency of the Deity in reducing Chaos into a form of order and consistency. 'Et' is therefore here, as grammarians term it, an expositive particle; as if the Poet had said, 'Deus sive natura,' 'God, or in other words, nature.']

[Footnote 9: The element of the vaulted heaven.—Ver. 26. This is a periphrasis, signifying the regions of the firmament or upper air, in which the sun and stars move; which was supposed to be of the purest fire and the source of all flame. The heavens are called 'convex,' from being supposed to assume the same shape as the terrestrial globe which they surround.]

[Footnote 10: The lowermost place.—Ver. 31. 'Ultima' must not be here understood in the presence of 'infima,' or as signifying 'last,' or 'lowest,' in a strict philosophical sense, for that would contradict the account of the formation of the world given by Hesiod, and which is here closely followed by Ovid; indeed, it would contradict his own words,—'Circumfluus humor coercuit solidum orbem.' The meaning seems to be, that the waters possess the lowest place only in respect to the earth whereon we tread, and not relatively to the terrestrial globe, the supposed centre of the system, inasmuch as the external surface of the earth in some places rises considerably, and leaves the water to subside in channels.]

EXPLANATION

The ancient philosophers, unable to comprehend how something could be produced out of nothing, supposed a matter pre-existent to the Earth in its present shape, which afterwards received form and order from some powerful cause. According to them, God was not the Creator, but the Architect of the universe, in ranging and disposing the elements in situations most suitable to their respective qualities. This is the Chaos so often sung of by the poets, and which Hesiod was the first to mention.

It is clear that this system was but a confused and disfigured tradition of the creation of the world, as mentioned by Moses; and thus, beneath these fictions, there lies some faint glimmering of truth. The first two chapters of the book of Genesis will be found to throw considerable light on the foundation of this Mythological system of the world's formation.

Hesiod, the most ancient of the heathen writers who have enlarged upon this subject, seems to have derived much of his information from the works of Sanchoniatho, who is supposed to have borrowed his ideas concerning Chaos from that passage in the second verse of the first Chapter of Genesis, which mentions the darkness that was spread over the whole universe—'and darkness was upon the face of the deep'—for he expresses himself almost in those words. Sanchoniatho lived before the Trojan war, and professed to have received his information respecting the original construction of the world from a priest of 'Jehovah,' named Jerombaal. He wrote in the Phœnician language; but we have only a translation of his works, by Philo Judæus, which is by many supposed to be spurious. It is, however, very probable, that from him the Greeks borrowed their notions regarding Chaos, which they mingled with fables of their own invention.

After the separation of matter, God gives form and regularity to the universe; and all other living creatures being produced, Prometheus moulds earth tempered with water, into a human form, which is animated by Minerva.

When thus he, whoever of the Gods he was,[11] had divided the mass so separated, and reduced it, so divided, into distinct members; in the first place, that it might not be unequal on any side, he gathered it up into the form of a vast globe; then he commanded the sea to be poured around it, and to grow boisterous with the raging winds, and to surround the shores of the Earth, encompassed by it; he added also springs, and numerous pools and lakes, and he bounded the rivers as they flowed downwards, with slanting banks. These, different in different places, are some of them swallowed up[12] by the Earth itself; some of them reach the ocean, and, received in the expanse of waters that take a freer range, beat against shores instead of banks.

He commanded the plains,[13] too, to be extended, the valleys to sink down, the woods to be clothed with green leaves, the craggy mountains to arise; and, as on the right-hand side,[14] two Zones intersect the heavens, and as many on the left; and as there is a fifth hotter than these, so did the care of the Deity distinguish this enclosed mass of the Earth by the same number, and as many climates are marked out upon the Earth. Of these, that which is the middle one[15] is not habitable on account of the heat; deep snow covers two[16] of them. Between either these he placed as many more,[17] and gave them a temperate climate, heat being mingled with cold.

Over these hangs the air, which is heavier than fire, in the same degree that the weight of water is lighter than the weight of the earth. Here he ordered vapors, here too, the clouds to take their station; the thunder, too, to terrify the minds of mortals, and with the lightnings, the winds that bring on cold. The Contriver of the World did not allow these indiscriminately to take possession of the sky. Even now, (although they each of them govern their own blasts in a distinct tract) they are with great difficulty prevented from rending the world asunder, so great is the discord of the brothers.[18] Eurus took his way[19] towards the rising of Aurora and the realms of Nabath[20] and Persia, and the mountain ridges exposed to the rays of the morning. The Evening star, and the shores which are warm with the setting sun, are bordering upon Zephyrus.[21] The terrible Boreas invaded Scythia,[22] and the regions of the North. The opposite quarter is wet with continual clouds, and the drizzling South Wind.[23] Over these he placed the firmament, clear and devoid of gravity, and not containing anything of the dregs of earth.

Scarcely had he separated all these by fixed limits, when the stars, which had long lain hid, concealed beneath that mass of Chaos, began to glow through the range of the heavens. And that no region might be destitute of its own peculiar animated beings, the stars and the forms of the Gods[24] possess the tract of heaven; the waters fell to be inhabited by the smooth fishes;[25] the Earth received the wild beasts, and the yielding air the birds.

But an animated being, more holy than these, more fitted to receive higher faculties, and which could rule over the rest,[26] was still wanting. Then Man was formed. Whether it was that the Artificer of all things, the original of the world in its improved state, framed him from divine elements;[27] or whether, the Earth, being newly made, and but lately divided from the lofty æther, still retained some atoms of its kindred heaven, which, tempered with the waters of the stream, the son of Iapetus fashioned after the image of the Gods, who rule over all things. And, whereas other animals bend their looks downwards upon the Earth, to Man he gave a countenance to look on high and to behold the heavens, and to raise his face erect to the stars. Thus, that which had been lately rude earth, and without any regular shape, being changed, assumed the form of Man, till then unknown.

[Footnote 11: Whoever of the Gods he was.—Ver. 32. By this expression the Poet perhaps may intend to intimate that the God who created the world was some more mighty Divinity than those who were commonly accounted Deities.]

[Footnote 12: Are some of them swallowed up.—Ver. 40. He here refers to those rivers which, at some distance from their sources, disappear and continue their course under ground. Such was the stream of Arethusa, the Lycus in Asia, the Erasinus in Argolis, the Alpheus in Peloponnesus, the Arcas in Spain, and the Rhone in France. Most of these, however, after descending into the earth, appear again and discharge their waters into the sea.]

[Footnote 13: He commanded the plains.—Ver. 43. The use here of the word 'jussit,' signifying 'ordered,' or 'commanded,' is considered as being remarkably sublime and appropriate, and serving well to express the ease wherewith an infinitely powerful Being accomplishes the most difficult works. There is the same beauty here that was long since remarked by Longinus, one of the most celebrated critics among the ancients, in the words used by Moses, 'And God said, Let there be light, and there was light,' Genesis, ch. i. ver. 3.]

[Footnote 14: On the right-hand side.—Ver. 45. The "right hand" here refers to the northern part of the globe, and the "left hand" to the southern. He here speaks of the zones. Astronomers have divided the heavens into five parallel circles. First, the equinoctial, which lies in the middle, between the poles of the earth, and obtains its name from the equality of days and nights on the earth while the sun is in its plane. On each side are the two tropics, at the distance of 23 deg. 30 min., and described by the sun when in his greatest declination north and south, or at the summer and winter solstices. That on the north side of the equinoctial is called the tropic of Cancer, because the sun describes it when in that sign of the ecliptic; and that on the south side is, for a similar reason, called the tropic of Capricorn. Again, at the distance of 23½ degrees from the poles are two other parallels called the polar circles, either because they are near to the poles, or because, if we suppose the whole frame of the heavens to turn round on the plane of the equinoctial, these circles are marked out by the poles of the ecliptic. By means of these parallels, astronomers have divided the heavens into four zones or tracks. The whole space between the two tropics is the middle or torrid zone, which the equinoctial divides into two equal parts. On each side of this are the temperate zones, which extend from the tropics to the two polar circles. And lastly, the portions enclosed by the polar circles make up the frigid zones. As the planes of these circles produced till they reached the earth, would also impress similar parallels upon it, and divide it in the same manner as they divide the heavens, astronomers have conceived five zones upon the earth, corresponding to those in the heavens, and bounded by the same circles.]

[Footnote 15: That which is the middle one.—Ver. 49. The ecliptic in which the sun moves, cuts the equator in two opposite points, at an angle of 23½ degrees; and runs obliquely from one tropic to another, and returns again in a corresponding direction. Hence, the sun, which in the space of a year, performs the revolution of this circle, must in that time be twice vertical to every place in the torrid zone, except directly under the tropics, and his greatest distance from their zenith at noon, cannot exceed 47 degrees. Thus his rays being often perpendicular, or nearly so, and never very oblique, must strike more forcibly, and cause more intense heat in that spot. Being little acquainted with the extent and situation of the earth, the ancients believed it uninhabitable. Modern discovery has shown that this is not the case as to a considerable part of the torrid zone, though with some parts of it our acquaintance is still very limited.]

[Footnote 16: Deep snow covers two.—Ver. 50. The two polar or frigid zones. For as the sun never approaches these nearer than the tropic on that side, and is, during one part of the year, removed by the additional extent of the whole torrid zone, his rays must be very oblique and faint, so as to leave these tracts exposed to almost perpetual cold.]

[Footnote 17: He placed as many more.—Ver. 51. The temperate zones, lying between the torrid and the frigid, partake of the character of each in a modified degree, and are of a middle temperature between hot and cold. Here, too, the distinction of the seasons is manifest. For in either temperate zone, when the sun is in that tropic, which borders upon it, being nearly vertical, the heat must be considerable, and produce summer; but when he is removed to the other tropic by a distance of 47 degrees, his rays will strike but faintly, and winter will be the consequence. The intermediate spaces, while he is moving from one tropic to the other, make spring and autumn.]

[Footnote 18: The brothers.—Ver. 60. That is, the winds, who, according to the Theogony of Hesiod, were the sons of Astreus, the giant, and Aurora.]

[Footnote 19: Eurus took his way.—Ver. 61. The Poet, after remarking that the air is the proper region of the winds, proceeds to take notice that God, to prevent them from making havoc of the creation, subjected them to particular laws, and assigned to each the quarter whence to direct his blasts. Eurus is the east wind, being so called from its name, because it blows from the east. As Aurora, or the morning, was always ushered in by the sun, who rises eastward, she was supposed to have her habitation in the eastern quarter of the world; and often, in the language of ancient poetry, her name signifies the east.]

[Footnote 20: The realms of Nabath.—Ver. 61. From Josephus we learn that Nabath, the son of Ishmael, with his eleven brothers, took possession of all the country from the river Euphrates to the Red Sea, and called it Nabathæa. Pliny the Elder and Strabo speak of the Nabatæi as situated between Babylon and Arabia Felix, and call their capital Petra. Tacitus, in his Annals (Book ii. ch. 57), speaks of them as having a king. Perhaps the term 'Nabathæa regna' implies here, generally, the whole of Arabia.]

[Footnote 21: Are bordering upon Zephyrus.—Ver. 63. The region where the sun sets, that is to say, the western part of the world, was assigned by the ancients to the Zephyrs, or west winds, so called by a Greek derivation because they cherish and enliven nature.]

[Footnote 22: Boreas invaded Scythia.—Ver. 34. Under the name of Scythia, the ancients generally comprehended all the countries situate in the extreme northern regions. 'Septem trio,' meaning the northern region of the world, is so called from the 'Triones,' a constellation of seven stars, near the North Pole, known also as the Ursa Major, or Greater Bear, and among the country people of our time by the name of Charles's Wain. Boreas, one of the names of 'Aquilo,' or the 'north wind,' is derived from a Greek word, signifying 'an eddy.' This name was probably given to it from its causing whirlwinds occasionally by its violence.]

[Footnote 23: The drizzling South Wind.—Ver. 66. The South Wind is especially called rainy, because, blowing from the Mediterranean sea on the coast of France and Italy, it generally brings with it clouds and rain.]

[Footnote 24: The forms of the Gods.—Ver. 73. There is some doubt what the Poet here means by the 'forms of the Gods.' Some think that the stars are meant, as if it were to be understood that they are forms of the Gods. But it is most probably only a poetical expression for the Gods themselves, and he here assigns the heavens as the habitation of the Gods and the stars; these last, according to the notion of the Platonic philosophers being either intelligent beings, or guided and actuated by such.]

[Footnote 25: Inhabited by the smooth fishes.—Ver. 74. 'Cesserunt nitidis habitandæ piscibus;' Clarke translates 'fell to the neat fishes to inhabit.']

[Footnote 26: Could rule over the rest.—Ver. 77. This strongly brings to mind the words of the Creator, described in the first chapter of Genesis, ver. 28. 'And God said unto them—have dominion over the fish of the sea, and over the fowl of the air, and over every living thing that moveth upon the earth.']

[Footnote 27: Framed him from divine elements.—Ver. 78. We have here strong grounds for contending that the ancient philosophers, and after them the poets, in their account of the creation of the world followed a tradition that had been copied from the Books of Moses. The formation of man, in Ovid, as well as in the Book of Genesis, is the last work of the Creator, and was, for the same purpose, that man might have dominion over the other animated works of the creation.]

EXPLANATION

According to Ovid, as in the book of Genesis, man is the last work of the Creator. The information derived from Holy Writ is here presented to us, in a disfigured form. Prometheus, who tempers the earth, and Minerva, who animates his workmanship, is God, who formed man, and 'breathed into his nostrils the breath of life.'

Some writers have labored to prove that this Prometheus, of the heathen Mythology, was a Scriptural character. Bochart believes him to have been the same with Magog, mentioned in the book of Genesis. Prometheus was the son of Iapetus, and Magog was the son of Japhet, who, according to that learned writer, was identical with Iapetus. He says, that as Magog went to settle in Scythia, so did Prometheus; as Magog either invented, or improved, the art of founding metals, and forging iron, so, according to the heathen poets, did Prometheus. Diodorus Siculus asserts that Prometheus was the first to teach mankind how to produce fire from the flint and steel.

The fable of Prometheus being devoured by an eagle, according to some, is founded on the name of Magog, which signifies 'a man devoured by sorrow.' Le Clerc, in his notes on Hesiod, says, that Epimetheus, the brother of Prometheus, was the same with the Gog of Scripture, the brother of Magog. Some writers, again, have exerted their ingenuity to prove that Prometheus is identical with the patriarch Noah.

FABLE III [I.89-112]

The formation of man is followed by a succession of the four ages of the world. The first is the Golden Age, during which Innocence and Justice alone govern the world.

The Golden Age was first founded, which, without any avenger, of its own accord, without laws, practised both faith and rectitude. Punishment, and the fear of it, did not exist, and threatening decrees were not read upon the brazen tables,[28] fixed up to view, nor yet did the suppliant multitude dread the countenance of its judge; but all were in safety without any avenger. The pine-tree, cut from its native mountains, had not yet descended to the flowing waves, that it might visit a foreign region; and mortals were acquainted with no shores beyond their own. Not as yet did deep ditches surround the towns; no trumpets of straightened, or clarions of crooked brass,[29] no helmets, no swords then existed. Without occasion for soldiers, the minds of men, free from care, enjoyed an easy tranquillity.

The Earth itself, too, in freedom, untouched by the harrow, and wounded by no ploughshares, of its own accord produced everything; and men, contented with the food created under no compulsion, gathered the fruit of the arbute-tree, and the strawberries of the mountain, and cornels, and blackberries adhering to the prickly bramble-bushes, and acorns which had fallen from the wide-spreading tree of Jove. Then it was an eternal spring; and the gentle Zephyrs, with their soothing breezes, cherished the flowers produced without any seed. Soon, too, the Earth unploughed yielded crops of grain, and the land, without being renewed, was whitened with the heavy ears of corn. Then, rivers of milk, then, rivers of nectar were flowing, and the yellow honey was distilled from the green holm oak.

[Footnote 28: Read upon the brazen tables.—Ver. 91. It was the custom among the Romans to engrave their laws on tables of brass, and fix them in the Capitol, or some other conspicuous place, that they might be open to the view of all.]

[Footnote 29: Clarions of crooked brass.—Ver. 98. 'Cornu' seems to have been a general name for the horn or trumpet; whereas the "tuba" was a straight trumpet, while the 'lituus' was bent into a spiral shape. Lydus says that the 'lituus' was the sacerdotal trumpet, and that it was employed by Romulus when he proclaimed the title of his newly-founded city. Acro says that it was peculiar to the cavalry, while the 'tuba' belonged to the infantry. The notes of the 'lituus' are usually described as harsh and shrill.]

EXPLANATION

The heathen poets had learned, most probably from tradition, that our first parents lived for some time in peaceful innocence; that, without tillage, the garden of Eden furnished them with fruit and food in abundance; and that the animals were submissive to their commands: that after the fall the ground became unfruitful, and yielded nothing without labor; and that nature no longer spontaneously acknowledged man for its master. The more happy days of our first parents they seem to have styled the Golden Age, each writer being desirous to make his own country the scene of those times of innocence. The Latin writers, for instance, have placed in Italy, and under the reign of Saturn and Janus, events, which, as they really happened, the Scriptures relate in the histories of Adam and of Noah.

FABLE IV [I.113-150]

In the Silver Age, men begin not to be so just, nor, consequently, so happy, as in the Golden Age. In the Brazen Age, which succeeds, they become yet less virtuous; but their wickedness does not rise to its highest pitch until the Iron Age, when it makes its appearance in all its deformity.

Afterwards (Saturn being driven into the shady realms of Tartarus), the world was under the sway of Jupiter; then the Silver Age succeeded, inferior to that of gold, but more precious than that of yellow brass. Jupiter shortened the duration of the former spring, and divided the year into four periods by means of winters, and summers, and unsteady autumns, and short springs. Then, for the first time, did the parched air glow with sultry heat, and the ice, bound up by the winds, was pendant. Then, for the first time, did men enter houses; those houses were caverns, and thick shrubs, and twigs fastened together with bark. Then, for the first time, were the seeds of Ceres buried in long furrows, and the oxen groaned, pressed by the yoke of the ploughshare.

The Age of Brass succeeded, as the third in order, after these; fiercer in disposition, and more prone to horrible warfare, but yet free from impiety. The last Age was of hard iron. Immediately every species of crime burst forth, in this age of degenerated tendencies;[30] modesty, truth, and honor took flight; in their place succeeded fraud, deceit, treachery, violence, and the cursed hankering for acquisition. The sailor now spread his sails to the winds, and with these, as yet, he was but little acquainted; and the trees, which had long stood on the lofty mountains, now, as ships bounded[31] through the unknown waves. The ground, too, hitherto common as the light of the sun and the breezes, the cautious measurer marked out with his lengthened boundary.

And not only was the rich soil required to furnish corn and due sustenance, but men even descended into the entrails of the Earth; and riches were dug up, the incentives to vice, which the Earth had hidden, and had removed to the Stygian shades.[32] Then destructive iron came forth, and gold, more destructive than iron; then War came forth, that fights through the means of both,[33] and that brandishes in his blood-stained hands the clattering arms. Men live by rapine; the guest is not safe from his entertainer, nor the father-in-law from the son-in-law; good feeling, too, between brothers is a rarity. The husband is eager for the death of the wife, she for that of her husband. Horrible stepmothers then mingle the ghastly wolfsbane; the son prematurely makes inquiry[34] into the years of his father. Piety lies vanquished, and the virgin Astræa[35] is the last of the heavenly Deities to abandon the Earth, now drenched in slaughter.

[Footnote 30: Age of degenerated tendencies.—Ver. 128. 'Vena' signifies among other things, a vein or track of metal as it lies in the mine. Literally, 'venæ pejoris' signifies 'of inferior metal.']

[Footnote 31: Now as ships bounded.—Ver. 134. 'Insultavere carinæ.' This line is translated by Clarke, 'The keel-pieces bounced over unknown waves.']

[Footnote 32: To the Stygian shades.—Ver. 139. That is, in deep caverns, and towards the centre of the earth; for Styx was feigned to be a river of the Infernal Regions, situate in the depths of the earth.]

[Footnote 33: Through the means of both.—Ver. 142. Gold forms, perhaps, more properly the sinews of war than iron. The history of Philip of Macedon gives a proof of this, as he conquered Greece more by bribes than the sword, and used to say, that he deemed no fortress impregnable, where there was a gate large enough to admit a camel laden with gold.]

EXPLANATION

The Poet here informs us, that during the Golden Age, a perpetual spring reigned on the earth, and that the division of the year into seasons was not known until the Silver Age. This allusion to Eden is very generally to be found in the works of the heathen poets. The Silver Age is succeeded by the Brazen, and that is followed by the Iron Age, which still continues. The meaning is, that man gradually degenerated from his primeval innocence, and arrived at that state of wickedness and impiety, of which the history of all ages, ancient and modern, presents us with so many lamentable examples.

The limited nature of their views, and the fact that their exuberant fancy was the source from which they derived many of their alleged events, naturally betrayed the ancient writers into great inconsistencies. For in the Golden Age of Saturn, we find wars waged, and crimes committed. Saturn expelled his father, and seized his throne; Jupiter, his son, treated Saturn as he had done his father Uranus; and Jupiter, in his turn, had to wage war against the Giants, in their attempt to dispossess him of the heavens.

FABLE V [I.151-162]

The Giants having attempted to render themselves masters of heaven, Jupiter buries them under the mountains which they have heaped together to facilitate their assault; and the Earth, animating their blood, forms out of it a cruel and fierce generation of men.

And that the lofty realms of æther might not be more safe than the Earth, they say that the Giants aspired to the sovereignty of Heaven, and piled the mountains, heaped together, even to the lofty stars. Then the omnipotent Father, hurling his lightnings, broke through Olympus,[36] and struck Ossa away from Pelion, that lay beneath it. While the dreadful carcasses lay overwhelmed beneath their own structure, they say that the Earth was wet, drenched with the plenteous blood of her sons, and that she gave life to the warm gore; and that, lest no memorial of this ruthless race should be surviving, she shaped them into the form of men. But that generation, too, was a despiser of the Gods above, and most greedy of ruthless slaughter, and full of violence: you might see that they derived their origin from blood.

EXPLANATION

The war of the giants, which is here mentioned, is not to be confounded with that between Jupiter and the Titans, who were inhabitants of heaven. The fall of the angels, as conveyed by tradition, probably gave rise to the story of the Titans; while, perhaps, the building of the tower of Babel may have laid the foundation of that of the attempt by the giants to reach heaven. Perhaps, too, the descendants of Cain, who are probably the persons mentioned in Scripture as the children 'of men' and 'giants,' were the race depicted under the form of the Giants, and the generation that sprung from their blood. See Genesis, ch. vi. ver. 2, 4.

FABLE VI [I.163-215]

Jupiter, having seen the crimes of this impious race of men, calls a council of the Gods, and determines to destroy the world.

When the Father of the Gods, the son of Saturn, beheld this from his loftiest height, he groaned aloud; and recalling to memory the polluted banquet on the table of Lycaon, not yet publicly known, from the crime being but lately committed, he conceives in his mind vast wrath, and such as is worthy of Jove, and calls together a council; no delay detains them, thus summoned.

There is a way on high,[37] easily seen in a clear sky, and which, remarkable for its very whiteness, receives the name of the Milky Way. Along this is the way for the Gods above to the abode of the great Thunderer and his royal palace. On the right and on the left side the courts of the ennobled Deities[38] are thronged, with open gates. The Gods of lower rank[39] inhabit various places; in front of the Way, the powerful and illustrious inhabitants of Heaven have established their residence. This is the place which, if boldness may be allowed to my expression, I should not hesitate to style the palatial residence of Heaven. When, therefore, the Gods above had taken their seats in the marble hall of assembly; he himself, elevated on his seat, and leaning on his sceptre of ivory, three or four times shook the awful locks[40] of his head, with which he makes the Earth, the Seas, and the Stars to tremble. Then, after such manner as this, did he open his indignant lips:—

"Not even at that time was I more concerned for the empire of the universe, when each of the snake-footed monsters was endeavoring to lay his hundred arms on the captured skies. For although that was a dangerous enemy, yet that war was with but one stock, and sprang from a single origin. Now must the race of mortals be cut off by me, wherever Nereus[41] roars on all sides of the earth; this I swear by the Rivers of Hell, that glide in the Stygian grove beneath the earth. All methods have been already tried; but a wound that admits of no cure, must be cut away with the knife, that the sound parts may not be corrupted. I have as subjects, Demigods, and I have the rustic Deities, the Nymphs,[42] and the Fauns, and the Satyrs, and the Sylvans, the inhabitants of the mountains; these, though as yet, we have not thought them worthy of the honor of Heaven, let us, at least, permit to inhabit the earth which we have granted them. And do you, ye Gods of Heaven, believe that they will be in proper safety, when Lycaon remarkable for his cruelty, has formed a plot against even me, who own and hold sway over the thunder and yourselves?"

All shouted their assent aloud, and with ardent zeal they called for vengeance on one who dared such crimes. Thus, when an impious band[43] madly raged to extinguish the Roman name in the blood of Cæsar, the human race was astonished with sudden terror at ruin so universal, and the whole earth shook with horror. Nor was the affectionate regard, Augustus, of thy subjects less grateful to thee, than that was to Jupiter. Who, after he had, by means of his voice and his hand, suppressed their murmurs, all of them kept silence. Soon as the clamor had ceased, checked by the authority of their ruler, Jupiter again broke silence in these words:

"He, indeed, (dismiss your cares) has suffered dire punishment; but what was the offence and what the retribution, I will inform you. The report of the iniquity of the age had reached my ears; wishing to find this not to be the truth, I descended from the top of Olympus, and, a God in a human shape, I surveyed the earth. 'Twere an endless task to enumerate how great an amount of guilt was everywhere discovered; the report itself was below the truth."

[Footnote 37: There is a way on high.—Ver. 168. The Poet here gives a description of the court of heaven; and supposing the galaxy, or Milky Way, to be the great road to the palace of Jupiter, places the habitations of the Gods on each side of it, and adjoining the palace itself. The mythologists also invented a story, that the Milky Way was a track left in the heavens by the milk of Juno flowing from the mouth of Hercules, when suckled by her. Aristotle, however, suspected what has been since confirmed by the investigations of modern science, that it was formed by the light of innumerable stars.]

[Footnote 38: The ennobled Deities.—Ver. 172. These were the superior Deities, who formed the privy councillors of Jupiter, and were called 'Di majorum gentium,' or, 'Di consentes.' Reckoning Jupiter as one, they were twelve in number, and are enumerated by Ennius in two limping hexameter lines:—

'Juno, Vesta, Minerva, Ceres, Diana, Venus, Mars,
Mercurius, Jovis, Neptunus, Vulcanus, Apollo.']

[Footnote 39: The Gods of lower rank.—Ver. 173. These were the 'Dii minorum gentium,' or inferior Deities.]

[Footnote 40: Shook the awful locks.—Ver. 179. This awful nod of Jupiter, the sanction by which he confirms his decrees, is an idea taken from Homer; by whom it is so vividly depicted at the end of the first book of the Iliad, that Phidias, in his statue of that God, admired for the awful majesty of its looks, is said to have derived his conception of the features from that description. Virgil has the same idea in the Æneid, book x; 'Annuit, et totum metu tremefecit Olympum.']

[Footnote 41: Nereus.—Ver. 187. He was one of the most ancient of the Deities of the sea, and was the son of Oceanus and Tethys.]

[Footnote 42: The Nymphs.—Ver. 192. The terrestrial Nymphs were the Dryads and Hamadryads, who haunting the woods, and the duration of their existence depending upon the life of particular trees, derived their name from the Greek word δρῦς, 'an oak.' The Oreades were nymphs who frequented the mountains, while the Napeæ lived in the groves and valleys. There were also Nymphs of the sea and of the rivers; of which, the Nereids were so called from their father Nereus, and the Oceanitides, from Oceanus. There were also the Naiads, or nymphs of the fountains, and many others.]

[Footnote 43: Thus when an impious band.—Ver. 200. It is a matter of doubt whether he here refers to the conspiracies of Brutus and Cassius against Julius Cæsar, or whether to that against Augustus, which is mentioned by Suetonius, in the nineteenth chapter of his History. As Augustus survived the latter conspiracy, and the parallel is thereby rendered more complete, probably this is the circumstance here alluded to.]

EXPLANATION

It is to be presumed, that Ovid here follows the prevailing tradition of his time; and it is surprising how closely that tradition adheres to the words of Scripture, relative to the determination of the Almighty to punish the earth by a deluge, as disclosed in the sixth chapter of Genesis. The Poet tells us, that the King of heaven calls the Gods to a grand council, to deliberate upon the punishment of mankind, in retribution for their wickedness. The words of Scripture are, "And God saw that the wickedness of man was great in the earth, and that every imagination of the thoughts of his heart was only evil continually. And it repented the Lord that he had made man on the earth, and it grieved him at his heart. And the Lord said, 'I will destroy man, whom I have created from the face of the earth; both man and beast, and the creeping thing, and the fowls of the air: for it repenteth me that I have made them.'"—Genesis, ch. vi. ver. 5, 6, 7.

Tradition seems to have faithfully carried down the fact, that, amid this universal corruption, there was still at least one just man, and here it attributes to Deucalion the merit that belonged to Noah.

FABLE VII [I.216-243]

Lycaon, king of Arcadia, in order to discover if it is Jupiter himself who has come to lodge in his palace, orders the body of an hostage, who had been sent to him, to be dressed and served up at a feast. The God, as a punishment, changes him into a wolf.

I had now passed Mænalus, to be dreaded for its dens of beasts of prey, and the pine-groves of cold Lycæus, together with Cyllene.[44] After this, I entered the realms and the inhospitable abode of the Arcadian tyrant, just as the late twilight was bringing on the night. I gave a signal that a God had come, and the people commenced to pay their adorations. In the first place, Lycaon derided their pious supplications. Afterwards, he said, I will make trial, by a plain proof, whether this is a God, or whether he is a mortal; nor shall the truth remain a matter of doubt. He then makes preparations to destroy me, when sunk in sleep, by an unexpected death; this mode of testing the truth pleases him. And not content with that, with the sword he cuts the throat of an hostage that had been sent from the nation of the Molossians,[45] and then softens part of the quivering limbs, in boiling water, and part he roasts with fire placed beneath. Soon as he had placed these on the table, I, with avenging flames, overthrew the house upon the household Gods,[46] worthy of their master. Alarmed, he himself takes to flight, and having reached the solitude of the country, he howls aloud, and in vain attempts to speak; his mouth gathers rage from himself, and through its usual desire for slaughter, it is directed against the sheep, and even still delights in blood. His garments are changed into hair, his arms into legs; he becomes a wolf, and he still retains vestiges of his ancient form. His hoariness is still the same, the same violence appears in his features; his eyes are bright as before; he is still the same image of ferocity.

"Thus fell one house; but one house alone did not deserve to perish; wherever the earth extends, the savage Erinnys[47] reigns. You would suppose that men had conspired to be wicked; let all men speedily feel that vengeance which they deserve to endure, for such is my determination."

[Footnote 44: Together with Cyllene.—Ver. 217. Cyllenus, or Cyllene, was a mountain of Arcadia, sacred to Mercury, who was hence called by the poets Cyllenius. Lycæus was also a mountain of Arcadia, sacred to Pan, and was covered with groves of pine-trees.]

[Footnote 45: Of the Molossians.—Ver. 226. The Molossi were a people of Epirus, on the eastern side of the Ambracian gulf. Ovid here commits a slight anachronism, as the name was derived from Molossus, the son of Neoptolemus, long after the time of Lycaon. Besides, as Burmann observes, who could believe that 'wars could be waged at such an early period between nations so distant as the Molossi and the Arcadians?' Apollodorus says, that it was a child of the same country, whose flesh Lycaon set before Jupiter. Other writers say that it was Nyctimus, the son of Lycaon, or Arcas, his grandson, that was slain by him.]

[Footnote 46: Upon the household Gods.—Ver. 231. This punishment was awarded to the Penates, or household Gods of Lycaon, for taking such a miscreant under their protection.]

[Footnote 47: The savage Erinnys.—Ver. 241. Erinnys was a general name given to the Furies by the Greeks. They were three in number—Alecto, Tisiphone, and Megæra. These were so called, either from the Greek ἔρις νοῦ, 'the discord of the mind,' or from ἐν τῇ ἔρα ναίειν, 'their inhabiting the earth,' watching the actions of men.]

EXPLANATION

If Ovid is not here committing an anachronism, and making Jupiter, before the deluge, relate the story of a historical personage, who existed long after it, the origin of the story of Lycaon must be sought in the antediluvian narrative. It is just possible that the guilty Cain may have been the original of Lycaon. The names are not very dissimilar: they are each mentioned as the first murderer; and the fact, that Cain murdered Abel at the moment when he was offering sacrifice to the Almighty, may have given rise to the tradition that Lycaon had set human flesh before the king of heaven. The Scripture, too, tells us, that Cain was personally called to account by the Almighty for his deed of blood.

The punishment here inflicted on Lycaon was not very dissimilar to that with which Cain was visited. Cain was sentenced to be a fugitive and a wanderer on the face of the earth; and such is essentially the character of the wolf, shunned by both men and animals. Of course, there are many points to which it is not possible to extend the parallel. Some of the ancient writers tell us, that there were two Lycaons, the first of whom was the son of Phoroneus, who reigned in Arcadia about the time of the patriarch Jacob; and the second, who succeeded him, polluted the festivals of the Gods by the sacrifice of the human race; for, having erected an altar to Jupiter, at the city of Lycosura, he slew human victims on it, whence arose the story related by the Poet. This solution is given by Pausanias, in his Arcadica. We are also told by that historian, and by Suidas, that Lycaon was, notwithstanding, a virtuous prince, the benefactor of his people, and the promoter of improvement.

Jupiter, not thinking the punishment of Lycaon sufficient to strike terror into the rest of mankind, resolves, on account of the universal corruption, to extirpate them by a universal deluge.

Some, by their words approve the speech of Jupiter, and give spur to him, indignantly exclaiming; others, by silent assent fulfil their parts. Yet the entire destruction of the human race is a cause of grief to them all, and they inquire what is to be the form of the earth in future, when destitute of mankind? who is to place frankincense[48] on the altars? and whether it is his design to give up the nations for a prey to the wild beasts? The ruler of the Gods forbids them making these enquiries, to be alarmed (for that the rest should be his care); and he promises, that from a wondrous source he will raise a generation unlike the preceding race.

And now he was about to scatter his thunder over all lands; but he was afraid lest, perchance, the sacred æther might catch fire, from so many flames, and the extended sky might become inflamed. He remembers, too, that it was in the decrees of Fate, that a time should come,[49] at which the sea, the earth, and the palace of heaven, seized by the flames, should be burned, and the laboriously-wrought fabric of the universe should be in danger of perishing. The weapons forged by the hands of the Cyclops are laid aside; a different mode of punishment pleases him: to destroy mankind beneath the waves, and to let loose the rains from the whole tract of Heaven. At once he shuts the North Wind in the caverns of Æolus, and all those blasts which dispel the clouds drawn over the Earth; and then he sends forth the South Wind. With soaking wings the South Wind flies abroad, having his terrible face covered with pitchy darkness; his beard is loaded with showers, the water streams down from his hoary locks, clouds gather upon his forehead, his wings and the folds of his robe[50] drip with wet; and, as with his broad hand he squeezes the hanging clouds, a crash arises, and thence showers are poured in torrents from the sky. Iris,[51] the messenger of Juno, clothed in various colors, collects the waters, and bears a supply upwards to the clouds.

The standing corn is beaten down, and the expectations of the husbandman, now lamented by him, are ruined, and the labors of a long year prematurely perish. Nor is the wrath of Jove satisfied with his own heaven; but Neptune, his azure brother, aids him with his auxiliary waves. He calls together the rivers, which, soon as they had entered the abode of their ruler, he says, "I must not now employ a lengthened exhortation; pour forth all your might, so the occasion requires. Open your abodes, and, each obstacle removed, give full rein to your streams." Thus he commanded; they return, and open the mouths of their fountains,[52] and roll on into the ocean with unobstructed course. He himself struck the Earth with his trident, on which it shook, and with a tremor laid open the sources of its waters. The rivers, breaking out, rush through the open plains, and bear away, together with the standing corn, the groves, flocks, men, houses, and temples, together with their sacred utensils. If any house remained, and, not thrown down, was able to resist ruin so vast, yet the waves, rising aloft, covered the roof of that house, and the towers tottered, overwhelmed beneath the stream. And now sea and land had no mark of distinction; everything now was ocean; and to that ocean shores were wanting. One man takes possession of a hill, another sits in a curved boat, and plies the oars there where he had lately ploughed; another sails over the standing corn, or the roof of his country-house under water; another catches a fish on the top of an elm-tree. An anchor (if chance so directs) is fastened in a green meadow, or the curving keels come in contact with the vineyards, now below them; and where of late the slender goats had cropped the grass, there unsightly sea-calves are now reposing their bodies.

The Nereids wonder at the groves, the cities, and the houses under water; dolphins get into the woods, and run against the lofty branches, and beat against the tossed oaks. The wolf swims[53] among the sheep; the wave carries along the tawny lions; the wave carries along the tigers. Neither does the powers of his lightning-shock avail the wild boar, nor his swift legs the stag, now borne away. The wandering bird, too, having long sought for land, where it may be allowed to light, its wings failing, falls down into the sea. The boundless range of the sea had overwhelmed the hills, and the stranger waves beat against the heights of the mountains. The greatest part is carried off by the water: those whom the water spares, long fastings overcome, through scantiness of food.

[Footnote 48: To place frankincense.—Ver. 249. In those early ages, corn or wheaten flour, was the customary offering to the Deities, and not frankincense, which was introduced among the luxuries of more refined times. Ovid is consequently guilty of an anachronism here.]

[Footnote 49: That a time should come.—Ver. 256. Lactantius informs us that the Sibyls predicted that the world should perish by fire. Seneca also, in his consolation to Marcia, and in his Quæstiones Naturales, mentions the same destined termination of the present state of the universe. It was a doctrine of the Stoic philosophers, that the stars were nurtured with moisture, and that on the cessation of this nourishment the conflagration of the universe would ensue.]

[Footnote 50: The folds of his robe.—Ver. 267. 'Rorant pennæ sinusque,' is quaintly translated by Clarke, 'his wings and the plaits of his coat drop.']

[Footnote 51: Iris.—Ver. 271. The mention of Iris, the goddess of the rainbow, in connection with the flood of Deucalion, cannot fail to remind us of the 'bow set in the cloud, for a token of the covenant between God and the earth,' on the termination of Noah's flood.—Gen. x. 14.]

[Footnote 52: The mouths of their fountains.—Ver. 281. The expressions in this line and in line 283, are not unlike the words of the 11th verse of the 7th chapter of Genesis, 'The fountains of the great deep were broken up.']

[Footnote 53: The wolf swims.—Ver. 304. One commentator remarks here, that there was nothing very wonderful in a dead wolf swimming among the sheep without devouring them. Seneca is, however, too severe upon our author in saying that he is trifling here, in troubling himself on so serious an occasion with what sheep and wolves are doing: for he gravely means to say, that the beasts of prey are terrified to that degree that they forget their carnivorous propensities.]

EXPLANATION

Pausanias makes mention of five deluges. The two most celebrated happened in the time of Ogyges, and in that of Deucalion. Of the last Ovid here speaks; and though that deluge was generally said to have overflowed Thessaly only, he has evidently adopted in his narrative the tradition of the universal deluge, which all nations seem to have preserved. He says, that the sea joined its waters to those falling from heaven. The words of Scripture are (Genesis, vii. 11), 'All the fountains of the great deep were broken up, and the windows of heaven were opened.' In speaking of the top of Parnassus alone being left uncovered, the tradition here followed by Ovid probably referred to Mount Ararat, where Noah's ark rested. Noah and his family are represented by Deucalion and Pyrrha. Both Noah and Deucalion were saved for their virtuous conduct; when Noah went out of the ark, he offered solemn sacrifices to God; and Pausanias tells us that Deucalion, when saved, raised an altar to Jupiter the Liberator. The Poet tells us, that Deucalion's deluge was to be the last: God promised the same thing to Noah. Josephus, in his Antiquities, Book i., tells us, that the history of the universal deluge was written by Nicolas of Damascus, Berosus, Mnaseas, and other ancient writers, from whom the Greeks and Romans received it.

FABLE IX [I.313-366]

Neptune appeases the angry waves; and he commands Triton to sound his shell, that the sea may retire within its shores, and the rivers within their banks. Deucalion and Pyrrha are the only persons saved from the deluge.

Phocis separates the Aonian[54] from the Actæan region; a fruitful land while it was a land; but at that time it had become a part of the sea, and a wide plain of sudden waters. There a lofty mountain rises towards the stars, with two tops, by name Parnassus,[55] and advances beyond the clouds with its summit. When here Deucalion (for the sea had covered all other places), borne in a little ship, with the partner of his couch, first rested; they adored the Corycian Nymphs,[56] and the Deities of the mountain, and the prophetic Themis,[57] who at that time used to give out oracular responses. No man was there more upright than he, nor a greater lover of justice, nor was any woman more regardful of the Deities than she.

Soon as Jupiter beholds the world overflowed by liquid waters, and sees that but one man remains out of so many thousands of late, and sees that but one woman remains out of so many thousands of late, both guiltless, and both worshippers of the Gods, he disperses the clouds; and the showers being removed by the North Wind, he both lays open the earth to the heavens, and the heavens to the earth. The rage, too, of the sea does not continue; and his three-forked trident now laid aside, the ruler of the deep assuages the waters, and calls upon the azure Triton standing above the deep, and having his shoulders covered with the native purple shells;[58] and he bids him blow[59] his resounding trumpet, and, the signal being given, to call back the waves and the streams. The hollow-wreathed trumpet[60] is taken up by him, which grows to a great width from its lowest twist; the trumpet, which, soon as it receives the air in the middle of the sea, fills with its notes the shores lying under either sun. Then, too, as soon as it touched the lips of the God dripping with his wet beard, and being blown, sounded the bidden retreat;[61] it was heard by all the waters both of earth and sea, and stopped all those waters by which it was heard. Now the sea[62] again has a shore; their channels receive the full rivers; the rivers subside; the hills are seen to come forth. The ground rises, places increase in extent as the waters decrease; and after a length of time, the woods show their naked tops, and retain the mud left upon their branches.

The world was restored; which when Deucalion beheld to be empty, and how the desolate Earth kept a profound silence, he thus addressed Pyrrha, with tears bursting forth:—"O sister, O wife, O thou, the only woman surviving, whom a common origin,[63] and a kindred descent, and afterwards the marriage tie has united to me, and whom now dangers themselves unite to me; we two are the whole people of the earth, whatever both the East and the West behold; of all the rest, the sea has taken possession. And even now there is no certain assurance of our lives; even yet do the clouds terrify my mind. What would now have been thy feelings, if without me thou hadst been rescued from destruction, O thou deserving of compassion? In what manner couldst thou have been able alone to support this terror? With whom for a consoler, to endure these sorrows? For I, believe me, my wife, if the sea had only carried thee off, should have followed thee, and the sea should have carried me off as well. Oh that I could replace the people that are lost by the arts of my father,[64] and infuse the soul into the moulded earth! Now the mortal race exists in us two alone. Thus it has seemed good to the Gods, and we remain as mere samples of mankind."

[Footnote 54: The Aonian.—Ver. 313. Aonia was a mountainous region of Bœotia; and Actæa was an ancient name of Attica, from ἄκτη, the sea-shore.]

[Footnote 55: By name Parnassus.—Ver. 317. Mount Parnassus has two peaks, of which the one was called 'Tichoreum,' and was sacred to Bacchus; and the other 'Hypampeum,' and was devoted to Apollo and the Muses.]

[Footnote 56: The Corycian Nymphs.—Ver. 320. The Corycian Nymphs were so called from inhabiting the Corycian cavern in Mount Parnassus; they were fabled to be the daughters of Plistus, a river near Delphi. There was another Corycian cave in Cilicia, in Asia Minor.]

[Footnote 57: The prophetic Themis.—Ver. 321. Themis is said to have preceded Apollo in giving oracular responses at Delphi. She was the daughter of Cœlus and Terra, and was the first to instruct men to ask of the Gods that which was lawful and right, whence she took the name of Themis, which signifies in Greek, 'that which is just and right.']

[Footnote 58: The native purple shells.—Ver. 332. 'Murex' was the name of the shell-fish from which the Tyrian purple, so much valued by the ancients, was procured. Some suppose that the meaning here is, that Triton had his shoulders tinted with the purple color of the murex. It is, however, more probable that the Poet means to say that he had his neck and shoulders studded with the shells of the murex, perhaps as a substitute for scales.]

[Footnote 59: He bids him blow.—Ver. 333. There were several Tritons, or minor sea gods. The one mentioned here, the chief Triton, was fabled to be the son of Neptune and Amphitrite, who always preceded Neptune in his course, and whose arrival he was wont to proclaim by the sound of his shell. He was usually represented as swimming, with the upper part of his body resembling that of a human being, while his lower parts terminated with the tail of a fish.]

[Footnote 60: The hollow-wreathed trumpet.—Ver. 335. The 'Buccina,' or, as we call it, 'the conch shell,' was a kind of horn, or trumpet, made out of a shell, called 'buccinum.' It was sometimes artificially curved, and sometimes straight, retaining the original form of the shell. The twisted form of the shell was one of the characteristic features of the trumpet, which, in later times, was made of horn, wood, or metal, so as to imitate the shell. It was chiefly used among the Romans, to proclaim the watches of the day and of the night, which watches were thence called 'buccina prima,' 'secunda,' etc. It was also blown at funerals, and at festive entertainments, both before sitting down to table and after. Macrobius tells us, that Tritons holding 'buccinæ' were fixed on the roof of the temple of Saturn.]

[Footnote 61: The bidden retreat.—Ver. 340. 'Canere receptus' was 'to sound the retreat,' as the signal for the soldiers to cease fighting, and to resume their march.]

[Footnote 62: Now the sea.—Ver. 343. This and the two following lines are considered as entitled to much praise for their terseness and brevity, as depicting by their short detached sentences the instantaneous effect produced by the commands of Neptune in reducing his dominions to a state of order.]

[Footnote 63: A common origin.—Ver. 352. Because Prometheus was the father of Deucalion and Epimetheus of Pyrrha; Prometheus and Epimetheus being the sons of Iapetus. It is in an extended sense that he styles her 'sister,' she being really his cousin.]

[Footnote 64: The arts of my father.—Ver. 363. He alludes to the story of his father, Prometheus, having formed men of clay, and animated them with fire stolen from heaven.]

EXPLANATION

Jupiter, Neptune, and Pluto, were, perhaps, originally three brothers, kings of three separate kingdoms. Having been deified each retaining his sovereignty, they were depicted as having the world divided between them; the empire of the sea falling to the share of Neptune. Among his occupations, were those of raising and calming the seas; and Ovid here represents him as being so employed.

FABLE X [I.367-415]

Deucalion and Pyrrha re-people the earth by casting stones behind them, in the manner prescribed by the Goddess Themis, whose oracle they had consulted.

He thus spoke, and they wept. They resolved to pray to the Deities of Heaven, and to seek relief through the sacred oracles. There is no delay; together they repair to the waters of Cephisus,[65] though not yet clear, yet now cutting their wonted channel. Then, when they have sprinkled the waters poured on their clothes[66] and their heads, they turn their steps to the temple of the sacred Goddess, the roof of which was defiled with foul moss, and whose altars were standing without fires. Soon as they reached the steps of the temple, each of them fell prostrate on the ground, and, trembling, gave kisses to the cold pavement. And thus they said:

"If the Deities, prevailed upon by just prayers, are to be mollified, if the wrath of the Gods is to be averted; tell us, O Themis, by what art the loss of our race is to be repaired, and give thy assistance, O most gentle Goddess to our ruined fortunes." The Goddess was moved, and gave this response: "Depart from my temple, and cover your heads,[67] and loosen the garments girt around you, and throw behind your backs the bones of your great mother." For a long time they are amazed; and Pyrrha is the first by her words to break the silence, and then refuses to obey the commands of the Goddess; and begs her, with trembling lips, to grant her pardon, and dreads to offend the shades of her mother by casting her bones. In the meantime they reconsider the words of the response given, but involved in dark obscurity, and they ponder them among themselves. Upon that, the son of Prometheus soothes the daughter of Epimetheus with these gentle words, and says, "Either is my discernment fallacious, or the oracles are just, and advise no sacrilege. The earth is the great mother; I suspect that the stones in the body of the earth are the bones meant; these we are ordered to throw behind our backs." Although she, descended from Titan,[68] is moved by this interpretation of her husband, still her hope is involved in doubt; so much do they both distrust the advice of heaven; but what harm will it do to try?

They go down, and they veil their heads, and ungird their garments, and cast stones, as ordered, behind their footsteps. The stones (who could have believed it, but that antiquity is a witness of the thing?) began to lay aside their hardness and their stiffness, and by degrees to become soft; and when softened, to assume a new form. Presently after, when they were grown larger, a milder nature, too, was conferred on them, so that some shape of man might be seen in them, yet though but imperfect; and as if from the marble commenced to be wrought, not sufficiently distinct, and very like to rough statues. Yet that part of them which was humid with any moisture, and earthy, was turned into portions adapted for the use of the body. That which is solid, and cannot be bent, is changed into bones; that which was just now a vein, still remains under the same name.[69] And in a little time, by the interposition of the Gods above, the stones thrown by the hands of the man, took the shape of a man, and the female race was renewed by the throwing of the woman. Thence are we a hardy generation, and able to endure fatigue, and we give proofs from what original we are sprung.

[Footnote 65: The waters of Cephisus.—Ver. 369. The river Cephisus rises on Mount Parnassus, and flows near Delphi.]

[Footnote 66: Poured on their clothes.—Ver. 371. It was the custom of the ancients, before entering a temple, either to sprinkle themselves with water, or to wash the body all over.]

[Footnote 67: Cover your heads.—Ver. 382. It was a custom among the ancients to cover their heads in sacrifice and other acts of worship, either as a mark of humility, or, according to Plutarch, that nothing of ill omen might meet their sight, and thereby interrupt the performance of the rites.]

[Footnote 68: Descended from Titan.—Ver. 395. Pyrrha was of the race of the Titans; for Iapetus, her grandfather, was the son of Titan and Terra.]

[Footnote 69: Under the same name.—Ver. 410. With his usual propensity for punning, he alludes to the use of the word 'vena,' as signifying either 'a vein' of the body, or a 'streak' or 'vein' in stone, according to the context.]

EXPLANATION

In the reign of Deucalion, king of Thessaly, the course of the river Peneus was stopped, probably by an earthquake. In the same year so great a quantity of rain fell, that all Thessaly was overflowed. Deucalion and some of his subjects fled to Mount Parnassus; where they remained until the waters abated. The children of those who were preserved are the stones of which the Poet here speaks. The Fable, probably, has for its foundation the double meaning of the word 'Eben,' or 'Aben,' which signifies either 'a stone,' or 'a child.' The Scholiast on Pindar tells us, too, that the word λάος, which means people, formerly also signified 'a stone.'

The brutal and savage nature of the early races of men may also have added strength to the tradition that they derived their original from stones. After the inundation, Deucalion is said to have repaired to Athens, where he built a temple to Jupiter, and instituted sacrifices in his honor. Some suppose that

Cranaus reigned at Athens when Deucalion retired thither; though Eusebius informs us it was under the reign of Cecrops. Deucalion was the son of Prometheus, and his wife Pyrrha was the daughter of his uncle, Epimetheus. After his death, he received the honor of a temple, and was worshipped as a Divinity.

FABLE XI [I.416-451]

The Earth, being warmed by the heat of the sun, produces many monsters: among others, the serpent Python, which Apollo kills with his arrows. To establish a memorial of this event, he institutes the Pythian games, and adopts the surname of Pythius.

The Earth of her own accord brought forth other animals of different forms; after that the former moisture was thoroughly heated by the rays of the sun, and the mud and the wet fens fermented with the heat; and the fruitful seeds of things nourished by the enlivening soil, as in the womb of a mother, grew, and, in lapse of time, assumed some regular shape. Thus, when the seven-streamed Nile[70] has forsaken the oozy fields, and has returned its waters to their ancient channel, and the fresh mud has been heated with the æthereal sun, the laborers, on turning up the clods, meet with very many animals, and among them, some just begun at the very moment of their formation, and some they see still imperfect, and as yet destitute of some of their limbs; and often, in the same body, is one part animated, the other part is coarse earth. For when moisture and heat have been subjected to a due mixture, they conceive; and all things arise from these two.

And although fire is the antagonist of heat, yet a moist vapor creates all things, and this discordant concord is suited for generation; when, therefore, the Earth, covered with mud by the late deluge, was thoroughly heated by the æthereal sunshine and a penetrating warmth, it produced species of creatures innumerable; and partly restored the former shapes, and partly gave birth to new monsters. She, indeed, might have been unwilling, but then she produced thee as well, thou enormous Python; and thou, unheard-of serpent, wast a source of terror to this new race of men, so vast a part of a mountain didst thou occupy.

The God that bears the bow, and that had never before used such arms, but against the deer and the timorous goats, destroyed him, overwhelmed with a thousand arrows, his quiver being well-nigh exhausted, as the venom oozed forth through the black wounds; and that length of time might not efface the fame of the deed, he instituted sacred games,[71] with contests famed in story, called "Pythia," from the name of the serpent so conquered. In these, whosoever of the young men conquered in boxing, in running, or in chariot-racing, received the honor of a crown of beechen leaves.[72] As yet the laurel existed not, and Phœbus used to bind his temples, graceful with long hair, with garlands from any tree.

[Footnote 70: The seven-streamed Nile.—Ver. 423. The river Nile discharges itself into the sea by seven mouths. It is remarkable for its inundations, which happen regularly every year, and overflow the whole country of Egypt. To this is chiefly owing the extraordinary fertility of the soil of that country; for when the waters subside, they leave behind them great quantities of mud, which, settling upon the land, enrich it, and continually reinvigorate it.]

[Footnote 71: Instituted sacred games.—Ver. 446. Yet Pausanias, in his Corinthiaca, tells us that they were instituted by Diomedes; others, again, say by Eurylochus the Thessalian; and others, by

Amphictyon, or Adrastus. The Pythian games were celebrated near Delphi, on the Crissæan plain, which contained a race-course, a stadium of 1000 feet in length, and a theatre, in which the musical contests took place. They were once held at Athens, by the advice of Demetrius Poliorcetes, because the Ætolians were in possession of the passes round Delphi. They were most probably originally a religious ceremonial, and were perhaps only a musical contest, which consisted in singing a hymn in honor of the Pythian God, accompanied by the music of the cithara. In later times, gymnastic and equestrian games and exercises were introduced there. Previously to the 48th Olympiad, the Pythian games had been celebrated at the end of every eighth year; after that period they were held at the end of every fourth year. When they ceased to be solemnized is unknown; but in the time of the Emperor Julian they still continued to be held.]

[Footnote 72: Crown of beechen leaves.—Ver. 449. This was the prize which was originally given to the conquerors in the Pythian games. In later times, as Ovid tells us, the prize of the victor was a laurel chaplet, together with the palm branch, symbolical of his victory.]

EXPLANATION

The story of the serpent Python, being explained on philosophical principles, seems to mean, that the heat of the sun, having dissipated the noxious exhalations emitted by the receding waters, the reptiles, which had been produced from the slime left by the flood, immediately disappeared.

If, however, we treat this narrative as based on historical facts, it is probable that the serpent represented some robber who infested the neighborhood of Parnassus, and molested those who passed that way for the purpose of offering sacrifice. A prince, either bearing the name of Apollo, or being a priest of that God, by his destruction liberated that region from this annoyance. This event gave rise to the institution of the Pythian games, which were celebrated near Delphi. Besides the several contests mentioned by Ovid, singing, dancing, and instrumental music, formed part of the exercises of these games. The event which Ovid here places soon after the deluge, must have happened much later, since in the time of Deucalion, the worship of Apollo was not known at Delphi. The Goddess Themis then delivered oracles there, which, previously to her time, had been delivered by the Earth.

FABLE XII [I.452-567]

Apollo, falling in love with Daphne, the daughter of the river Peneus, she flies from him. He pursues her; on which, the Nymph, imploring the aid of her father, is changed into a laurel.

Daphne, the daughter of Peneus, was the first love of Phœbus; whom, not blind chance, but the vengeful anger of Cupid assigned to him.

The Delian God,[73] proud of having lately subdued the serpent, had seen him bending the bow and drawing the string, and had said, "What hast thou to do, wanton boy, with gallant arms? Such a burden as that better befits my shoulders; I, who am able to give unerring wounds to the wild beasts, wounds to the enemy, who lately slew with arrows innumerable the swelling Python, that covered so many acres of land with his pestilential belly. Do thou be contented to excite I know not what flames with thy torch; and do not lay claim to praises properly my own."

To him the son of Venus replies, "Let thy bow shoot all things, Phœbus; my bow shall shoot thee; and as much as all animals fall short of thee, so much is thy glory less than mine." He thus said; and cleaving the air with his beating wings, with activity he stood upon the shady heights of Parnassus, and drew two weapons out of his arrow-bearing quiver, of different workmanship; the one repels, the other excites desire. That which causes love is of gold, and is brilliant, with a sharp point; that which repels it is blunt, and contains lead beneath the reed. This one the God fixed in the Nymph, the daughter of Peneus, but with the other he wounded the very marrow of Apollo, through his bones pierced by the arrow. Immediately the one is in love; the other flies from the very name of a lover, rejoicing in the recesses of the woods, and in the spoils of wild beasts taken in hunting, and becomes a rival of the virgin Phœbe. A fillet tied together[74] her hair, put up without any order. Many a one courted her; she hated all wooers; not able to endure, and quite unacquainted with man, she traverses the solitary parts of the woods, and she cares not what Hymen,[75] what love, or what marriage means. Many a time did her father say, "My daughter, thou owest me a son-in-law;" many a time did her father say, "My daughter, thou owest me grandchildren." She, utterly abhorring the nuptial torch,[76] as though a crime, has her beauteous face covered with the blush of modesty; and clinging to her father's neck, with caressing arms, she says, "Allow me, my dearest father, to enjoy perpetual virginity; her father, in times, bygone, granted this to Diana."

He indeed complied. But that very beauty forbids thee to be what thou wishest, and the charms of thy person are an impediment to thy desires. Phœbus falls in love, and he covets an alliance with Daphne, now seen by him, and what he covets he hopes for, and his own oracles deceive him; and as the light stubble is burned, when the ears of corn are taken off, and as hedges are set on fire by the torches, which perchance a traveller has either held too near them, or has left there, now about the break of day, thus did the God burst into a flame; thus did he burn throughout his breast, and cherish a fruitless passion with his hopes. He beholds her hair hanging unadorned upon her neck, and he says, "And what would it be if it were arranged?" He sees her eyes, like stars, sparkling with fire; he sees her lips, which it is not enough to have merely seen; he praises both her fingers and her hands, and her arms and her shoulders naked, from beyond the middle; whatever is hidden from view, he thinks to be still more beauteous. Swifter than the light wind she flies, and she stops not at these words of his, as he calls her back:

"O Nymph, daughter of Peneus, stay, I entreat thee! I am not an enemy following thee. In this way the lamb flies from the wolf; thus the deer flies from the lion; thus the dove flies from the eagle with trembling wing; in this way each creature flies from its enemy: love is the cause of my following thee. Ah! wretched me! shouldst thou fall on thy face, or should the brambles tear thy legs, that deserve not to be injured, and should I prove the cause of pain to thee. The places are rugged, through which thou art thus hastening; run more leisurely, I entreat thee, and restrain thy flight; I myself will follow more leisurely. And yet, inquire whom thou dost please; I am not an inhabitant of the mountains, I am not a shepherd; I am not here, in rude guise,[77] watching the herds or the flocks. Thou knowest not, rash girl, thou knowest not from whom thou art flying, and therefore it is that thou dost fly. The Delphian land, Claros and Tenedos,[78] and the Pataræan palace pays service to me. Jupiter is my sire; by me, what shall be, what has been, and what is, is disclosed; through me, songs harmonize with the strings. My own arrow, indeed, is unerring; yet one there is still more unerring than my own, which has made this wound in my heart, before unscathed. The healing art is my discovery, and throughout the world I am honored as the bearer of help, and the properties of simples are[79] subjected to me. Ah, wretched me![80] that love is not to be cured by any herbs; and that those arts which afford relief to all, are of no avail for their master."

The daughter of Peneus flies from him, about to say still more, with timid step, and together with him she leaves his unfinished address. Then, too, she appeared lovely; the winds exposed her form to view, and the gusts meeting her fluttered about her garments, as they came in contact, and the light breeze spread behind her her careless locks; and thus, by her flight, was her beauty increased. But the youthful God[81] has not patience any longer to waste his blandishments; and as love urges him on, he follows her steps with hastening pace. As when the greyhound[82] has seen the hare in the open field, and the one by the speed of his legs pursues his prey, the other seeks her safety; the one is like as if just about to fasten on the other, and now, even now, hopes to catch her, and with nose outstretched plies upon the footsteps of the hare. The other is in doubt whether she is caught already, and is delivered from his very bite, and leaves behind the mouth just touching her. And so is the God, and so is the virgin;[83] he swift with hopes, she with fear.

Yet he that follows, aided by the wings of love, is the swifter, and denies her any rest; and is now just at her back as she flies, and is breathing upon her hair scattered upon her neck. Her strength being now spent, she grows pale, and being quite faint, with the fatigue of so swift a flight, looking upon the waters of Peneus, she says, "Give me, my father, thy aid, if you rivers have divine power. Oh Earth, either yawn to swallow me, or by changing it, destroy that form, by which I have pleased too much, and which causes me to be injured."

Hardly had she ended her prayer, when a heavy torpor seizes her limbs; and her soft breasts are covered with a thin bark. Her hair grows into green leaves, her arms into branches; her feet, the moment before so swift, adhere by sluggish roots; a leafy canopy overspreads her features; her elegance alone[84] remains in her. This, too, Phœbus admires, and placing his right hand upon the stock, he perceives that the breast still throbs beneath the new bark; and then, embracing the branches as though limbs in his arms, he gives kisses to the wood, and yet the wood shrinks from his kisses. To her the God said: "But since thou canst not be my wife, at least thou shalt be my tree; my hair, my lyre,[85] my quiver shall always have thee, oh laurel! Thou shalt be presented to the Latian chieftains, when the joyous voice of the soldiers shall sing the song of triumph,[86] and the long procession shall resort to the Capitol. Thou, the same, shalt stand as a most faithful guardian at the gate-posts of Augustus before his doors,[87] and shalt protect the oak placed in the centre; and as my head is ever youthful with unshorn locks, do thou, too, always wear the lasting honors of thy foliage."

Pæan had ended his speech; the laurel nodded assent with its new-made boughs, and seemed to shake its top just like a head.

[Footnote 73: The Delian God.—Ver. 454. Apollo is so called, from having been born in the Isle of Delos, in the Ægean Sea. The Peneus was a river of Thessaly.]

[Footnote 74: A fillet tied together.—Ver. 477. The 'vitta' was a band encircling the head, and served to confine the tresses of the hair. It was worn by maidens and by married women also; but the 'vitta' assumed on the day of marriage was of a different form from that used by virgins. It was not worn by women of light character, or even by the 'libertinæ,' or female slaves who had been liberated; so that it was not only deemed an emblem of chastity, but of freedom also. It was of various colors: white and purple are mentioned. In the later ages the 'vitta' was sometimes set with pearls.]

[Footnote 75: Hymen.—Ver. 480. Hymen, or Hymenæus, was one of the Gods of Marriage; hence the name 'Hymen' was given to the union of two persons in marriage.]

[Footnote 76: The nuptial torch.—Ver. 483. Plutarch tells us, that it was the custom in the bridal procession to carry five torches before the bride, on her way to the house of her husband. Among the Romans, the nuptial torch was lighted at the parental hearth of the bride, and was borne before her by a boy, whose parents were alive. The torch was also used at funerals, for the purpose of lighting the pile, and because funerals were often nocturnal ceremonies. Hence the expression of Propertius,—'Vivimus inter utramque facem,' 'We are living between the two torches.' Originally, the 'tædæ' seem to have been slips or lengths of resinous pine wood: while the 'fax' was formed of a bundle of wooden staves, either bound by a rope drawn round them in a spiral form, or surrounded by circular bands at equal distances. They were used by travellers and others, who were forced to be abroad after sunset; whence the reference in line 493 to the hedge ignited through the carelessness of the traveller, who has thrown his torch there on the approach of morning.]

[Footnote 77: Here in rude guise.—Ver. 514. 'Non hic armenta gregesve Horridus observo' is quaintly translated by Clarke, 'I do not here in a rude pickle watch herds or flocks.']

[Footnote 78: Claros and Tenedos.—Ver. 516. Claros was a city of Ionia, famed for a temple and oracle of Apollo, and near which there was a mountain and a grove sacred to him. There was an island in the Myrtoan Sea of that name, to which some suppose that reference is here made. Tenedos was an island of the Ægean Sea, in the neighborhood of Troy. Patara was a city of Lycia, where Apollo gave oracular responses during six months of the year. It was from Patara that St. Paul took ship for Phœnicia, Acts, xxi. 1, 2.]

[Footnote 79: The properties of simples.—Ver. 522. The first cultivators of the medical art pretended to nothing beyond an acquaintance with the medicinal qualities of herbs and simples; it is not improbable that inasmuch as the vegetable world is nourished and raised to the surface of the earth in a great degree by the heat of the sun, a ground was thereby afforded for allegorically saying that Apollo, or the Sun, was the discoverer of the healing art.]

[Footnote 80: Ah! wretched me!—Ver. 523. A similar expression occurs in the Heroides, v. 149, 'Me miseram, quod amor non est medicabilis herbis.']

[Footnote 81: The youthful God.—Ver. 531. Apollo was always represented as a youth, and was supposed never to grow old. The Scholiast on the Thebais of Statius, b. i., v. 694, says, 'The reason is, because Apollo is the Sun; and because the Sun is fire, which never grows old.' Perhaps the youthfulness of the Deity is here mentioned, to account for his ardent pursuit of the flying damsel.]

[Footnote 82: As when the greyhound.—Ver. 533. The comparison here of the flight of Apollo after Daphne, to that of the greyhound after the hare, is considered to be very beautifully drawn, and to give an admirable illustration of the eagerness with which the God pursues on the one hand, and the anxiety with which the Nymph endeavors to escape on the other. Pope, in his Windsor Forest, has evidently imitated this passage, where he describes the Nymph Lodona pursued by Pan, and transformed into a river. His words are—

'Not half so swift the trembling doves can fly,
When the fierce eagle cleaves the liquid sky;

Not half so swiftly the fierce eagle moves,
When through the clouds he drives the trembling doves;
As from the God she flew with furious pace,
Or as the God more furious urged the chase.
Now fainting, sinking, pale, the nymph appears;
Now close behind, his sounding steps she hears;
And now his shadow reach'd her as she run,
His shadow lengthened by the setting sun;
And now his shorter breath, with sultry air,
Pants on her neck, and fans her parting hair.'

The greyhound was probably called 'canis Gallicus,' from having been originally introduced into Italy from Gaul. 'Vertagus' was their Gallic name, which we find used by Martial, and Gratian in his Cynegeticon, ver. 203.]

[Footnote 83: And so is the virgin.—Ver. 539. 'Sic Deus et virgo est' is translated by Clarke, 'So is the God and the young lady;' indeed, he mostly translates 'virgo,' 'young lady.']

[Footnote 84: Her elegance alone.—Ver. 552. Clarke translates 'Remanet nitor unus in illa,' 'her neatness alone continues in her.']

[Footnote 85: My lyre.—Ver. 559. The players of the cithara, the instrument of Apollo, were crowned with laurel, in the scenic representations of the stage.]

[Footnote 86: The song of triumph.—Ver. 560. The Poet here pays a compliment to Augustus and the Roman people. The laurel was the emblem of victory among the Romans. On such occasions the 'fasces' of the general and the spears and javelins of the soldiers were wreathed with laurel; and after the time of Julius Cæsar, the Roman general, when triumphing, wore a laurel wreath on his head, and held a branch of laurel in his hand.]

[Footnote 87: Before his doors.—Ver. 562. He here alludes to the civic crown of oak leaves which, by order of the Senate, was placed before the gate of the Palatium, where Augustus Cæsar resided, with branches of laurel on either side of it.]

EXPLANATION

To explain this Fable, it must be laid down as a principle that there were originally many Jupiters, and Apollos, and Mercuries, whose intrigues being, in lapse of time, attributed to but one individual, that fact accounts for the great number of children which claimed those respective Gods for their fathers.

Some prince probably, for whom his love of learning had acquired the name of Apollo, falling in love with Daphne, pursued her to the brink of the river Peneus, into which, being accidentally precipitated, she perished in her lover's sight. Some laurels growing near the spot, perhaps gave rise to the story of her transformation; or possibly the etymology of the word 'Daphne,' which in Greek signifies a laurel, was the foundation of the Fable. Pausanias, however, in his Arcadia, gives another version of this story. He says that Leucippus, son of Œnomaus, king of Pisa, falling in love with Daphne, disguised himself in female apparel, and devoted himself to her service. He soon procured her friendship and confidence; but Apollo, who was his rival, having discovered his fraud, one day redoubled the heat of the sun. Daphne and her companions going to bathe, obliged Leucippus to follow their example, on which, having discovered his stratagem, they killed him with the arrows which they carried for the purposes of hunting.

Diodorus Siculus tells us that Daphne was the same with Manto, the daughter of Tiresias, who was banished to Delphi, where she delivered oracles, of the language of which Homer availed himself in the composition of his poems. The inhabitants of Antioch asserted that the adventure here narrated happened in the suburbs of their city, which thence derived its name of Daphne.

FABLE XIII [I.568-600]

Jupiter, pursuing Io, the daughter of Inachus, covers the earth with darkness, and ravishes the Nymph.

There is a grove of Hæmonia,[88] which a wood, placed on a craggy rock, encloses on every side. They call it Tempe;[89] through this the river Peneus, flowing from the bottom of mount Pindus,[90] rolls along with its foaming waves, and in its mighty fall, gathers clouds that scatter a vapor like thin smoke,[91] and with its spray besprinkles the tops of the woods, and wearies places, far from near to it, with its noise. This is the home, this the abode, these are the retreats of the great river; residing here in a cavern formed by rocks, he gives law to the waters, and to the Nymphs that inhabit those waters. The rivers of that country first repair thither, not knowing whether they should congratulate, or whether console the parent; the poplar-bearing Spercheus,[92] and the restless Enipeus,[93] the aged Apidanus,[94] the gentle Amphrysus,[95] and Æas,[96] and, soon after, the other rivers, which, as their current leads them, carry down into the sea their waves, wearied by wanderings. Inachus[97] alone is absent, and, hidden in his deepest cavern, increases his waters with his tears, and in extreme wretchedness bewails his daughter Io as lost; he knows not whether she now enjoys life, or whether she is among the shades below; but her, whom he does not find anywhere, he believes to be nowhere, and in his mind he dreads the worst.

Jupiter had seen Io as she was returning from her father's stream, and had said, "O maid, worthy of Jove, and destined to make I know not whom happy in thy marriage, repair to the shades of this lofty grove (and he pointed at the shade of the grove) while it is warm, and while the Sun is at his height, in the midst of his course. But if thou art afraid to enter the lonely abodes of the wild beasts alone, thou shalt enter the recesses of the groves, safe under the protection of a God, and that a God of no common sort; but with me, who hold the sceptre of heaven in my powerful hand; me, who hurl the wandering lightnings—Do not fly from me;" for now she was flying. And now she had left behind the pastures of Lerna,[98] and the Lircæan plains planted with trees, when the God covered the earth far and wide with darkness overspreading, and arrested her flight, and forced her modesty.

[Footnote 88: A grove of Hæmonia.—Ver. 568. Hæmonia was an ancient name of Thessaly, so called from its king, Hæmon, a son of Pelasgus, and father of Thessalus, from which it received its later name.]

[Footnote 89: Call it Tempe.—Ver. 569. Tempe was a valley of Thessaly, proverbial for its pleasantness and the beauty of its scenery. The river Peneus ran through it, but not with the violence which Ovid here depicts; for Ælian tells us that it runs with a gentle sluggish stream, more like oil than water.]

[Footnote 90: Mount Pindus.—Ver. 570. Pindus was a mountain situate on the confines of Thessaly.]

[Footnote 91: Like thin smoke.—Ver. 571. He speaks of the spray, which in the fineness of its particles resembles smoke.]

[Footnote 92: Spercheus.—Ver. 579. The Spercheus was a rapid stream, flowing at the foot of Mount Æta into the Malian Gulf, and on whose banks many poplars grew.]

[Footnote 93: Enipeus.—Ver. 579. The Enipeus rises in Mount Othrys, and runs through Thessaly. Virgil (Georgics, iv. 468) calls it 'Altus Enipeus,' the deep Enipeus.]

[Footnote 94: Apidanus.—Ver. 580. The Apidanus, receiving the stream of the Enipeus at Pharsalia, flows into the Peneus. It is supposed by some commentators to be here called 'senex,' aged, from the slowness of its tide. But where it unites the Enipeus it flows with violence, so that it is probably called 'senex,' as having been known and celebrated by the poets from of old.]

[Footnote 95: Amphrysus.—Ver. 580. This river ran through that part of Thessaly known by the name of Phthiotis.]

[Footnote 96: Æas.—Ver. 580. Pliny the Elder (Book iii, ch. 23) calls this river Aous. It was a small limpid stream, running through Epirus and Thessaly, and discharging itself into the Ionian sea.]

[Footnote 97: Inachus.—Ver. 583. This was a river of Argolis, now known as the Naio. It took its rise either in Lycæus or Artemisium, mountains of Arcadia. Stephens, however, thinks that Lycæus was a mountain of Argolis.]

[Footnote 98: Lerna.—Ver. 597. This was a swampy spot on the Argive territory, where the poets say that the dragon with seven heads, called Hydra, which was slain by Hercules, had made his haunt. It is not improbable that the pestilential vapors of this spot were got rid of by means of its being drained under the superintendence of Hercules, on which fact the story was founded. Some commentators, however, suppose the Lerna to have been a flowing stream.]

EXPLANATION

The Greeks frequently embellished their mythology with narratives of Phœnician or Egyptian origin. The story of Io probably came from Egypt. Isis was one of the chief divinities of that country, and her worship naturally passed, with their colonies, into foreign countries. Greece received it when Inachus went to settle there, and in lapse of time Isis, under the name of Io, was supposed to have been his daughter, and the fable was invented which is here narrated by Ovid.

The Greek authors, Apollodorus, Strabo, Diodorus Siculus, and Pausanias, say that Io was the daughter of Inachus, the first king of Argos; that Jupiter carried her away to Crete; and that by her he had a son named Epaphus, who went to reign in Egypt, whither his mother accompanied him. They also tell us that she married Apis, or Osiris, who, after his death, was numbered among the Deities of Egypt by the name of Serapis. From them we also learn that Juno, being actuated by jealousy, on the discovery of the intrigue, put Io under the care of her uncle Argus, a man of great vigilance, but that Jupiter having slain him, placed his mistress on board of a vessel which had the figure of a cow at its head; from which circumstance arose the story of the transformation of Io. The Greek writers also state, that the Bosphorus, a part of the Ægean sea, derived its name from the passage of Io in the shape of a cow.

FABLE XIV [I.601-688]

Jupiter, having changed Io into a cow, to conceal her from the jealousy of Juno, is obliged to give her to that Goddess, who commits her to the charge of the watchful Argus. Jupiter sends Mercury with an injunction to cast Argus into a deep sleep, and to take away his life.

In the meantime Juno looked down upon the midst of the fields, and wondering that the fleeting clouds had made the appearance of night under bright day, she perceived that they were not the vapors from a river, nor were they raised from the moist earth, and then she looked around to see where her husband was, as being one who by this time was full well acquainted with the intrigues of a husband who had been so often detected.[99] After she had found him not in heaven, she said, "I am either deceived, or I am injured;" and having descended from the height of heaven, she alighted upon the earth, and commanded the mists to retire. He had foreseen the approach of his wife, and had changed the features of the daughter of Inachus into a sleek heifer.[100] As a cow, too, she is beautiful. The daughter of Saturn, though unwillingly, extols the appearance of the cow; and likewise inquires, whose it is, and whence, or of what herd it is, as though ignorant of the truth. Jupiter falsely asserts that it was produced out of the earth, that the owner may cease to be inquired after. The daughter of Saturn begs her of him as a gift. What can he do? It is a cruel thing to deliver up his own mistress, and not to give her up is a cause of suspicion. It is shame which persuades him on the one hand, love dissuades him on the other. His shame would have been subdued by his love; but if so trifling a gift as a cow should be refused to the sharer of his descent and his couch, she might well seem not to be a cow.

The rival now being given up to her, the Goddess did not immediately lay aside all apprehension; and she was still afraid of Jupiter, and was fearful of her being stolen, until she gave her to Argus, the son of Aristor, to be kept by him. Argus had his head encircled with a hundred eyes. Two of them used to take rest in their turns, the rest watched, and used to keep on duty.[101] In whatever manner he stood, he looked towards Io; although turned away, he still used to have Io before his eyes. In the daytime he suffers her to feed; but when the sun is below the deep earth, he shuts her up, and ties a cord round her neck undeserving of such treatment. She feeds upon the leaves of the arbute tree, and bitter herbs, and instead of a bed the unfortunate animal lies upon the earth, that does not always have grass on it, and drinks of muddy streams. And when, too, she was desirous, as a suppliant, to stretch out her arms to Argus, she had no arms to stretch out to Argus; and she uttered lowings from her mouth, when endeavoring to complain. And at this sound she was terrified, and was affrighted at her own voice.

She came, too, to the banks, where she was often wont to sport, the banks of her father, Inachus; and soon as she beheld her new horns in the water, she was terrified, and, astonished, she recoiled from herself. The Naiads knew her not, and Inachus himself knew her not, who she was; but she follows her father, and follows her sisters, and suffers herself to be touched, and presents herself to them, as they admire her. The aged Inachus held her some grass he had plucked; she licks his hand, and gives kisses to the palms of her father. Nor does she restrain her tears; and if only words would follow, she would implore his aid, and would declare her name and misfortunes. Instead of words, letters, which her foot traced in the dust, completed the sad discovery of the transformation of her body. "Ah, wretched me!" exclaims her father Inachus; and clinging to the horns and the neck of the snow-white cow, as she wept, he repeats, "Ah, wretched me! and art thou my daughter, that hast been sought for by me throughout all lands? While undiscovered, thou wast a lighter grief to me, than now, when thou art found. Thou art silent, and no words dost thou return in answer to mine; thou only heavest sighs from the depth of thy breast, and what alone thou art able to do, thou answerest in lowings to my words. But I, in ignorance of this, was preparing the bridal chamber, and the nuptial torches for thee; and my chief hope was that of a son-in-law, my next was that of grandchildren. But now must thou have a mate from the herd, now, too, an offspring of the herd. Nor is it possible for me to end grief so great by death; but it is a detriment to be a God; and the gate of death being shut against me, extends my grief to eternal ages."

While thus he lamented, the starry Argus removed her away, and carried the daughter, thus taken from her father, to distant pastures. He himself, at a distance, occupies the lofty top of a mountain, whence, as he sits, he may look about on all sides.

Nor can the ruler of the Gods above, any longer endure so great miseries of the granddaughter of Phoroneus;[102] and he calls his son Mercury, whom the bright Pleiad, Maia,[103] brought forth, and orders him to put Argus to death. There is but little delay to take wings upon his feet, and his soporiferous wand[104] in his hand, and a cap for his hair.[105] After he had put these things in order, the son of Jupiter leaps down from his father's high abode upon the earth, and there he takes off his cap, and lays aside his wings; his wand alone was retained. With this, as a shepherd, he drives some she-goats through the pathless country, taken up as he passed along, and plays upon oaten straws joined together.

The keeper appointed by Juno, charmed by the sound of this new contrivance, says, "Whoever thou art, thou mayst be seated with me upon this stone; for, indeed, in no other place is the herbage more abundant for thy flock; and thou seest, too, that the shade is convenient for the shepherds." The son of Atlas sat down, and with much talking he occupied the passing day with his discourse, and by playing upon his joined reeds he tried to overpower his watchful eyes. Yet the other strives hard to overcome soft sleep; and although sleep was received by a part of his eyes, yet with a part he still keeps watch. He inquires also (for the pipe had been but lately invented) by what method it had been found out.

[Footnote 99: So often detected.—Ver. 606. Clarke translates 'deprensi toties mariti' by the expression, 'who had been so often catched in his roguery.']

[Footnote 100: Into a sleek heifer.—Ver. 611. Clarke renders the words, 'nitentem juvencam,' a neat heifer.]

[Footnote 101: To keep on duty.—Ver. 627. 'In statione manebant.' This is a metaphorical expression, taken from military affairs, as soldiers in turns relieve each other, and take their station, when they keep watch and ward.]

[Footnote 102: Phoroneus.—Ver. 668. He was the father of Jasius and of Inachus, the parent of Io. Some accounts, however, say that Inachus was the father of Phoroneus, and the son of Oceanus.]

[Footnote 103: Pleiad Maia.—Ver. 670. Maia was one of the seven daughters of Atlas, who were styled Pleiädes after they were received among the constellations.]

[Footnote 104: Soporiferous wand.—Ver. 671. This was the 'caduceus,' or staff, with which Mercury summoned the souls of the departed from the shades, induced slumber, and did other offices pertaining to his capacity as the herald and messenger of Jupiter. It was represented as an olive branch, wreathed with two snakes. In time of war, heralds and ambassadors, among the Greeks, carried a 'caduceus.' It was not used by the Romans.]

[Footnote 105: A cap for his hair.—Ver. 672. This was a cap called 'Petasus.' It had broad brims, and was not unlike the 'causia,' or Macedonian hat, except that the brims of the latter were turned up at the sides.]

EXPLANATION

The story of the Metamorphosis of Io has been already enlarged upon in the Explanation of the preceding Fable. It may, however, not be irrelevant to observe, that myths, or mythological stories or fables, are frequently based upon some true history, corrupted by tradition in lapse of time. The poets, too, giving loose to their fancy in their love of the marvellous, have still further disfigured the original story; so that it is in most instances extremely difficult to trace back the facts to their primitive simplicity, by a satisfactory explanation of each circumstance attending them, either upon a philosophical, or an historical principle of solution.

FABLE XV [I.689-712]

Pan, falling in love with the Nymph Syrinx, she flies from him; on which he pursues her. Syrinx, arrested in her flight by the waves of the river Ladon, invokes the aid of her sisters, the Naiads, who change her into reeds. Pan unites them into an instrument with seven pipes, which bears the name of the Nymph.

Then the God says, "In the cold mountains of Arcadia, among the Hamadryads of Nonacris,[106] there was one Naiad very famous; the Nymphs called her Syrinx. And not once alone had she escaped the Satyrs as they pursued, and whatever Gods either the shady grove or the fruitful fields have in them. In her pursuits and her virginity itself she used to devote herself to the Ortygian Goddess;[107] and being clothed after the fashion of Diana, she might have deceived one, and might have been supposed to be the daughter of Latona, if she had not had a bow of cornel wood, the other, a bow of gold; and even then did she sometimes deceive people. Pan spies her as she is returning from the hill of Lycæus, and having his head crowned with sharp pine leaves, he utters such words as these;" it remained for Mercury to repeat the words, and how that the Nymph, slighting his suit, fled through pathless spots, until she came to the gentle stream of sandy Ladon;[108] and that here, the waters stopping her course, she prayed to her watery sisters, that they would change her; and how that Pan, when he was thinking that Syrinx was now caught by him, had seized hold of some reeds of the marsh, instead of the body of the Nymph; and how, while he was sighing there, the winds moving amid the reeds had made a murmuring noise, and like one complaining; and how that, charmed by this new discovery and the sweetness of the sound, he had said, "This mode of converse with thee shall ever remain with me;" and that accordingly, unequal reeds being stuck together among themselves by a cement of wax, had since retained the name of the damsel.

[Footnote 106: Nonacris.—Ver. 690. Nonacris was the name of both a mountain and a city of Arcadia, in the Peloponnesus.]

[Footnote 107: The Ortygian Goddess.—Ver. 694. Diana is called "Ortygian," from the isle of Delos, where she was born, one of whose names was Ortygia, from the quantity of quails, ὄρτυγες, there found.]

[Footnote 108: Ladon.—Ver. 702. This was a beautiful river of Arcadia, flowing into the Alpheus: its banks were covered with vast quantities of reeds. Ovid here calls its stream 'placidum;' whereas in the fifth book of the Fasti, l. 89, he calls it 'rapax,' 'violent;' and in the second book of the Fasti, l. 274, its waters are said to be 'citæ aquæ,' swift waters. Some commentators have endeavored to reconcile these discrepancies; but the probability is, that Ovid, like many other poets, used his epithets at random, or rather according to the requirements of the measure for the occasion.]

EXPLANATION

This appears to have been an Egyptian fable, imported into the works of the Grecian poets. Pan was probably a Divinity of the Egyptians, who worshipped nature under that name, as we are told by Herodotus and Diodorus Siculus. As, however, according to Nonnus, there were not less than twelve Pans, it is possible that the adventure here related may have been supposed to have happened to one of them who was a native of Greece. He was most probably the inventor of the Syrinx, or Pandæan pipe, and, perhaps, formed his first instrument from the produce of the banks of the River Ladon, from which circumstance Syrinx may have been styled the daughter of that river.

FABLE XVI [I.713-723]

Mercury, having lulled Argus to sleep, cuts off his head, and Juno places his eyes in the peacock's tail.

The Cyllenian God[109] being about to say such things, perceived that all his eyes were sunk in sleep, and that his sight was wrapped[110] in slumber. At once he puts an end to his song, and strengthens his slumbers, stroking his languid eyes with his magic wand. There is no delay; he wounds him, as he nods, with his crooked sword, where the head is joined to the neck; and casts him, all blood-stained, from the rock, and stains the craggy cliff with his gore.

Argus, thou liest low, and the light which thou hadst in so many eyes is now extinguished; and one night takes possession of a whole hundred eyes. The daughter of Saturn takes them, and places them on the feathers of her own bird, and she fills its tail with starry gems.

[Footnote 109: The Cyllenian God.—Ver. 713. Mercury is so called from Cyllene, in Arcadia, where he was born.]

[Footnote 110: That his sight was wrapped.—Ver. 714. Clarke translates 'Adopertaque lumina somno,' 'and his peepers covered with sleep.']

EXPLANATION

The ancient writers, Asclepiades and Pherecydes, tell us, that Argus was the son of Arestor. He is supposed by some to have been the fourth king of Argos after Inachus, and to have been a person of great wisdom and penetration, on account of which he was said to have a hundred eyes. Io most probably was committed to his charge, and he watched over her with the greatest care.

It is impossible to divine the reason why his eyes were said to have been set by Juno in the tail of the peacock; though, perhaps, the circumstance has no other foundation than the resemblance of the human eye to the spots in the tail of that bird, which was consecrated to Juno. Besides, if Juno is to be considered the symbol of Air, or Æther, through which light is transmitted to us, it is not surprising that the ancients bestowed so many eyes upon the bird which was consecrated to her.

FABLE XVII [I.724-779]

Io, terrified and maddened with dreadful visions, runs over many regions, and stops in Egypt, when Juno, at length, being pacified, restores her to her former shape, and permits her to be worshipped there, under the name of Isis.

Immediately, she was inflamed with rage, and deferred not the time of expressing her wrath; and she presented a dreadful Fury before the eyes and thoughts of the Argive mistress,[111] and buried in her bosom invisible stings, and drove her, in her fright, a wanderer through the whole earth. Thou, O Nile, didst remain, as the utmost boundary of her long wanderings. Soon as she arrived there, she fell upon her knees, placed on the edge of the bank, and raising herself up, with her neck thrown back, and casting to Heaven those looks which then alone she could, by her groans, and her tears, and her mournful lowing, she seemed to be complaining of Jupiter, and to be begging an end of her sorrows.

He, embracing the neck of his wife with his arms, entreats her, at length, to put an end to her punishment; and he says, "Lay aside thy fears for the future; she shall never more be the occasion of any trouble to thee;" and then he bids the Stygian waters to hear this oath. As soon as the Goddess is pacified, Io receives her former shape, and she becomes what she was before; the hairs flee from off of her body, her horns decrease, and the orb of her eye becomes less; the opening of her jaw is contracted; her shoulders and her hands return, and her hoof, vanishing, is disposed of into five nails; nothing of the cow remains to her, but the whiteness of her appearance; and the Nymph, contented with the service of two feet, is raised erect on them; and yet she is afraid to speak, lest she should low like a cow, and timorously tries again the words so long interrupted. Now, as a Goddess, she is worshipped by the linen-wearing throng[112] of Egypt.

To her, at length, Epaphus[113] is believed to have been born from the seed of great Jove, and throughout the cities he possesses temples joined to those of his parent. Phaëton, sprung from the Sun, was equal to him in spirit and in years; whom formerly, as he uttered great boasts, and yielded not at all to him, and proud of his father, Phœbus, the grandson of Inachus could not endure; and said, "Thou, like a madman, believest thy mother in all things, and art puffed up with the conceit of an imaginary father."

Phaëton blushed, and in shame repressed his resentment; and he reported to his mother, Clymene,[114] the reproaches of Epaphus; and said, "Mother, to grieve thee still more, I, the free, the bold youth, was silent; I am ashamed both that these reproaches can be uttered against us, and that they cannot be refuted; but do thou, if only I am born of a divine race, give me some proof of so great a descent, and claim me for heaven." Thus he spoke, and threw his arms around the neck of his mother; and besought her, by his own head and by that of Merops,[115] and by the nuptial torches of his sisters, that she would give him some token of his real father.

It is a matter of doubt whether Clymene was more moved by the entreaties of Phaëton, or by resentment at the charge made against her; and she raised both her arms to heaven, and, looking up to the light of the Sun, she said, "Son, I swear to thee, by this beam, bright with shining rays, which both hears and sees us, that thou, that thou, I say, wast begotten by this Sun, which thou beholdest; by this Sun, which governs the world. If I utter an untruth, let him deny himself to be seen by me, and let this light prove the last for my eyes. Nor will it be any prolonged trouble for thee to visit thy father's dwelling; the abode where he arises is contiguous to our regions.[116] If only thy inclination disposes thee, go forth, and thou shalt inquire of himself."

Phaëton immediately springs forth, overjoyed, upon these words of his mother, and reaches the skies in imagination; and he passes by his own Æthiopians, and the Indians situate beneath the rays of the Sun,[117] and briskly wends his way to the rising of his sire.

[Footnote 111: The Argive mistress.—Ver. 726. Clarke renders 'Pellicis Argolicæ,' 'of the Grecian miss.']

[Footnote 112: The linen-wearing throng.—Ver. 747. The priests, and worshippers of Isis, with whom Io is here said to be identical, paid their adoration to her clothed in linen vestments. Probably, Isis was the first to teach the Egyptians the cultivation of flax.]

[Footnote 113: Epaphus.—Ver. 748. Herodotus, in his second book, tells us, that this son of Jupiter, by Io, was the same as the Egyptian God, Apis. Eusebius, quoting from Apollodorus, says that Epaphus was the son of Io, by Telegonus, who married her.]

[Footnote 114: Clymene.—Ver. 756. She was a Nymph of the sea, the daughter of Oceanus and Tethys.]

[Footnote 115: Merops.—Ver. 763. He was king of Ethiopia, and marrying the Nymph Clymene, was either the stepfather of Phaëton, or, as some writers say, his putative father.]

[Footnote 116: To our regions.—Ver. 773. Ethiopia, which, in the time of Ovid, was generally looked upon as one of the regions of the East.]

[Footnote 117: The rays of the Sun.—Ver. 778. 'Ignibus sidereis,' means here the 'heat,' or 'fire of the sun,' the sun being considered as a 'sidus,' or 'luminous heavenly body.']

EXPLANATION

To the elucidation of this narrative, already given, we will only add, that some of the mythologists inform us, that when Mercury had lulled Argus to sleep, a youth named Hierax awoke him; on which Mercury killed Argus with a stone, and turned Hierax into a spar-hawk.

BOOK THE SECOND

FABLE I [II.1-303]

Phaëton, insulted by Epaphus, goes to the Palace of Apollo, to beseech him to give some token that he is his son. Apollo, having sworn, by the river Styx, to refuse him nothing that he should desire, he immediately asks to guide his chariot for one day. He is unsuccessful in the attempt, and, the horses running away, the world is in danger of being consumed.

The palace of the Sun was raised high, on stately columns, bright with radiant gold, and carbuncle that rivals the flames; polished ivory covered its highest top, and double folding doors shone with the brightness of silver. The workmanship even exceeded the material; for there Mulciber had carved the sea circling round the encompassed Earth; and the orb of the Earth, and the Heavens which hang over that orb. There the waves have in them the azure Deities, both Triton, sounding with his shell, and the changing Proteus, and Ægeon,[1] pressing the huge backs of whales with his arms; Doris,[2] too, and her daughters, part of whom appear to be swimming, part, sitting on the bank, to be drying their green hair; some are seen borne upon fishes. The features in all are not the same, nor, however, remarkably different: they are such as those of sisters ought to be. The Earth has upon it men and cities, and woods, and wild beasts, and rivers, and Nymphs, and other Deities of the country. Over these is placed the figure of the shining Heaven, and there are six Signs of the Zodiac on the right door, and as many on the left.

Soon as the son of Clymene had arrived thither by an ascending path, and entered the house of his parent, thus doubted of; he immediately turned his steps to the presence of his father, and stood at a distance, for he could not bear the refulgence nearer. Arrayed in a purple garment, Phœbus was seated on a throne sparkling with brilliant emeralds. On his right hand, and on his left, the Days, the Months, the Years, the Ages, and the Hours were arranged, at corresponding distances, and the fresh Spring was standing, crowned with a chaplet of blossoms; Summer was standing naked, and wearing garlands made of ears of corn; Autumn, too, was standing besmeared with the trodden-out grapes; and icy Winter, rough with his hoary hair.

Then the Sun, from the midst of this place, with those eyes with which he beholds all things, sees the young man struck with fear at the novelty of these things, and says, "What is the occasion of thy journey hither? What dost thou seek, Phaëton, in this my palace, a son not to be denied by his parent?"

He answers, "O thou universal Light of the unbounded World, Phœbus, my father, if thou grantest me the use of that name; and if Clymene is not concealing an error under a false pretext, give me, my parent, some token, by which I may be believed to be really thy progeny; and remove this uncertainty from my mind." Thus he spoke; but his parent took off the rays shining all around his head, and commanded him to come nearer; and, having embraced him, he says, "And neither art thou deserving to be denied to be mine, and Clymene has told thee thy true origin; and that thou mayst have the less doubt, ask any gift thou mayst please, that thou mayst receive it from me bestowing it. Let the lake, by which the Gods are wont to swear, and which is unseen, even by my eyes, be as a witness of my promise."

Hardly had he well finished, when he asks for his father's chariot, and for the command and guidance of the wing-footed horses for one day. His father repented that he had so sworn, and shaking his splendid head three or four times, he said, "By thine have my words been made rash. I wish I were allowed not to grant what I have promised! I confess, my son, that this alone I would deny thee. Still, I may dissuade thee: thy desire is not attended with safety. Thou desirest, Phaëton, a gift too great, and one which is suited neither to thy strength, nor to such youthful years. Thy lot is that of a mortal; that which thou desirest, belongs not to mortals. Nay, thou aimest, in thy ignorance, at even more than it is allowed the Gods above to obtain. Let every one be self-satisfied, if he likes; still, with the exception of myself, no one is able to take his stand upon the fire-bearing axle-tree. Even the Ruler of vast Olympus, who hurls the ruthless bolts with his terrific right hand, cannot guide this chariot; and yet, what have we greater than Jupiter? The first part of the road is steep, and such as the horses, though fresh in the morning, can hardly climb. In the middle of the heavens it is high aloft, from whence it is often a source of fear, even to myself, to look down upon the sea and the earth, and my breast trembles with fearful apprehensions. The last stage is a steep descent, and requires a sure command of the horses. Then, too, Tethys[3] herself, who receives me in her waves, extended below, is often wont to fear, lest I should be borne headlong from above. Besides, the heavens are carried round[4] with a constant rotation, and carry with them the lofty stars, and whirl them with rapid revolution. Against this I have to contend; and that force which overcomes all other things, does not overcome me; and I am carried in a contrary direction to the rapid world. Suppose the chariot given to thee; what couldst thou do? Couldst thou proceed, opposed to the whirling poles, so that the rapid heavens should not carry thee away? Perhaps, too, thou dost fancy in thy mind that there are groves, and cities of the Gods, and temples enriched with gifts; whereas, the way is through dangers, and the forms of wild beasts;[5] and though thou shouldst keep on thy road, and be drawn aside by no wanderings, still thou must pass amid the horns of the threatening Bull, and the Hæmonian[6] bow, and before the visage of the raging Lion, and the Scorpion, bending his cruel claws with a wide compass, and the Crab, that bends his claws in a different manner; nor is it easy for thee to govern the steeds spirited by those fires which they have in their breasts, and which they breathe forth from their mouths and their nostrils. Hardly are they restrained by me, when their high-mettled spirit is once heated, and their necks struggle against the reins. But do thou have a care, my son, that I be not the occasion of a gift fatal to thee, and while the matter still permits, alter thy intentions. Thou askest, forsooth, a sure proof that thou mayst believe thyself sprung from my blood? I give thee a sure proof in thus being alarmed for thee; and by my paternal apprehensions, I am shown to be thy father. Lo, behold my countenance! I wish, too, that thou couldst direct thy eyes into my breast, and discover my fatherly concern within! Finally, look around thee, upon whatever the rich world contains, and ask for anything out of the blessings, so many and so great, of heaven, of earth, and of sea; and thou shalt suffer no denial. In this one thing alone I beg to be excused, which, called by its right name, is a penalty, and not an honor; thou art asking, Phaëton, a punishment instead of a gift. Why, in thy ignorance, art thou embracing my neck with caressing arms? Doubt not; whatever thou shalt desire shall be granted thee (by the Stygian waves I have sworn it); but do thou make thy desire more considerately."

He had finished his admonitions; and yet Phaëton resists his advice, and presses his point, and burns with eagerness for the chariot. Wherefore, his parent having delayed as long as he could, leads the young man to the lofty chariot, the gift of Vulcan. The axle-tree was of gold, the poles were of gold; the circumference of the exterior of the wheel was of gold; the range of the spokes was of silver. Chrysolites and gems placed along the yoke in order, gave a bright light from the reflected sun. And while the aspiring Phaëton is admiring these things, and is examining the workmanship, behold! the watchful Aurora opened her purple doors in the ruddy east, and her halls filled with roses. The stars disappear, the troops whereof Lucifer gathers, and moves the last from his station in the heavens. But the father Titan, when he beheld the earth and the universe growing red, and the horns of the far-distant Moon, as if about to vanish, orders the swift Hours to yoke the horses. The Goddesses speedily perform his commands, and lead forth the steeds from the lofty stalls, snorting forth flames, and filled with the juice of Ambrosia; and then they put on the sounding bits.

Then the father touched the face of his son with a hallowed drug, and made it able to endure the burning flames, and placed the rays upon his locks, and fetching from his troubled heart sighs presaging his sorrow, he said: "If thou canst here at least, my boy, obey the advice of thy father, be sparing of the whip, and use the bridle with nerve. Of their own accord they are wont to hasten on; the difficulty is to check them in their full career. And let not the way attract thee through the five direct circles.[7] There is a track cut obliquely, with a broad curvature, and bounded by the extremities of three zones, and so it shuns the South pole, and the Bear united to the North. Let thy way be here; thou wilt perceive distinct traces of the wheels. And that heaven and earth may endure equal heat, neither drive too low, nor urge the chariot along the summit of the sky. Going forth too high, thou wilt set on fire the signs of the heavens; too low, the earth; in the middle course thou will go most safely. Neither let the right wheel bear thee off towards the twisted Serpent, nor let the left lead thee to the low Altar; hold thy course between them. The rest I leave to Fortune, who, I pray, may aid thee, and take more care of thee, than thou dost of thyself. Whilst I am speaking, the moist Night has touched the goals placed on the Western shores; delay is not allowed me. I am required; the Morning is shining forth, the darkness being dispersed. Seize the reins with thy hands; or if thou hast a mind capable of change, make use of my advice, and not my chariot, while thou art still able, and art even yet standing upon solid ground; and while thou art not yet in thy ignorance filling the chariot that thou didst so unfortunately covet."

The other leaps into the light chariot with his youthful body, and stands aloft, and rejoices to take in his hand the reins presented to him, and then gives thanks to his reluctant parent. In the meantime the swift Pyroeis, and Eoüs and Æthon, the horses of the sun, and Phlegon, making the fourth, fill the air with neighings, sending forth flames, and beat the barriers with their feet. After Tethys, ignorant of the destiny of her grandson, had removed these, and the scope of the boundless universe was given them, they take the road, and moving their feet through the air, they cleave the resisting clouds, and raised aloft by their wings, they pass by the East winds that had arisen from the same parts. But the weight was light; and such as the horses of the sun could not feel; and the yoke was deficient of its wonted weight. And as the curving ships, without proper ballast, are tossed about, and unsteady, through their too great lightness, are borne through the sea, so does the chariot give bounds[8] in the air, unimpeded by its usual burden, and is tossed on high, and is just like an empty one.

Soon as the steeds have perceived this, they rush on, and leave the beaten track, and run not in the order in which they did before. He himself becomes alarmed; and knows not which way to turn the reins entrusted to him, nor does he know where the way is, nor, if he did know, could he control them. Then, for the first time, did the cold Triones grow warm with sunbeams, and attempt, in vain, to be dipped in the sea that was forbidden to them. And the Serpent which is situate next to the icy pole, being before torpid with cold, and formidable to no one, grew warm, and regained new rage from the heat. They say, too,[9] that thou, Boötes, being disturbed, took to flight; although thou wast but slow, and thy wain impeded thee. But when, from the height of the skies, the unhappy Phaëton looked down upon the earth, lying far, very far beneath, he grew pale, and his knees shook with a sudden terror; and in a light so great, darkness overspread his eyes. And now he could wish that he had never touched the horses of his father; and now he is sorry that he knew his descent, and that he prevailed in his request; now desiring to be called the son of Merops. He is borne along, just as a ship driven by the furious Boreas, to which its pilot has given up the overpowered helm, and which he has resigned to the Gods and the effect of his supplications. What can he do? much of heaven is left behind his back; still more is before his eyes. Either space he measures in his mind; and at one moment he is looking forward to the West, which it is not allowed him by fate to reach; and sometimes he looks back upon the East. Ignorant what to do, he is stupefied; and he neither lets go the reins, nor is he able to retain them; nor does he know the names of the horses. In his fright, too, he sees strange objects scattered everywhere in various parts of the heavens, and the forms of huge wild beasts. There is a spot where the Scorpion bends his arms into two curves, and with his tail and claws bending on either side, he extends his limbs through the space of two signs of the Zodiac. As soon as the youth beheld him wet with the sweat of black venom, and threatening wounds with the barbed point of his tail, bereft of sense, he let go the reins, in a chill of horror. Soon as they, falling down, have touched the top of their backs, the horses range at large: and no one restraining them, they go through the air of an unknown region; and where their fury drives them thither, without check, do they hurry along, and they rush on to the stars fixed in the sky, and drag the chariot through pathless places. One while they are mounting aloft, and now they are borne through steep places, and along headlong paths in a tract nearer to the earth.

The Moon, too, wonders that her brother's horses run lower than her own, and the scorched clouds send forth smoke. As each region is most elevated, it is caught by the flames, and cleft, it makes vast chasms, and becomes dry, its moisture being carried away. The grass grows pale; the trees, with their foliage, are burnt up; and the dry standing corn affords fuel for its own destruction. But I am complaining of trifling ills. Great cities perish, together with their fortifications, and the flames turn whole nations, with their populations, into ashes; woods, together with mountains, are on fire. Athos[10] burns, and the Cilician Taurus,[11] and Tmolus,[12] and Œta,[13] and Ida,[14] now dry, but once most famed for its springs; and Helicon,[15] the resort of the Virgin Muses, and Hæmus,[16] not yet called Œagrian. Ætna[17] burns intensely with redoubled flames, and Parnassus, with its two summits, and Eryx,[18] and Cynthus,[19] and Othrys, and Rhodope,[20] at length to be despoiled of its snows, and Mimas,[21] and Dindyma,[22] and Mycale,[23] and Cithæron,[24] created for the performance of sacred rites. Nor does its cold avail even Scythia; Caucasus[25] is on fire, and Ossa with Pindus, and Olympus, greater than them both, and the lofty Alps,[26] and the cloud-bearing Apennines.[27]

Then, indeed, Phaëton beholds the world set on fire on all sides, and he cannot endure heat so great, and he inhales with his mouth scorching air, as though from a deep furnace, and perceives his own chariot to be on fire. And neither is he able now to bear the ashes and the emitted embers; and, on every side, he is involved in heated smoke. Covered with a pitchy darkness, he knows not whither he is going, nor where he is, and is hurried away at the pleasure of the winged steeds. They believe that it was then that the nations of the Æthiopians contracted their black hue,[28] the blood being attracted into the surface of the body. Then was Libya[29] made dry by the heat, the moisture being carried off; then, with dishevelled hair, the Nymphs lamented the springs and the lakes. Bœotia bewails Dirce,[30] Argos Amymone,[31] and Ephyre[32] the waters of Pirene. Nor do rivers that have got banks distant in situation, remain secure; Tanais[33] smokes in the midst of its waters, and the aged Peneus, and Teuthrantian Caïcus,[34] and rapid Ismenus,[35] with Phocean Erymanthus,[36] and Xanthus[37] again to burn, and yellow Lycormas,[38] and Mæander,[39] which sports with winding streams, and the Mygdonian Melas,[40] and the Tænarian Eurotas.[41] The Babylonian Euphrates, too, was on fire, Orontes[42] was in flames, and the swift Thermodon[43] and Ganges,[44] and Phasis,[45] and Ister.[46] Alpheus[47] boils; the banks of Spercheus burn; and the gold which Tagus[48] carries with its stream, melts in the flames. The river birds too, which made famous the Mæonian[49] banks of the river with their song, grew hot in the middle of Caÿster. The Nile, affrighted, fled to the remotest parts of the earth, and concealed his head, which still lies hid; his seven last mouths are empty, become seven mere channels, without any stream. The same fate dries up the Ismarian rivers, Hebrus together with Strymon,[50] and the Hesperian[51] streams, the Rhine, and the Rhone, and the Po, and the Tiber, to which was promised the sovereignty of the world.

All the ground bursts asunder; and through the chinks, the light penetrates into Tartarus, and startles the Infernal King with his spouse. The Ocean too, is contracted, and that which lately was sea, is a surface of parched sand; and the mountains which the deep sea had covered, start up and increase the number of the scattered Cyclades.[52] The fishes sink to the bottom, and the crooked Dolphins do not care to raise themselves on the surface into the air, as usual. The bodies of sea calves float lifeless on their backs, on the top of the water. The story, too, is, that even Nereus himself, and Doris and their daughters, lay hid in the heated caverns. Three times had Neptune ventured, with a stern countenance, to thrust his arms out of the water; three times he was unable to endure the scorching heat of the air. However, the genial Earth, as she was surrounded with sea, amid the waters of the main, and the springs, dried up on every side, which had hidden themselves in the bowels of their cavernous parent, burnt-up, lifted up her all-productive face[53] as far as her neck, and placed her hands to her forehead, and shaking all things with a vast trembling, she sank down a little, and retired below the spot where she is wont to be, and thus she spoke, with a parched voice: "O sovereign of the Gods, if thou approvest of this, if I have deserved it, why do thy lightnings linger? Let me, if doomed to perish by the force of fire, perish by thy flames; and alleviate my misfortune, by being the author of it. With difficulty, indeed, do I open my mouth for these very words;" (the vapor had oppressed her utterance.) "Behold my scorched hair, and such a quantity of ashes over my eyes, so much too, over my features. And dost thou give this as my recompense? this, as the reward of my fertility and of my duty, in that I endure wounds from the crooked plough and harrows, and am harassed all the year through? In that I supply green leaves for the cattle, and corn, a wholesome food for mankind, and frankincense for yourselves? But still, suppose that I am deserving of destruction, why have the waves deserved this? Why has thy brother deserved it? Why do the seas, delivered to him by lot, decrease, and why do they recede still further from the sky? But if regard for neither thy brother nor for myself influences thee, still have consideration for thy own skies; look around, on either side, how each pole is smoking; if the fire shall injure them, thy palace will fall in ruins. See! Atlas[54] himself is struggling, and hardly can he bear the glowing heavens on his shoulders. If the sea, if the earth perishes, if the palace of heaven, we are thrown[55] into the confused state of ancient chaos. Save it from the flames, if aught still survives, and provide for the preservation of the universe."

Thus spoke the Earth; nor, indeed, could she any longer endure the vapor, nor say more; and she withdrew her face within herself, and the caverns neighboring to the shades below.

[Footnote 1: Ægeon.—Ver. 10. Homer makes him to be the same with Briareus. According to another account, which Ovid here follows, he was a sea God, the son of Oceanus and Terra.]

[Footnote 2: Doris.—Ver. 11. She was the daughter of Oceanus, the wife of Nereus, and the mother of the fifty Nereids.]

[Footnote 3: Tethys.—Ver. 69. She was the daughter of Cœlus and Terra, and the wife of Oceanus. Her name is here used to signify the ocean itself.]

[Footnote 4: Are carried round.—Ver. 70. Clarke thus renders this line,—"Add, too, that the heaven was whisked round with a continual rolling."]

[Footnote 5: Wild beasts.—Ver. 78. The signs of the Zodiac.]

[Footnote 6: Hæmonian.—Ver. 81. Or Thessalian. He here alludes to the Thessalian Chiron, the Centaur, who, according to Ovid and other writers, was placed in the Zodiac as the Constellation Sagittarius: while others say that Crotus, or Croto, the son of Eupheme, the nurse of the Muses, was thus honored.]

[Footnote 7: Through the five direct circles.—Ver. 129. There is some obscurity in this passage, arising from the mode of expression. Phœbus here counsels Phaëton what track to follow, and tells him to pursue his way by an oblique path, and not directly in the plane of the equator. This last is what he calls 'directos via quinque per arcus.' These five arcs, or circles, are the five parallel circles by which astronomers distinguish the heavens, namely, the two polar circles, the two tropics, and the equinoctial. The latter runs exactly in the middle, between the other two circles, so that the expression must be understood to mean, 'pursue not your way directly through that circle which is the middlemost of the five, but observe the track that cuts it obliquely.']

[Footnote 8: The chariot give bounds.—Ver. 165-6. Clarke thus renders these lines.—'Thus does the chariot give jumps into the air without its usual weight, and is kicked up on high, and is like one empty.']

[Footnote 9: They say, too.—Ver. 176-7. The following is Clarke's translation of these two lines,—'They say, too, that you, Boötes, scowered off in a mighty bustle, although you were but slow, and thy cart hindered thee.']

[Footnote 10: Athos.—Ver. 217. Athos (now Monte Santo) was a mountain of Macedonia, so lofty that its shadow was said to extend even to the Isle of Lemnos, which was eighty-seven miles distant.]

[Footnote 11: Taurus.—Ver. 217. This was an immense mountain range which ran through the middle of Cilicia, in Asia Minor.]

[Footnote 12: Tmolus.—Ver. 217. Tmolus (now Bozdaz) was a mountain of Lydia, famed for its wines and saffron. Pactolus, a stream with sands reputed to be golden, took its rise there.]

[Footnote 13: Œta.—Ver. 217. This was a mountain chain, which divided Thessaly from Doris and Phocis; famed for the death of Hercules on one of its ridges.]

[Footnote 14: Ida.—Ver. 218. There were two mountains of the name of Ide, or Ida; one in Crete, the other near Troy. The latter is here referred to, as being famed for its springs.]

[Footnote 15: Helicon.—Ver. 219. This was a mountain of Bœotia, sacred to the Virgin Muses.]

[Footnote 16: Hæmus.—Ver. 219. This, which is now called the Balkan range, was a lofty chain of mountains running through Thrace. Orpheus, the son of Œagrus and Calliope, was there torn in pieces by the Mænades, or Bacchanalian women, whence the mountain obtained the epithet of 'Œagrian.']

[Footnote 17: Ætna.—Ver. 220. This is the volcanic mountain of Sicily; the flames caused by the fall of Phaëton, added to its own, caused them to be redoubled.]

[Footnote 18: Eryx.—Ver. 221. This was a mountain of Sicily, now called San Juliano. On it, a magnificent temple was erected, in honor of Venus.]

[Footnote 19: Cynthus.—Ver. 221. This was a mountain of Delos, on which Apollo and Diana were said to have been born.]

[Footnote 20: Rhodope.—Ver. 222. It was a high mountain, capped with perpetual snows, in the northern part of Thrace.]

[Footnote 21: Mimas.—Ver. 222. A mountain of Ionia, near the Ionian Sea. It was of very great height; whence Homer calls it ὑψίκρημνος.]

[Footnote 22: Dindyma.—Ver. 223. This was a mountain of Phrygia, near Troy, sacred to Cybele, the mother of the Gods.]

[Footnote 23: Mycale.—Ver. 223. A mountain of Caria, opposite to the Isle of Samos.]

[Footnote 24: Cithæron.—Ver. 223. This was a mountain of Bœotia, famous for the orgies of Bacchus, there celebrated. In its neighborhood, Pentheus was torn to pieces by the Mænades, for slighting the worship of Bacchus.]

[Footnote 25: Caucasus.—Ver. 224. This was a mountain chain in Asia, between the Euxine and Caspian Seas.]

[Footnote 26: Alps.—Ver. 226. This mountain range divides France from Italy.]

[Footnote 27: Apennines.—Ver. 226. This range of mountains runs down the centre of Italy.]

[Footnote 28: Their black hue.—Ver. 235. The notion that the blackness of the African tribes was produced by the heat of the sun, is borrowed by the Poet from Hesiod. Hyginus, too, says, 'the Indians, because, by the proximity of the fire, their blood was turned black by the heat thereof, became of black appearance themselves.' Notwithstanding the learned and minute investigations of physiologists on the subject, this question is still involved in considerable obscurity.]

[Footnote 29: Libya.—Ver. 237. This was a region between Mauritania and Cyrene. The Greek writers, however, often use the word to signify the whole of Africa. Servius gives a trifling derivation for the name, in saying that Libya was so called, because λείπει ὁ ὕετος, 'it is without rain.']

[Footnote 30: Dirce.—Ver. 239. Dirce was a celebrated fountain of Bœotia, into which it was said that Dirce, the wife of Lycus, king of Thebes, was transformed.]

[Footnote 31: Amymone.—Ver. 240. It was a fountain of Argos, near Lerna, into which the Nymph, Amymone, the daughter of Lycus, king of the Argives, was said to have been transformed.]

[Footnote 32: Ephyre.—Ver. 240. It was the most ancient name of Corinth, in the citadel of which, or the Acrocorinthus, was the spring Pyrene, of extreme brightness and purity and sacred to the Muses.]

[Footnote 33: Tanais.—Ver. 242. This river, now the Don, after a long winding course, discharges itself into the 'Palus Mæotis,' now the sea of 'Azof.']

[Footnote 34: Caïcus.—Ver. 243. This is a river of Mysia, here called 'Teuthrantian,' from Mount Teuthras, in its vicinity.]

[Footnote 35: Ismenus.—Ver. 244. Ismenus was a river of Bœotia, that flowed past Thebes into the Euripus.]

[Footnote 36: Erymanthus.—Ver. 245. This was a river of Arcadia, which, rising in a mountain of that name, fell into the Alpheus.]

[Footnote 37: Xanthus.—Ver. 245. This was a river of Troy; here spoken of as destined to behold flames a second time, in the conflagration of that city.]

[Footnote 38: Lycormas.—Ver. 245. This was a rapid river of Ætolia, which was afterwards known by the name of Evenus.]

[Footnote 39: Mæander.—Ver. 246. This was a river of Phrygia, flowing between Lydia and Caria; it was said to have 600 windings in its course.]

[Footnote 40: Melas.—Ver. 247. This name was given to many rivers of Thrace, Thessaly, and Asia, on account of the darkness of the color of their waters; the name was derived from the Greek word μέλας, 'black.']

[Footnote 41: Tænarian Eurotas.—Ver. 247. The Eurotas was a river of Laconia, which flowed under the walls of the city of Sparta, and discharged itself into the sea near the promontory of Tænarus, now called Cape Matapan. The Eurotas is now called 'Basilipotamo,' or 'king of streams.']

[Footnote 42: Orontes.—Ver. 248. The Orontes was a river of Asia Minor, which flowed near Antioch.]

[Footnote 43: Thermodon.—Ver. 249. This was a river of Cappadocia, near which the Amazons were said to dwell.]

[Footnote 44: Ganges.—Ver. 249. This is one of the largest rivers in Asia, and discharges itself into the Persian Gulf; and not, as Gierig says, in his note on this passage, in the Red Sea.]

[Footnote 45: Phasis.—Ver. 249. This was a river of Colchis, falling into the Euxine Sea.]

[Footnote 46: Ister.—Ver. 249. The Danube had that name from its source to the confines of Germany; and thence, in its course through Scythia to the sea, it was called by the name of 'Ister.']

[Footnote 47: Alpheus.—Ver. 250. It was a river of Arcadia, in Peloponnesus.]

[Footnote 48: Tagus.—Ver. 251. This was a river of Spain, which was said to bring down from the mountains great quantities of golden sand. The Poet here feigns this to be melted by the heat of the sun, and in that manner to be carried along by the current of the river.]

[Footnote 49: Mæonian.—Ver. 252. Mæonia was so called from the river Mæon, and was another name of Lydia. The Caÿster, famous for its swans, flowed through Lydia.]

[Footnote 50: Strymon.—Ver. 257. The Hebrus and the Strymon were rivers of Thrace. Ismarus was a mountain of that country, famous for its vines.]

[Footnote 51: Hesperian.—Ver. 258. Hesperia, or 'the western country,' was a general name of not only Spain and Gaul, but even Italy. The Rhine is a river of France and Germany, the Rhone of France. The Padus, or Po, and the Tiber, are rivers of Italy.]

[Footnote 52: Cyclades.—Ver. 264. The Cyclades were a cluster of islands in the Ægean Sea, surrounding Delos as though with a circle, whence their name.]

[Footnote 53: Her all-productive face.—Ver. 275. The earth was similarly called by the Greeks παμμήτωρ, 'the mother of all things.' So Virgil calls it 'omniparens.']

[Footnote 54: Atlas.—Ver. 296. This was a mountain of Mauritania, which, by reason of its height, was said to support the heavens.]

[Footnote 55: We are thrown.—Ver. 299. Clarke translates, 'In chaos antiquum confundimur,' 'We are then jumbled into the old chaos again.']

EXPLANATION

If we were to regard this fable solely as an allegory intended to convey a moral, we should at once perceive that the adventure of Phaëton represents the wilful folly of a rash young man, who consults his own inclination, rather than the dictates of wisdom and prudence. Some ancient writers tell us that Phaëton was the son of Phœbus and Clymene, while others make the nymph Rhoda to have been his mother. Apollodorus, following Hesiod, says that Herse, the daughter of Cecrops, king of Athens, was the mother of Cephalus, who was carried away by Aurora; which probably means that he left Greece for the purpose of settling in the East. Cephalus had a son named Tithonus, the father of Phaëton. Thus Phaëton was the fourth in lineal descent from Cecrops, who reigned at Athens about 1580, B.C. The story is most probably based upon the fact of some excessive heat that happened in his time. Aristotle supposes that at that period flames fell from heaven, which ravaged several countries. Possibly the burning of the cities of the plain, or the stay of the sun in his course at the command of Joshua, may have been the foundation of the story. St. Chrysostom suggests that it is based upon an imperfect version of the ascent of Elijah in a chariot of fire; that name, or rather 'Elias,' the Greek form of it, bearing a strong resemblance to Ἥλιος, the Greek name of the sun. Vossius suggests that this is an Egyptian history, and considers the story of the grief of Phœbus for the loss of his son to be another version of the sorrows of the Egyptians for the death of Osiris. The tears of the Heliades, or sisters of Phaëton, he conceives to be identical with the lamentations of the women who wept for the death of Thammuz. The Poet, when he tells us that Phaëton abandoned his chariot on seeing The Scorpion, probably intends to show that the event of which he treats happened in the month in which the sun enters that sign.

Plutarch and Tzetzes tell us that Phaëton was a king of the Molossians, who drowned himself in the Po; that he was a student of astronomy, and foretold an excessive heat which happened in his reign, and laid waste his kingdom. Lucian, also, in his Discourse on Astronomy, gives a similar explanation of the story, and says that this prince dying very young, left his observations imperfect, which gave rise to the fable that he did not know how to drive the chariot of the sun to the end of its course.

FABLE II [II.305-324]

Jupiter, to save the universe from being consumed, hurls his thunder at Phaëton, on which he falls headlong into the river Eridanus.

But the omnipotent father, having called the Gods above to witness, and him, too, who had given the chariot to Phaëton, that unless he gives assistance, all things will perish in direful ruin, mounts aloft to the highest eminence, from which he is wont to spread the clouds over the spacious earth; from which he moves his thunders, and hurls the brandished lightnings. But then, he had neither clouds that he could draw over the earth, nor showers that he could pour down from the sky. He thundered aloud, and darted the poised lightning from his right ear against the charioteer, and at the same moment deprived him both of his life and his seat, and by his ruthless fires restrained the flames. The horses are affrighted, and, making a bound in an opposite direction, they shake the yoke from off their necks, and disengage themselves from the torn harness. In one place lie the reins; in another, the axle-tree wrenched away from the pole; in another part are the spokes of the broken wheels; and the fragments of the chariot torn in pieces are scattered far and wide. But Phaëton, the flames consuming his yellow hair, is hurled headlong, and is borne in a long tract through the air; as sometimes a star from the serene sky may appear to fall, although it really has not fallen. Him the great Eridanus receives, in a part of the world far distant from his country, and bathes his foaming face.

FABLE III [II.325-366]

The sisters of Phaëton are changed into poplars, and their tears become amber distilling from those trees.

The Hesperian Naiads[56] commit his body, smoking from the three-forked flames, to the tomb, and inscribe these verses on the stone:—"Here is Phaëton buried, the driver of his father's chariot, which if he did not manage, still he miscarried in a great attempt." But his wretched father had hidden his face, overcast with bitter sorrow, and, if only we can believe it, they say that one day passed without the sun.[57] The flames afforded light; and so far, there was some advantage in that disaster. But Clymene, after she had said whatever things were to be said amid misfortunes so great, traversed the whole earth, full of woe, and distracted, and tearing her bosom. And first seeking his lifeless limbs, and then his bones, she found his bones, however, buried on a foreign bank. She laid herself down on the spot; and bathed with tears the name she read on the marble, and warmed it with her open breast. The daughters of the Sun mourn no less, and give tears, an unavailing gift, to his death; and beating their breasts with their hands, they call Phaëton both night and day, who is doomed not to hear their sad complaints; and they lie scattered about the tomb.

The Moon had four times filled her disk, by joining her horns; they, according to their custom (for use had made custom), uttered lamentations; among whom Phaëthusa, the eldest of the sisters, when she was desirous to lie on the ground, complained that her feet had grown stiff; to whom the fair Lampetie attempting to come, was detained by a root suddenly formed. A third, when she is endeavoring to tear her hair with her hands, tears off leaves; one complains that her legs are held fast by the trunk of a tree, another that her arms are become long branches. And while they are wondering at these things, bark closes upon their loins; and by degrees, it encompasses their stomachs, their breasts, their shoulders, and their hands; and only their mouths are left uncovered, calling upon their mother. What is their mother to do? but run here and there, whither frenzy leads her, and join her lips with theirs, while yet she may? That is not enough; she tries to pull their bodies out of the trunks of the trees, and with her hands to tear away the tender branches; but from thence drops of blood flow as from a wound. Whichever of them is wounded, cries out, "Spare me, mother, O spare me, I pray; in the tree my body is being torn. And now farewell." The bark came over the last words.

Thence tears flow forth; and amber distilling from the new-formed branches, hardens in the sun; which the clear river receives and sends to be worn by the Latian matrons.

[Footnote 56: The Hesperian Naiads.—Ver. 325. These were the Naiads of Italy. They were by name Phaëthusa, Lampetie, and Phœbe.]

[Footnote 57: Passed without the sun.—Ver. 331. There is, perhaps, in this line some faint reference to a tradition of the sun having, in the language of Scripture, 'stood still upon Gibeon, in his course, by the command of Joshua, when dispensing the divine vengeance upon the Amorites,' Joshua, x. 13. Or of the time when 'the shadow returned ten degrees backward', by the sun-dial of Ahaz, 2 Kings, xx. 11.]

FABLE IV [II.367-400]

Cycnus, king of Liguria, inconsolable for the death of Phaëton, is transformed into a swan.

Cycnus, the son of Sthenelus,[58] was present at this strange event; who, although he was related to thee, Phaëton, on his mother's side, was yet more nearly allied in affection. He having left his kingdom (for he reigned over the people and the great cities of the Ligurians[59]) was filling the verdant banks and the river Eridanus, and the wood, now augmented by the sisters, with his complaints; when the man's voice became shrill, and gray feathers concealed his hair. A long neck, too, extends from his breast, and a membrane joins his reddening toes; feathers clothe his sides, and his mouth holds a bill without a point. Cycnus becomes a new bird; but he trusts himself not to the heavens or the air, as being mindful of the fire unjustly sent from thence. He frequents the pools and the wide lakes, and abhorring fire, he chooses the streams, the very contrary of flames.

Meanwhile, the father of Phaëton, in squalid garb, and destitute of his comeliness, just as he is wont to be when he suffers an eclipse of his disk, abhors both the light, himself, and the day; and gives his mind up to grief, and adds resentment to his sorrow, and denies his services to the world. "My lot," says he, "has been restless enough from the very beginning of time, and I am tired of labors endured by me, without end and without honor. Let any one else drive the chariot that carries the light. If there is no one, and all the Gods confess that they cannot do it, let Jupiter himself drive it; that, at least, while he is trying my reins, he may for a time lay aside the lightnings that bereave fathers. Then he will know, having made trial of the strength of the flame-footed steeds, that he who did not successfully guide them, did not deserve death."

All the Deities stand around the Sun, as he says such things; and they entreat him, with suppliant voice, not to determine to bring darkness over the world. Jupiter, as well, excuses the hurling of his lightnings, and imperiously adds threats to entreaties. Phœbus calls together his steeds, maddened and still trembling with terror, and, subduing them, vents his fury both with whip and lash; for he is furious, and upbraids them with his son, and charges his death upon them.

[Footnote 58: Sthenelus.—Ver. 367. He was a king of Liguria. Commentators have justly remarked that it was not very likely that a king of Liguria should be related to Clymene, a queen of the Ethiopians, as Ovid, in the next line, says was the case. This story was probably invented by some writer, who fancied that there were two persons of the name of Phaëton; one the subject of eastern tradition, and the other a personage of the Latin mythology.]

[Footnote 59: The Ligurians.—Ver. 370. These were a people situate on the eastern side of Etruria, between the rivers Var and Macra. The Grecian writers were in the habit of styling the whole of the north of Italy Liguria.]

EXPLANATION

Plutarch places the tomb of Phaëton on the banks of the river Po; and it is not improbable that his mother and sisters, grieving at his fate, ended their lives in the neighborhood of his tomb, being overcome with grief, which gave rise to the story that they were changed into the poplars on its banks, which distilled amber. Some writers say, that they were changed into larch trees, and not poplars. Hesiod and Pindar also make mention of this tradition. Possibly, Cycnus, being a friend of Phaëton, may have died from grief at his loss, on which the poets graced his attachment with the story that he was changed into a swan. Apollodorus mentions two other persons of the name of Cycnus. One was the son of Mars, and was killed before Troy; the other, as Hesiod tells us, was killed by Hercules. Lucian, in his satirical vein, tells us, that inquiring on the banks of the Po for the swans, and the poplars distilling amber, he was told that no such things had ever been seen there; and that even the tradition of Phaëton and his sisters was utterly unknown to the inhabitants of those parts.

FABLE V [II.401-465]

Jupiter, while taking a survey of the world, to extinguish the remains of the fire, falls in love with Calisto, whom he sees in Arcadia; and, in order to seduce that Nymph, he assumes the form of Diana. Her sister Nymphs disclose her misfortune before the Goddess, who drives her from her company, on account of the violation of her vow of chastity.

But the omnipotent father surveys the vast walls of heaven, and carefully searches, that no part, impaired by the violence of the fire, may fall to ruin. After he has seen them to be secure and in their own full strength, he examines the earth, and the works of man; yet a care for his own Arcadia is more particularly his object. He restores, too, the springs and the rivers, that had not yet dared to flow, he gives grass to the earth: green leaves to the trees; and orders the injured forests again to be green. While thus he often went to and fro, he stopped short on seeing a virgin of Nonacris, and the fires engendered within his bones received fresh heat. It was not her employment to soften the wool by teasing, nor to vary her tresses in their arrangement; while a buckle fastened her garment, and a white fillet her hair, carelessly flowing; and at one time she bore in her hand a light javelin, at another, a bow. She was a warrior of Phœbe; nor did any Nymph frequent Mænalus, more beloved by Trivia,[60] than she; but no influence is of long duration. The lofty Sun had now obtained a position beyond the mid course, when she enters a grove which no generation had ever cut. Here she puts her quiver off from her shoulders, and unbends her pliant bow, and lies down on the ground, which the grass had covered, and presses her painted quiver, with her neck laid on it. When Jupiter saw her thus weary, and without a protector, he said, "For certain, my wife will know nothing of this stolen embrace; or, if she should chance to know, is her scolding, is it, I say, of such great consequence?"

Immediately he puts on the form and dress of Diana, and says, "O Virgin! one portion of my train, upon what mountains hast thou been hunting?" The virgin raises herself from the turf, and says, "Hail, Goddess! that art, in my opinion, greater than Jove, even if he himself should hear it." He both smiles and he hears it, and is pleased at being preferred to himself; and he gives her kisses, not very moderate, nor such as would be given by a virgin. He stops her as she is preparing to tell him in what wood she has been hunting, by an embrace, and he does not betray himself without the commission of violence. She, indeed, on the other hand, as far as a woman could do (would that thou hadst seen her, daughter of Saturn, then thou wouldst have been more merciful), she, indeed, I say, resists; but what damsel, or who besides, could prevail against Jupiter? Jove, now the conqueror, seeks the heavens above; the grove and the conscious wood is now her aversion. Making her retreat thence, she is almost forgetting to take away her quiver with her arrows, and the bow which she had hung up.

Behold, Dictynna,[61] attended by her train, as she goes along the lofty Mænalus, and exulting in the slaughter of the wild beasts, beholds her, and calls her, thus seen. Being so called, she drew back, and at first was afraid lest Jupiter might be under her shape; but after she saw the Nymphs walking along with her, she perceived that there was no deceit,[62] and she approached their train. Alas! how difficult it is not to betray a crime by one's looks! She scarce raises her eyes from the ground, nor, as she used to do, does she walk by the side of the Goddess, nor is she the foremost in the whole company; but she is silent, and by her blushes she gives signs of her injured honor. And Diana, but for the fact, that she is a virgin, might have perceived her fault by a thousand indications; the Nymphs are said to have perceived it.

The horns of the Moon were now rising again in her ninth course, when the hunting Goddess, faint from her brother's flames, lighted on a cool grove, out of which a stream ran, flowing with its murmuring noise, and borne along the sand worn fine by its action. When she had approved of the spot, she touched the surface of the water with her foot; and commending it as well, she says, "All overlookers are far off; let us bathe our bodies, with the stream poured over them." She of Parrhasia[63] blushed; they all put off their clothes; she alone sought an excuse for delay. Her garment was removed as she hesitated, which being put off, her fault was exposed with her naked body. Cynthia said to her, in confusion, and endeavoring to conceal her stomach with her hands, "Begone afar hence! and pollute not the sacred springs;" and she ordered her to leave her train.

[Footnote 60: Trivia.—Ver. 416. This was an epithet of Diana, as presiding over and worshipped in the places where three roads met, which were called 'trivia.' Being known as Diana on earth, the Moon in

the heavens, and Proserpine in the infernal regions, she was represented at these places with three faces; those of a horse, a dog, and a female; the latter being in the middle.]

[Footnote 61: Dictynna.—Ver. 441. Diana was so called from the Greek word δικτὺς, 'a net,' which was used by her for the purposes of hunting.]

[Footnote 62: There was no deceit.—Ver. 446. Clarke translates 'sensit abesse dolos,' 'she was convinced there was no roguery in the case.']

[Footnote 63: She of Parrhasia.—Ver. 460. Calisto is so called from Parrhasia, a region of Arcadia. Parrhasius was the name of a mountain, a grove, and a city of that country and was derived from the name of Parrhasus, a son of Lycaon.]

FABLES VI AND VII [II.466-550]

Juno, being jealous that Calisto has attracted Jupiter, transforms her into a Bear. Her son, Arcas, not recognizing his mother in that shape, is about to kill her; but Jupiter removes them both to the skies, where they form the Constellations of the Great and the Little Bear. The raven, as a punishment for his garrulity, is changed from white to black.

The spouse of the great Thunderer had perceived this some time before, and had put off the severe punishment designed for her, to a proper time. There is now no reason for delay; and now the boy Arcas (that, too, was a grief to Juno) was born of the mistress of her husband. Wherefore, she turned her thoughts, full of resentment, and her eyes upon her, and said, "This thing, forsooth, alone was wanting, thou adulteress, that thou shouldst be pregnant, and that my injury should become notorious by thy labors, and that thereby the disgraceful conduct of my husband, Jupiter, should be openly declared. Thou shalt not go unpunished; for I will spoil that shape of thine, on which thou pridest thyself, and by which thou, mischievous one,[64] dost charm my husband."

Thus she spoke; and seizing her straight in front by the hair,[65] threw her on her face to the ground. She suppliantly stretched forth her arms; those arms began to grow rough with black hair,[66] and her hands to be bent, and to increase to hooked claws, and to do the duty of feet, and the mouth, that was once admired by Jupiter, to become deformed with a wide opening; and lest her prayers, and words not needed, should influence her feelings, the power of speech is taken from her; an angry and threatening voice, and full of terror, is uttered from her hoarse throat. Still, her former understanding remains in her, even thus become a bear; and expressing her sorrows by her repeated groans, she lifts up her hands, such as they are, to heaven and to the stars, and she deems Jove ungrateful, though she cannot call him so. Ah! how often, not daring to rest in the lonely wood, did she wander about before her own house, and in the fields once her own. Ah! how often was she driven over the crags by the cry of the hounds; and, a huntress herself, she fled in alarm, through fear of the hunters! Often, seeing the wild beasts, did she lie concealed, forgetting what she was; and, a bear herself, dreaded the he-bears seen on the mountains, and was alarmed at the wolves, though her father was among them.

Behold! Arcas, the offspring of the daughter of Lycaon, ignorant of who is his parent, approaches her, thrice five birthdays being now nearly past; and while he is following the wild beasts, while he is choosing the proper woods, and is enclosing the Erymanthian forests[67] with his platted nets, he meets with his mother. She stood still, upon seeing Arcas, and was like one recognizing another. He drew back, and, in his ignorance, was alarmed at her keeping her eyes fixed upon him without ceasing; and, as she was desirous to approach still nearer, he would have pierced her breast with the wounding spear. Omnipotent Jove averted this, and removed both them and such wickedness; and placed them, carried through vacant space with a rapid wind, in the heavens, and made them neighboring Constellations.

Juno swelled with rage after the mistress shone amid the stars, and descended on the sea to the hoary Tethys, and the aged Ocean, a regard for whom has often influenced the Gods; and said to them, inquiring the reason of her coming, "Do you inquire why I, the queen of the Gods, am come hither from the æthereal abodes? Another has possession of heaven in my stead. May I be deemed untruthful, if, when the night has made the world dark, you see not in the highest part of heaven stars but lately thus honored to my affliction; there, where the last and most limited circle surrounds the extreme part of the axis of the world. Is there, then, any ground why one should hesitate to affront Juno, and dread my being offended, who only benefit them by my resentment? See what a great thing I have done! How vast is my power! I forbade her to be of human shape; she has been made a Goddess; 'tis thus that I inflict punishment on offenders; such is my mighty power! Let him obtain for her her former shape, and let him remove this form of a wild beast; as he formerly did for the Argive Phoronis. Why does he not marry her as well, divorcing Juno, and place her in my couch, and take Lycaon for his father-in-law? But if the wrong done to your injured foster-child affects you, drive the seven Triones away from your azure waters, and expel the stars received into heaven as the reward of adultery, that a concubine may not be received into your pure waves."

The Gods of the sea granted her request. The daughter of Saturn enters the liquid air in her graceful chariot,[68] with her variegated peacocks; peacocks just as lately tinted, upon the killing of Argus, as thou, garrulous raven, hadst been suddenly transformed into a bird having black wings, whereas thou hadst been white before. For this bird was formerly of a silver hue, with snow-white feathers, so that he equalled the doves entirely without spot; nor would he give place to the geese that were to save the Capitol by their watchful voice, nor to the swan haunting the streams. His tongue was the cause of his disgrace; his chattering tongue being the cause, that the color which was white is now the reverse of white.

There was no one more beauteous in all Hæmonia than Larissæan[69] Coronis. At least, she pleased thee, Delphian God, as long as she continued chaste, or was not the object of remark. But the bird of Phœbus found out her infidelity;[70] and the inexorable informer winged his way to his master, that he might disclose the hidden offence. Him the prattling crow follows, with flapping wings, to make all inquiries of him. And having heard the occasion of his journey, she says, "Thou art going on a fruitless errand; do not despise the presages of my voice."

[Footnote 64: Thou, mischievous one.—Ver. 475. Clarke, rather too familiarly, renders 'importuna,' 'plaguy baggage.']

[Footnote 65: In front by the hair.—Ver. 476. 'Adversâ prensis a fronte capillis,' is rendered by Clarke, 'seizing her fore-top.' Had he been describing the combats of two fish-wives, such a version would have been, perhaps, more appropriate than in the present instance.]

[Footnote 66: With black hair.—Ver. 478. To the explanation given at the end of the story, we may here add the curious one offered by Palæphatus. He says that Calisto was a huntress who entered the den of a bear, by which she was devoured; and that the bear coming out, and Calisto being no more seen, it was reported that she had been transformed into a bear.]

[Footnote 67: Erymanthian forests.—Ver. 499. Erymanthus was a mountain of Arcadia, which was afterwards famous for the slaughter there, by Hercules, of the wild boar, which made it his haunt.]

[Footnote 68: Graceful chariot.—Ver. 531. Clarke translates 'habili curru,' 'her neat chariot.']

[Footnote 69: Larissæan.—Ver. 542. Larissa was the chief city of Thessaly, and was situate on the river Peneus.]

[Footnote 70: Her infidelity.—Ver. 545. 'Sed ales sensit adulterium Phœbeius,' is translated by Clarke, 'but the Phœban bird found out her pranks.']

EXPLANATION

Cicero (On the Nature of the Gods, Book iii.) tells us, that Lycaon had a daughter who delighted in the chase, and that Jupiter, the second of that name, the king of Arcadia, fell in love with her. This was the ground on which she was said to have been a favorite of Diana. The story of Calisto having been received into Heaven, and forming the Constellation of the Bear, was perhaps grounded on the fact of Lycaon, her father, having been the first known to take particular notice of this Constellation. The story of the request of Juno, that Tethys will not receive this new Constellation into the Ocean, is probably derived from the circumstance, that the Bear, as well as the other stars within the Arctic Circle, never sets.

Possibly, Arcas, the son of Calisto, dying at a youthful age, may have been the origin of the Constellation of the Lesser Bear.

FABLE VIII [II.551-590]

A virgin, the favorite of Apollo, of the same name with Coronis, is changed into a crow, for a story which she tells Minerva, concerning the basket in which Ericthonius was enclosed.

"Consider what I was, and what I am, and inquire into my deserts. Thou wilt find that my fidelity was my ruin. For once upon a time, Pallas had enclosed Ericthonius, an offspring born without a mother, in a basket made of Actæan twigs; and had given it to keep to the three virgins born of the two-shaped[71] Cecrops, and had given them this injunction, that they should not inquire into her secrets. I, being hidden among the light foliage, was watching from a thick elm what they were doing. Two of them, Pandrosos and Herse, observe their charge without any treachery; Aglauros alone calls her sisters cowards, and unties the knots with her hand; but within they behold a child, and a dragon extended by him. I told the Goddess what was done; for which such a return as this is made to me, that I am said to have been banished from the protection of Minerva, and am placed after the bird of the night. My punishment may warn birds not to incur dangers, by their chattering. But I consider that she courted me with no inclination of my own, nor asking for any such favors. This thou mayst ask of Pallas thyself;

although she is angry, she will not, with all her anger, deny this. For Coroneus, one famous in the land of Phocis (I mention what is well known) begot me: and so I was a virgin of royal birth, and was courted by rich suitors (so despise me not). My beauty was the cause of my misfortune; for while I was passing with slow steps along the sea-shore, on the surface of the sand, as I was wont to do, the God of the Ocean beheld me, and was inflamed; and when he had consumed his time to no purpose, in entreating me with soft words, he prepared to use violence, and followed me. I fled, and I left the firm shore, and wearied myself in vain on the yielding sand. Then I invoked both Gods and men; but my voice did not reach any mortal. A virgin was moved for a virgin, and gave me assistance. I was extending my arms toward heaven; when those arms began to grow black with light feathers. I struggled to throw my garments from off my shoulders, but they were feathers, and had taken deep root in my skin. I tried to beat my naked breast with my hands, but I had now neither hands nor naked breast. I ran; and the sand did not retard my feet as before, and I was lifted up from the surface of the ground. After that, being lifted up, I was carried through the air, and was assigned, as a faultless companion, to Minerva. Yet what does this avail me, if Nyctimene, made a bird for a horrid crime, has succeeded me in my honor?"

[Footnote 71: Two-shaped.—Ver. 555. Cecrops is here so called, and in the Greek, διφυὴς from the fact of his having been born in Egypt, and having settled in Greece, and was thus to be reckoned both as an Egyptian, and in the number of the Greeks.]

EXPLANATION

Ericthonius was fabled to be the son, or foster-child, of Athene, or Minerva, perhaps because he was the son of the daughter of Cranaus, who had the name of Athene, by a priest of Vulcan, which Divinity was said to have been his progenitor. St. Augustine alleges that he was exposed, and found in a temple dedicated to Minerva and Vulcan. His name being composed of two words, ἔρις and χθὼν, signifying 'contention,' and 'earth,' Strabo imagines that he was the son of Vulcan and the Earth. But it seems that the real ground on which he was called by that name was, that he disputed the right to the crown of Athens with Amphictyon, on the death of Cranaus, the second king. Amphictyon prevailed, but Ericthonius succeeded him. To hide his legs, which were deformed, he is said to have invented chariots; though that is not likely, as Egypt, from which Greece had received many colonies, was acquainted with the use of them from the earliest times. He is also said to have instituted the festival of the Panathenæa, at Athens, whence, in process of time, it was adopted by the whole of Greece.

Hyginus tells us, that after his death he was received into heaven as the constellation 'Auriga,' or 'the Charioteer;' and he further informs us, that the deformity of his legs gave occasion to the saying, that he was half man and half a serpent. Apollodorus says that he was born in Attica; that he was the son of Cranaë, the daughter of Attis; and that he dethroned Amphictyon, and became the fourth king of Athens.

FABLE IX [II.591-632]

Nyctimene having entertained a criminal passion for her father, Nycteus, the Gods, to punish her incest, transform her into an owl. Apollo pierces the breast of Coronis with an arrow, on the raven informing him of the infidelity of his mistress.

"Has not the thing, which is very well known throughout the whole of Lesbos,[72] been heard of by thee, that Nyctimene defiled the bed of her father? She is a bird indeed; but being conscious of her crime, she avoids the human gaze and the light, and conceals her shame in the darkness; and by all the birds she is expelled entirely from the sky."

The raven says to him, saying such things, "May this, thy calling of me back, prove a mischief to thee, I pray; I despise the worthless omen." Nor does he drop his intended journey; and he tells his master, that he has seen Coronis lying down with a youth of Hæmonia. On hearing the crime of his mistress, his laurel fell down; and at the same moment his usual looks, his plectrum,[73] and his color, forsook the God. And as his mind was now burning with swelling rage, he took up his wonted arms, and levelled his bow bent from the extremities, and pierced, with an unerring shaft, that bosom, that had been so oft pressed to his own breast. Wounded, she uttered a groan, and, drawing the steel from out of the wound, she bathed her white limbs with purple blood; and she said, "I might justly, Phœbus, have been punished by thee, but still I might have first brought forth; now we two shall die in one." Thus far she spoke; and she poured forth her life, together with her blood. A deadly coldness took possession of her body deprived of life.

The lover, too late, alas! repents of his cruel vengeance, and blames himself that he listened to the bird, and that he was so infuriated. He hates the bird, through which he was forced to know of the crime and the cause of his sorrow; he hates, too, the string, the bow, and his hand; and together with his hand, those rash weapons, the arrows. He cherishes her fallen to the ground, and by late resources endeavors to conquer her destiny; and in vain he practices his physical arts.

When he found that these attempts were made in vain, and that the funeral pile was being prepared, and that her limbs were about to be burnt in the closing flames, then, in truth, he gave utterance to sighs fetched from the bottom of his heart (for it is not allowed the celestial features to be bathed with tears). No otherwise than, as when an axe, poised from the right ear of the butcher, dashes to pieces, with a clean stroke, the hollow temples of the sucking calf, while the dam looks on. Yet after Phœbus had poured the unavailing perfumes on her breast, when he had given the last embrace and had performed the due obsequies prematurely hastened, he did not suffer his own offspring to sink into the same ashes; but he snatched the child from the flames and from the womb of his mother, and carried him into the cave of the two-formed Chiron. And he forbade the raven, expecting for himself the reward of his tongue that told no untruth, to perch any longer among the white birds.

[Footnote 72: Lesbos.—Ver. 591. This was an island in the Ægean sea, lying to the south of Troy.]

[Footnote 73: Plectrum.—Ver. 601. This was a little rod, or staff, with which the player used to strike the strings of the lyre, or cithara, on which he was playing.]

EXPLANATION

History does not afford us the least insight into the foundation of the story of Coronis transformed into a crow, for making too faithful a report, nor that of the raven changed from white to black, for talking too much. If they are based upon some events which really happened, we must be content to acknowledge that these Fables refer to the history of two persons entirely unknown to us, and who, perhaps, lived as far back as the time of the daughters of Cecrops, to whom the story seems to bear some relation. Coronis being the name of a crow as well as of a Nymph, Lucian and other writers have fabled that her son, Æsculapius, was produced from the egg of that bird, and was born in the shape of a serpent, under which form he was very generally worshipped.

FABLE X [II.633-675]

Ocyrrhoe, the daughter of the Centaur Chiron, attempting to predict future events, tells her father the fate of the child Æsculapius, on which the Gods transform her into a mare.

In the meantime the half-beast Chiron was proud of a pupil of Divine origin, and rejoiced in the honor annexed to the responsibility. Behold! the daughter of the Centaur comes, having her shoulders covered with her yellow hair; whom once the nymph Chariclo,[74] having borne her on the banks of a rapid stream, called Ocyrrhoë. She was not contented to learn her father's arts only; but she sang the secrets of the Fates. Therefore, when she had conceived in her mind the prophetic transports, and grew warm with the God, whom she held confined within her breast, she beheld the infant, and she said, "Grow on, child, the giver of health to the whole world; the bodies of mortals shall often owe their own existence to thee. To thee will it be allowed to restore life when taken away; and daring to do that once against the will of the Gods, thou wilt be hindered by the bolts of thy grandsire from being able any more to grant that boon. And from a God thou shalt become a lifeless carcase; and a God again, who lately wast a carcase; and twice shalt thou renew thy destiny. Thou likewise, dear father, now immortal, and produced at thy nativity, on the condition of enduring for ever, wilt then wish that thou couldst die, when thou shalt be tormented on receiving the blood of a baneful serpent[75] in thy wounded limbs; and the Gods shall make thee from an immortal being, subject to death, and the three Goddesses[76] shall cut thy threads."

Something still remained in addition to what she had said. She heaved a sigh from the bottom of her breast, and the tears bursting forth, trickled down her cheeks, and thus she said: "The Fates prevent me, and I am forbidden to say any more, and the use of my voice is precluded. My arts, which have brought the wrath of a Divinity upon me, were not of so much value; I wish that I had not been acquainted with the future. Now the human shape seems to be withdrawing from me; now grass pleases me for my food; now I have a desire to range over the extended plains; I am turned into a mare, and into a shape kindred to that of my father. But yet, why entirely? For my father partakes of both forms."

As she was uttering such words as these, the last part of her complaint was but little understood; and her words were confused. And presently neither were they words indeed, nor did it appear to be the voice of a mare, but of one imitating a mare. And in a little time she uttered perfect neighing, and stretched her arms upon the grass. Then did her fingers grow together, and a smooth hoof united five nails in one continued piece of horn. The length of her face and of her neck increased; the greatest part of her long hair became a tail. And as the hairs lay scattered about her neck, they were transformed into a mane lying upon the right side; at once both her voice and her shape were changed. And this wondrous change gave her the new name of Enippe.

[Footnote 74: Chariclo.—Ver. 636. She was the daughter of Apollo, or of Oceanus, but is supposed not to have been the same person that is mentioned by Apollodorus as the mother of the prophet Tiresias.]

[Footnote 75: A baneful serpent.—Ver. 652. This happened when one of the arrows of Hercules, dipped in the poison of the Lernæan Hydra, pierced the foot of Chiron while he was examining it.]

[Footnote 76: The three Goddesses.—Ver. 654. Namely, Clotho, Lachesis, and Atropos, the 'Parcæ,' or 'Destinies.']

FABLE XI [II.676-707]

Mercury, having stolen the oxen of Apollo, and Battus having perceived the theft, he engages him, by a present, to keep the matter secret. Mistrusting, however, his fidelity, he assumes another shape, and tempting him with presents, he succeeds in corrupting him. To punish his treachery, the God changes him into a touchstone.

The Philyrean[77] hero wept, and in vain, God of Delphi, implored thy assistance; but neither couldst thou reverse the orders of great Jupiter, nor, if thou couldst have reversed them wast thou then present; for then thou wast dwelling in Elis and the Messenian[78] fields. This was the time when a shepherd's skin garment was covering thee, and a stick cut out of the wood was the burden of thy left hand, and of the other, a pipe unequal with its seven reeds. And while love is thy concern, while thy pipe is soothing thee, some cows are said to have strayed unobserved into the plains of Pylos.[79] The son of Maia the daughter of Atlas, observes them, and with his usual skill hides them, driven off, in the woods. Nobody but an old man, well-known in that country, had noticed the theft: all the neighborhood called him Battus. He was keeping the forests and the grassy pastures, and the set of fine-bred mares of the rich Neleus.[80]

Mercury was afraid of him, and took him aside with a gentle hand, and said to him, "Come, stranger, whoever thou art, if, perchance any one should ask after these herds, deny that thou hast seen them; and, lest no requital be paid thee for so doing, take a handsome cow as thy reward;" and thereupon he gave him one. On receiving it, the stranger returned this answer: "Thou mayst go in safety. May that stone first make mention of thy theft;" and he pointed to a stone. The son of Jupiter feigned to go away. But soon he returned, and changing his form, together with his voice, he said, "Countryman, if thou hast seen any cows pass along this way, give me thy help, and break silence about the theft; a female, coupled together with its bull shall be presented thee as a reward." But the old man,[81] after his reward was thus doubled, said, "They will be beneath those hills;" and beneath those hills they really were. The son of Atlas laughed and said, "Dost thou, treacherous man, betray me to my own self? Dost betray me to myself?" and then he turned his perjured breast into a hard stone, which even now is called the "Touchstone;"[82] and this old disgrace is attached to the stone that really deserves it not.

[Footnote 77: Philyrean.—Ver. 676. Chiron was the son of Philyra, by Saturn.]

[Footnote 78: Messenian.—Ver. 679. Elis and Messenia were countries of Peloponnesus; the former was on the northwest, and the latter on the southwest side of it.]

[Footnote 79: Plains of Pylos.—Ver. 684. There were three cities named Pylos in Peloponnesus. One was in Elis, another in Messenia, and the third was situate between the other two. The latter is supposed to have been the native place of Nestor, though they all laid claim to that honor.]

[Footnote 80: Neleus.—Ver. 689. He was the king of Pylos, and the father of Nestor.]

[Footnote 81: The old man.—Ver. 702. Clarke quaintly translates 'at senior,' 'but then the old blade.']

[Footnote 82: The 'Touchstone.'—Ver. 706. It is a matter of doubt among commentators whether 'index' here means a general term for the touchstone, by which metals are tested; or whether it means that Battus was changed into one individual stone, which afterwards was called 'index.' Lactantius, by his words, seems to imply that the latter was the case. He says, 'He changed him into a stone, which, from this circumstance, is called "index" about Pylos.' 'Index' was a name of infamy, corresponding with the Greek word συκοφάντης, and with our term 'spy.']

EXPLANATION

The Centaurs, fabulous monsters, half men and half horses, were perhaps the first horsemen in Thessaly and its neighborhood. It is also probable that Chiron, who was one of these, acquired great fame by the knowledge he had acquired at a time and in a country where learning was little cultivated. The ancients regarded him as the first promulgator of the utility of medicines, in which he was said to have instructed his pupil Æsculapius. He was also considered to be an excellent musician and a good astronomer, as we learn from Homer, Diodorus Siculus, and other authors. Most of the heroes of that age, and among them Hercules and Jason, studied under him. Very probably, the only foundation for the story of the transformation of Ocyrrhoë, was the skill and address which, under her father's instruction, she acquired in riding and the management of horses. For if, as it seems really was the case, the horsemen of that age were taken for monsters, half men and half horses, it is not surprising to find the story that the daughter of a Centaur was transformed into a mare.

Chiron is generally supposed to have marked out the Constellations, for the purpose of directing the Argonauts in their voyage for the recovery of the Golden Fleece.

FABLE XII [II.708-764]

Mercury, falling in love with Herse, the daughter of Cecrops, endeavors to engage Aglauros in his interest, and by her means, to obtain access to her sister. She refuses to assist him, unless he promises to present her with a large sum of money.

Hence, the bearer of the caduceus raised himself upon equal wings; and as he flew, he looked down upon the fields of Munychia,[83] and the land pleasing to Minerva, and the groves of the well-planted Lycæus. On that day, by chance, the chaste virgins were, in their purity, carrying the sacred offerings in baskets crowned with flowers, upon their heads to the joyful citadel of Pallas. The winged God beholds them returning thence; and he does not shape his course directly forward, but wheels round in the same circle. As that bird swiftest in speed, the kite, on espying the entrails, while he is afraid, and the priests stand in numbers around the sacrifice, wings his flight in circles, and yet ventures not to go far away, and greedily hovers around the object of his hopes with waving wings, so does the active Cyllenian God bend his course over the Actæan towers, and circles round in the same air. As much as Lucifer shines more brightly than the other stars, and as much as the golden Phœbe shines more brightly than thee, O Lucifer, so much superior was Herse, as she went, to all the other virgins, and was the ornament of the solemnity and of her companions. The son of Jupiter was astonished at her beauty; and as he hung in the air, he burned no otherwise than as when the Balearic[84] sling throws forth the plummet of lead; it flies and becomes red hot in its course, and finds beneath the clouds the fires which it had not before.

He alters his course, and, having left heaven, goes a different way; nor does he disguise himself; so great is his confidence in his beauty. This, though it is every way complete, still he improves by care, and smooths his hair and adjusts his mantle,[85] that it may hang properly, so that the fringe and all the gold may be seen; and minds that his long smooth wand, with which he induces and drives away sleep, is in his right hand, and that his wings[86] shine upon his beauteous feet.

A private part of the house had three bed-chambers, adorned with ivory and with tortoiseshell, of which thou, Pandrosos, hadst the right-hand one, Aglauros the left-hand, and Herse had the one in the middle. She that occupied the left-hand one was the first to remark Mercury approaching, and she ventured to ask the name of the God, and the occasion of his coming. To her thus answered the grandson of Atlas and of Pleione: "I am he who carries the commands of my father through the air. Jupiter himself is my father. Nor will I invent pretences; do thou only be willing to be attached to thy sister, and to be called the aunt of my offspring. Herse is the cause of my coming; I pray thee to favor one in love." Aglauros looks upon him with the same eyes with which she had lately looked upon the hidden mysteries of the yellow-haired Minerva, and demands for her agency gold of great weight; and, in the meantime, obliges him to go out of the house. The warlike Goddess turned upon her the orbs of her stern eyes, and drew a sigh from the bottom of her heart, with so great a motion, that she heaved both her breast and the Ægis placed before her valiant breast. It occurred to her that she had laid open her secrets with a profane hand, at the time when she beheld progeny created for the God who inhabits Lemnos,[87] without a mother, and contrary to the assigned laws; and that she could now be agreeable both to the God and to the sister of Aglauros, and that she would be enriched by taking the gold, which she, in her avarice, had demanded. Forthwith she repairs to the abode of Envy, hideous with black gore. Her abode is concealed in the lowest recesses of a cave, wanting sun, and not pervious to any wind, dismal and filled with benumbing cold; and which is ever without fire, and ever abounding with darkness.

[Footnote 83: Munychia.—Ver. 709. Munychia was the name of a promontory and harbor of Attica, between the Piræus and the promontory of 'Sunium.' The spot was so called from Munychius, who there built a temple in honor of Diana.]

[Footnote 84: Balearic.—Ver. 727. The Baleares were the islands of Majorca, Minorca, and Iviza, in the Mediterranean, near the coast of Spain. The natives of these islands were famous for their skill in the use of the sling. That weapon does not appear to have been used in the earliest times among the Greeks, as Homer does not mention it; it had, however, been introduced by the time of the war with Xerxes, though even then the sling was, perhaps, rarely used as a weapon. The Acarnanians and the Achæans of Agium, Patræ, and Dymæ were very expert in the use of the sling. That used by the Achæans was made of three thongs of leather, and not of one only, like those of other nations. The natives of the Balearic isles are said to have attained their skill from the circumstance of their mothers, when they were children, obliging them to obtain their food by striking it, from a tree, with a sling. While other slings were made of leather, theirs were made of rushes. Besides stones, plummets of lead, called 'glandes,' (as in the present instance), and μολύβδιδες, of a form between acorns and almonds, were cast in moulds, to be thrown from slings. They have been frequently dug up in various parts of Greece, and particularly on the plains of Marathon. Some have the device of a thunderbolt; while others are inscribed with δέξαι, 'take *this.' It was a prevalent idea with the ancients that the stone discharged from the sling became red hot in its course, from the swiftness of its motion.]*

[Footnote 85: Adjusts his mantle.—Ver. 733. 'Chlamydemque ut pendeat apte, Collocat,' etc., is translated by Clarke—'And he places his coat that it might hang agreeably, that the border and all its gold might appear.']

[Footnote 86: That his wings.—Ver. 736. Clarke renders 'ut tersis niteant talaria plantis,' 'that his wings shine upon his spruce feet.']

[Footnote 87: God who inhabits Lemnos.—Ver. 757. Being precipitated from heaven for his deformity, Vulcan fell upon the Isle of Lemnos, in the Ægean Sea, where he exercised the craft of a blacksmith, according to the mythologists. The birth of Ericthonius, by the aid of Minerva, is here referred to.]

EXPLANATION

Cicero tells us, that there were several persons in ancient times named Mercury. The probability is, that one of them fell in love with Herse, one of the daughters of Cecrops, king of Athens; and that Aglauros becoming jealous of her, this tradition was built upon facts of so ordinary a nature.

FABLE XIII [II.765-832]

Pallas commands Envy to make Aglauros jealous of her sister Herse. Envy obeys the request of the Goddess; and Aglauros, stung with that passion, continues obstinate in opposing Mercury's passage to her sister's apartment, for which the God changes her into a statue.

When the female warrior, to be dreaded in battle, came hither, she stood before the abode (for she did not consider it lawful to go under the roof), and she struck the door-posts with the end of the spear. The doors, being shaken, flew open; she sees Envy within, eating the flesh of vipers, the nutriment of her own bad propensities; and when she sees her, she turns away her eyes. But the other rises sluggishly from the ground, and leaves the bodies of the serpents half devoured, and stalks along with sullen pace. And when she sees the Goddess graced with beauty and with splendid arms, she groans, and fetches a deep sigh at her appearance. A paleness rests on her face, and leanness in all her body; she never looks direct on you; her teeth are black with rust; her breast is green with gall; her tongue is dripping with venom. Smiles there are none, except such as the sight of grief has excited. Nor does she enjoy sleep, being kept awake with watchful cares; but sees with sorrow the successes of men, and pines away at seeing them. She both torments and is tormented at the same moment, and is ever her own punishment. Yet, though Tritonia[88] hated her, she spoke to her briefly in such words as these: "Infect one of the daughters of Cecrops with thy poison; there is occasion so to do; Aglauros is she."

Saying no more, she departed, and spurned the ground with her spear impressed on it. She, beholding the Goddess as she departed, with a look askance, uttered a few murmurs, and grieved at the success of Minerva; and took her staff, which wreaths of thorns entirely surrounded; and veiled in black clouds, wherever she goes she tramples down the blooming fields, and burns up the grass, and crops the tops of the flowers. With her breath, too, she pollutes both nations and cities, and houses; and at last she descries the Tritonian[89] citadel, flourishing in arts and riches, and cheerful peace. Hardly does she restrain her tears, because she sees nothing to weep at. But after she has entered the chamber of the daughter of Cecrops, she executes her orders; and touches her breast with her hand stained with rust, and fills her heart with jagged thorns. She breathes into her as well the noxious venom, and spreads the poison black as pitch throughout her bones, and lodges it in the midst of her lungs.

And that these causes of mischief may not wander through too wide a space, she places her sister before her eyes, and the fortunate marriage of that sister, and the God under his beauteous appearance, and aggravates each particular. By this, the daughter of Cecrops being irritated, is gnawed by a secret grief, and groans, tormented by night, tormented by day, and wastes away in extreme wretchedness, with a slow consumption, as ice smitten upon by a sun often clouded. She burns at the good fortune of the happy Herse, no otherwise than as when fire is placed beneath thorny reeds, which do not send forth flames, and burn with a gentle heat. Often does she wish to die, that she may not be a witness to any such thing; often, to tell the matters, as criminal, to her severe father. At last, she sat herself down in the front of the threshold, in order to exclude the God when he came; to whom, as he proffered blandishments and entreaties, and words of extreme kindness, she said, "Cease all this; I shall not remove myself hence, until thou art repulsed." "Let us stand to that agreement," says the active Cyllenian God; and he opens the carved door with his wand. But in her, as she endeavors to arise, the parts which we bend in sitting cannot be moved, through their numbing weight. She, indeed, struggles to raise herself, with her body, upright; but the joints of her knees are stiff, and a chill runs through her nails, and her veins are pallid, through the loss of blood.

And as the disease of an incurable cancer is wont to spread in all directions, and to add the uninjured parts to the tainted; so, by degrees, did a deadly chill enter her breast, and stop the passages of life, and her respiration. She did not endeavor to speak; but if she had endeavored, she had no passage for her voice. Stone had now possession of her neck; her face was grown hard, and she sat, a bloodless statue. Nor was the stone white; her mind had stained it.

[Footnote 88: Tritonia.—Ver. 783. Minerva is said to have been called Tritonia, either from the Cretan word τριτω, signifying 'a head,' as she sprang from the head of Jupiter; or from Trito, a lake of Libya, near which she was said to have been born.]

[Footnote 89: Tritonian.—Ver. 794. Athens, namely, which was sacred to Pallas, or Minerva, its tutelary divinity.]

EXPLANATION

Pausanias, in his Attica, somewhat varies this story, and says that the daughters of Cecrops, running mad, threw themselves from the top of a tower. It is very probable that on the introduction of the worship of Pallas, or Minerva, into Attica, these daughters of Cecrops may have hesitated to encourage the innovation, and the story was promulgated that the Goddess had in that manner punished their impiety. This seems the more likely, from the fact mentioned by Pausanias that Pandrosos, the third daughter of Cecrops, had, after her death, a temple built in honor of her, near that of Minerva, because she had continued faithful to that Goddess, and had not disobeyed her, as her sisters had done. The reputation and good fame of Herse and Aglauros had, however, been restored by the time of Herodotus, since he informs us that they both had their temples at Athens.

FABLE XIV [II.833-875]

Jupiter assumes the shape of a Bull, and carrying off Europa, swims with her on his back to the isle of Crete.

When the grandson of Atlas had inflicted this punishment upon her words and her profane disposition, he left the lands named after Pallas, and entered the skies with his waving wings. His father calls him on one side; and, not owning the cause of his love, he says, "My son, the trusty minister of my commands, banish delay, and swiftly descend with thy usual speed, and repair to the region which looks towards thy Constellation mother on the left side, (the natives call it Sidonis[90] by name) and drive towards the sea-shore, the herd belonging to the king, which thou seest feeding afar upon the grass of the mountain."

Thus he spoke; and already were the bullocks, driven from the mountain, making for the shore named, where the daughter of the great king, attended by Tyrian virgins, was wont to amuse herself. Majesty and love but ill accord, nor can they continue in the same abode. The father and the ruler of the Gods, whose right hand is armed with the three-forked flames, who shakes the world with his nod, laying aside the dignity of empire, assumes the appearance of a bull; and mixing with the oxen, he lows, and, in all his beauty, walks about upon the shooting grass. For his color is that of snow, which neither the soles of hard feet have trodden upon, nor the watery South wind melted. His neck swells with muscles; dewlaps hang from between his shoulders. His horns are small indeed, but such as you might maintain were made with the hand, and more transparent than a bright gem. There is nothing threatening in his forehead; nor is his eye formidable; his countenance expresses peace.

The daughter of Agenor is surprised that he is so beautiful, and that he threatens no attack; but although so gentle, she is at first afraid to touch him. By and by she approaches him, and holds out flowers to his white mouth. The lover rejoices, and till his hoped-for pleasure comes, he gives kisses to her hands; scarcely, oh, scarcely, does he defer the rest. And now he plays with her, and skips upon the green grass; and now he lays his snow-white side upon the yellow sand. And, her fear now removed by degrees, at one moment he gives his breast to be patted by the hand of the virgin; at another, his horns to be wreathed with new-made garlands. The virgin of royal birth even ventured to sit down upon the back of the bull, not knowing upon whom she was pressing. Then the God, by degrees moving from the land, and from the dry shore, places the fictitious hoofs of his feet in the waves near the brink. Then he goes still further, and carries his prize over the expanse of the midst of the ocean. She is affrighted, and, borne off, looks back on the shore she has left; and with her right hand she grasps his horn, while the other is placed on his back; her waving garments are ruffled by the breeze.

[Footnote 90: Sidonis.—Ver. 840. Sidon, or Sidonis, was a maritime city of Phœnicia, near Tyre, of whose greatness it was not an unworthy rival.]

EXPLANATION

This Fable depicts one of the most famous events in the ancient Mythology. As we have already remarked, it is supposed that there were several persons of the name of Zeus, or Jupiter; though there is great difficulty in assigning to each individual his own peculiar adventures. Vossius refers the adventure of Niobe, the daughter of Phoroneus, to Jupiter Apis, the king of Argos, who reigned about B.C. 1770; and that of Danaë to Jupiter Prœtus, who lived about 1350 years before the Christian era. It was Jupiter Tantalus, according to him, that carried off Ganymede; and it was Jupiter, the father of Hercules, that deceived Leda. He says that the subject of the present Fable was Jupiter Asterius, who reigned about B.C. 1400. Diodorus Siculus tells us that he was the son of Teutamus, who, having married the daughter of Creteus, went with some Pelasgians to settle in the island of Crete, of which he was the first king. We may then conclude, that Jupiter Asterius, having heard of the beauty of Europa, the daughter of Agenor, King of Tyre, fitted out a ship, for the purpose of carrying her off by force. This is the less improbable, as we learn from Herodotus, that the custom of carrying those away by force, who could not be obtained by fair means, was very common in these rude ages.

The ship in which Asterius made his voyage, had, very probably, the form of a bull for its figure-head; which, in time, occasioned those who related the adventure, to say, that Jupiter concealed himself under the shape of that animal, to carry off his mistress. Palæphatus and Tzetzes suggest, that the story took its rise from the name of the general of Asterius, who was called Taurus, which is also the Greek name for a bull. Bochart has an ingenious suggestion, based upon etymological grounds. He thinks that the twofold meaning of the word 'Alpha,' or 'Ilpha,' which, in the Phœnician dialect, meant either a ship or a bull, gave occasion to the fable; and that the Greeks, on reading the annals of the Phœnicians, by mistake, took the word in the latter sense.

Europa was honored as a Divinity after her death, and a festival was instituted in her memory, which Hesychius calls 'Hellotia,' from Ἑλλωτὶς, the name she received after her death.

BOOK THE THIRD

FABLE I [III.1-34]

Jupiter, having carried away Europa, her father, Agenor, commands his son Cadmus to go immediately in search of her, and either to bring back his sister with him, or never to return to Phœnicia. Cadmus, wearied with his toils and fruitless inquiries, goes to consult the oracle at Delphi, which bids him observe the spot where he should see a cow lie down, and build a city there, and give the name of Bœotia to the country.

And now the God, having laid aside the shape of the deceiving Bull, had discovered himself, and reached the Dictæan land; when her father, ignorant of her fate, commands Cadmus to seek her thus ravished, and adds exile as the punishment, if he does not find her; being both affectionate and unnatural in the self-same act. The son of Agenor, having wandered over the whole world,[1] as an exile flies from his country and the wrath of his father, for who is there that can discover the intrigues of Jupiter? A suppliant, he consults the oracle of Phœbus, and inquires in what land he must dwell. "A heifer," Phœbus says, "will meet thee in the lonely fields, one that has never borne the yoke, and free from the crooked plough. Under her guidance, go on thy way; and where she shall lie down on the grass, there cause a city to be built, and call it the Bœotian[2] city."

Scarcely had Cadmus well got down from the Castalian cave,[3] when he saw a heifer, without a keeper, slowly going along, bearing no mark of servitude upon her neck. He follows, and pursues her steps with leisurely pace, and silently adores Phœbus, the adviser of his way. And now he had passed the fords of the Cephisus, and the fields of Panope, when the cow stood still and raising her forehead, expansive with lofty horns, towards heaven, she made the air reverberate with her lowings. And so, looking back on her companions that followed behind, she lay down, and reposed her side upon the tender grass. Cadmus returned thanks, and imprinted kisses upon the stranger land, and saluted the unknown mountains and fields. He was now going to offer sacrifice to Jupiter, and commanded his servants to go and fetch some water for the libation from the running springs. An ancient grove was standing there, as yet profaned by no axe. There was a cavern in the middle of it, thick covered with twigs and osiers, forming a low arch by the junction of the rocks; abounding with plenty of water. Hid in this cavern, there was a dragon sacred to Mars,[4] adorned with crests and a golden color. His eyes sparkle with fire, and all his body is puffed out with poison; three tongues, too, are brandished, and his teeth stand in a triple row.

[Footnote 1: Over the whole world.—Ver. 6. Apollodorus tells us that Cadmus lived in Thrace until the death of his mother, Telephassa, who accompanied him; and that, after her decease, he proceeded to Delphi to make inquiries of the oracle.]

[Footnote 2: Bœotian.—Ver. 13. He implies here that Bœotia received its name from the Greek word βοῦς, 'an ox' or 'cow.' Other writers say that it was so called from Bœotus, the son of Neptune and Arne. Some authors also say that Thebes received its name from the Syrian word 'Thebe,' which signified 'an ox.']

[Footnote 3: Castalian cave.—Ver. 14. Castalius was a fountain at the foot of Mount Parnassus, and in the vicinity of Delphi. It was sacred to the Muses.]

[Footnote 4: Sacred to Mars.—Ver. 32. Euripides says, that the dragon had been set there by Mars to watch the spot and the neighboring stream. Other writers say that it was a son of Mars, Dercyllus by name, and that a Fury, named Tilphosa, was its mother. Ancient history abounds with stories of enormous serpents. The army of Regulus is said by Pliny the Elder, to have killed a serpent of enormous size, which obstructed the passage of the river Bagrada, in Africa. It was 120 feet in length.]

EXPLANATION

Reverting to the history of Europa, it may be here remarked, that Apollodorus has preserved her genealogy. Libya, according to that author, had two sons by Neptune, Belus and Agenor. The latter married Telephassa, by whom he had Cadmus, Phœnix, and Cilix, and a daughter named Europa. Some ancient writers, however, say, that Europa was the daughter of Phœnix, and the grandchild of Agenor.

Some authors, and Ovid among the rest, have supposed that Europe received its name from Europa. Bochart has, with considerable probability, suggested that it was originally so called from the fair complexion of the people who inhabited it. Europa herself may have received her name also from the fairness of her complexion: hence, the poets, as the Scholiast on Theocritus tells us, invented a fable, that a daughter of Juno stole her mother's paint, to give it to Europa, who used it with so much success as to ensure, by its use, an extremely fair and beautiful complexion.

The companions of Cadmus, fetching water from the fountain of Mars, are devoured by the Dragon that guards it. Cadmus, on discovering their destruction, slays the monster, and, by the advice of Minerva, sows the teeth, which immediately produce a crop of armed men. They forthwith quarrel among themselves, and kill each other, with the exception of five who assist Cadmus in building the city of Thebes.

After the men who came from the Tyrian nation had touched this grove with ill-fated steps, and the urn let down into the water made a splash; the azure dragon stretched forth his head from the deep cave, and uttered dreadful hissings. The urns dropped from their hands; and the blood left their bodies, and a sudden trembling seized their astonished limbs. He wreathes his scaly orbs in rolling spires, and with a spring becomes twisted into mighty folds; and uprearing himself from below the middle into the light air, he looks down upon all the grove, and is of as large a size,[5] as, if you were to look on him entire, the serpent which separates the two Bears.

There is no delay; he seizes the Phœnicians (whether they are resorting to their arms or to flight, or whether fear itself is preventing either step); some he kills with his sting,[6] some with his long folds, some breathed upon[7] by the venom of his baneful poison.

The sun, now at its height, had made the shadows but small: the son of Agenor wonders what has detained his companion and goes to seek his men. His garment was a skin torn from a lion; his weapon was a lance with shining steel, and a javelin; and a courage superior to any weapon. When he entered the grove, and beheld the lifeless bodies, and the victorious enemy of immense size upon them, licking the horrid wounds with bloodstained tongue, he said, "Either I will be the avenger of your death, bodies of my faithful companions, or I will be a sharer in it." Thus he said; and with his right hand he raised a huge stone,[8] and hurled the vast weight with a tremendous effort. And although high walls with lofty towers would have been shaken with the shock of it, yet the dragon remained without a wound; and, being defended by his scales as though with a coat of mail, and the hardness of his black hide, he repelled the mighty stroke with his skin. But he did not overcome the javelin as well with the same hardness; which stood fast, fixed in the middle joint of his yielding spine, and sank with the entire point of steel into his entrails. Fierce with pain, he turned his head towards his back, and beheld his wounds, and bit the javelin fixed there. And after he had twisted it on every side with all his might, with difficulty he wrenched it from his back; yet the steel stuck fast in his bones. But then, when this newly inflicted wound has increased his wonted fury, his throat swelled with gorged veins, and white foam flowed around his pestilential jaws. The Earth, too, scraped with the scales, sounds again, and the livid steam that issues from his infernal mouth,[9] infects the tainted air. One while he is enrolled in spires making enormous rings; sometimes he unfolds himself straighter than a long beam. Now with a vast impulse, like a torrent swelled with rain, he is borne along, and bears down the obstructing forests with his breast. The son of Agenor gives way a little; and by the spoil of the lion he sustains the shock, and with his lance extended before him, pushes back his mouth, as it advances. The dragon rages, and vainly inflicts wounds on the hard steel, and fixes his teeth upon the point. And now the blood began to flow from his poisonous palate, and had dyed the green grass with its spray. But the wound was slight; because he recoiled from the stroke, and drew back his wounded throat, and by shrinking prevented the blow from sinking deep, and did not suffer it to go very far. At length, the son of Agenor, still pursuing, pressed the spear lodged in his throat, until an oak stood in his way as he retreated, and his neck was pierced, together with the trunk. The tree was bent with the weight of the serpent, and groaned at having its trunk lashed with the extremity of its tail.

While the conqueror was surveying the vast size of his vanquished enemy, a voice was suddenly heard (nor was it easy to understand whence it was, but heard it was). "Why, son of Agenor, art thou thus contemplating the dragon slain by thee? Even thou thyself shalt be seen in the form of a dragon."[10] He, for a long time in alarm, lost his color together with his presence of mind, and his hair stood on end with a chill of terror. Lo! Pallas, the favorer of the hero, descending through the upper region of the air, comes to him, and bids him sow the dragon's teeth under the earth turned up, as the seeds of a future people. He obeyed; and when he had opened a furrow with the pressed plough, he scattered the teeth on the ground as ordered, the seed of a race of men. Afterwards ('tis beyond belief) the turf began to move, and first appeared a point of a spear out of the furrows, next the coverings of heads nodding with painted cones;[11] then the shoulders and the breast, and the arms laden with weapons start up, and a crop of men armed with shields grows apace. So, when the curtains[12] are drawn up in the joyful theaters, figures are wont to rise, and first to show their countenances; by degrees the rest; and being drawn out in a gradual continuation, the whole appear, and place their feet on the lowest edge of the stage. Alarmed with this new enemy, Cadmus is preparing to take arms, when one of the people that the earth had produced cries out, "Do not take up arms, nor engage thyself in civil war." And then, engaged hand to hand, he strikes one of his earth-born brothers with the cruel sword, while he himself falls by a dart sent from a distance. He, also, who had put him to death, lives no longer than the other, and breathes forth the air which he has so lately received. In a similar manner, too, the whole troop becomes maddened, and the brothers so newly sprung up, fall in fight with each other, by mutual wounds. And now the youths that had the space of so short an existence allotted them, beat with throbbing breast their blood-stained mother, five only remaining, of whom Echion[13] was one. He, by the advice of Tritonia, threw his arms upon the ground, and both asked and gave the assurance of brotherly concord.

The Sidonian stranger had these as associates in his task, when he built the city that was ordered by the oracle of Phœbus.

[Footnote 5: As large a size.—Ver. 44. This description of the enormous size of the dragon or serpent is inconsistent with what the Poet says in line 91, where we find Cadmus enabled to pin his enemy against an oak.]

[Footnote 6: With his sting.—Ver. 48. He enumerates in this one instance the various modes by which serpents put their prey to death, either by means of their sting, or, in the case of the larger kinds of serpent, by twisting round it, and suffocating it in their folds.]

[Footnote 7: Some breathed upon.—Ver. 49. It was a prevalent notion among the ancients, that some serpents had the power of killing their prey by their poisonous breath. Though some modern commentators on this passage may be found to affirm the same thing, it is extremely doubtful if such is the fact. The notion was, perhaps, founded on the power which certain serpents have of fascinating their prey by the agency of the eye, and thus depriving it of the means of escape.]

[Footnote 8: A huge stone.—Ver. 59. 'Molaris' here means a stone as large as a mill-stone, and not a mill-stone itself, for we must remember that this was an uninhabited country, and consequently a stranger to the industry of man.]

[Footnote 9: His infernal mouth.—Ver. 76. 'Stygio' means 'pestilential as the exhalations of the marshes of Styx.']

[Footnote 10: Form of a dragon.—Ver. 98. This came to pass when, having been expelled from his dominions by Zethus and Amphion, he retired to Illyria, and was there transformed into a serpent, a fate which was shared by his wife Hermione.]

[Footnote 11: With painted cones.—Ver. 108. The 'conus' was the conical part of the helmet into which the crest of variegated feathers was inserted.]

[Footnote 12: When the curtains.—Ver. 111. The 'Siparium' was a piece of tapestry stretched on a frame, and, rising before the stage, answered the same purpose as the curtain or drop-scene with us, in concealing the stage till the actors appeared. Instead of drawing up this curtain to discover the stage and actors, according to our present practice, it was depressed when the play began, and fell beneath the level of the stage; whence 'aulæa premuntur,' 'the curtain is dropped,' meant that the play had commenced. When the performance was finished, this was raised again gradually from the foot of the stage; therefore 'aulæa tolluntur,' 'the curtain is raised,' would mean that the play had finished. From the present passage we learn, that in drawing it up from the stage, the curtain was gradually displayed, the unfolding taking place, perhaps, below the boards, so that the heads of the figures rose first, until the whole form appeared in full with the feet resting on the stage, when the 'siparium' was fully drawn up. From a passage in Virgil's Georgics (book iii. l. 25), we learn that the figures of Britons (whose country had then lately been the scene of new conquests) were woven on the canvas of the 'siparium,' having their arms in the attitude of lifting the curtain.]

[Footnote 13: Echion.—Ver. 126. The names of the others were Udeus, Chthonius, Hyperenor, and Pelor, according to Apollodorus. To these some added Creon, as a sixth.]

EXPLANATION

Agenor, on losing his daughter, commands his sons to go in search of her, and not to return till they have found her. The young princes, either unable to learn what was become of her, or, perhaps, being too weak to recover her out of the hands of the king of Crete, did not return to their father, but established themselves in different countries; Cadmus settling in Bœotia, Cilix in Cilicia, to which he gave his name, and Phœnix, as Hyginus tells us, remaining in Africa. Photius, quoting from Conon, the historian, informs us, that the hope of conquering some country in Europe, and establishing a colony there, was the true ground of the voyage of Cadmus.

Palæphatus, and other writers, say, that the Dragon which was killed by Cadmus was a king of the country, who was named Draco, and was a son of Mars: that his teeth were his subjects, who rallied again after their defeat, and that Cadmus put them all to the sword, except Chthonius, Udeus, Hyperenor, Pelor, and Echion, who became reconciled to him. Heraclitus, however, assures us, that Cadmus really did slay a serpent, which was very annoying to the Bœotian territory. Bochart and LeClerc are of opinion that the Fable has the following foundation:—They say, that in the Phœnician language, the same word signifies either the teeth of a serpent, or short javelins, pointed with brass; that the word which signifies the number five likewise means an army; and that probably, from these circumstances, the Fable may have taken its rise. For the Greeks, in following the annals written in the Phœnician language, while writing the history of the founder of Thebes, instead of describing his soldiers as wearing helmets on their heads, with back and breast-plates, and with darts in their hands pointed with brass, which equipment was then entirely novel in Greece, chose rather to follow the more wonderful version, and to say, that Cadmus had five companions produced from the teeth of a serpent; as, according to Bochart's suggestion, the same Phœnician phrase may either signify a company of men sprung from the teeth of a serpent, or a company of men armed with brazen darts.

This conjecture is, perhaps, confirmed by a story related by Herodotus (book ii.), which resembles it very much. He tells us, that Psammeticus, king of Egypt, being driven to the marshy parts of his kingdom, sent to consult the oracle of Latona, which answered that he should be restored by brass men coming from the sea. At the time, this answer appeared to him entirely frivolous; but certain Ionian soldiers, being obliged, some years after, to retire to Egypt, and appearing on the shore with their weapons and armor, all of brass, those who perceived them ran immediately to inform the king, that men clad in brass were plundering the country. The prince then fully comprehended the meaning of the oracle, and making an alliance with them, recovered his throne by the assistance they gave him. These brass men come from the sea, and those sprung from the earth were soldiers who assisted Psammeticus and Cadmus in carrying out their objects. Bochart's conjecture is strengthened by the fact, that Cadmus was either the inventor of the cuirass and javelin, or the first that brought them into Greece. Without inquiring further into the subject, we may conclude, that the men sprung from the earth, or the dragon's teeth which were sown, were the people of the country, whom Cadmus found means to bring over to his interest; and that they first helped him to conquer his enemies, and then to build the citadel of Thebes, to ensure his future security. Apollodorus says that Cadmus, to expiate the slaughter of the dragon, was obliged to serve Mars a whole year; which year, containing eight of our years, it is not improbable that Cadmus rendered services for a long time to his new allies before he received any assistance from them.

FABLE III [III.131-252]

Actæon, the grandson of Cadmus, fatigued with hunting and excessive heat, inadvertently wanders to the cool valley of Gargaphie, the usual retreat of Diana, when tired with the same exercise. There, to his misfortune, he surprises the Goddess and her Nymphs while bathing, for which she transforms him into a stag, and his own hounds tear him to pieces.

And now Thebes was standing; now Cadmus, thou mightst seem happy in thy exile. Both Mars and Venus[14] had become thy father-in-law and mother-in-law; add to this, issue by a wife so illustrious, so many sons[15] and daughters, and grandchildren, dear pledges of love; these, too, now of a youthful age. But, forsooth, the last day of life must always be awaited by man, and no one ought to be pronounced happy before his death,[16] and his last obsequies. Thy grandson, Cadmus, was the first occasion of sorrow to thee, among so much prosperity, the horns, too, not his own, placed upon his forehead, and you, O dogs, glutted with the blood of your master. But, if you diligently inquire into his case, you will find the fault of an accident, and not criminality in him; for what criminality did mistake embrace?

There was a mountain stained with the blood of various wild beasts; and now the day had contracted the meridian shadow of things, and the sun was equally distant from each extremity of the heavens; when the Hyantian youth[17] thus addressed the partakers of his toils, as they wandered along the lonely haunts of the wild beasts, with gentle accent: "Our nets are moistened, my friends, and our spears, too, with the blood of wild beasts; and the day has yielded sufficient sport; when the next morn, borne upon her rosy chariot, shall bring back the light, let us seek again our proposed task. Now Phœbus is at the same distance from both lands, the Eastern and the Western, and is cleaving the fields with his heat. Cease your present toils, and take away the knotted nets." The men execute his orders, and cease their labors. There was a valley, thick set with pitch-trees and the sharp-pointed cypress; by name Gargaphie,[18] sacred to the active Diana. In the extreme recess of this, there was a grotto in a grove, formed by no art; nature, by her ingenuity, had counterfeited art; for she had formed a natural arch, in the native pumice and the light sand-stones. A limpid fountain ran murmuring on the right hand with its little stream, having its spreading channels edged with a border of grass. Here, when wearied with hunting, the Goddess of the woods was wont to bathe her virgin limbs in clear water.

After she had entered there, she handed to one of the Nymphs, her armor-bearer, her javelin, her quiver, and her unstrung bow. Another Nymph put her arms under her mantle, when taken off: two removed the sandals from her feet. But Crocale,[19] the daughter of Ismenus, more skilled than they, gathered her hair, which lay scattered over her neck, into a knot, although she herself was with her hair loose. Nephele,[20] and Hyale,[21] and Rhanis,[22] fetch water, Psecas[23] and Phyale[24] do the same, and pour it from their large urns. And while the Titanian Goddess was there bathing in the wonted stream, behold! the grandson of Cadmus, having deferred the remainder of his sport till next day, came into the grove, wandering through the unknown wood, with uncertain steps; thus did his fate direct him.

Soon as he entered the grotto, dropping with its springs, the Nymphs, naked as they were, on seeing a man, smote their breasts, and filled all the woods with sudden shrieks, and gathering round Diana, covered her with their bodies. Yet the Goddess herself was higher than they, and was taller than them all by the neck. The color that is wont to be in clouds, tinted by the rays of the sun when opposite, or that of the ruddy morning, was on the features of Diana, when seen without her garments. She, although surrounded with the crowd of her attendants, stood sideways, and turned her face back; and how did she wish that she had her arrows at hand; and so she took up water,[25] which she did have at hand, and threw it over the face of the man, and sprinkling his hair with the avenging stream, she added these words, the presages of his future woe: "Now thou mayst tell, if tell thou canst, how that I was seen by thee without my garments." Threatening no more, she places on his sprinkled head the horns of a lively stag; she adds length to his neck, and sharpens the tops of his ears; and she changes his hands into feet, and his arms into long legs, and covers his body with a spotted coat of hair; fear, too is added. The Autonoëian[26] hero took to flight, and wondered that he was so swift in his speed; but when he beheld his own horns in the wonted stream, he was about to say, "Ah, wretched me!" when no voice followed. He groaned; that was all his voice, and his tears trickled down a face not his own, but that of a stag. His former understanding alone remained. What should he do? Should he return home, and to the royal abode? or should he lie hid in the woods? Fear hinders the one step, shame the other. While he was hesitating, the dogs espied him, and first Melampus,[27] and the good-nosed Ichnobates gave the signal, in full cry. Ichnobates,[28] was a Gnossian dog; Melampus was of Spartan breed. Then the rest rush on, swifter than the rapid winds; Pamphagus,[29] and Dorcæus,[30] and Oribasus,[31] all Arcadian dogs; and able Nebrophonus,[32] and with Lælaps,[33] fierce Theron,[34] and Pterelas,[35] excelling in speed, Agre[36] in her scent, and Hylæus,[37] lately wounded by a fierce boar, and Nape,[38] begotten by a wolf, and Pœmenis,[39] that had tended cattle, and Harpyia,[40] followed by her two whelps, and the Sicyonian Ladon,[41] having a slender girth; Dromas,[42] too, and Canace,[43] Sticte,[44] and Tigris, and Alce,[45] and Leucon,[46] with snow-white hair, and Asbolus,[47] with black, and the able-bodied Lacon,[48] and Aëllo,[49] good at running, and Thoüs,[50] and swift Lycisca,[51] with her Cyprian brother, Harpalus,[52] too, having his black face marked with white down the middle, and

Melaneus,[53] and Lachne,[54] with a wire-haired body, and Labros,[55] and Agriodos,[56] bred of a Dictæan sire, but of a Laconian dam, and Hylactor,[57] with his shrill note; and others which it were tedious to recount.

This pack, in eagerness for their prey, are borne over rocks and cliffs, and crags difficult of approach, where the path is steep, and where there is no road. He flies along the routes by which he has so often pursued; alas! he is now flying from his own servants. Fain would he have cried, "I am Actæon, recognize your own master." Words are wanting to his wishes; the air resounds with their barking. Melanchætes[58] was the first to make a wound on his back, Theridamas[59] the next; Oresitrophus[60] fastened upon his shoulder. These had gone out later, but their course was shortened by a near cut through the hill. While they hold their master, the rest of the pack come up, and fasten their teeth in his body. Now room is wanting for more wounds. He groans, and utters a noise, though not that of a man, still, such as a stag cannot make; and he fills the well-known mountains with dismal moans, and suppliant on his bended knees, and like one in entreaty, he turns round his silent looks as though they were his arms.

But his companions, in their ignorance, urge on the eager pack with their usual cries, and seek Actæon with their eyes; and cry out "Actæon" aloud, as though he were absent. At his name he turns his head, as they complain that he is not there, and in his indolence, is not enjoying a sight of the sport afforded them. He wished, indeed, he had been away, but there he was; and he wished to see, not to feel as well, the cruel feats of his own dogs. They gather round him on all sides, and burying their jaws in his body, tear their master in pieces under the form of an imaginary stag. And the rage of the quiver-bearing Diana is said not to have been satiated, until his life was ended by many a wound.

[Footnote 14: Mars and Venus.—Ver. 132. The wife of Cadmus was Hermione, or Harmonia, who was said to have been the daughter of Mars and Venus. The Deities honored the nuptials with their presence, and presented marriage gifts, while the Muses and the Graces celebrated the festivity with hymns of their own composition.]

[Footnote 15: So many sons.—Ver. 134. Apollodorus, Hyginus, and others, say that Cadmus had but one son, Polydorus. If so, 'tot,' 'so many,' must here refer to the number of his daughters and grandchildren. His daughters were four in number, Autonoë, Ino, Semele, and Agave. Ino married Athamas, Autonoë Aristæus, Agave Echion, while Semele captivated Jupiter. The most famous of the grandsons of Cadmus were Bacchus, Melicerta, Pentheus, and Actæon.]

[Footnote 16: Before his death.—Ver. 135. This was the famous remark of Solon to Crœsus, when he was the master of the opulent and flourishing kingdom of Lydia, and seemed so firmly settled on his throne, that there was no probability of any interruption of his happiness. Falling into the hands of Cyrus the Persian, and being condemned to be burnt alive, he recollected this wise saying of Solon, and by that means saved his life, as we are told by Herodotus, who relates the story at length. Euripides has a similar passage in his Troades, line 510.]

[Footnote 17: The Hyantian youth.—Ver. 147. Actæon is thus called, as being a Bœotian. The Hyantes were the ancient or aboriginal inhabitants of Bœotia.]

[Footnote 18: Gargaphie.—Ver. 156. Gargaphie, or Gargaphia, was a valley situate near Platæa, having a fountain of the same name.]

[Footnote 19: Crocale.—Ver. 169. So called, perhaps, from κεκρύφαλος, an ornament for the head, being a coif, band, or fillet of network for the hair called in Latin 'reticulum,' by which name her office is denoted. The handmaid, whose duty it was to attend to the hair, held the highest rank in ancient times among the domestics.]

[Footnote 20: Nephele.—Ver. 171. From the Greek word νεφέλη, 'a cloud.']

[Footnote 21: Hyale.—Ver. 171. This is from ὕαλος, 'glass,' the name signifying 'glassy,' 'pellucid.' The very name calls to mind Milton's line in his Comus—'Under the glassy, cool, translucent wave.']

[Footnote 22: Rhanis.—Ver. 171. This name is adapted from the Greek verb ῥαίνω, 'to sprinkle.']

[Footnote 23: Psecas.—Ver. 172. From the Greek ψεκὰς, 'a dew-drop.']

[Footnote 24: Phyale.—Ver. 172. This is from the Greek φιαλὴ, 'an urn.']

[Footnote 25: Took up water.—Ver. 189. The ceremonial of sprinkling previous to the transformation seems not to have been neglected any more by the offended Goddesses of the classical Mythology, than by the intriguing enchantresses of the Arabian Nights' Entertainments; as the unfortunate Beder, when under the displeasure of the vicious queen Labè, experienced to his great inconvenience. The love for the supernatural, combined with an anxious desire to attribute its operations to material and visible agencies, forms one of the most singular features of the human character.]

[Footnote 26: Autonoëian.—Ver. 198. Autonoë was the daughter of Cadmus and Hermione, or Harmonia, and the wife of Aristæus, by whom she was the mother of Actæon. We may here remark, that in one of his satires, Lucian introduces Juno as saying to Diana, that she had let loose his dogs on Actæon, for fear lest, having seen her naked, he should divulge the deformity of her person.]

[Footnote 27: Melampus.—Ver. 206. These names are all from the Greek, and are interesting, as showing the epithets by which the ancients called their dogs. The pack of Actæon is said to have consisted of fifty dogs. Their names were preserved by several Greek poets, from whom Apollodorus copied them; but the greater part of his list has perished, and what remains is in a very corrupt state. Hyginus has preserved two lists, the first of which contains thirty-nine names, most of which are similar to those here given by Ovid, and in almost the same order; while the second contains thirty-six names, different from those here given. Æschylus has named but four of them, and Ovid here names thirty-six. Crete, Arcadia, and Laconia produced the most valuable hounds. Melampus, 'Black-foot,' is from the Greek words μέλας, 'black,' and ποῦς, 'a foot.']

[Footnote 28: Ichnobates.—Ver. 207. 'Tracer.' From the Greek ἰχνὸς, 'a footstep,' and βαίνω, 'to go.']

[Footnote 29: Pamphagus.—Ver. 210. 'Glutton.' From πᾶν, 'all,' and φάγω, 'to eat.']

[Footnote 30: Dorcæus.—Ver. 210. 'Quicksight.' From δέρκω, 'to see.']

[Footnote 31: Oribasus.—Ver. 210. 'Ranger.' From ὄρος, 'a mountain,' and βαίνω, 'to go.']

[Footnote 32: Nebrophonus.—Ver. 211. 'Kill-buck.' From νεβρὸς, 'a fawn,' and φονέω, 'to kill.']

[Footnote 33: Lælaps.—Ver. 211. 'Tempest.' So called from its swiftness and power, λαίλαψ, signifying 'a whirlwind.']

[Footnote 34: Theron.—Ver. 211. 'Hunter.' From the Greek, θερεύω, 'to trace,' or 'hunt.']

[Footnote 35: Pterelas.—Ver. 212. 'Wing.' 'Swift-footed,' from πτερὸν, 'a wing,' and ἐλαύνω, 'to drive onward.']

[Footnote 36: Agre.—Ver. 212. 'Catcher.' 'Quick-scented,' from ἄγρα, 'hunting,' or 'the chase.']

[Footnote 37: Hylæus.—Ver. 213. 'Woodger,' or 'Wood-ranger;' the Greek ὕλη, signifying 'a wood.']

[Footnote 38: Nape.—Ver. 214. 'Forester.' A 'forest,' or 'wood,' being in Greek, νάπη.]

[Footnote 39: Pœmenis.—Ver. 215. 'Shepherdess,' From the Greek ποίμενις, 'a shepherdess.']

[Footnote 40: Harpyia.—Ver. 215. 'Ravener.' From the Greek word ἅρπυια, 'a harpy,' or 'ravenous bird.']

[Footnote 41: Ladon.—Ver. 216. This dog takes its name from Ladon, a river of Sicyon, a territory on the shores of the gulf of Corinth.]

[Footnote 42: Dromas.—Ver. 217. 'Runner.' From the Greek δρόμος, 'a race.']

[Footnote 43: Canace.—Ver. 217. 'Barker.' The word καναχὴ, signifies 'a noise,' or 'din.']

[Footnote 44: Sticte.—Ver. 217. 'Spot.' So called from the variety of her colors, as στικτὸς, signifies 'diversified with various spots,' from στίζω, 'to vary with spots.' 'Tigris' means 'Tiger.']

[Footnote 45: Alce.—Ver. 217. 'Strong.' From the Greek ἀλκὴ 'strength.']

[Footnote 46: Leucon.—Ver. 218. 'White.' From λευκὸς, 'white.']

[Footnote 47: Asbolus.—Ver. 218. 'Soot,' or 'Smut.' From the Greek ἄσβολος, 'soot.']

[Footnote 48: Lacon.—Ver. 219. From his native country, Laconia.]

[Footnote 49: Aëllo.—Ver. 219. 'Storm.' From ἄελλα, 'a tempest.']

[Footnote 50: Thoüs.—Ver. 220. 'Swift.' From θοὸς, 'swift.' Pliny the Elder states, that 'thos' was the name of a kind of wolf, of larger make, and more active in springing than the common wolf. He says that it is of inoffensive habits towards man; but that it lives by prey, and is hairy in winter, but without hair in summer. It is supposed by some that he alludes to the jackal. Perhaps, from this animal, the dog here mentioned derived his name.]

[Footnote 51: Lycisca.—Ver. 220. 'Wolf.' From the diminutive of the Greek word λύκος, 'a wolf.' Virgil uses 'Lycisca' as the name of a dog, in his Eclogues.]

[Footnote 52: Harpalus.—Ver. 222. 'Snap.' From ἁρπάζω, 'to snatch,' or 'plunder.']

[Footnote 53: Melaneus.—Ver. 222. 'Black-coat.' From the Greek, μέλας, 'black.']

[Footnote 54: Lachne.—Ver. 222. 'Stickle.' From the Greek work λαχνὴ, signifying 'thickness of the hair.']

[Footnote 55: Labros.—Ver. 224. 'Worrier.' From the Greek λάβρος 'greedy.' Dicte was a mountain of Crete; whence the word 'Dictæan' is often employed to signify 'Cretan.']

[Footnote 56: Agriodos.—Ver. 224. 'Wild-tooth.' From ἄγριος 'wild,' and ὀδοῦς, 'a tooth.']

[Footnote 57: Hylactor.—Ver. 224. 'Babbler.' From the Greek word ὑλακτέω, signifying 'to bark.']

[Footnote 58: Melanchætes.—Ver. 232. 'Black-hair.' From the μέλας, 'black,' and χαιτὴ, 'mane.']

[Footnote 59: Theridamas.—Ver. 233. 'Kilham.' From θὴρ, 'a wild beast,' and δαμάω, 'to subdue.']

[Footnote 60: Oresitrophus.—Ver. 223. 'Rover.' From ὄρος 'a mountain,' and τρέφω 'to nourish.']

EXPLANATION

If the maxim of Horace, 'Nec Deus intersit, nisi dignus vindice nodus,' had been a little more frequently observed by the ancient poets, their Deities would not have been so often placed in a degrading or disgusting light before posterity. There cannot be a better illustration of the truth of this than the present Fable, where Ovid represents the chaste and prudent Diana as revenging herself in a cruel and barbarous manner for the indiscretion, or rather misfortune, of an innocent young man.

Cicero mentions several Goddesses of the name of Diana. The first was the daughter of Jupiter and Proserpine; the second of Jupiter and Latona; and the third of Upis and Glauce. Strabo mentions another Diana, named Britomartis, the daughter of Eubalus. The worship, however, of Diana as the Goddess of the Moon, was, most probably, derived from Egypt, with the Isis of whom she is perhaps identical. The adventure narrated in this Fable is most probably to be attributed to Diana Britomartis, as Strabo tells us, that she was particularly fond of the chase. Pausanias, in his Attica, tells the story in much the same terms, but he adds, that on seeing Diana bathing, the novelty of the sight excited Actæon's curiosity, and prompted him to approach nearer. To explain this fable, some authors suggest, that Actæon's dogs becoming mad, devoured him; while others suppose, that having ruined himself by the expense of supporting a large pack of hounds, and a hunting establishment, it was reported that he had been devoured by his dogs. Diodorus Siculus, and Euripides, tell us, that Actæon showed contempt to Diana, and was about to eat of the sacrifice that had been offered to her; and of course, in such a case, punishment at the hands of the Goddess would be deemed a just retribution. Apollodorus says, that Actæon was brought up by Chiron, and that he was put to death on Mount Cithæron, for having seen Diana bathing; though, according to one ancient authority, he was punished for having made improper overtures to Semele. Apollodorus also says, that his dogs died of grief, on the loss of their master, and he has preserved some of their names.

Juno, incensed against Semele for her intrigue with Jupiter, takes the form of Beroë, the more easily to ensure her revenge. Having first infused in Semele suspicions of her lover, she then recommends her to adopt a certain method of proving his constancy. Semele, thus deceived, obtains a reluctant promise from Jupiter, to make his next visit to her in the splendor and majesty in which he usually approached his wife.

They speak in various ways of this matter. To some, the Goddess seems more severe than is proper; others praise her, and call her deserving of her state of strict virginity: both sides find their reasons. The wife of Jupiter alone does not so much declare whether she blames or whether she approves, as she rejoices at the calamity of a family sprung from Agenor, and transfers the hatred that she has conceived from the Tyrian mistress to the partners of her race. Lo! a fresh occasion is now added to the former one; and she grieves that Semele is pregnant from the seed of great Jupiter. She then lets loose her tongue to abuse.

"And what good have I done by railing so often?" said she. "She herself must be attacked by me. If I am properly called the supreme Juno, I will destroy her; if it becomes me to hold the sparkling sceptre in my right hand; if I am the queen, and both the sister and wife of Jupiter. The sister I am, no doubt. But I suppose she is content with a stolen embrace, and the injury to my bed is but trifling. She is now pregnant; that alone was wanting; and she bears the evidence of his crime in her swelling womb, and wishes to be made a mother by Jupiter, a thing which hardly fell to my lot alone. So great is her confidence in her beauty. I will take care[61] he shall deceive her; and may I be no daughter of Saturn, if she does not descend to the Stygian waves, sunk there by her own dear Jupiter."

Upon this she rises from her throne, and, hidden in a cloud of fiery hue, she approaches the threshold of Semele. Nor did she remove the clouds before she counterfeited an old woman, and planted gray hair on her temples; and furrowed her skin with wrinkles, and moved her bending limbs with palsied step, and made her voice that of an old woman. She became Beroë[62] herself, the Epidaurian[63] nurse of Semele. When, therefore, upon engaging in discourse with her, and after long talking, they came to the name of Jupiter, she sighed, and said, "I only wish it may be Jupiter; yet I am apt to fear everything. Many a one under the name of a God has invaded a chaste bed. Nor yet is it enough that he is Jupiter; let him, if, indeed, he is the real one, give some pledge of his affection; and beg of him to bestow his caresses on thee, just in the greatness and form in which he is received by the stately Juno; and let him first assume his ensigns of royalty." With such words did Juno tutor the unsuspecting daughter of Cadmus. She requested of Jupiter a favor, without naming it. To her the God said, "Make thy choice, thou shalt suffer no denial; and that thou mayst believe it the more, let the majesty of the Stygian stream bear witness. He is the dread and the God of the Gods."

Overjoyed at what was her misfortune, and too easily prevailing, as now about to perish by the complaisance of her lover, Semele said, "Present thyself to me, just such as the daughter of Saturn is wont to embrace thee, when ye honor the ties of Venus." The God wished to shut her mouth as she spoke, but the hasty words had now escaped into air. He groaned; for neither was it now possible for her not to have wished, nor for him not to have sworn. Therefore, in extreme sadness, he mounted the lofty skies, and with his nod drew along the attendant clouds; to which he added showers and lightnings mingled with winds, and thunders, and the inevitable thunderbolt.

[Footnote 61: I will take care.—Ver. 271. 'Faxo,' 'I will make,' is sometimes used by the best authors for 'fecero;' and 'faxim' for 'faciam,' or 'fecerim.']

[Footnote 62: Beroë.—Ver. 278. Iris, in the fifth book of the Æneid (l. 620), assumes the form of another Beroë; and a third person of that name is mentioned in the fourth book of the Georgics, l. 34.]

[Footnote 63: Epidaurian.—Ver. 278. Epidaurus was a famous city of Argolis, in Peloponnesus, famous for its temple, dedicated to the worship of Æsculapius, who was the tutelary Divinity of that city.]

EXPLANATION

It is most probable, that an intrigue between a female named Semele and one of the princes called Jupiter having had a tragical end, gave occasion to this Fable. Pausanias, in his Laconica, tells us, that Cadmus, exasperated against his daughter Semele, caused her and her son to be thrown into the sea; and that being thrown ashore at Oreate, an ancient town of Laconia, Semele was buried there.

Semele, according to Apollodorus, was, after her death, ranked among the Goddesses by the name of Thyone. He says that her son Bacchus going down to hell, brought her thence, and carried her up to heaven; where, according to Nonnus, she conversed with Pallas and Diana, and ate at the same table with Jupiter, Mercury, Mars, and Venus. The author, known by the name of Orpheus, gives Semele the title of Goddess, and Πανβασίλεια, or 'Queen of the Universe.'

FABLE V [III.302-338]

Semele is visited by Jupiter, according to the promise she had obliged him to make; but, being unable to support the effulgence of his lightning, she is burnt to ashes in his presence. Bacchus, with whom she is pregnant, is preserved; and Tiresias decided the dispute between Jupiter and Juno, concerning the sexes.

And yet, as much as possible, he tries to mitigate his powers. Nor is he now armed with those flames with which he had overthrown the hundred-handed Typhœus; in those, there is too much fury. There is another thunder, less baneful, to which the right hand of the Cyclops gave less ferocity and flames, and less anger. The Gods above call this second-rate thunder; it he assumes, and he enters the house of Agenor. Her mortal body could not endure[64] the æthereal shock, and she was burned amid her nuptial presents. The infant, as yet unformed, is taken out of the womb of his mother, and prematurely (if we can believe it) is inserted in the thigh of the father, and completes the time that he should have spent in the womb. His aunt, Ino, nurses him privately in his early cradle. After that, the Nyseian Nymphs[65] conceal him, entrusted to them, in their caves, and give him the nourishment of milk.

And while these things are transacted on earth by the law of destiny, and the cradle of Bacchus, twice born,[66] is secured; they tell that Jupiter, by chance, well drenched with nectar, laid aside all weighty cares, and engaged in some free jokes with Juno, in her idle moments, and said: "Decidedly the pleasure of you, females, is greater than that which falls to the lot of us males." She denied it. It was agreed between them, to ask what was the opinion of the experienced Tiresias. To him both pleasures were well known. For he had separated with a blow of his staff two bodies of large serpents, as they were coupling in a green wood; and (passing strange) become a woman from a man, he had spent seven autumns. In the eighth, he again saw the same serpents, and said, "If the power of a stroke given you is so great as to change the condition of the giver into the opposite one, I will now strike you again." Having struck the same snakes, his former sex returned, and his original shape came again. He, therefore, being chosen as umpire in this sportive contest, confirmed the words of Jove. The daughter of Saturn is said to have grieved more than was fit, and not in proportion to the subject; and she condemned the eyes of the umpire to eternal darkness.

But the omnipotent father (for it is not allowed any God to cancel the acts of another Deity) gave him the knowledge of things to come, in recompense for his loss of sight, and alleviated his punishment by this honor.

[Footnote 64: Could not endure.—Ver. 308. 'Corpus mortale tumultus Non tulit æthereos,' is rendered by Clarke, 'her mortal body could not bear this æthereal bustle.']

[Footnote 65: The Nyseian Nymphs.—Ver. 314. Nysa was the name of a city and mountain of Arabia, or India. The tradition was, that there the Nyseian Nymphs, whose names were Cysseis, Nysa, Erato, Eryphia, Bromia, and Polyhymnia, brought up Bacchus. The cave where he was concealed from the fury of Juno, was said to have had two entrances, from which circumstance Bacchus received the epithet of Dithyrites. Servius, in his commentary on the sixth Eclogue of Virgil (l. 15), says that Nysa was the name of the female that nursed Bacchus. Hyginus also speaks of her as being the daughter of Oceanus. From the name 'Nysa,' Bacchus received, in part, his Greek name 'Dionysus.']

[Footnote 66: Twice born.—Ver. 318. Clarke thus translates and explains this line—'They tell you, that Jupiter well drenched;' i.e. 'fuddled with nectar,' etc.]

FABLE VI [III.339-401]

Echo, having often amused Juno with her stories, to give time to Jupiter's mistresses to make their escape, the Goddess, at last, punishes her for the deception. She is slighted and despised by Narcissus, with whom she falls in love.

He, much celebrated by fame throughout the cities of Aonia,[67] gave unerring answers to the people consulting him. The azure Liriope[68] was the first to make essay and experiment of his infallible voice; whom once Cephisus encircled in his winding stream, and offered violence to, when enclosed by his waters. The most beauteous Nymph produced an infant from her teeming womb, which even then might have been beloved, and she called him Narcissus. Being consulted concerning him, whether he was destined to see the distant season of mature old age; the prophet, expounding destiny, said, "If he never recognizes himself." Long did the words of the soothsayer appear frivolous; but the event, the thing itself, the manner of his death, and the novel nature of his frenzy, confirmed it.

And now the son of Cephisus had added one to three times five years, and he might seem to be a boy and a young man as well. Many a youth,[69] and many a damsel, courted him; but there was so stubborn a pride in his youthful beauty, that no youths, no damsels made any impression on him. The noisy Nymph, who has neither learned to hold her tongue after another speaking, nor to speak first herself, resounding Echo, espied him, as he was driving the timid stags into his nets. Echo was then a body, not a voice; and yet the babbler had no other use of her speech than she now has, to be able to repeat the last words out of many. Juno had done this; because when often she might have been able to detect the Nymphs in the mountains in the embrace of her husband, Jupiter, she purposely used to detain[70] the Goddess with a long story, until the Nymphs had escaped. After the daughter of Saturn perceived this, she said, "But small exercise of this tongue, with which I have been deluded, shall be allowed thee, and a very short use of thy voice." And she confirmed her threats by the event. Still, in the end of one's speaking she redoubles the voice, and returns the words she hears. When, therefore, she beheld Narcissus[71] wandering through the pathless forests, and fell in love with him, she stealthily followed his steps; and the more she followed him, with the nearer flame did she burn. In no other manner than as when the native sulphur, spread around[72] the tops of torches, catches the flame applied to it. Ah! how often did she desire to accost him in soft accents, and to employ soft entreaties! Nature resists, and suffers her not to begin; but what Nature does permit, that she is ready for; to await his voice, to which to return her own words.

By chance, the youth, being separated from the trusty company of his attendants, cries out, "Is there any one here?" and Echo answers "Here!" He is amazed; and when he has cast his eyes on every side, he cries out with a loud voice, "Come!" Whereon she calls the youth who calls. He looks back; and again, as no one comes, he says, "Why dost thou avoid me?" and just as many words as he spoke, he receives. He persists; and being deceived by the imitation of an alternate voice, he says, "Let us come together here;" and Echo, that could never more willingly answer any sound whatever, replies, "Let us come together here!" and she follows up her own words, and rushing from the woods,[73] is going to throw her arms around the neck she has so longed for. He flies; and as he flies, he exclaims, "Remove thy hands from thus embracing me; I will die first, before thou shalt have the enjoyment of me." She answers nothing but "Have the enjoyment of me." Thus rejected, she lies hid in the woods, and hides her blushing face with green leaves, and from that time lives in lonely caves; but yet her love remains, and increases from the mortification of her refusal. Watchful cares waste away her miserable body; leanness shrivels her skin, and all the juices of her body fly off in air. Her voice and her bones alone are left.

Her voice still continues, but they say that her bones received the form of stones. Since then, she lies concealed in the woods, and is never seen on the mountains: but is heard in all of them. It is her voice alone which remains alive in her.

[Footnote 67: Aonia.—Ver. 339. Aonia was a mountainous district of Bœotia, so called from Aon, the son of Neptune, who reigned there. The name is often used to signify the whole of Bœotia.]

[Footnote 68: Liriope.—Ver. 342. She was the daughter of Oceanus and Tethys, and was the mother of the youth Narcissus, by the river Cephisus. Her name is derived from the Greek λείριον, 'a lily.']

[Footnote 69: Many a youth.—Ver. 353. Clarke translates 'multi juvenes,' 'many young fellows.']

[Footnote 70: Used to detain.—Ver. 364. Clarke translates 'Illa Deam longo prudens sermone tenebat Dum fugerent Nymphæ,' 'She designedly detained the Goddess with some long-winded discourse or other till the Nymphs ran away.' He translates 'garrula,' in line 360, 'the prattling hussy.']

[Footnote 71: Narcissus.—Ver. 370. This name is from the Greek word ναρκᾷν, 'to fade away,' which was characteristic of the youth's career, and of the duration of the flower.]

[Footnote 72: Sulphur spread around.—Ver. 372. These lines show, that it was the custom of the ancients to place sulphur on the ends of their torches, to make them ignite the more readily, in the same manner as the matches of the present day are tipped with that mineral.]

[Footnote 73: Rushing from the woods.—Ver. 388. 'Egressaque sylvis.' Clarke renders, 'and bouncing out of the wood.']

EXPLANATION

It appears much more reasonable to attempt the explanation of this story on the grounds of natural philosophy than of history. The poets, in their fondness for basing every subject upon fiction, probably invented the fable, to explain what to them appeared an extraordinary phenomenon. By way of embellishing their story, they tell us that Echo was the daughter of the Air and the Tongue, and that the God Pan fell in love with her; by which, probably, the simple fact is meant, that some person, represented under the name of that god, endeavored to trace the cause of this phenomenon.

If, however, we should endeavor to base the story upon purely historical grounds, we may suppose that it took its rise from some Nymph, who wandered so far into the woods as to be unable to find her way out again; and from the fact that those who went to seek her, hearing nothing but the echo of their own voices, brought back the strange but unsatisfactory intelligence that the Nymph had been changed into a voice.

FABLE VII [III.402-510]

Narcissus falls in love with his own shadow, which he sees in a fountain; and, pining to death, the Gods change him into a flower, which still bears his name.

Thus had he deceived her, thus, too, other Nymphs that sprung from the water or the mountains, thus the throng of youths before them. Some one, therefore, who had been despised by him, lifting up his hands towards heaven, said, "Thus, though he should love, let him not enjoy what he loves!" Rhamnusia[74] assented to a prayer so reasonable. There was a clear spring, like silver, with its unsullied waters, which neither shepherds, nor she-goats feeding on the mountains, nor any other cattle, had touched; which neither bird nor wild beast had disturbed, nor bough falling from a tree. There was grass around it, which the neighboring water nourished, and a wood, that suffered the stream to become warm with no rays of the sun. Here the youth, fatigued both with the labor of hunting and the heat, lay down, attracted by the appearance of the spot, and the spring; and, while he was endeavoring to quench his thirst, another thirst grew upon him.

While he is drinking, being attracted with the reflection of his own form, seen in the water, he falls in love with a thing that has no substance; and he thinks that to be a body, which is but a shadow. He is astonished at himself, and remains unmoved with the same countenance, like a statue formed of Parian marble.[75] Lying on the ground, he gazes on his eyes like two stars, and fingers worthy of Bacchus, and hair worthy of Apollo, and his youthful cheeks and ivory neck, and the comeliness of his mouth, and his blushing complexion mingled with the whiteness of snow; and everything he admires, for which he himself is worthy to be admired. In his ignorance, he covets himself; and he that approves, is himself the thing approved. While he pursues he is pursued, and at the same moment he inflames and burns. How often does he give vain kisses to the deceitful spring; how often does he thrust his arms, catching at the neck he sees, into the middle of the water, and yet he does not catch himself in them. He knows not what he sees, but what he sees, by it is he inflamed; and the same mistake that deceives his eyes, provokes them. Why, credulous youth, dost thou vainly catch at the flying image? What thou art seeking is nowhere; what thou art in love with, turn but away and thou shalt lose it; what thou seest, the same is but the shadow of a reflected form; it has nothing of its own. It comes and stays with thee; with thee it will depart, if thou canst but depart thence.

No regard for food,[76] no regard for repose, can draw him away thence; but, lying along upon the overshadowed grass, he gazes upon the fallacious image with unsatiated eyes, and by his own sight he himself is undone. Raising himself a little while, extending his arms to the woods that stand around him, he says, "Was ever, O, ye woods! any one more fatally in love? For this ye know, and have been a convenient shelter for many a one. And do you remember any one, who ever thus pined away, during so long a time, though so many ages of your life has been spent? It both pleases me and I see it; but what I see, and what pleases me, yet I cannot obtain; so great a mistake possesses one in love; and to make me grieve the more, neither a vast sea separates us, nor a long way, nor mountains, nor a city with its gates closed; we are kept asunder by a little water. He himself wishes to be embraced; for as often as I extend my lips to the limpid stream, so often does he struggle towards me with his face held up; you would think he might be touched. It is a very little that stands in the way of lovers. Whoever thou art, come up hither. Why, dear boy, the choice one, dost thou deceive me? or whither dost thou retire, when pursued? Surely, neither my form nor my age is such as thou shouldst shun; the Nymphs, too, have courted me. Thou encouragest I know not what hopes in me with that friendly look, and when I extend my arms to thee, thou willingly extendest thine; when I smile, thou smilest in return; often, too, have I observed thy tears, when I was weeping; my signs, too, thou returnest by thy nods, and, as I guess by the motion of thy beauteous mouth, thou returnest words that come not to my ears. In thee 'tis I, I now perceive; nor does my form deceive me. I burn with the love of myself, and both raise the flames and endure them. What shall I do? Should I be entreated, or should I entreat? What, then, shall I entreat? What I desire is in my power; plenty has made me poor. Oh! would that I could depart from my own body! a new wish, indeed, in a lover; I could wish that what I am in love with was away. And now grief is taking away my strength, and no long period of my life remains; and in my early days am I cut off; nor is death grievous to me, now about to get rid of my sorrows by death. I wish that he who is beloved could enjoy a longer life. Now we two, of one mind, shall die in the extinction of one life."

Thus he said, and, with his mind but ill at ease, he returned to the same reflection, and disturbed the water with his tears; and the form was rendered defaced by the moving of the stream; when he saw it beginning to disappear, he cried aloud, "Whither dost thou fly? Stay, I beseech thee! and do not in thy cruelty abandon thy lover; let it be allowed me to behold that which I may not touch, and to give nourishment to my wretched frenzy." And, while he was grieving, he tore his garment from the upper border, and beat his naked breast with his palms, white as marble. His breast, when struck, received a little redness, no otherwise than as apples are wont, which are partly white and partly red; or as a grape, not yet ripe, in the parti-colored clusters, is wont to assume a purple tint. Soon as he beheld this again in the water, when clear, he could not endure it any longer; but, as yellow wax with the fire, or the hoar frost of the morning, is wont to waste away with the warmth of the sun, so he, consumed by love, pined away, and wasted by degrees with a hidden flame. And now, no longer was his complexion of white mixed with red; neither his vigor nor his strength, nor the points which had charmed when seen so lately, nor even his body, which formerly Echo had been in love with, now remained. Yet, when she saw these things, although angry, and mindful of his usage of her, she was grieved, and, as often as the unhappy youth said, "Alas!" she repeated, "Alas!" with re-echoing voice; and when he struck his arms with his hands, she, too, returned the like sound of a blow.

His last accents, as he looked into the water, as usual, were these: "Ah, youth, beloved in vain!" and the spot returned just as many words; and after he had said, "Farewell!" Echo, too, said, "Farewell!" He laid down his wearied head upon the green grass, when night closed the eyes that admired the beauty of their master; and even then, after he had been received into the infernal abodes, he used to look at himself in the Stygian waters. His Naiad sisters lamented him, and laid their hair,[77] cut off, over their brother; the Dryads, too, lamented him, and Echo resounded to their lamentations. And now they were preparing the funeral pile, and the shaken torches, and the bier. The body was nowhere to be found. Instead of his body, they found a yellow flower, with white leaves encompassing it in the middle.

[Footnote 74: Rhamnusia.—Ver. 406. Nemesis, the Goddess of Retribution, and the avenger of crime, was the daughter of Jupiter. She had a famous temple at Rhamnus, one of the 'pagi,' or boroughs of Athens. Her statue was there, carved by Phidias out of the marble which the Persians brought into Greece for the purpose of making a statue of Victory out of it, and which was thus appropriately devoted to the Goddess of Retribution. This statue wore a crown, and had wings, and holding a spear of ash in the right hand, it was seated on a stag.]

[Footnote 75: Parian marble.—Ver. 419. Paros was an island in the Ægean sea, one of the Cyclades; it was famous for the valuable quality of its marble, which was especially used for the purpose of making statues of the Gods.]

[Footnote 76: Regard for food.—Ver. 437. 'Cereris.' The name of the Goddess of corn is here used instead of bread itself.]

[Footnote 77: Laid their hair.—Ver. 506. It was the custom among the ancients for females, when lamenting the dead, not only to cut off their hair, but to lay it on the body, when extended upon the funeral pile.]

EXPLANATION

If this story is based upon any historical facts, they are entirely lost to us; as all we learn from history concerning Narcissus, is the fact that he was a Thespian by birth. The Fable seems rather to be intended as a useful moral lesson, disclosing the fatal effects of self-love. His pursuit, too, of his own image, ever retiring from his embrace, strongly resembles the little reality that exists in many of those pleasures which mankind so eagerly pursue.

Pausanias, in his Bœotica, somewhat varies the story. He tells us that Narcissus having lost his sister, whom he tenderly loved, and who resembled him very much, and was his constant companion in the chase, thought, on seeing himself one day in a fountain, that it was the shade of his lost sister, and, thereupon, pined away and died of grief. According to him, the fountain was near a village called Donacon, in the country of the Thespians. Pausanias regards the account of his change into the flower which bears his name as a mere fiction, since Pamphus says that Proserpina, when carried away, long before the time of Narcissus, gathered that flower in the fields of Enna; and that the same flower was sacred to her. Persons sacrificing to the Furies, or Eumenides, used to wear chaplets made of the Narcissus, because that flower commonly grew about graves and sepulchres.

Tiresias, who predicted the untoward fate of Narcissus, was, as we are informed by Apollodorus, the son of Evenus and Chariclo, and was the most renowned soothsayer of his time. He lost his life by drinking of the fountain of Telphusa when he was overheated; or, as some suppose, through the unwholesome quality of the water. As he lived to a great age, and became blind towards the end of his life, the story, which Ovid mentions, was invented respecting him. Another version of it was, that he lost his sight, by reason of his having seen Minerva while bathing. This story was very probably based either upon the fact that he had composed a Treatise upon the Animal Functions of the Sexes, or that he had promulgated the doctrine that the stars had not only souls (a common opinion in those times), but also that they were of different sexes. He is supposed to have lived about 1200 years before the Christian era.

FABLE VIII [III.511-733]

Pentheus ridicules the predictions of Tiresias; and not only forbids his people to worship Bacchus, who had just entered Greece in triumph, but even commands them to capture him, and to bring him into his presence. Under the form of Accœtes, one of his companions, Bacchus suffers that indignity, and relates to Pentheus the wonders which the God had wrought. The recital enrages Pentheus still more, who thereupon goes to Mount Cithæron, to disturb the orgies then celebrating there; on which his own mother and the other Bacchantes tear him to pieces.

This thing, when known, brought deserved fame to the prophet through the cities of Achaia;[78] and great was the reputation of the soothsayer. Yet Pentheus,[79] the son of Echion, a contemner of the Gods above, alone, of all men, despises him, and derides the predicting words of the old man, and upbraids him with his darkened state, and the misfortune of having lost his sight. He, shaking his temples, white with hoary hair, says: "How fortunate wouldst thou be, if thou as well couldst become deprived of this light, that thou mightst not behold the rites of Bacchus. For soon the day will come, and even now I predict that it is not far off, when the new God Liber, the son of Semele, shall come hither. Unless thou shalt vouchsafe him the honor of a temple, thou shalt be scattered, torn in pieces, in a thousand places, and with thy blood thou shalt pollute both the woods, and thy mother and the sisters of thy mother. These things will come to pass; for thou wilt not vouchsafe honor to the Divinity; and thou wilt complain that under this darkness I have seen too much."

The son of Echion drives him away as he says such things as these. Confirmation follows his words, and the predictions of the prophet are fulfilled. Liber comes, and the fields resound with festive howlings. The crowd runs out; both matrons and new-married women mixed with the men, both high and low, are borne along to the celebration of rites till then unknown. "What madness," says Pentheus, "has confounded your minds, O ye warlike men,[80] descendants of the Dragon? Can brass knocked against brass prevail so much with you? And the pipe with the bending horn, and these magical delusions? And shall the yells of women, and madness produced by wine, and troops of effeminate wretches, and empty tambourines[81] prevail over you, whom neither the warrior's sword nor the trumpet could affright, nor troops with weapons prepared for fight? Am I to wonder at you, old men, who, carried over distant seas, have fixed in these abodes a new Tyre, and your banished household Gods, but who now allow them to be taken without a struggle? Or you, of more vigorous age and nearer to my own, ye youths; whom it was befitting to be brandishing arms, and not the thyrsus,[82] and to be covered with helmets, not green leaves? Do be mindful, I entreat you, of what race you are sprung, and assume the courage of that dragon, who though but one, destroyed many. He died for his springs and his stream; but do you conquer for your own fame. He put the valiant to death; do you expel the feeble foe, and regain your country's honor. If the fates forbid Thebes to stand long, I wish that engines of war[83] and men should demolish the walls, and that fire and sword should resound. Then should we be wretched without any fault of our own, and our fate were to be lamented, but not concealed, and our tears would be free from shame. But now Thebes will be taken by an unarmed boy, whom neither wars delight, nor weapons, nor the employment of horses, but hair wet with myrrh, and effeminate chaplets, and purple, and gold interwoven with embroidered garments; whom I, indeed, (do you only stand aside) will presently compel to own that his father is assumed, and that his sacred rites are fictitious. Has Acrisius[84] courage enough to despise the vain Deity, and to shut the gates of Argos against his approach; and shall this stranger affright Pentheus with all Thebes? Go quickly, (this order he gives to his servants), go, and bring hither in chains the ringleader. Let there be no slothful delay in executing my commands."

His grandfather,[85] Cadmus, Athamas, and the rest of the company of his friends rebuke him with expostulations, and in vain try to restrain him. By their admonition he becomes more violent, and by being curbed his fury is irritated, and is on the increase, and the very restraint did him injury. So have I beheld a torrent, where nothing obstructed it in its course, run gently and with moderate noise; but wherever beams and stones in its way withheld it, it ran foaming and raging, and more violent from its obstruction. Behold! the servants return, all stained with blood; and when their master inquires where Bacchus is, they deny that they have seen Bacchus. "But this one," say they, "we have taken, who was his attendant and minister in his sacred rites." And then they deliver one, who, from the Etrurian nation, had followed the sacred rites of the Deity, with his hands bound behind his back.

Pentheus looks at him with eyes that anger has made terrible, and although he can scarcely defer the time of his punishment, he says, "O wretch, doomed to destruction, and about, by thy death, to set an example to others, tell me thy name, and the name of thy parents, and thy country, and why thou dost attend the sacred rites of a new fashion." He, void of fear, says, "My name is Acœtes; Mæonia[86] is my country; my parents were of humble station. My father left me no fields for the hardy oxen to till, no wool-bearing flocks, nor any herds. He himself was but poor, and he was wont with line, and hooks, to deceive the leaping fishes, and to take them with the rod. His trade was his only possession. When he gave that calling over to me, he said, 'Receive, as the successor and heir of my employment, those riches which I possess;' and at his death he left me nothing but the streams. This one thing alone can I call my patrimony. But soon, that I might not always be confined to the same rocks, I learned with a steadying right hand to guide the helm of the ship, and I made observations with my eyes of the showery Constellation of the Olenian she-goat,[87] and Taygete,[88] and the Hyades,[89] and the Bear, and the quarters of the winds, and the harbors fit for ships. By chance, as I was making for Delos, I touched at the coast of the land of Dia,[90] and came up to the shore by plying the oars on the right side; and I gave a nimble leap, and lighted upon the wet sand. When the night was past, and the dawn first began to grow red, I arose and ordered my men to take in fresh water, and I pointed out the way which led to the stream. I myself, from a lofty eminence, looked around to see what the breeze promised me; and then I called my companions, and returned to the vessel. 'Lo! we are here,' says Opheltes, my chief mate; and having found, as he thought, a prize in the lonely fields, he was leading along the shore, a boy with all the beauty of a girl. He, heavy with wine and sleep, seemed to stagger, and to follow with difficulty. I examined his dress, his looks, and his gait, and I saw nothing there which could be taken to be mortal. I both was sensible of it, and I said to my companions, 'I am in doubt what Deity is in that body; but in that body a Deity there is. Whoever thou art, O be propitious and assist our toils; and pardon these as well.' 'Cease praying for us,' said Dictys, than whom there was not another more nimble at climbing to the main-top-yards, and at sliding down by catching hold of a rope. This Libys, this the yellow-haired Melanthus, the guardian of the prow, and this Alcimedon approved of; and Epopeus[91] as well, the cheerer of their spirits, who by his voice gave both rest and time to the oars; and so did all the rest; so blind is the greed for booty. 'However,' I said, 'I will not allow this ship to be damaged by this sacred freight. Here I have the greatest share of right.' and I opposed them at the entrance.

"Lycabas, the boldest of all the number, was enraged, who, expelled from a city of Etruria, was suffering exile as the punishment for a dreadful murder.[92] He, while I was resisting, seized hold of my throat with his youthful fist, and shaking me, had thrown me overboard into the sea, if I had not, although stunned, held fast by grasping a rope. The impious crew approved of the deed. Then at last Bacchus (for Bacchus it was), as though his sleep had been broken by the noise, and his sense was returning into his breast after much wine, said: 'What are you doing? What is this noise? Tell me, sailors, by what means have I come hither? Whither do you intend to carry me?' 'Lay aside thy fears,' said Proreus, 'and tell us what port thou wouldst wish to reach. Thou shalt stop at the land that thou desirest.' 'Direct your course then to Naxos,'[93] says Liber, 'that is my home; it shall prove a hospitable land for you.'

"In their deceit they swore by the ocean and by all the Deities, that so it should be; and bade me give sail to the painted ship. Naxos was to our right; and as I was accordingly setting sail for the right hand, every one said for himself, 'What art thou about, madman? What insanity possesses thee, Accœtes? Stand away to the left.' The greater part signified their meaning to me by signs; some whispered in my ear what they wanted. I was at a loss, and I said, 'Let some one else take the helm;' and I withdrew myself from the execution both of their wickedness, and of my own calling. I was reviled by them all, and the whole crew muttered reproaches against me. Æthalion, among them, says, 'As if, forsooth, all our safety is centred in thee,' and he himself comes up, and takes my duty; and leaving Naxos, he steers a different course. Then the God, mocking them as if he had at last but that moment discovered their knavery, looks down upon the sea from the crooked stern; and, like one weeping, he says: 'These are not the shores, sailors, that you have promised me; this is not the land desired by me. By what act have I deserved this treatment? What honor is it to you, if you that are young men, deceive a mere boy? if you that are many, deceive me, who am but one?' I had been weeping for some time. The impious gang laughed at my tears, and beat the sea with hastening oars. Now by himself do I swear to thee (and no God is there more powerful than he), that I am relating things to thee as true, as they are beyond all belief. The ship stood still upon the ocean, no otherwise than if it was occupying a dry dock. They, wondering at it, persisted in the plying of their oars; they unfurled their sails, and endeavored to speed onward with this twofold aid. Ivy impeded the oars,[94] and twined around them in encircling wreaths; and clung to the sails with heavy clusters of berries. He himself, having his head encircled with bunches of grapes, brandished a lance covered with vine leaves. Around him, tigers and visionary forms of lynxes, and savage bodies of spotted panthers, were extended.

"The men leaped overboard, whether it was madness or fear that caused this; and first of all, Medon began to grow black with fins, with a flattened body, and to bend in the curvature of the back-bone. To him Lycabas said, 'Into what prodigy art thou changing?' and, as he spoke, the opening of his mouth was wide, his nose became crooked, and his hardened skin received scales upon it. But Libys, while he was attempting to urge on the resisting oars, saw his hands shrink into a small compass, and now to be hands no longer, and that now, in fact, they may be pronounced fins. Another, desirous to extend his arms to the twisting ropes, had no arms, and becoming crooked, with a body deprived of limbs, he leaped into the waves; the end of his tail was hooked, just as the horns of the half-moon are curved.

They flounce about on every side, and bedew the ship with plenteous spray, and again they emerge, and once more they return beneath the waves. They sport with all the appearance of a dance, and toss their sportive bodies, and blow forth the sea, received within their wide nostrils. Of twenty the moment before (for so many did that ship carry), I was the only one remaining. The God encouraged me, frightened and chilled with my body all trembling, and scarcely myself, saying, 'Shake off thy fear, and make for Dia.' Arriving there, I attended upon the sacred rites of Bacchus, at the kindled altars."

"We have lent ear to a long story,"[95] says Pentheus, "that our anger might consume its strength in its tediousness. Servants! drag him headlong, and send to Stygian night his body, racked with dreadful tortures." At once the Etrurian Accœtes, dragged away, is shut up in a strong prison; and while the cruel instruments of the death that is ordered, and the iron and the fire are being made ready, the report is that the doors opened of their own accord, and that the chains, of their own accord, slipped from off his arms, no one loosening them.

The son of Echion persists: and now he does not command others to go, but goes himself to where Cithæron,[96] chosen for the celebration of these sacred rites, was resounding with singing, and the shrill voices of the votaries of Bacchus. Just as the high-mettled steed neighs, when the warlike trumpeter gives the alarm with the sounding brass, and conceives a desire for battle, so did the sky, struck with the long-drawn howlings, excite Pentheus, and his wrath was rekindled on hearing the clamor. There was, about the middle of the mountain, the woods skirting its extremity, a plain free from trees, and visible on every side. Here his mother was the first to see him looking on the sacred rites with profane eyes; she first was moved by a frantic impulse, and she first wounded her son, Pentheus, by hurling her thyrsus, and cried out, "Ho! come, my two sisters;[97] that boar which, of enormous size, is roaming amid our fields, that boar I must strike." All the raging multitude rushes upon him alone; all collect together, and all follow him, now trembling, now uttering words less atrocious than before, now blaming himself, now confessing that he has offended.

However, on being wounded, he says, "Give me thy aid, Autonoë, my aunt; let the ghost of Actæon[98] influence thy feelings." She knows not what Actæon means, and tears away his right hand as he is praying; the other is dragged off by the violence of Ino. The wretched man has now no arms to extend to his mother; but showing his maimed body, with the limbs torn off, he says, "Look at this, my mother!" At the sight Agave howls aloud, and tosses her neck, and shakes her locks in the air; and seizing his head, torn off, with her blood-stained fingers, she cries out, "Ho! my companions, this victory is our work!"

The wind does not more speedily bear off, from a lofty tree, the leaves nipped by the cold of autumn, and now adhering with difficulty, than were the limbs of the man, torn asunder by their accursed hands. Admonished by such examples, the Ismenian matrons frequent the new worship, and offer frankincense, and reverence the sacred altars.

[Footnote 78: Cities of Achaia.—Ver. 511. Achaia was properly the name of a part of Peloponnesus, on the gulf of Corinth; but the name is very frequently applied to the whole of Greece.]

[Footnote 79: Pentheus.—Ver. 513. He was the son of Echion and Agave, the daughter of Cadmus.]

[Footnote 80: Warlike men.—Ver. 531. 'Mavortia.' Mavors was a name of Mars, frequently used by the poets. The Thebans were 'proles Mavortia,' as being sprung from the teeth of the dragon, who was said to be a son of Mars.]

[Footnote 81: Tambourines.—Ver. 537. 'Tympana.' These instruments, among the ancients, were of various kinds. Some resembled the modern tambourine; while others presented a flat circular disk on the upper surface, and swelled out beneath, like the kettle-drum of the present day. They were covered with the hides of oxen, or of asses, and were beaten either with a stick or the hand. They were especially used in the rites of Bacchus, and of Cybele.]

[Footnote 82: The thyrsus.—Ver. 542. The thyrsus was a long staff, carried by Bacchus, and by the Satyrs and Bacchanalians engaged in the worship of the God of the grape. It was sometimes terminated by the apple of the pine, or fir-cone, the fir-tree being esteemed sacred to Bacchus, from the turpentine flowing therefrom and its apples being used in making wine. It is, however, frequently represented as terminating in a knot of ivy, or vine leaves, with grapes or berries arranged in a conical form. Sometimes, also, a white fillet was tied to the pole just below the head. We learn from Diodorus Siculus, and Macrobius, that Bacchus converted the thyrsi carried by himself and his followers into weapons, by concealing an iron point in the head of leaves. A wound with its point was supposed to produce madness.]

[Footnote 83: Engines of war.—Ver. 549. 'Tormenta.' These were the larger engines of destruction used in ancient warfare. They were so called from the verb 'torqueo,' 'to twist,' from their being formed by the twisting of hair, fibre, or strips of leather. The different sorts were called 'balistæ' and 'catapultæ.' The former were used to impel stones; the latter, darts and arrows. In sieges, the 'Aries,' or 'battering ram,' which received its name from having an iron head resembling that of a ram, was employed in destroying the lower part of the wall, while the 'balista' was overthrowing the battlements, and the 'catapulta' was employed to shoot any of the besieged who appeared between them. The 'balistæ' and 'catapultæ' were divided into the 'greater' and the 'less.' When New Carthage, the arsenal of the Carthaginians, was taken, according to Livy (b. xxvi. c. 47), there were found in it 120 large and 281 small catapultæ, and twenty-three large and fifty-two small balistæ. The various kinds of 'tormenta' are said to have been introduced about the time of Alexander the Great. If so, Ovid must here be committing an anachronism, in making Pentheus speak of 'tormenta,' who lived so many ages before that time. To commit anachronisms with impunity seems, however, to be the poet's privilege, from Ovid downwards to our Shakspere, where he makes Falstaff talk familiarly of the West Indies. We find the dictionaries giving 'tormentum' as the Latin word for 'cannon;' so that in this case we may say not that 'necessity is the mother of invention,' but rather that she is 'the parent of anachronism.']

[Footnote 84: Acrisius.—Ver. 559. He was a king of Argos, the son of Abas, and the father of Danaë. He refused, and probably with justice, to admit Bacchus or his rites within the gates of his city.]

[Footnote 85: His grandfather.—Ver. 563. Athamas was the son of Æolus, and being the husband of Ino, was the son-in-law of Cadmus; who being the father of Agave, the mother of Pentheus, is the grandfather mentioned in the present line.]

[Footnote 86: Mæonia.—Ver. 583. Colonists were said to have proceeded from Lydia, or Mæonia, to the coasts of Etruria. Bacchus assumes the name of Acœtes, as corresponding to the Greek epithet ἀκοίτης, 'watchful,' or 'sleepless;' which ought to be the characteristic of the careful 'pilot,' or 'helmsman.']

[Footnote 87: Olenian she-goat.—Ver. 594. Amalthea, the goat that suckled Jupiter, is called Olenian, either because she was reared in Olenus, a city of Bœotia, or because she was placed as a Constellation between the arms, ὠλέναι, of the Constellation Auriga, or the Charioteer. The rising and setting of this Constellation were supposed to produce showers.]

[Footnote 88: Taygete.—Ver. 594. She was one of the Pleiades, the daughters of Atlas, who were placed among the Constellations.]

[Footnote 89: Hyades.—Ver. 594. These were the Dodonides, or nurses of Bacchus, whom Jupiter, as a mark of his favor, placed in the number of the Constellations. Their name is derived from ὕειν, 'to rain.']

[Footnote 90: Dia.—Ver. 596. This was another name of the Isle of Naxos. Gierig thinks that the reading here is neither 'Diæ' nor 'Chiæ,' which are the two common readings; as the situation of neither the Isle of Naxos nor that of Chios, would suit the course of the ship, as stated in the text. He thinks that the Isle of Ceos, or Cea, is meant, which Ptolemy calls Κια, and which he thinks ought here to be written 'Ciæ.']

[Footnote 91: Epopeus.—Ver. 619. He was the κελεύστης, 'pausarius,' or keeper of time for the rowers.]

[Footnote 92: A dreadful murder.—Ver. 626. They seem to have been composed of much the same kind of lawless materials that formed the daring crews of the buccanier Morgan and Captain Kydd in more recent times.]

[Footnote 93: Naxos.—Ver. 636. This was the most famous island of the group of the Cyclades.]

[Footnote 94: Ivy impeded the oars.—Ver. 664. Hyginus tells us, that Bacchus changed the oars into thyrsi, the sails into clusters of grapes, and the rigging into ivy branches. In the Homeric hymn on this subject we find the ship flowing with wine, vines growing on the sails, ivy twining round the mast, and the benches wreathed with chaplets.]

[Footnote 95: To a long story.—Ver. 692. Clarke renders this line, 'We have lent our ears to a long tale of a tub.']

[Footnote 96: Cithæron.—Ver. 702. This was a mountain of Bœotia, famous for the orgies of Bacchus there celebrated.]

[Footnote 97: My two sisters.—Ver. 713. These were Ino and Autonoë.]

[Footnote 98: Ghost of Actæon.—Ver. 720. He appeals to Autonoë, the mother of Actæon, to remember the sad fate of her own son, and to show him some mercy; but in vain: for, as one commentator on the passage says, 'Drunkenness had taken away both her reason and her memory.']

EXPLANATION

Cicero mentions two Deities of the name of Bacchus; while other authors speak of several of that name. The first was the son of Jupiter and Proserpina; the second was the son of the Nile, and the founder of the city of Nysa, in Arabia; Caprius was the father of the third. The fourth was the son of the Moon and Jupiter, in honor of whom the Orphic ceremonies were performed. The fifth was the son of Nisus and Thione, and the instituter of the Trieterica. Diodorus Siculus mentions but three of the name of Bacchus; namely, the Indian, surnamed the bearded Bacchus, who conquered India; the son of Jupiter and Ceres, who was represented with horns; and the son of Jupiter and Semele, who was called the Theban Bacchus.

The most reasonable opinion seems to be that of Herodotus and Plutarch, who inform us, that the true Bacchus, and the most ancient of them all, was born in Egypt, and was originally called Osiris. The worship of that Divinity passed from Egypt to Greece, where it received great alterations; and, according to Diodorus Siculus, it was Orpheus who introduced it, and made those innovations. In gratitude to the family of Cadmus, from which he had received many favors, he dedicated to Bacchus, the grandson of Cadmus, those mysteries which had been instituted in honor of Osiris, whose worship was then but little known in Greece. Diodorus Siculus says, that as Semele was delivered of Bacchus in the seventh month, it was reported that Jupiter shut him up in his thigh, to carry him there the remaining time of gestation. This Fable was probably founded on the meaning of an equivocal word. The Greek word μηρὸς signifies either 'a thigh,' or 'the hollow of a mountain.' Thus the Greeks, instead of saying that Bacchus had been nursed on Mount Nysa, in Arabia, according to the Egyptian version of the story, published that he had been carried in the thigh of Jupiter.

As Bacchus applied himself to the cultivation of the vine, and taught his subjects several profitable and necessary arts, he was honored as a Divinity; and having won the esteem of many neighboring countries, his worship soon spread. Among his several festivals there was one called the Trieterica, which was celebrated every three years. In that feast the Bacchantes carried the figure of the God in a chariot drawn by two tigers, or panthers; and, crowned with vine leaves, and holding thyrsi in their hands, they ran in a frantic manner around the chariot, filling the air with the noise of tambourines and brazen instruments, shouting 'Evoë. Bacche!' and calling the God by his several names of Bromius, Lyæus, Evan, Lenæus, and Sabazius. To this ceremonial, received from the Egyptians, the Greeks added other ceremonies replete with abominable licentiousness, and repulsive to common decency. These were often suppressed by public enactment, but were as often re-established by the votaries of lewdness and immodesty, and such as found in these festivals a pretext and opportunity for the commission of the most horrible offences.

The story of the unfortunate fate of Pentheus is supposed by the ancient writers to have been strictly true. Pentheus, the son of Echion and Agave, the daughter of Cadmus, having succeeded his grandfather in his kingdom, is supposed, like him, to have opposed those abuses that had crept into the mysteries of Bacchus, and went to Mount Cithæron for the purpose of chastising the Bacchantes, who were celebrating his festival; whereupon, in their frantic madness, the worshippers, among whom were his mother and his aunt, tore him in pieces. Pausanias, however, says that Pentheus really was a wicked prince; and he somewhat varies his story, as he tells us that having got into a tree to overlook the secret ceremonies of the orgies, Pentheus was discovered by the Bacchantes, who punished his curiosity by putting him to death. The story of the transformation of the mariners is supposed by Bochart to have been founded on the adventure of certain merchants from the coast of Etruria, whose vessel had the figure of a dolphin at the prow, or rather of the fish called 'tursio,' probably the porpoise, or sea-hog. They were probably shipwrecked near the Isle of Naxos, which was sacred to Bacchus, whose mysteries they had perhaps neglected, or even despised. On this slender ground, perhaps, the report spread, that the God himself had destroyed them, as a punishment for their impiety.

The daughters of Minyas, instead of celebrating the festival of Bacchus, apply themselves to other pursuits during the ceremonies; and among several narratives which they relate to pass away the time, they divert themselves with the story of the adventures of Pyramus and Thisbe. These lovers having made an appointment to meet without the walls of Babylon, Thisbe arrives first; but at the sight of a lioness, she runs to hide herself in a cave, and in her alarm, drops her veil. Pyramus, arriving soon after, finds the veil of his mistress stained with blood; and believing her to be dead, kills himself with his own sword. Thisbe returns from the cave; and finding Pyramus weltering in his blood, she plunges the same fatal weapon into her own breast.

But Alcithoë, the daughter of Minyas,[1] does not think that the rites[2] of the God ought to be received; but still, in her rashness, denies that Bacchus is the progeny of Jupiter; and she has her sisters[3] as partners in her impiety.

The priest had ordered both mistresses and maids, laying aside their employments, to have their breasts covered with skins, and to loosen the fillets of their hair, and to put garlands on their locks, and to take the verdant thyrsi in their hands; and had prophesied that severe would be the resentment of the Deity, if affronted. Both matrons and new-married women obey, and lay aside their webs and work-baskets,[4] and their tasks unfinished; and offer frankincense, and invoke both Bacchus and Bromius,[5] and Lyæus,[6] and the son of the Flames, and the Twice-Born, and the only one that had two mothers.[7] To these is added the name of Nyseus, and the unshorn Thyoneus,[8] and with Lenæus,[9] the planter of the genial grape, and Nyctelius,[10] and father Eleleus, and Iacchus,[11] and Evan,[12] and a great many other names, which thou, Liber, hast besides, throughout the nations of Greece. For thine is youth everlasting; thou art a boy to all time, thou art beheld as the most beauteous of all in high heaven; thou hast the features of a virgin, when thou standest without thy horns. By thee the East was conquered, as far as where swarthy India is bounded by the remote Ganges. Thou God, worthy of our veneration, didst smite Pentheus, and the axe-bearing Lycurgus,[13] sacrilegious mortals; thou didst hurl the bodies of the Etrurians into the sea. Thou controllest the neck of the lynxes yoked to thy chariot, graced with the painted reins. The Bacchanals and the Satyrs follow thee; the drunken old man, too, Silenus, who supports his reeling limbs with a staff, and sticks by no means very fast to his bending ass. And wherever thou goest, the shouts of youths, and together the voices of women, and tambourines beaten with the hands, and hollow cymbals resound, and the box-wood pipe, with its long bore. The Ismenian matrons ask thee to show thyself mild and propitious, and celebrate thy sacred rites as prescribed.

The daughters of Minyas alone, within doors, interrupting the festival with unseasonable labor,[14] are either carding wool, or twirling the threads with their fingers, or are plying at the web, and keeping the handmaids to their work. One of them, as she is drawing the thread with her smooth thumb, says, "While others are idling, and thronging to these fanciful rites, let us, whom Pallas, a better Deity, occupies, alleviate the useful toil of our hands with varying discourse; and let us relate by turns to our disengaged ears, for the general amusement, something each in our turn, that will not permit the time to seem long." They approve of what she says, and her sisters bid her to be the first to tell her story.

She considers which of many she shall tell (for she knows many a one), and she is in doubt whether she shall tell of thee, Babylonian Dercetis,[15] whom the people of Palestine[16] believe to inhabit the pools, with thy changed form, scales covering thy limbs; or rather how her daughter, taking wings, passed her latter years in whitened turrets; or how a Naiad,[17] by charms and too potent herbs, changed the bodies of the young men into silent fishes, until she suffered the same herself. Or how the tree which bore white fruit formerly, now bears it of purple hue, from the contact of blood. This story pleases her; this, because it was no common tale, she began in manner such as this, while the wool followed the thread:—

"Pyramus and Thisbe, the one the most beauteous of youths,[18] the other preferred before all the damsels that the East contained, lived in adjoining houses; where Semiramis is said to have surrounded her lofty city[19] with walls of brick.[20] The nearness caused their first acquaintance, and their first advances in love; with time their affection increased. They would have united themselves, too, by the tie of marriage, but their fathers forbade it. A thing which they could not forbid, they were both inflamed, with minds equally captivated. There is no one acquainted with it; by nods and signs, they hold converse. And the more the fire is smothered, the more, when so smothered, does it burn. The party-wall, common to the two houses, was cleft by a small chink, which it had got formerly, when it was built. This defect, remarked by no one for so many ages, you lovers (what does not love perceive?) first found one, and you made it a passage for your voices, and the accents of love used to pass through it in safety, with the gentlest murmur. Oftentimes, after they had taken their stations, Thisbe on one side, and Pyramus on the other, and the breath of their mouths had been mutually caught by turns, they used to say, 'Envious wall, why dost thou stand in the way of lovers? what great matter were it, for thee to suffer us to be joined with our entire bodies? Or if that is too much, that, at least, thou shouldst open, for the exchange of kisses. Nor are we ungrateful; we confess that we are indebted to thee, that a passage has been given for our words to our loving ears.' Having said this much, in vain, on their respective sides, about night they said, 'Farewell'; and gave those kisses each on their own side, which did not reach the other side.

"The following morning had removed the fires of the night, and the Sun, with its rays, had dried the grass wet with rime, when they met together at the wonted spot. Then, first complaining much in low murmurs, they determine, in the silent night, to try to deceive their keepers, and to steal out of doors; and when they have left the house, to quit the buildings of the city as well: but that they may not have to wander, roaming in the open fields, to meet at the tomb of Ninus,[21] and to conceal themselves beneath the shade of a tree. There was there a lofty mulberry tree, very full of snow-white fruit, quite close to a cold spring. The arrangement suits them; and the light, seeming to depart but slowly, is buried in the waters, and from the same waters the night arises. The clever Thisbe, turning the hinge, gets out in the dark, and deceives her attendants, and, having covered her face, arrives at the tomb, and sits down under the tree agreed upon; love made her bold. Lo! a lioness approaches, having her foaming jaws besmeared with the recent slaughter of oxen, about to quench her thirst with the water of the neighboring spring. The Babylonian Thisbe sees her at a distance, by the rays of the moon, and with a trembling foot she flies to a dark cave; and, while she flies, her veil falling from her back, she leaves it behind. When the savage lioness has quenched her thirst with plenteous water, as she is returning into the woods, she tears the thin covering, found by chance without Thisbe herself, with her blood-stained mouth.

"Pyramus, going out later than Thisbe, saw the evident footmarks of a wild beast, in the deep dust, and grew pale all over his face. But, as soon as he found her veil, as well, dyed with blood, he said: 'One night will be the ruin of two lovers, of whom she was the most deserving of a long life. My soul is guilty; 'tis I that have destroyed thee, much to be lamented; who bade thee to come by night to places full of terror, and came not hither first. O, whatever lions are lurking beneath this rock, tear my body in pieces, and devour my accursed entrails with ruthless jaws. But it is the part of a coward to wish for death.' He takes up the veil of Thisbe, and he takes it with himself to the shade of the tree agreed on, and, after he has bestowed tears on the well-known garment, he gives kisses to the same, and he says, 'Receive, now, a draught of my blood as well!' and then plunges the sword, with which he is girt, into his bowels; and without delay, as he is dying, he draws it out of the warm wound. As he falls on his back upon the ground, the blood spurts forth on high, not otherwise than as when a pipe is burst on the lead decaying,[22] and shoots out afar the liquid water from the hissing flaw, and cleaves the air with its jet. The fruit of the tree, by the sprinkling of the blood, are changed to a dark tint, and the root, soaked with the gore, tints the hanging mulberries with a purple hue. Behold! not yet having banished her fear, Thisbe returns, that she may not disappoint her lover, and seeks for the youth both with her eyes and her affection, and longs to tell him how great dangers she has escaped. And when she observes the spot, and the altered appearance of the tree, she doubts if it is the same, so uncertain does the color of the fruit make her. While she is in doubt, she sees palpitating limbs throbbing upon the bloody ground; she draws back her foot, and having her face paler than box-wood,[23] she shudders like the sea, which trembles[24] when its surface is skimmed by a gentle breeze. But, after pausing a time, she had recognized her own lover, she smote her arms, undeserving of such usage, and tearing her hair, and embracing the much-loved body, she filled the gashes with her tears, and mingled her tokens of sorrow with his blood; and imprinting kisses on his cold features, she exclaimed, 'Pyramus! what disaster has taken thee away from me? Pyramus! answer me; 'tis thy own Thisbe, dearest, that calls thee; hear me, and raise thy prostrate features.'

"At the name of Thisbe, Pyramus raised his eyes, now heavy with death, and, after he had seen her, he closed them again. After she had perceived her own garment, and beheld, too, the ivory sheath[25] without its sword, she said, ''Tis thy own hand, and love, that has destroyed thee, ill-fated youth! I, too, have a hand bold enough for this one purpose; I have love as well; this shall give me strength for the wound. I will follow thee in thy death, and I shall be called the most unhappy cause and companion of thy fate, and thou who, alas! couldst be torn from me by death alone, shalt not be able, even by death, to be torn from me. And you, O most wretched parents of mine and his, be but prevailed upon, in this one thing, by the entreaties of us both, that you will not deny those whom their constant love and whom their last moments have joined, to be buried in the same tomb. But thou, O tree, which now with thy boughs dost overshadow the luckless body of but one, art fated soon to cover those of two. Retain a token of this our fate, and ever bear fruit black and suited for mourning, as a memorial of the blood of us two.' Thus she said; and having fixed the point under the lower part of her breast, she fell upon the sword, which still was reeking with his blood.

"Her prayers, however, moved the Gods, and moved their parents. For the color of the fruit, when it has fully ripened, is black;[26] and what was left of them, from the funeral pile, reposed in the same urn."

[Footnote 1: Minyas.—Ver. 1. Alcithoë was the daughter of Minyas, who, according to some, was the son of Orchomenus, according to others, his father. Pausanias says that the Bœotians, over whom he reigned, were called 'Minyæ' from him; but he makes no allusion to the females who are here mentioned by Ovid.]

[Footnote 2: Rites.—Ver. 1. 'Orgia:' this was the original name of the Dionysia, or festival of Bacchus; but in time the word came to be applied to any occasion of festivity.]

[Footnote 3: Her sisters.—Ver. 3. The names of the sisters of Alcithoë, according to Plutarch, were Aristippe and Leucippe. The names of the three, according to Ælian, were Alcathoë, Leucippe, and Aristippe, who is sometimes called Arsinoë. The latter author says, that the truth of the case was, that they were decent women, fond of their husbands and families, who preferred staying at home, and *attending to their domestic concerns, to running after the new rites; on which it was said, by their enemies, that Bacchus had punished them.]*

[Footnote 4: Work-baskets.—Ver. 10. The 'calathus,' which was called by the Greeks κάλαθος, καλαθίσκος, and τάλαρος, generally signifies the basket in which women placed their work, and especially the materials used for spinning. They were generally made of osiers and reeds, but sometimes of more valuable materials, such as silver, perhaps in filagree work. 'Calathi' were also used for carrying fruits and flowers. Virgil (Ecl. v. l. 71) speaks of cups for holding wine, under the name of 'Calathi.']

[Footnote 5: Bromius.—Ver. 11. Bacchus was called Bromius, from βρέμω, 'to cry out,' or 'shout,' from the yells and noise made by his worshippers, whose peculiar cries were, Εὐοῖ Βάκχε, ὦ Ἰακχε, Ἰώ Βάκχε, Εὐοῖ σαβοῖ. 'Evoë, Bacche! O, Iacche! Io, Bacche! Evoë sabæ!']

[Footnote 6: Lyæus.—Ver. 11. Bacchus was called Lyæus, from the Greek word, λύειν, 'to loosen,' or 'relax,' because wine dispels care.]

[Footnote 7: That had two mothers.—Ver. 12. The word 'bimater' seems to have been fancied by Ovid as an appropriate epithet for Bacchus, Jupiter having undertaken the duties of a mother for him, in the latter months of gestation.]

[Footnote 8: Thyoneus.—Ver. 13. Bacchus was called Thyoneus, either from Semele, his mother, one of whose names was Thyone, or from the Greek, θύειν, 'to be frantic,' from which origin the Bacchanals also received their name of Thyades.]

[Footnote 9: Lenæus.—Ver. 14. From the Greek word ληνός, 'a wine-press.']

[Footnote 10: Nyctelius.—Ver. 15. From the Greek word νὺξ, 'night,' because his orgies were celebrated by night. Eleleus is from the shout, or 'huzza' of the Greeks, which was ελελεῦ.]

[Footnote 11: Iacchus.—Ver. 15. From the Greek ἰαχὴ, 'clamor,' or 'noise.']

[Footnote 12: Evan.—Ver. 15. From the exclamation, Εὐοῖ, or 'Evoë' which the Bacchanals used in performing his orgies.]

[Footnote 13: Lycurgus.—Ver. 22. He was a king of Thrace, who having slighted the worship of Bacchus, was afflicted with madness, and hewed off his own legs with a hatchet, and, according to Apollodorus, mistaking his own son Dryas for a vine, destroyed him with the same weapon.]

[Footnote 14: Unseasonable labor.—Ver. 32. 'Minerva;' the name of the Goddess Minerva is here used for the exercise of the art of spinning, of which she was the patroness. The term 'intempestiva' is appropriately applied, as the arts of industry and frugality, which were first invented by Minerva, but ill accorded with the idle and vicious mode of celebrating the festival of Bacchus.]

[Footnote 15: Dercetis.—Ver. 45. Lucian, speaking of Dercetis, or Derceto, says, 'I have seen in Phœnicia a statue of this goddess, of a very singular kind. From the middle upwards, it represents a woman, but below it terminates in a fish. The statue of her, which is shown at Hieropolis, represents her wholly as a woman.' He further says, that the temple of this last city was thought by some to have been built by Semiramis, who consecrated it not to Juno, as is generally believed, but to her own mother, Derceto.

Atergatis was another name of this Goddess. She was said, by an illicit amour, to have been the mother of Semiramis, and in despair, to have thrown herself into a lake near Ascalon, on which she was changed into a fish.]

[Footnote 16: Palestine.—Ver. 46. Palæstina, or Philistia, in which Ascalon was situate, was a part of Syria, lying in its south-western extremity.]

[Footnote 17: How a Naiad.—Ver. 49. The Naiad here mentioned is supposed to have been a Nymph of the Island of the Sun, called also Nosola, between Taprobana (the modern Ceylon) and the coast of Carmania (perhaps Coromandel), who was in the habit of changing such youths as fell into her hands into fishes. As a reward for her cruelty, she herself was changed into a fish by the Sun.]

[Footnote 18: Most beauteous of youths.—Ver. 55. Clarke translates 'juvenum pulcherrimus alter,' 'one of the most handsome of all the young fellows.']

[Footnote 19: Her lofty city.—Ver. 57. The magnificence of ancient Babylon has been remarked by many ancient writers, from Herodotus downwards. Its walls are said to have been 60 miles in compass, 87 feet in thickness, and 350 feet in height.]

[Footnote 20: Walls of brick.—Ver. 58. The walls were built by Semiramis of bricks dried in the sun, cemented together with layers of bitumen.]

[Footnote 21: The tomb of Ninus.—Ver. 88. According to Diodorus Siculus, the sepulchre of Ninus, the first king of Babylon, was ten stadia in length, and nine in depth; it had the appearance of a vast citadel, and was at a considerable distance from the city of Babylon. Commentators have expressed some surprise that Ovid here uses the word 'busta,' for 'tomb,' as the place of meeting for these chaste lovers, as the prostitutes of Rome used to haunt the 'busta,' or 'tombs;' whence they obtained the epithet of 'bustuariæ.']

[Footnote 22: The lead decaying.—Ver. 122. 'Fistula' here means 'a water-pipe.' Vitruvius speaks of three methods of conveying water; by channels of masonry, earthen pipes, and leaden pipes. The latter were smaller, and more generally used; to them reference is here made. They were formed by bending plates of lead into a form, not cylindrical, but the section of which was oblong, and tapering towards the top like a pear. The description here given, though somewhat homely, is extremely natural, and, as frequent experience shows us, depicts the results when the soldering of a water-pipe has become decayed.]

[Footnote 23: Paler than box-wood.—Ver. 134. From the light color of boxwood, the words 'buxo pallidiora,' 'paler than boxwood,' became a proverbial expression among the Romans.]

[Footnote 24: The sea which trembles.—Ver. 136. The ripple, or shudder, which runs along the surface of the sea, when a breath of wind is stirring in a calm, is very beautifully described here, and is worthy of notice.]

[Footnote 25: The ivory sheath.—Ver. 148. The 'vagina,' or 'sheath' of the sword, was often highly decorated; and we learn from Homer and Virgil, as well as Ovid, that ivory was much used for that purpose. The sheath was worn by the Greeks and Romans on the left side of the body, so as to enable them to draw the sword from it, by passing the right hand in front of the body, to take hold of the hilt, with the thumb next to the blade.]

[Footnote 26: Is black.—Ver. 165. He thus accounts for the deep purple hue of the mulberry which, before the event mentioned here, he says was white.]

EXPLANATION

It is pretty clear, as we have already seen, that the establishment of the worship of Bacchus in Greece met with great opposition, and that his priests and devotees published several miracles and prodigies, the more easily to influence the minds of their fellow-men. Thus, the daughters of Minyas are said to have been changed into bats, solely because they neglected to join in the orgies of that God; when, probably, the fact was, that they were either secretly despatched, or were forced to fly for their lives; and their absence was accounted for to the ignorant and credulous, by the invention of this Fable. The story of Dercetis, as related by Diodorus Siculus, Pliny, and Herodotus, is, that having offended Venus, that Goddess caused her to fall in love with a young man, by whom she had a daughter. In despair at her misfortune, she killed her lover, and exposed her child, and afterwards drowned herself. The Syrians, lamenting her fate, built a temple near where she was drowned, and honored her as a Goddess. They stated that she was turned into a fish, and they there represented her under the figure of a woman down to the waist, and of a fish thence downwards. They also abstained from eating fish; though they offered them to her in sacrifice, and suspended gilded ones in her temple. Selden, in his Treatise on the Syrian Gods, suggests that the story of Dercetis, or Atergatis, was founded on the figure and worship of Dagon, the God of the Philistines, who was represented under the figure of a fish; and that the name of Atergatis is a corruption of 'Adir Dagon,' 'a great fish,' which is not at all improbable. The same author supposes that Dercetis was originally the same Deity with Venus, Astarte, Minerva, Juno, Isis, and the Moon; and that she was worshipped under the name of Mylitta by the Assyrians, and as Alilac by the Arabians. Lucian tells us, that Dercetis was reported to have been the mother of Semiramis.

Ovid and Hyginus are the only authors that make mention of the story of Pyramus and Thisbe, and both agree in making Babylon the scene of it. It seems to be rather intended as a moral tale, than to have been built upon any actual circumstance. It affords a lesson to youth not to enter rashly into engagements: and to parents not to pursue, too rigorously, the gratification of their own resentment, but rather to consult the inclination of their children, when not likely to be productive of unhappiness at a future period.

The reader cannot fail to call to mind the admirable travesty of this story by Shakspere, in the 'Midsummer Night's Dream.'

FABLE II [IV.167-233]

The Sun discovers to Vulcan the intrigue between Mars and Venus, and then, himself, falls in love with Leucothoë. Venus, in revenge for the discovery, resolves to make his amours unfortunate.

Here she ended; and there was but a short time betwixt, and then Leuconoë began[27] to speak. Her sisters held their peace. "Love has captivated even this Sun, who rules all things by his æthereal light. I will relate the loves of the Sun. This God is supposed to have been the first to see the adultery of Venus with Mars; this God is the first to see everything. He was grieved at what was done, and showed to the husband, the son of Juno,[28] the wrong done to his bed, and the place of the intrigue. Both his senses, and the work which his skilful right hand was then holding, quitted him on the instant. Immediately, he files out some slender chains of brass, and nets, and meshes, which can escape the eye. The finest threads cannot surpass that work, nor yet the cobweb that hangs from the top of the beam. He makes it so, too, as to yield to a slight touch, and a gentle movement, and skilfully arranges it drawn around the bed. When the wife and the gallant come into the same bed, being both caught through the artifice of the husband, and chains prepared by this new contrivance, they are held fast in the very midst of their embraces.

"The Lemnian God immediately threw open the folding doors[29] of ivory, and admitted the Deities. There they lay disgracefully bound. And yet many a one of the Gods, not the serious ones, could fain wish thus to become disgraced. The Gods of heaven laughed, and for a long time was this the most noted story in all heaven. The Cytherean[30] goddess exacts satisfaction of the Sun, in remembrance of this betrayal; and, in her turn, disturbs him with the like passion, who had disturbed her secret amours. What now, son of Hyperion,[31] does thy beauty, thy heat, and thy radiant light avail thee? For thou, who dost burn all lands with thy flames, art now burnt with a new flame; and thou, who oughtst to be looking at everything, art gazing on Leucothoë, and on one maiden art fixing those eyes which thou oughtst to be fixing on the universe. At one time thou art rising earlier in the Eastern sky; at another thou art setting late in the waves; and in taking time to gaze on her, thou art lengthening the hours of mid-winter. Sometimes thou art eclipsed, and the trouble of thy mind affects thy light, and, darkened, thou fillest with terror the breasts of mortals. Nor art thou pale, because the form of the moon, nearer to the earth, stands in thy way. It is that passion which occasions this complexion. Thou lovest her alone, neither does Clymene, nor Rhodos,[32] nor the most beauteous mother[33] of the Ææan Circe engage thee, nor yet Clytie, who, though despised, was longing for thy embraces; at that very time thou wast suffering these grievous pangs. Leucothoë occasioned the forgetting of many a damsel; she, whom Eurynome, the most beauteous of the perfume-bearing[34] nation produced.[35] But after her daughter grew up, as much as the mother excelled all other Nymphs, so much did the daughter excel the mother. Her father, Orchamus, ruled over the Achæmenian[36] cities, and he is reckoned the seventh in descent from the ancient Belus.[37]

"The pastures of the horses of the Sun are under the Western sky; instead of grass, they have ambrosia.[38] That nourishes their limbs wearied with their daily service, and refits them for labor. And while the coursers are there eating their heavenly food, and night is taking her turn; the God enters the beloved chamber, changed into the shape of her mother Eurynome, and beholds Leucothoë among twice six handmaids, near the threshold, drawing out the smooth threads with her twirling spindle. When, therefore, as though her mother, he has given kisses to her dear daughter, he says, "There is a secret matter, which I have to mention; maids, withdraw, and take not from a mother the privilege of speaking in private with her daughter." They obey; and the God being left in the chamber without any witness, he says, 'I am he, who measures out the long year, who beholds all things, and through whom the earth sees all things; the eye, in fact, of the universe. Believe me, thou art pleasing to me.' She is affrighted; and in her alarm, both her distaff and her spindle fall from her relaxed fingers. Her very fear becomes her; and, he, no longer delaying, returns to his true shape, and his wonted beauty. But the maiden, although startled at the unexpected sight, overcome by the beauty of the God,[39] and dismissing all complaints, submits to his embrace.

[Footnote 27: Leuconoë began.—Ver. 168. It is worthy of remark, how strongly the affecting tale of Pyramus and Thisbe contrasts with the loose story of the loves of Mars and Venus.]

[Footnote 28: The son of Juno.—Ver. 173. Vulcan is called 'Junonigena,' because, according to some, he was the son of Juno alone. Other writers, however, say that he was the only son of Jupiter and Juno.]

[Footnote 29: The folding doors.—Ver. 185. The plural word 'valvæ' is often used to signify a door, or entrance, because among the ancients each doorway generally contained two doors folding together. The internal doors even of private houses were bivalve; hence, as in the present case, we often read of the folding doors of a bed-chamber. Each of these doors or valves was usually wide enough to permit persons to pass each other in egress and ingress without opening the other door as well. Sometimes each valve was double, folding like our window-shutters.]

[Footnote 30: Cytherean.—Ver. 190. Cythera was an island on the southern coast of Laconia; where Venus was supposed to have landed, after she had risen from the sea. It was dedicated to her worship.]

[Footnote 31: Hyperion.—Ver. 192. He was the son of Cœlus, or Uranus, and the father of the Sun. The name of Hyperion is, however, often given by the poets to the Sun himself.]

[Footnote 32: Rhodos.—Ver. 204. She was a damsel of the Isle of Rhodes, the daughter of Neptune, and, according to some, of Venus. She was greatly beloved by Apollo, to whom she bore seven children.]

[Footnote 33: Beauteous mother.—Ver. 205. This was Persa, the daughter of Oceanus, and the mother of the enchantress Circe, who is here called 'Ææa,' from Ææa, a city and peninsula of Colchis. Circe is referred to more at length in the 14th Book of the Metamorphoses.]

[Footnote 34: Perfume-bearing.—Ver. 209. Being born in Arabia, the producer of all kinds of spices and perfumes, which were much in request among the ancients, for the purposes of sacrifice.]

[Footnote 35: Produced.—Ver. 210. Eurynome was the wife of Orchamus, and was the daughter of Oceanus and Tethys.]

[Footnote 36: Achæmenian.—Ver. 212. Persia is called Achæmenian, from Achæmenes, one of its former kings.]

[Footnote 37: Ancient Belus.—Ver. 213. The order of descent is thus reckoned from Belus; Abas, Acrisius, Danaë, Perseus, Bachæmon, Achæmenes, and Orchamus.]

[Footnote 38: Ambrosia.—Ver. 215. Ambrosia was said to be the food of the Deities, and nectar their drink.]

[Footnote 39: Beauty of the God.—Ver. 233. Clarke translates, 'Virgo victa nitore Dei.' 'The young lady—charmed with the spruceness of the God.']

EXPLANATION

Plutarch, in his Treatise 'How to read the Poets,' suggests a curious explanation of the discovery by the Sun of the intrigue of Mars and Venus. He says that such persons as are born under the conjunction of the planets Mars and Venus, are naturally of an amorous temperament; but that if the Sun does not happen then to be at a distance, their indiscretions will be very soon discovered.

Palæphatus gives a historical solution to the story. He says that Helius, the son of Vulcan, king of Egypt, resolving to cause his father's laws against adultery to be strictly observed, and having been informed that a lady of the court had an intrigue with one of the courtiers, entered her apartment in the night, and obtaining ocular proof of the courtier's guilt, caused him to be severely punished. He also tells us that the similarity of the name gave birth to the Fable which Homer was the first to relate, with a small variation, and which is here copied by Ovid. Libanius, deploring the burning of the Temple of Apollo near Antioch, complains of the ingratitude of Vulcan to that God, who had formerly discovered to him the infidelity of his wife; a subject upon which St. Chrysostom seems to think that the rhetorician would have done better to have been silent.

FABLE III [IV.234-270]

Clytie, in a fit of revenge, discovers the adventure of Leucothoë to her father, who orders her to be buried alive. The Sun, grieved at her misfortune, changed her into the frankincense tree; he also despises the informer, who pines away for love of him, and is at last changed into the sunflower.

Clytie envied her, (for the love of the Sun[40] for her had not been moderate), and, urged on by resentment at a rival, she published the intrigue, and, when spread abroad, brought it to the notice of her father. He, fierce and unrelenting, cruelly buried her alive deep in the ground, as she entreated and stretched out her hands towards the light of the Sun, and cried, "'Twas he that offered violence to me against my will;" and upon her he placed a heap of heavy sand. The son of Hyperion scattered it with his rays, and gave a passage to thee, by which thou mightst be able to put forth thy buried features.

But thou, Nymph, couldst not now raise thy head smothered with the weight of the earth; and there thou didst lie, a lifeless body. The governor of the winged steeds is said to have beheld nothing more afflicting than that, since the lightnings that caused the death of Phaëton. He, indeed, endeavors, if he can, to recall her cold limbs to an enlivening heat, by the strength of his rays. But, since fate opposes attempts so great, he sprinkles both her body and the place with odoriferous nectar, and having first uttered many a complaint he says, "Still shalt thou reach the skies."[41] Immediately, the body, steeped in the heavenly nectar, dissolves, and moistens the earth with its odoriferous juices; and a shoot of frankincense having taken root by degrees through the clods, rises up and bursts the hillock with its top.

But the author of light came no more to Clytie (although love might have excused her grief, and her grief the betrayal); and he put an end to his intercourse with her. From that time she, who had made so mad a use of her passion, pined away, loathing the other Nymphs; and in the open air, night and day, she sat on the bare ground, with her hair dishevelled and unadorned. And for nine days, without water or food, she subsisted in her fast, merely on dew and her own tears; and she did not raise herself from the ground. She only used to look towards the face of the God as he moved along, and to turn her own features towards him. They say that her limbs became rooted fast in the ground; and a livid paleness turned part of her color into that of a bloodless plant. There is a redness in some part; and a flower, very like a violet,[42] conceals her face. Though she is held fast by a root, she turns towards the Sun, and though changed, she still retains her passion.

[Footnote 40: For the love of the Sun.—Ver. 234. This remark is added, to show that the God had not been sufficiently cautious in his courtship of her sister to conceal it from the observation of Clytie.]

[Footnote 41: Reach the skies.—Ver. 251. That is to say, 'You shall arise from the earth as a tree bearing frankincense: the gums of which, burnt in sacrifice to the Gods, shall reach the heavens with their sweet odors.' Persia and Arabia have been celebrated by the poets, ancient and modern, for their great fertility in frankincense and other aromatic plants.]

[Footnote 42: Like a violet.—Ver. 268. This cannot mean the large yellow plant which is called the sunflower. The small aromatic flower which we call heliotrope, with its violet hue and delightful perfume, more nearly answers the description. The larger flower probably derived its name from the resemblance which it bears to the sun, surrounded with rays, as depicted by the ancient painters.]

EXPLANATION

No ascertained historical fact can be found as the basis of the story of Leucothoë being buried alive by her father Orchamus, or of her rival Clytie being metamorphosed into a sunflower. The story seems to have been most probably simply founded on principles of natural philosophy. Leucothoë, it is not unreasonable to suppose, may have been styled the daughter of Orchamus, king of Persia, for no other reason but because that Prince was the first to introduce the frankincense tree, which was called Leucothoë, into his kingdom; and it was added that she fell in love with Apollo, because the tree produces an aromatic drug much used in physic, of which that God was fabled to have been the inventor. The jealousy of Clytie was, perhaps, founded upon a fact, stated by some naturalists, that the sunflower is a plant which kills the frankincense tree, when growing near it. Pliny, however, who ascribes several properties to the sunflower, does not mention this among them.

Orchamus is nowhere mentioned by the ancient writers, except in the present instance.

FABLE IV [IV.271-284]

Daphnis is turned into a stone. Scython is changed from a man into a woman. Celmus is changed into adamant. Crocus and Smilax are made into flowers. The Curetes are produced from a shower.

Thus she spoke; and the wondrous deed charms their ears. Some deny that it was possible to be done, some say that real Gods can do all things; but Bacchus is not one of them. When her sisters have become silent, Alcithoë is called upon; who running with her shuttle through the warp of the hanging web, says, "I keep silence upon the well-known amours of Daphnis, the shepherd of Ida,[43] whom the resentment of the Nymph, his paramour, turned into a stone. Such mighty grief inflames those who are in love. Nor do I relate how once Scython, the law of nature being altered, was of both sexes first a man, then a woman. Thee too, I pass by, O Celmus, now adamant, formerly most attached to Jupiter when little; and the Curetes,[44] sprung from a plenteous shower of rain; Crocus, too, changed, together with Smilax,[45] into little flowers; and I will entertain your minds with a pleasing novelty."

[Footnote 43: Shepherd of Ida.—Ver. 277. This may mean either Daphnis of Crete, or of Phrygia; for in both those countries there was a mountain named Ida.]

[Footnote 44: The Curetes.—Ver. 282. According to Dionysius of Halicarnassus, the Curetes were the ancient inhabitants of Crete. We may here remark, that the story of their springing from the earth after a shower of rain, seems to have no other foundation than the fact of their having been of the race of the Titans; that is, they were descended from Uranus, or Cœlus and Tita, by which names were meant the heaven and the earth.]

[Footnote 45: Smilax.—Ver. 283. The dictionary meanings given for this word are—1. Withwind, a kind of herb. 2. The yew tree. 3. A kind of oak. The Nymph was probably supposed to have been changed into the first.]

EXPLANATION

Most probably, the story of the shepherd Daphnis being turned into a stone, was no other than an allegorical method of expressing the insensibility of an individual. Thalia was the name of the Nymph who was thus affronted by Daphnis.

The story of Scython changing his sex, is perhaps based upon the fact, that the country of Thrace, which took the name of Thracia from a famous sorceress, was before called Scython; and that as it lost a name of the masculine gender for one of the feminine, in after times it became reported that Scython had changed sexes.

Pliny tells us that Celmus was a young man of remarkable wisdom and moderation, and that the passions making no impression on him, he was changed into adamant. Some, however, assert that he was foster-father to Jupiter, by whom he was enclosed in an impenetrable tower, for revealing the immortality of the Gods.

According to one account, Crocus and Smilax were a constant and happy married couple, who for their chaste and innocent life were said to have been changed into flowers; but another story is, that Crocus was a youth beloved by Smilax, and that on his rejecting the Nymph's advances, they were both turned into flowers.

The story of the Curetes being sprung from rain, is possibly founded on the report that they were descended from Uranus and Tita, the Heaven and the Earth. Some suppose them to have been the original inhabitants of the isle of Crete; and they are said to have watched over the infancy of Jupiter, by whom they were afterwards slain, for having concealed Epaphus from his wrath.

FABLE V [IV.285-388]

The Naiad Salmacis falls in love with the youth Hermaphroditus, who rejects her advances. While he is bathing, she leaps into the water, and seizing the youth in her arms, they become one body, retaining their different sexes.

Learn how Salmacis became infamous, and why it enervates, with its enfeebling waters, and softens the limbs bathed in it. The cause is unknown; but the properties of the fountain are very well known. The Naiads nursed a boy, born to Mercury of the Cytherean Goddess in the caves of Ida; whose face was such that therein both mother and father could be discerned; he likewise took his name from them. As soon as he had completed thrice five years, he forsook his native mountains, and leaving Ida, the place of his nursing, he loved to wander over unknown spots, and to see unknown rivers, his curiosity lessening the fatigue. He went, too, to the Lycian[46] cities, and the Carians, that border upon Lycia. Here he sees a pool of water, clear to the very ground at the bottom; here there are no fenny reeds, no barren sedge, no rushes with their sharp points. The water is translucent; but the edges of the pool are enclosed with green turf, and with grass ever verdant. A Nymph dwells there; but one neither skilled in hunting, nor accustomed to bend the bow, nor to contend in speed; the only one, too, of all the Naiads not known to the swift Diana. The report is, that her sisters often said to her, "Salmacis, do take either the javelin, or the painted quiver, and unite thy leisure with the toils of the chase." She takes neither the javelin, nor the painted quiver, nor does she unite her leisure with the toils of the chase. But sometimes she is bathing her beauteous limbs in her own spring; and often is she straitening her hair with a comb of Citorian boxwood,[47] and consulting the waters, into which she looks, what is befitting her. At other times, covering her body with a transparent garment, she reposes either on the soft leaves or on the soft grass. Ofttimes is she gathering flowers. And then, too, by chance was she gathering them when she beheld the youth, and wished to possess him, thus seen.

But though she hastened to approach the youth, still she did not approach him before she had put herself in order, and before she had surveyed her garments, and put on her best looks, and deserved to be thought beautiful. Then thus did she begin to speak: "O youth, most worthy to be thought to be a God! if thou art a God, thou mayst well be Cupid; but, if thou art a mortal, happy are they who begot thee, and blessed is thy brother, and fortunate indeed thy sister, if thou hast one, and the nurse as well who gave thee the breast. But far, far more fortunate than all these is she; if thou hast any wife, if thou shouldst vouchsafe any one the honor of marriage. And if any one is thy wife, then let my pleasure be stolen; but, if thou hast none, let me be thy wife, and let us unite in one tie." After these things said, the Naiad is silent; a blush tinges the face of the youth: he knows not what love is, but even to blush becomes him. Such is the color of apples, hanging on a tree exposed to the sun, or of painted ivory, or of the moon blushing beneath her brightness when the aiding cymbals[48] of brass are resounding in vain. Upon the Nymph desiring, without ceasing, such kisses at least as he might give to his sister, and now laying her hands upon his neck, white as ivory, he says, "Wilt thou desist, or am I to fly, and to leave this place, together with thee?"

Salmacis is affrighted, and says, "I freely give up this spot to thee, stranger," and, with a retiring step, she pretends to go away. But then looking back, and hid in a covert of shrubs, she lies concealed, and puts her bended knees down to the ground. But he, just like a boy, and as though unobserved on the retired sward, goes here and there, and in the sportive waves dips the soles of his feet, and then his feet as far as his ankles. Nor is there any delay; being charmed with the temperature of the pleasant waters, he throws off his soft garments from his tender body. Then, indeed, Salmacis is astonished, and burns with desire for his naked beauty. The eyes, too, of the Nymph are on fire, no otherwise than as when the Sun,[49] most brilliant with his clear orb, is reflected from the opposite image of a mirror. With difficulty does she endure delay; hardly does she now defer her joy. Now she longs to embrace him; and now, distracted, she can hardly contain herself. He, clapping his body with his hollow palms, swiftly leaps into the stream, and throwing out his arms alternately, shines in the limpid water, as if any one were to cover statues of ivory, or white lilies, with clear glass.

"I have gained my point," says the Naiad; "see, he is mine!" and, all her garments thrown aside, she plunges in the midst of the waters, and seizes him resisting her, and snatches reluctant kisses, and thrusts down her hands, and touches his breast against his will, and clings about the youth, now one way, and now another. Finally, as he is struggling against her, and desiring to escape, she entwines herself about him, like a serpent which the royal bird takes up and is bearing aloft; and as it hangs, it holds fast his head and feet, and enfolds his spreading wings with its tail. Or, as the ivy is wont to wind itself along the tall trunks of trees; and as the polypus[50] holds fast its enemy, caught beneath the waves, by letting down his suckers on all sides; so does the descendant of Atlas[51] still persist, and deny the Nymph the hoped-for joy. She presses him hard; and clinging to him with every limb, as she holds fast, she says, "Struggle as thou mayst, perverse one, still thou shalt not escape. So ordain it, ye Gods, and let no time separate him from me, nor me from him." Her prayers find propitious Deities, for the mingled bodies of the two are united,[52] and one human shape is put upon them; just as if any one should see branches beneath a common bark join in growing, and spring up together. So, when their bodies meet together in the firm embrace, they are no more two, and their form is twofold, so that they can neither be styled woman nor boy; they seem to be neither and both.

Therefore, when Hermaphroditus sees that the limpid waters, into which he had descended as a man, have made him but half a male, and that his limbs are softened in them, holding up his hands, he says, but now no longer with the voice of a male, "O, both father and mother, grant this favor to your son, who has the name of you both, that whoever enters these streams a man, may go out thence but half a man, and that he may suddenly become effeminate in the waters when touched." Both parents, moved, give their assent to the words of their two-shaped son, and taint the fountain with drugs of ambiguous quality.

[Footnote 46: Lycian.—Ver. 296. Lycia was a province of Asia Minor, on the shores of the Mediterranean Sea. Caria was another province, adjoining to Lycia.]

[Footnote 47: Citorian boxwood.—Ver. 311. Citorus, or Cythorus, was a mountain of Paphlagonia, famous for the excellence of the wood of the box trees that grow there. The Greeks and Romans made their combs of it. The Egyptians used them made of ivory and wood, and toothed on one side only; those of the Greeks had teeth on both sides. Great care was usually taken of the hair; to go with it uncombed was a sign of affliction.]

[Footnote 48: The aiding cymbals.—Ver. 333. The witches and magicians, in ancient times, and especially those of Thessaly, professed to be able, with their charms and incantations, to bring the moon down from heaven. The truth of these assertions being commonly believed, at the period of an eclipse it was supposed by the multitude that the moon was being subjected to the spells of these magicians, and that she was struggling (laborabat) against them, on which the sound of drums, trumpets, and cymbals was resorted to, to distract the attention of the moon, and to drown the charms repeated by the enchanters, for which reason, the instruments employed for the purpose were styled 'auxiliares.']

[Footnote 49: As when the Sun.—Ver. 349. Bailey gives this explanation of the passage,—'The eyes of the Nymph seemed to sparkle and shine, just as the rays of the sun in a clear sky when a looking-glass is placed against them, for then they seem most splendid, and contract the fire.' From the mention of the eyes of the Nymph burning 'flagrant,' we might be almost justified in concluding that 'speculum' means here not a mirror, but a burning-glass. The 'specula,' or looking-glasses, of the ancients were usually made of metal, either a composition of tin and copper, or silver; but in later times, alloy was mixed with

the silver. Pliny mentions the obsidian stone, or, as it is now called, the Icelandic agate, as being used for this purpose. Nero is said to have used emeralds for mirrors. Pliny the Elder says that mirrors were made in the glass-houses of Sidon, which consisted of glass plates, with leaves of metal at the back; they were probably of an inferior character. Those of copper and tin were made chiefly at Brundisium. The white metal formed from this mixture soon becoming dim, a sponge with powdered pumice stone was usually fastened to the mirrors made of that composition. They were generally small, of a round or oval shape, and having a handle; and female slaves usually held them, while their mistresses were performing the duties of the toilet. Sometimes they were fastened to the walls, and they were occasionally of the length of a person's body. Venus was supposed often to use the mirror; but Minerva repudiated the use of it.]

[Footnote 50: Polypus.—Ver. 366. This is a fish which entangles its prey, mostly consisting of shell fish, in its great number of feet or feelers. Ovid here calls them 'flagella;' but in the Halieuticon he styles them 'brachia' and 'crines.' Pliny the Elder calls them 'crines' and 'cirri.']

[Footnote 51: Descendant of Atlas.—Ver. 368. Hermaphroditus was the great-grandson of Atlas; as the latter was the father of Maia, the mother of Mercury, who begot Hermaphroditus.]

[Footnote 52: The two are united.—Ver. 374. Clarke translates, 'nam mixta duorum corpora junguntur,' 'for the bodies of both, being jumbled together, are united.']

EXPLANATION

The only probable solution of this story seems to have been the fact that there was in Caria, near the town of Halicarnassus, as we read in Vitruvius, a fountain which was instrumental in civilizing certain barbarians who had been driven from that neighborhood by the Argive colony established there. These men being obliged to repair to the fountain for water, and meeting the Greek colonists there, their intercourse not only polished them, but in course of time corrupted them, by the introduction of the luxurious manners of Greece. Hence the fountain had the reputation of changing men into women.

Possibly the water of that fountain, by some peculiar chemical quality, made those who drank of it become soft and effeminate, as waters are to be occasionally found with extraordinary qualities. Lylius Gyraldus suggests, that several disgraceful adventures happened near this fountain (which was enclosed by walls), which in time gave it a bad name.

FABLE VI [IV.389-415]

Bacchus, to punish the daughters of Minyas for their contempt of his worship, changes them into bats, and their work into ivy and vine leaves.

There was now an end of their stories; and still do the daughters of Minyas go on with their work, and despise the God, and desecrate his festival; when, on a sudden, tambourines unseen resound with their jarring noise; the pipe, too, with the crooked horn, and the tinkling brass, re-echo; myrrh and saffron shed their fragrant odors; and, a thing past all belief, their webs begin to grow green, and the cloth hanging in the loom to put forth foliage like ivy. Part changes into vines, and what were threads before, are now turned into vine shoots. Vine branches spring from the warp, and the purple lends its splendor to the tinted grapes.

And now the day was past, and the time came on, which you could neither call darkness nor light, but yet the very commencement of the dubious night along with the light. The house seemed suddenly to shake, and unctuous torches to burn, and the building to shine with glowing fires, and the fictitious phantoms of savage wild beasts to howl. Presently, the sisters are hiding themselves throughout the smoking house, and in different places are avoiding the fires and the light. While they are seeking a hiding-place, a membrane is stretched over their small limbs, and covers their arms with light wings; nor does the darkness suffer them to know by what means they have lost their former shape. No feathers bear them up; yet they support themselves on pellucid wings; and, endeavoring to speak, they utter a voice very diminutive even in proportion to their bodies, and express their low complaints with a squeaking sound. They frequent houses, not woods; and, abhorring the light, they fly abroad by night. And from the late evening do they derive their name.[53]

[Footnote 53: Derive their name.—Ver. 415. In Greek they are called νυκτερίδες, from νυξ, 'night;' and in Latin, 'vespertiliones,' from 'vesper,' 'evening,' on account of their habits.]

FABLE VII [IV.416-562]

Tisiphone, being sent by Juno to the Palace of Athamas, causes him to become mad; on which he dashes his son Learchus to pieces against a wall. He then pursues his wife Ino, who throws herself headlong from the top of a rock into the sea, with her other son Melicerta in her arms: when Neptune, at the intercession of Venus, changes them into Sea Deities. The attendants of Ino, who have followed her in her flight, are changed, some into stone, and others into birds, as they are about to throw themselves into the sea after their mistress.

But then the Divine power of Bacchus is famed throughout all Thebes; and his aunt is everywhere telling of the great might of the new Divinity; she alone,[54] out of so many sisters, is free from sorrow, except that which her sisters have occasioned. Juno beholds her, having her soul elevated with her children, and her alliance with Athamas, and the God her foster-child. She cannot brook this, and says to herself, "Was the child of a concubine able to transform the Mæonian sailors, and to overwhelm them in the sea, and to give the entrails of the son to be torn to pieces by his mother, and to cover the three daughters of Minyas with newly formed wings? Shall Juno be able to do nothing but lament these griefs unrevenged? And is that sufficient for me? Is this my only power? He himself instructs me what to do. It is right to be taught even by an enemy. And what madness can do, he shows enough, and more than enough, by the slaughter of Pentheus. Why should not Ino, too, be goaded by madness, and submit to an example kindred to those of her sisters?"

There is a shelving path, shaded with dismal yew, which leads through profound silence to the infernal abodes. Here languid Styx exhales vapors; and the new-made ghosts descend this way, and phantoms when they have enjoyed[55] funeral rites. Horror and winter possess these dreary regions far and wide, and the ghosts newly arrived know not where the way is that leads to the Stygian city, or where is the dismal palace of the black Pluto. The wide city has a thousand passages, and gates open on every side. And as the sea receives the rivers for the whole earth, so does that spot[56] receive all the souls; nor is it too little for any amount of people, nor does it perceive the crowd to increase. The shades wander about, bloodless, without body and bones; and some throng the place of judgment; some the abode of the infernal prince. Some pursue various callings, in imitation of their former life; their own punishment confines others.

Juno, the daughter of Saturn, leaving her celestial habitation, submits to go thither, so much does she give way to hatred and to anger. Soon as she has entered there, and the threshold groans, pressed by her sacred body, Cerberus raises his threefold mouth, and utters triple barkings at the same moment. She summons the Sisters,[57] begotten of Night, terrible and implacable Goddesses. They are sitting before the doors of the prison shut close with adamant, and are combing black vipers from their hair. Soon as they recognize her amid the shades of darkness, these Deities arise. This place is called "the accursed." Tityus[58] is giving his entrails to be mangled, and is stretched over nine acres. By thee, Tantalus,[59] no waters are reached, and the tree which overhangs thee, starts away. Sisyphus,[60] thou art either catching or thou art pushing on the stone destined to fall again. Ixion[61] is whirled round, and both follows and flies from himself. The granddaughters, too, of Belus, who dared to plot the destruction of their cousins, are everlastingly taking up the water which they lose. After the daughter of Saturn has beheld all these with a stern look, and Ixion before all; again, after him, looking upon Sisyphus, she says,

"Why does he alone, of all the brothers, suffer eternal punishment? and why does a rich palace contain the proud Athamas, who, with his wife, has ever despised me?" And then she explains the cause of her hatred and of her coming, and what it is she desires. What she desires is, that the palace of Cadmus shall not stand, and that the Sister Furies shall involve Athamas in crime. She mingles together promises, commands, and entreaties, and solicits the Goddesses. When Juno has thus spoken, Tisiphone, with her locks dishevelled as they are, shakes them, and throws back from her face the snakes crawling over it; and thus she says: "There is no need of a long preamble; whatever thou commandest, consider it as done: leave these hateful realms, and betake thyself to the air of a better heaven."

Juno returns, overjoyed; and, preparing to enter heaven, Iris,[62] the daughter of Thaumas, purifies her by sprinkling water. Nor is there any delay; the persecuting Tisiphone[63] takes a torch reeking with gore, and puts on a cloak red with fluid blood, and is girt with twisted snakes, and then goes forth from her abode. Mourning attends her as she goes, and Fright, and Terror, and Madness with quivering features. She now reaches the threshold; the Æolian door-posts are said to have shaken, and paleness tints the maple door; the Sun, too, flies from the place. His wife is terrified at these prodigies; Athamas, too, is alarmed, and they are both preparing to leave the house. The baneful Erinnys stands in the way, and blocks up the passage; and extending her arms twisted round with folds of vipers, she shakes her locks; the snakes thus moved, emit a sound. Some lying about her shoulders, some gliding around her temples, send forth hissings and vomit forth corruption, and dart forth their tongues. Then she tears away two snakes from the middle of her hair, which, with pestilential hand, she throws against them. But these creep along the breasts of Ino and Athamas, and inspire them with direful intent. Nor do they inflict any wounds upon their limbs; it is the mind that feels the direful stroke. She had brought, too, with her a monstrous composition of liquid poison, the foam of the mouth of Cerberus, and the venom of Echidna;[64] and purposeless aberrations, and the forgetfulness of a darkened understanding, and crime, and tears, and rage, and the love of murder. All these were blended together; and, mingled with fresh blood she had boiled them in a hollow vessel of brass, stirred about with a stalk of green hemlock. And while they are trembling, she throws the maddening poison into the breasts of them both, and moves their inmost vitals. Then repeatedly waving her torch in the same circle, she swiftly follows up the flames thus excited with fresh flames. Thus triumphant, and having executed her commands, she returns to the empty realms of the great Pluto; and she ungirds the snakes which she had put on.

Immediately the son of Æolus, filled with rage, cries out, in the midst of his palace, "Ho! companions, spread your nets in this wood; for here a lioness was just now beheld by me with two young ones." And, in his madness, he follows the footsteps of his wife, as though of a wild beast; and he snatches Learchus, smiling and stretching forth his little arms from the bosom of his mother, and three or four times he whirls him round in the air like a sling, and, frenzied, he dashes in pieces[65] the bones of the infant against the hard stones. Then, at last, the mother being roused (whether it was grief that caused it, or whether the power of the poison spread over her), yells aloud, and runs away distracted, with dishevelled hair; and carrying thee, Melicerta, a little child, in her bare arms, she cries aloud "Evoë, Bacche." At the name of Bacchus, Juno smiles, and says, "May thy foster-child[66] do thee this service."

There is a rock[67] that hangs over the sea; the lowest part is worn hollow by the waves, and defends the waters covered thereby from the rain. The summit is rugged, and stretches out its brow over the open sea. This Ino climbs (madness gives her strength), and, restrained by no fear, she casts herself and her burden[68] into the deep; the water, struck by her fall, is white with foam. But Venus, pitying the misfortunes of her guiltless granddaughter,[69] in soothing words thus addresses her uncle: "O Neptune, thou God of the waters, to whom fell a power next after the empire of heaven, great things indeed do I request; but do thou take compassion on my kindred, whom thou seest being tossed upon the boundless Ionian sea;[70] and add them to thy Deities. I have surely some interest with the sea, if, indeed, I once was foam formed in the hollowed deep, and my Grecian name is derived[71] from that." Neptune yields to her request; and takes away from them all that is mortal, and gives them a venerable majesty; and alters both their name and their shape, and calls Palæmon a Divinity,[72] together with his mother Leucothoë.

Her Sidonian attendants,[73] so far as they could, tracing the prints of their feet, saw the last of them on the edge of the rock; and thinking that there was no doubt of their death, they lamented the house of Cadmus, with their hands tearing their hair and their garments; and they threw the odium on the Goddess, as being unjust and too severe against the concubine. Juno could not endure their reproaches, and said, "I will make you yourselves tremendous memorials of my displeasure." Confirmation followed her words. For the one who had been especially attached, said, "I will follow the queen into the sea;" and about to give the leap, she could not be moved any way, and adhering to the rock, there she stuck fast. Another, while she was attempting to beat her breast with the accustomed blows, perceived in the attempt that her arms had become stiff. One, as by chance she had extended her hands over the waters of the sea, becoming a rock, held out her hands in those same waters. You might see the fingers of another suddenly hardened in her hair, as she was tearing her locks seized on the top of her head. In whatever posture each was found at the beginning of the change, in the same she remained. Some became birds; which, sprung from Ismenus, skim along the surface of the waves in those seas, with the wings which they have assumed.

[Footnote 54: She alone.—Ver. 419. This was Ino, whose only sorrows hitherto had been caused by the calamities which befell her sisters and their offspring: Semele having died a shocking death, Autonoë having seen her son Actæon changed into a stag, and then devoured by his dogs, and Agave having assisted in tearing to pieces her own son Pentheus.]

[Footnote 55: When they have enjoyed.—Ver. 435. The spirits whose bodies had not received the rites of burial, we learn from Homer and Virgil, were not allowed to pass the river Styx, but wandered on its banks for a hundred years.]

[Footnote 56: So does that spot.—Ver. 441. That is to say, whatever number of ghosts arrives there, it receives them all with ease, and is not sensible of the increase of number; either because the place itself is of such immense extent, or because the souls of the dead do not occupy space.]

[Footnote 57: The Sisters.—Ver. 450. These were the Furies, fabled to be the daughters of Night and Acheron. They were three in number, Tisiphone, Alecto, and Megæra, and were supposed to be the avengers of crime and wickedness.]

[Footnote 58: Tityus.—Ver. 456. Tityus was the son of Jupiter and Elara. On account of his enormous size, the poets sometimes style him a son of the earth. Attempting to commit violence upon Latona, he was slain by the arrows of Apollo, and precipitated to the infernal regions, where he was condemned to have his liver constantly devoured by a vulture, and then renewed, to perpetuate his torments.]

[Footnote 59: Tantalus.—Ver. 457. He was the son of Jupiter, by the Nymph Plote. The crime for which he was punished is differently related by the poets. Some say, that he divulged the secrets of the Gods, that had been entrusted to him; while others relate, that at an entertainment which he gave to the Deities, he caused his own son, Pelops, to be served up, on which Ceres inadvertently ate his shoulder. He was doomed to suffer intense hunger and thirst, amid provisions of all kinds within his reach, which perpetually receded from him.]

[Footnote 60: Sisyphus.—Ver. 459. Sisyphus, the son of Æolus, was a daring robber, who infested Attica. He was slain by Theseus; and being sent to the infernal regions, was condemned to the punishment of rolling a great stone to the top of a mountain, which it had no sooner reached than it fell down again, and renewed his labor.]

[Footnote 61: Ixion.—Ver. 461. Being advanced by Jupiter to heaven, he presumed to make an attempt on Juno. Jupiter, to deceive him, formed a cloud in her shape, on which Ixion begot the Centaurs. He was cast into Tartarus, and was there fastened to a wheel, which turned round incessantly.]

[Footnote 62: Iris.—Ver. 480. Iris was the daughter of Thaumas and Electra, and the messenger of Juno. She was the Goddess of the Rainbow.]

[Footnote 63: Tisiphone.—Ver. 481. Clarke translates 'Tisiphone importuna,' 'the plaguy Tisiphone.']

[Footnote 64: Echidna.—Ver. 501. This word properly means, 'a female viper;' but it here refers to the Hydra, or dragon of the marsh of Lerna, which Hercules slew. It was fabled to be partly a woman, and partly a serpent, and to have been begotten by Typhon. According to some accounts, this monster had seven heads.]

[Footnote 65: Dashes in pieces.—Ver. 519. Euripides and Hyginus relate, that Athamas slew his son while hunting; and Apollodorus says, that he mistook him for a stag.]

[Footnote 66: Thy foster-child.—Ver. 524. Bacchus was the foster-child of Ino, who was the sister of his mother Semele. The remaining portion of the story of Ino and Melicerta is again related by Ovid in the sixth book of the Fasti.]

[Footnote 67: There is a rock.—Ver. 525. Pausanias calls this the Molarian rock, and says, that it was one of the Scironian rocks, near Megara, in Attica. It was a branch of the Geranian mountain.]

[Footnote 68: And her burden.—Ver. 530. This was her son Melicerta, who, according to Pausanias, was received by dolphins, and was landed by them on the isthmus of Corinth.]

[Footnote 69: Guiltless granddaughter.—Ver. 531. Venus was the grandmother of Ino, inasmuch as Hermione, or Harmonia, the wife of Cadmus, was the daughter of Mars and Venus.]

[Footnote 70: Boundless Ionian sea.—Ver. 535. The Ionian sea must be merely mentioned here as a general name for the broad expanse of waters, of which the Saronic gulf, into which the Molarian rock projected, formed part. Ovid may, however, mean to say that Ino threw herself from some rock in the Ionian sea, and not from the Molarian rock; following, probably, the account of some other writer, whose works are lost.]

[Footnote 71: Grecian name is derived.—Ver. 538. Venus was called Aphrodite, by the Greeks, from ἄφρος, 'the foam of the sea,' from which she was said to have sprung.]

[Footnote 72: A Divinity.—Ver. 542. Ino and Melicerta were worshipped as Divinities both in Greece and at Rome.]

[Footnote 73: Sidonian attendants.—Ver. 543. The Theban matrons are meant, who had married the companions of Cadmus that accompanied him from Phœnices.]

EXPLANATION

The story of Ino, Athamas, and Melicerta appears to have been based upon historical facts, as we are informed by Herodotus, Diodorus Siculus, and Pausanias.

Athamas, the son of Æolus, and great-grandson of Deucalion, having, on the death of Themisto, his first wife, married Ino, the daughter of Cadmus, divorced her soon afterwards, to marry Nephele, by whom he had Helle and Phryxus. She having been divorced in her turn, he took Ino back again, and by her had Learchus and Melicerta. Ino, not being able to endure the presence of the children of Nephele, endeavored to destroy them. The city of Thebes being at that time afflicted with famine, which was said to have been caused by Ino, who ordered the seed to be parched before it was sown, Athamas ordered the oracle of Delphi to be consulted. The priests, either having been bribed, or the messengers having been corrupted, word was brought, that, to remove this affliction, the children of Nephele must be sacrificed.

Phryxus being warned of the designs of his stepmother, embarked in a ship, with his sister Helle, and sailed for Colchis, where he met with a kind reception from his kinsman Æetes. The young princess, however, either becoming sea-sick, and leaning over the bulwarks of the vessel, fell overboard and was drowned, or died a natural death in the passage of the Hellespont, to which she gave its name from that circumstance. Athamas, having discovered the deceitful conduct of Ino, in his rage killed her son Learchus, and sought her, for the purpose of sacrificing her to his vengeance. To avoid his fury, she fled with her son Melicerta, and, being pursued, threw herself from a rock into the sea. To console her relatives, the story was probably invented, that the Gods had changed Ino and Melicerta into Sea Deities, under the names of Leucothoë and Palæmon. Melicerta was afterwards worshipped in the Isle of Tenedos, where children were offered to him in sacrifice. In his honor, Glaucus established the Isthmian games, which were celebrated for many ages at Corinth; and, being interrupted for a time, were revived by Theseus, in honor of Neptune. Leucothoë was also worshipped at Rome, and the Roman women used to offer up their vows to her for their brothers' children, not daring to supplicate the Goddess for their own, because she had been unfortunate in hers. This Ovid tells us in the Sixth Book of the Fasti. The Romans gave the name of Matuta to Ino, and Melicerta, or Palæmon, was called Portunus.

The circumstance mentioned by Ovid, that some of Ino's attendants were changed into birds, and others into rocks, is, perhaps, only a poetical method of saying that some of her attendants escaped, while others perished with her.

FABLE VIII [IV.563-603]

The misfortunes of his family oblige Cadmus to leave Thebes, and to retire with his wife Hermione to Illyria, where they are changed into serpents.

The son of Agenor knows not that his daughter and his little grandson are now Deities of the sea. Forced by sorrow, and a succession of calamities, and the prodigies which, many in number, he had beheld, the founder flies from his city, as though the ill-luck of the spot, and not his own, pressed hard upon him, and driven, in a long series of wandering, he reaches the coast of Illyria, with his exiled wife. And now, loaded with woes and with years, while they are reflecting on the first disasters of their house, and in their discourse are recounting their misfortunes, Cadmus says, "Was that dragon a sacred one, that was pierced by my spear, at the time when, setting out from Sidon, I sowed the teeth of the dragon in the ground, a seed till then unknown? If the care of the Gods avenges this with resentment so unerring, I pray that I myself, as a serpent, may be lengthened out into an extended belly." Thus he says; and, as a serpent, he is lengthened out into an extended belly, and perceives scales growing on his hardened skin, and his black body become speckled with azure spots; and he falls flat on his breast, and his legs, joined into one, taper out by degrees into a thin round point. His arms are still remaining; those arms which remain he stretches out; and, as the tears are flowing down his face, still that of a man, he says, "Come hither, wife, come hither, most unhappy one, and, while something of me yet remains, touch me; and take my hand, while it is still a hand, and while I am not a serpent all over." He, indeed, desires to say more, but, on a sudden, his tongue is divided into two parts. Nor are words in his power when he offers to speak; and as often as he attempts to utter any complaints, he makes a hissing: this is the voice that Nature leaves him. His wife, smiting her naked breast with her hand, cries aloud, "Stay, Cadmus! and deliver thyself, unhappy one, from this monstrous form. Cadmus, what means this? Where are thy feet? where are both thy shoulders and thy hands? where is thy color and thy form, and, while I speak, where all else besides? Why do ye not, celestial Gods, turn me as well into a similar serpent?" Thus she spoke; he licked the face of his wife, and crept into her dear bosom, as though he recognized her; and gave her embraces, and reached her well-known neck.

Whoever is by, (some attendants are present), is alarmed; but the crested snakes soothe them with their slippery necks, and suddenly they are two serpents, and in joined folds they creep along, until they enter the covert of an adjacent grove. Now, too, do they neither shun mankind, nor hurt them with wounds, and the gentle serpents keep in mind what once they were.

EXPLANATION

After Cadmus had reigned at Thebes many years, a conspiracy was formed against him. Being driven from the throne, and his grandson Pentheus assuming the crown, he and his wife Hermione retired into Illyria, where, as Apollodorus says, he commanded the Illyrian army, and at length was chosen king: on his death, the story here related by Ovid was invented. It is possible that it may have been based on the following grounds:—

The Phœnicians were anciently called 'Achivi,' which name they still retained after their establishment in Greece. 'Chiva' being also the Hebrew, and perhaps Phœnician word for 'a serpent,' the Greeks, probably in reference to the Phœnician origin of Cadmus, reported after his death, that he and his wife were serpents; and in time, that transformation may have been stated to have happened at the end of his life. According to Aulus Gellius, the ancient inhabitants of Illyria had two eyelids to each eye, and with their looks, when angered, they were able to kill those whom they beheld stedfastly. The Greeks hence called them serpents and basilisks; and, it is not unlikely, that when Cadmus retired among them, they said that he had become one of the Illyrians, otherwise a dragon, or a serpent. All the ancient writers who mention his history agree that Cadmus really did retire into Illyria, where he first assisted the Enchelians in their war against the Illyrians. The latter were defeated, and, to obtain a peace from the Enchelians, they gave the crown to Cadmus; to which, on his death, his son Illyrus succeeded. The historian Christodorus, quoted by Pausanias, says that he built the city of Nygnis, in the country of the Enchelians.

Some writers have supposed, upon the authority of Euhemerus as quoted by Eusebius that Cadmus was not the son of Agenor, but was one of his officers, who eloped thence with Hermione, a singing girl. Others suppose that Cadmus is not really a proper name, but that it signifies a 'leader,' or 'conductor;' and that he received the name from leading a colony into Greece. Bochart says that he was called Cadmus, because he came from the eastern part of Phœnicia, which is called in Scripture 'Cadmonia,' or 'oriental;' and that Hermione probably received her name from Mount Hermon.

FABLE IX [IV.604-662]

Perseus, the son of Jupiter and Danaë, having killed Medusa, carries her head into Africa, where the blood that runs from it produces serpents. Atlas, king of that country, terrified at the remembrance of an oracle, which had foretold that his golden fruit should be taken by one of the sons of Jupiter, not only orders him to depart, but even resorts to violence to drive him away, on which Perseus shows him the Gorgon's head, and changes him into a mountain.

But yet their grandson, Bacchus gave them both a great consolation, under this change of form; whom India, subdued by him, worshipped as a God, and whom Achaia honored with erected temples. Acrisius the son of Abas,[74] descended of the same race,[75] alone remained, to drive him from the walls of the Argive city, and to bear arms against the God, and to believe him not to be the offspring of Jove. Neither did he think Perseus to be the offspring of Jupiter, whom Danaë had conceived in a shower of gold; but soon (so great is the power of truth) Acrisius was sorry, both that he had insulted the God, and that he had not acknowledged his grandson. The one was now placed in heaven, while the other, bearing the memorable spoil of the viperous monster, cut the yielding air with hissing wings; and while the conqueror was hovering over the Libyan sands, bloody drops, from the Gorgon's head, fell down, upon receiving which, the ground quickened them into various serpents. For this cause, that region is filled and infested with snakes.

Carried thence, by the fitful winds, through boundless space, he is borne now here, now there, just like a watery cloud, and, from the lofty sky, looks down upon the earth, removed afar; and he flies over the whole world. Three times he saw the cold Bears, thrice did he see the claws of the Crab; ofttimes he was borne to the West, many a time to the East. And now, the day declining, afraid to trust himself to the night, he stopped in the Western part of the world, in the kingdom of Atlas; and there he sought a little rest, until Lucifer should usher forth the fires of Aurora, Aurora, the chariot of the day. Here was Atlas, the son of Iapetus, surpassing all men in the vastness of his body. Under this king was the extremity of the earth, and the sea which holds its waters under the panting horses of the Sun, and receives the wearied chariot. For him, a thousand flocks, and as many herds, wandered over the pastures, and no neighboring places disturbed the land. Leaves of the trees, shining with radiant gold, covered branches of gold, and apples of gold. "My friend," said Perseus to him, "if the glory of a noble race influences thee, Jupiter is the author of my descent; or if thou art an admirer of exploits, thou wilt admire mine. I beg of thee hospitality, and a resting place." The other was mindful of an ancient oracle. The Parnassian Themis had given this response: "A time will come, Atlas, when thy tree shall be stripped of its gold, and a son of Jove shall have the honor of the prize." Dreading this, Atlas had enclosed his orchard with solid walls, and had given it to be kept by a huge dragon;[76] and expelled all strangers from his territories. To Perseus, too, he says, "Far hence begone, lest the glory of the exploits, to which thou falsely pretendest, and Jupiter as well, be far from protecting thee." He adds violence as well to his threats, and tries to drive him from his doors, as he hesitates and mingles resolute words with persuasive ones. Inferior in strength (for who could be a match for Atlas in strength?), he says "Since my friendship is of so little value to thee, accept this present;" and then, turning his face away, he exposes on the left side the horrible features of Medusa. Atlas, great as he is, becomes a mountain. Now his beard and his hair are changed into woods; his shoulders and his hands become mountain ridges, and what was formerly his head, is the summit on the top of the mountain. His bones become stones; then, enlarged on every side, he grows to an immense height (so you willed it, ye Gods), and the whole heaven, with so many stars, rests upon him.

[Footnote 74: Son of Abas.—Ver. 608. Acrisius was the son of Abas, king of Argos. He was the father of Danaë, by whom Jupiter was the father of Perseus.]

[Footnote 75: Of the same race.—Ver. 607. Some suppose that by this it is meant that as Belus, the father of Abas, and grandfather of Acrisius, was the son of Jupiter, who was also the father of Bacchus, the latter and Acrisius were consequently related.]

[Footnote 76: A huge dragon.—Ver. 647. The name of the dragon was Ladon.]

EXPLANATION

The story of the seduction of Danaë, the mother of Perseus, by Jupiter, in the form of a shower of gold, has been thus explained by some of the ancient writers. Acrisius, hearing of a prediction that Danaë, his daughter, should bring forth a child that would kill him, caused her to be shut in a tower with brazen gates, or, according to some, in a subterraneous chamber, covered with plates of that metal; which place, according to Pausanias, remained till the time of Perilaus, the king of Argos, by whom it was destroyed. The precautions of Acrisius were, however, made unavailing by his brother Prœtus; who, falling in love with his niece, corrupted the guards with gold, and gained admission into the tower. Danaë, being delivered of Perseus, her father caused them to be exposed in a boat to the mercy of the waves. Being cast on shore near Seriphus, the king, Polydectes, gave them a hospitable reception, and took care of the education of Perseus.

Diodorus Siculus says that the Gorgons were female warriors, who inhabited the neighborhood of Lake Tritonis, in Libya. Pausanias explains the story of Medusa, by saying that she ruled the people in that neighborhood, and laid waste the lands of the nations in her vicinity. Perseus, having fled, with some companions, from Peloponnesus, surprised her by night, and killed her, together with her escort. The next morning, the beauty of her face appeared so remarkable that he cut it off, and afterwards took it with him to Greece, to show it to the people, who could not look on it without being struck with astonishment. On this explanation we may remark, that if it is true, Perseus must have had more skill than the surgeons of our day, in being able to preserve the beauty of the features so long after death.

Again, many of the ancient historians, with Pliny, Athenæus, and Solinus, think that the Gorgons were wild women of a savage nature, living in caves and forests, who, falling on wayfarers, committed dreadful atrocities. Palæphatus and Fulgentius think that the Gorgons really were three young women, possessed of great wealth, which they employed in a very careful manner; Phorcus, their father, having left them three islands, and a golden statue of Minerva, which they placed in their common treasury. They had one minister in common for the management of their affairs, who used to go for that purpose from one island to another, whence arose the story that they had but one eye, and that they lent it to one another alternately. Perseus, a fugitive from Argos, hearing of the golden statue, determined to obtain it; and with that view, seized their minister, or, in the allegorical language of the poets, took their eye away from them. He then sent them word, that if they would give him the statue, he would deliver up his captive, and threatened, in case of refusal, to put him to death. Stheno and Euryale consented to this; but Medusa resisting, she was killed by Perseus. Upon his obtaining the statue, which was called the Gorgon, or Gorgonian, he broke it in pieces, and placed the head on the prow of his ship. As the sight of this, and the fame of the exploits of Perseus, spread terror everywhere, and caused passive submission to him, the fable originated, that with Medusa's head he turned his enemies into stone. Landing in the Isle of Seriphus, the king fled, with all his subjects; and, on entering the chief city, finding nothing but the bare stones there, he caused the report to be spread, that he had petrified the inhabitants.

Servius, in his Commentary on the Æneid, quotes an opinion of Ammonius Serenus, that the Gorgons were young women of such beauty as to make a great impression on all that saw them; for which reason they were said to turn them into statues. Le Clerc thinks that the story bears reference to a voyage which the Phœnicians had made in ancient times to the coast of Africa, whence they brought a great number of horses; and that the name 'Perseus' comes from the Phœnician word 'pharscha,' 'a horseman;' while the horse Pegasus was so called from the Phœnician 'pagsous,' 'a bridled horse,' according to the conjecture of Bochart. Alexander of Myndus, a historian quoted by Athenæus, says that Libya had an animal which the natives called 'gorgon;' that it resembled a sheep, and with its breath killed all those who approached it; that a tuft of hair fell over its eyes, which was so heavy as to be removed with difficulty, for the purpose of seeing the objects around it; but that when it was removed, by its looks it struck dead any person whom it gazed upon. He says, that in the war with Jugurtha, some of the soldiers of Marius were thus slain by it, and that it was at last killed by means of arrows discharged from a great distance.

The Gorgons are said to have inhabited the Gorgades, islands in the Æthiopian Sea, the chief of which was called Cerna, according to Diodorus and Palæphatus. It is not improbable that the Cape Verde Islands were called by this name. The fable of the transformation of Atlas into the mountain of that name may possibly have been based upon the simple fact, that Perseus killed him in the neighborhood of that range, from which circumstance it derived the name which it has borne ever since. The golden apples, which Atlas guarded with so much care, were probably either gold mines, which Atlas had discovered in the mountains of his country, and had secured with armed men and watchful dogs; or sheep, whose fleeces were extremely valuable for their fineness; or else oranges and lemons, and other fruits peculiar to very hot climates, for the production of which the poets especially remarked the country of Tingitana (the modern Tangier), as being very celebrated.

FABLE X [IV.663-803]

Perseus, after his victory over Atlas, and his change into a mountain, arrives in Æthiopia, at the time when Andromeda is exposed to be devoured by a monster. He kills it, and hides the Gorgon's head under the sand, covered with sea-weed and plants; which are immediately turned into coral. He then renders thanks to the Gods for his victory, and marries Andromeda. At the marriage feast he relates the manner in which he had killed Medusa; and the reason why Minerva had changed her hair into serpents.

The grandson of Hippotas[77] had shut up the winds in their eternal prison; and Lucifer, who reminds men of their work, was risen in the lofty sky, in all his splendor. Resuming his wings, Perseus binds his feet with them on either side, and is girt with his crooked weapon, and cleaves the liquid air with his winged ankles. Nations innumerable being left behind, around and below, he beholds the people of the Æthiopians and the lands of Cepheus. There the unjust Ammon[78] had ordered the innocent Andromeda to suffer punishment for her mother's tongue.[79]

Soon as the descendant of Abas beheld her, with her arms bound to the hard rock, but that the light breeze was moving her hair, and her eyes were running with warm[80] tears, he would have thought her to be a work of marble. Unconsciously he takes fire, and is astonished; captivated with the appearance of her beauty, thus beheld, he almost forgets to wave his wings in the air. When he has lighted on the ground, he says, "O thou, undeserving of these chains, but rather of those by which anxious lovers are mutually united, disclose to me, inquiring both the name of this land and of thyself, and why thou wearest these chains." At first she is silent, and, a virgin, she does not dare address[81] a man; and with her hands she would have concealed her blushing features, if she had not been bound; her eyes, 'twas all she could do, she filled with gushing tears. Upon his often urging her, lest she should seem unwilling to confess her offence, she told the name both of her country and herself, and how great had been the confidence of her mother in her beauty. All not yet being told, the waves roared, and a monster approaching,[82] appeared with its head raised out of the boundless ocean, and covered the wide expanse with its breast. The virgin shrieks aloud; her mournful father, and her distracted mother, are there, both wretched, but the latter more justly so. Nor do they bring her any help with them, but tears suitable to the occasion, and lamentations, and they cling round her body, bound to the rock.

Then thus the stranger says: "Plenty of time will be left for your tears hereafter, the season for giving aid is but short. If I were to demand her in marriage, I, Perseus, the son of Jove, and of her whom, in prison, Jove embraced in the impregnating shower of gold, Perseus, the conqueror of the Gorgon with her serpent locks, and who has dared, on waving wings, to move through the æthereal air, I should surely be preferred before all as your son-in-law. To so many recommendations I endeavor to add merit (if only the Deities favor me). I only stipulate that she may be mine, if preserved by my valor." Her parents embrace the condition, (for who could hesitate?) and they entreat his aid, and promise as well, the kingdom as a dowry. Behold! as a ship onward speeding, with the beak fixed in its prow, plows the waters, impelled by the perspiring arms[83] of youths; so the monster, moving the waves by the impulse of its breast, was as far distant from the rocks, as that distance in the mid space of air, which a Balearic string can pass with the whirled plummet of lead; when suddenly the youth, spurning the earth with his feet, rose on high into the clouds. As the shadow of the hero was seen on the surface of the sea, the monster vented its fury on the shadow so beheld. And as the bird of Jupiter,[84] when he has espied on the silent plain a serpent exposing its livid back to the sun, seizes it behind; and lest it should turn upon him its raging mouth, fixes his greedy talons in its scaly neck; so did the winged hero, in his rapid flight through the yielding air, press the back of the monster, and the descendant of Inachus thrust his sword up to the very hilt in its right shoulder, as it roared aloud.

Tortured by the grievous wound, it sometimes raises itself aloft in the air, sometimes it plunges beneath the waves, sometimes it wheels about, just like a savage boar, which a pack of hounds in full cry around him affrights. With swift wings he avoids the eager bites[85] of the monster, and, with his crooked sword, one while wounds its back covered with hollow shells, where it is exposed, at another time the ribs of its sides, and now, where its tapering tail terminates in that of a fish. The monster vomits forth from its mouth streams mingled with red blood; its wings, made heavy by it, are wet with the spray. Perseus, not daring any longer to trust himself on his dripping pinions,[86] beholds a rock, which with its highest top projects from the waters when becalmed, but is now covered by the troubled sea. Resting on that, and clinging to the upper ridge[87] of the rock with his left hand, three or four times he thrusts his sword through its entrails aimed at by him. A shout, with applause, fills the shores and the lofty abodes of the Gods. Cassiope and Cepheus, the father, rejoice, and salute him as their son-in-law, and confess that he is the support and the preserver of their house.

Released from her chains, the virgin walks along, both the reward and the cause of his labors. He himself washes his victorious hands in water taken from the sea; and that it may not injure the snake-bearing head with the bare sand, he softens the ground with leaves; and strews some weeds produced beneath the sea, and lays upon them the face of Medusa, the daughter of Phorcys. The fresh weeds, being still alive, imbibed the poison of the monster in their spongy pith, and hardened by its touch; and felt an unwonted stiffness in their branches and their leaves. But the Nymphs of the sea attempt the wondrous feat on many other weeds, and are pleased at the same result; and raise seed again from them scattered on the waves. Even now the same nature remains in the coral, that it receives hardness from contact with the air; and what was a plant in the sea, out of the sea becomes stone.

To three Deities he erects as many altars of turf; the left one to Mercury; the right to thee, warlike Virgin; the altar of Jove is in the middle. A cow is sacrificed to Minerva; a calf to the wing-footed God, and a bull to thee, greatest of the Deities. Forthwith he takes Andromeda, and the reward of an achievement so great, without any dowry. Hymenæus and Cupid wave their torches before them; the fires are heaped with abundant perfumes. Garlands, too, are hanging from the houses: flageolets and lyres, and pipes, and songs resound, the happy tokens of a joyous mind. The folding-doors thrown open, the entire gilded halls are displayed, and the nobles of king Cepheus sit down at a feast furnished with splendid preparations. After they have done the feast, and have cheered their minds with the gifts of the generous Bacchus, the grandson of Abas inquires the customs and habits of the country. Immediately one of them, Lyncides, tells him, on his inquiring, the manners and habits of the inhabitants. Soon as he had told him these things, he said, "Now, most valiant Perseus, tell us, I beseech thee, with how great valor and by what arts thou didst cut off the head all hairy with serpents." The descendant of Abas tells them that there is a spot situate beneath cold Atlas, safe in its bulwark of a solid mass; that, in the entrance of this, dwelt the two sisters, the daughters of Phorcys, who shared the use of a single eye; that he stealthily, by sly craft, while it was being handed over,[88] obtained possession of this by putting his hand in the way; and that through rocks far remote, and pathless, and bristling with woods on their craggy sides, he had arrived at the abodes of the Gorgons, and saw everywhere, along the fields and the roads, statues of men and wild beasts turned into stone, from their natural form, at the sight of Medusa; yet that he himself, from the reflection on the brass of the shield[89] which his left hand bore, beheld the visage of the horrible Medusa; and that, while a sound sleep held her and her serpents entranced, he took the head from off the neck; and that Pegasus and his brother,[90] fleet with wings, were produced from the blood of her, their mother. He added, too, the dangers of his lengthened journey, themselves no fiction;[91] what seas, what lands he had seen beneath him from on high, and what stars he had reached with his waving wings.

Yet, before it was expected,[92] he was silent; whereupon one of the nobles rejoined, inquiring why she alone, of the sisters, wore snakes mingled alternately with her hair. "Stranger," said he, "since thou inquirest on a matter worthy to be related, hear the cause of the thing thou inquirest after. She was the most famed for her beauty, and the coveted hope of many wooers; nor, in the whole of her person, was any part more worthy of notice than her hair: I have met with some who said they had seen it. The sovereign of the sea is said to have deflowered her in the Temple of Minerva. The daughter of Jove turned away, and covered her chaste eyes with her shield. And that this might not be unpunished, she changed the hair of the Gorgon into hideous snakes. Now, too, that she may alarm her surprised foes with terror, she bears in front upon her breast, those snakes which she thus produced."

[Footnote 77: Hippotas.—Ver. 663. Æolus, the God of the Winds, was the son of Jupiter, by Acesta, the daughter of Hippotas.]

[Footnote 78: Ammon.—Ver. 671. Jupiter, with the surname of Ammon, had a temple in the deserts of Libya, where he was worshipped under the shape of a ram; a form which he was supposed to have assumed, when, in common with the other Deities, he fled from the attacks of the Giants. The oracle of Jupiter Ammon being consulted relative to the sea monster, which Neptune, at the request of the Nereids, had sent against the Ethiopians, answered that Andromeda must be exposed to be devoured by it; which Ovid here, not without reason, calls an unjust demand.]

[Footnote 79: Mother's tongue.—Ver. 670. Cassiope, the mother of Andromeda, had dared to compare her own beauty with that of the Nereids. Cepheus, the son of Phœnix, was the father of Andromeda.]

[Footnote 80: Warm.—Ver. 674. 'Tepido,' 'warm,' is decidedly preferable here to 'trepido,' 'trembling.']

[Footnote 81: Dare address.—Ver. 682. Heinsius thinks that 'appellare' here is not the correct reading; and suggests 'aspectare,' which seems to be more consistent with the sense of the passage, which would then be, 'and does not dare to look down upon the hero.']

[Footnote 82: Monster approaching.—Ver. 689. Pliny the Elder and Solinus tell us that the bones of this monster were afterwards brought from Joppa, a seaport of Judæa, to Rome, and that the skeleton was forty feet in length, and the spinal bone was six feet in circumference.]

[Footnote 83: The perspiring arms.—Ver. 707. 'Juvenum sudantibus acta lacertis' is translated by Clarke, 'forced forward by the arms of sweating young fellows.']

[Footnote 84: Bird of Jupiter.—Ver. 714. The eagle was the bird sacred to Jove. The larger kinds of birds which afforded auguries from their mode of flight, were called 'præpetes.']

[Footnote 85: Avoids the eager bites.—Ver. 723. Clarke translates this line, 'He avoids the monster's eager snaps with his swift wings.']

[Footnote 86: His dripping pinions.—Ver. 730. 'Talaria' were either wings fitted to the ankles, or shoes having such wings fastened to them; they were supposed to be usually worn by Mercury.]

[Footnote 87: Clinging to the upper ridge.—Ver. 733. 'Tenens juga prima sinistra' is rendered by Clarke, 'seizing the tip-top of it with his left hand.']

[Footnote 88: Being handed over.—Ver. 766. Of course, as they had but one eye between them, they must have both been blind while it was passing from one hand to another, so that Perseus could have had but little difficulty in effecting the theft here mentioned.]

[Footnote 89: Brass of the shield.—Ver. 783. This reflecting shield Perseus is said to have received from Minerva, and by virtue of it he was enabled to see without being seen. Lucian says that Minerva herself held this reflecting shield before him, and by that means afforded him the opportunity of seeing the reflection of Medusa's figure; and that Perseus, seizing her by the hair with his left hand, and keeping his eye fixed on the image reflected in the shield, took his sword in his right, and cut off her head, and then, by the aid of his wings, flew away before the other Gorgon sisters were aware of what he had done.]

[Footnote 90: Pegasus and his brother.—Ver. 786. Pegasus and Chrysaor were two winged horses, which were fabled to have sprung up from the blood of Medusa, when slain by Perseus.]

[Footnote 91: Themselves no fiction.—Ver. 787. His dangers were not false or imaginary, inasmuch as he was pursued by Sthenyo and Euryale, the sisters of Medusa, who were fabled to have wings, and claws of iron on their hands. Ovid deals a sly hit in the words 'non falsa pericula cursus,' at the tales of travellers, who, even in his day, seem to have commenced dealing in the marvellous; as, indeed, we may learn for ourselves, on turning to the pages of Herodotus, who seems to have been often imposed upon.]

[Footnote 92: Before it was expected.—Ver. 790. Showing thereby how delighted his audience was with his narrative.]

EXPLANATION

It is extremely difficult to surmise what may have given rise to many of the fabulous circumstances here narrated. It has been conjectured by some, that Pegasus and his brother Chrysaor, the two horses produced from the blood of Medusa, were really two ships in the harbor of the island where that princess was residing at the time when she was slain by Perseus; and that, on that event, they were seized by him. Perhaps they had the figure of a winged horse on the prow; from which circumstance the fable had its origin. Possibly, the story of the production of coral from the blood of Medusa may have originated in the fact, that on the defeat of the Gorgons, navigation became more safe, and, consequently, the fishing for coral more common than it had been before.

The story of the exposure of Andromeda may be founded on the fact, that she was contracted by her parents against her will to some fierce, piratical prince, who infested the adjacent seas with his depredations; and that the betrothal was made, on condition that he should allow the realms of her father, Cepheus, to be free and undisturbed; Perseus, being informed of this, slew the pirate, and Phineus having been kept in a state of inactivity through dread of the valor of Perseus, it was fabled that he had been changed into a stone. This interpretation of the story is the one suggested by Vossius.

Some writers think, that Phineus, the uncle of Andromeda, was the enemy from which she was rescued by Perseus, and who is here represented under the form of a monster; while others suggest that this monster was the name of the ship in which the pirate before mentioned was to have carried away Andromeda.

BOOK THE FIFTH

FABLE I [V.1-242]

While Perseus is continuing the relation of the adventures of Medusa, Phineus, to whom Andromeda has been previously promised in marriage, rushes into the palace, with his adherents, and attacks his rival. A furious combat is the consequence, in which Perseus gives signal proofs of his valor. At length, perceiving himself likely to be overpowered by the number of his enemies, he shows them the head of the Gorgon; on which Phineus and his followers are turned into statues of stone. After this victory, he takes Andromeda with him to Argos, his native city, where he turns the usurper Prœtus into stone, and re-establishes his grandfather Acrisius on the throne.

And while the hero, the son of Danaë, is relating these things in the midst of the company of the subjects of Cepheus, the royal courts are filled with a raging multitude; nor is the clamor such as celebrates a marriage-feast, but one which portends dreadful warfare. You might compare the banquet, changed into a sudden tumult, to the sea, which, when calm, the boisterous rage of the winds disturbs by raising its waves.

Foremost among these, Phineus,[1] the rash projector of the onslaught, shaking an ashen spear with a brazen point, cries, "Behold! now, behold! I am come, the avenger of my wife, ravished from me; neither shall thy wings nor Jupiter turned into fictitious gold, deliver thee from me." As he is endeavoring to hurl his lance, Cepheus cries out, "What art thou doing? What fancy, my brother, impels thee, in thy madness, to this crime? Is this the due acknowledgment to return for deserts so great? Dost thou repay the life of her thus preserved, with this reward? 'Twas not Perseus, if thou wouldst know the truth, that took her away from thee; but the incensed majesty of the Nereids, and horned Ammon, and the monster of the sea, which came to be glutted with my bowels. She was snatched from thee at that moment, at which she was to have perished; unless it is that thou dost, in thy cruelty, insist upon that very thing, that she should perish, and wilt be appeased only by my affliction. It is not enough, forsooth, that in thy presence she was bound and that thou, both her uncle and her betrothed, didst give no assistance; wilt thou be grieving, besides, that she was saved by another, and wilt thou deprive him of his reward? If this appears great to thee, thou shouldst have recovered it from the rock to which it was fastened. Now, let him who has recovered it, through whom my old age is not childless, have what he stipulated for, both by his merits and his words; and know that he was preferred not before thee, but before certain death."

Phineus said nothing, on the other hand; but viewing both him and Perseus, with alternate looks, he was uncertain whether he should first attack the one or the other; and, having paused a short time, he vainly threw his spear, hurled with all the force that rage afforded. As it stood fixed in the cushion,[2] then, at length, Perseus leapt off from the couch, and in his rage would have pierced the breast of his enemy with the weapon, thrown back, had not Phineus gone behind an altar, and thus (how unworthily!) an altar[3] protected a miscreant. However, the spear, not thrown in vain, stuck in the forehead of Rhœtus; who, after he fell, and the steel was wrenched from the skull, he still struggled, and besprinkled the laid tables with his blood. But then does the multitude burst forth into ungovernable rage, and hurl their weapons. Some there are, who say that Cepheus ought to die with his son-in-law; but Cepheus has gone out by the entrance of the house, calling right and good faith to witness, and the Gods of hospitality,[4] that this disturbance is made contrary to his will. The warlike Pallas comes; and with her shield protects her brother Perseus, and gives him courage. There was an Indian, Athis by name,[5] whom Limnate, the daughter of the river Ganges, is believed to have brought forth beneath the glassy waters; excelling in beauty, which he improved by his rich dress; in his prime, as yet but twice eight years of age, dressed in a purple tunic, which a golden fringe bordered; a gilded necklace graced his neck, and a curved hair-pin his hair wet with myrrh. He, indeed, had been taught to hit things, although at a distance, with his hurled javelin, but he was more skilled at bending the bow. Perseus struck him even then, as he was bending with his hands the flexible horns of a bow, with a billet, which, placed in the middle of the altar, was smoking, and he crushed his face into his broken skull.

When the Assyrian Lycabas, who was a most attached friend of his, and no concealer of his real affection, saw him rolling his features, the objects of such praises, in his blood; after he had bewailed Athis, breathing forth his life from this cruel wound, he seized the bow which he had bent, and said, "And now let the contest against thee be with me; not long shalt thou exult in the fate of the youth, by which thou acquirest more hatred than praise." All this he had not yet said, when the piercing weapon darted from the string, and though avoided, still it hung in the folds of his garment. The grandson of Acrisius turned against him his falchion,[6] already proved in the slaughter of Medusa, and thrust it into his breast. But he, now dying, with his eyes swimming in black night, looked around for Athis, and sank upon him, and carried to the shades the consolation of a united death. Lo! Phorbas of Syene,[7] the son of Methion, and Amphimedon, the Libyan, eager to engage in the fight, fell down, slipping in the blood with which the earth was warm, soaked on every side; as they arose the sword met them, being thrust in the ribs of the one, and in the throat of Phorbas. But Perseus does not attack Erithus, the son of Actor, whose weapon is a broad battle-axe, by using his sword, but he takes up, with both hands, a huge bowl,[8] standing out with figures deeply embossed, and of vast mass in its weight, and hurls it against the man. The other vomits forth red blood, and, falling on his back, beats the ground with his dying head. Then he slays Polydæmon, sprung from the blood of Semiramis, and the Caucasian Abaris, and Lycetus, the son of Sperchius,[9] and Elyces, with unshorn locks, and Phlegias, and Clytus; and he tramples upon the heaps of the dying, which he has piled up.

But Phineus, not daring to engage hand to hand with his enemy, hurls his javelin, which accident carries against Idas, who, in vain, has declined the warfare[10] and has followed the arms of neither. He, looking at the cruel Phineus with stern eyes, says, "Since I am thus forced to take a side, take the enemy, Phineus, that thou hast made, and make amends for my wound with this wound." And now, just about to return the dart drawn from his body, he falls sinking down upon his limbs void of blood. Here, too, Odytes, the next in rank among the followers of Cepheus, after the king, lies prostrate under the sword of Clymenus; Hypseus kills Protenor, and Lyncides Hypseus. There is, too, among them the aged Emathion, an observer of justice, and a fearer of the Gods; as his years prevent him from fighting, he engages by talking, and he condemns and utters imprecations against their accursed arms. As he clings to the altars[11] with trembling hands, Chromis cuts off his head with his sword, which straightway falls upon the altar, and there, with his dying tongue he utters words of execration, and breathes forth his soul in the midst of the fires. Upon this, two brothers, Broteas and Ammon invincible at boxing, if swords could only be conquered by boxing, fell by the hand of Phineus; Ampycus, too, the priest of Ceres, having his temples wreathed with a white fillet. Thou too, son of Iapetus, not to be employed for these services; but one who tuned the lyre, the work of peace, to thy voice, hadst been ordered to attend the banquet and festival with thy music. As thou art standing afar, and holding the unwarlike plectrum, Pettalus says, laughing, "Go sing the rest to the Stygian ghosts," and fixes the point of the sword in his left temple. He falls, and with his dying fingers he touches once again the strings of the lyre; and in his fall he plays a mournful dirge.[12] The fierce Lycormas does not suffer him to fall unpunished; and tearing away a massive bar from the doorpost on the right, he dashes it against the bones of the middle of the neck of Pettalus; struck, he falls to the ground, just like a slaughtered bullock.

The Cinyphian[13] Pelates, too, was trying to tear away the oaken bar of the doorpost on the left; as he was trying, his right hand was fastened thereto by the spear of Corythus, the son of Marmarus, and it stood riveted to the wood. Thus riveted, Abas pierced his side; he did not fall, however, but dying, hung from the post, which still held fast his hand. Melaneus, too, was slain, who had followed the camp of Perseus, and Dorylas, very rich in Nasamonian land.[14] Dorylas, rich in land, than whom no one possessed it of wider extent, or received thence so many heaps of corn. The hurled steel stood fixed obliquely in his groin; the hurt was mortal. When the Bactrian[15] Halcyoneus, the author of the wound, beheld him sobbing forth his soul, and rolling his eyes, he said, "Take for thine own this spot of earth which thou dost press, out of so many fields," and he left his lifeless body. The descendant of Abas, as his avenger, hurls against Halcyoneus the spear torn from his wound yet warm, which, received in the middle of the nostrils, pierced through his neck, and projected on both sides. And while fortune is aiding his hand, he slays, with different wounds, Clytius and Clanis, born of one mother. For an ashen spear poised with a strong arm is driven through both the thighs of Clytius; with his mouth does Clanis bite the javelin. Celadon, the Mendesian,[16] falls, too; Astreus falls, born of a mother of Palestine, but of an uncertain father. Æthion, too, once sagacious at foreseeing things to come, but now deceived[17] by a false omen; and Thoactes, the armor-bearer of the king, and Agyrtes, infamous for slaying his father.

More work still remains, than what is already done; for it is the intention of all to overwhelm one. The conspiring troops fight on all sides, for a cause that attacks both merit and good faith. The one side, the father-in-law, attached in vain, and the new-made wife, together with her mother, encourage; and these fill the halls with their shrieks. But the din of arms, and the groans of those that fall, prevail; and for once, Bellona[18] is deluging the household Gods polluted with plenteous blood, and is kindling the combat anew. Phineus, and a thousand that follow Phineus, surround Perseus alone; darts are flying thicker than the hail of winter, on both his sides, past his eyes, and past his ears. On this, he places his shoulders against the stone of a large pillar, and, having his back secure, and facing the adverse throng, he withstands their attack. Chaonian[19] Molpeus presses on the left, Nabathæan Ethemon on the right.

As a tiger, urged on by hunger, when it hears the lowings of two herds, in different valleys, knows not on which side in preference to rush out, and yet is eager to rush out on both; so Perseus, being in doubt whether to bear onward to the right or to the left, repulses Molpeus by a wound in the leg, which he runs through, and is contented with his flight. Nor, indeed, does Ethemon give him time, but fiercely attacks him; and, desirous to inflict a wound deep in his neck, he breaks his sword, wielded with incautious force; and against the extremity of a column which he has struck, the blade flies to pieces, and sticks in the throat of its owner; yet that blow has not power sufficient to effect his death. Perseus stabs him with his Cyllenian[20] falchion, trembling, and vainly extending his unarmed hands.

But when Perseus saw his valor likely to yield to such numbers, he said, "Since you yourselves force me to do it, I will seek assistance from an enemy: turn away your faces, if any of my friends are here;" and then he produced the head of the Gorgon. "Go, seek some one else," said Thescelus, "for thy miracles to affect;" and, as he was preparing to hurl his deadly javelin with his hand, he stood fast in that posture, a statue of marble. Ampyx, being next him, made a pass with his sword at the breast of Lyncidas, full of daring spirit, and, while making it, his right hand became stiff, moving neither to one side nor the other. But Nileus, who had falsely boasted that he was begotten by the seven-mouthed Nile, and who had engraved on his shield its seven channels, partly in silver, partly in gold, said, "Behold, Perseus, the origin of my race; thou shalt carry to the silent shades a great consolation for thy death, that thou wast killed by one so great." The last part of his address was suppressed in the midst of the utterance; and you would think his half-open mouth was attempting to speak, but it gave no passage for his words. Eryx rebuked them,[21] and said, "Ye are benumbed by the cowardice of your minds, not by the locks of the Gorgon; rush on with me, and strike to the ground this youth that wields his magic arms." He was about to rush on, when the earth arrested his steps, and he remained an immovable stone, and an armed statue. But all these met with the punishment they had deserved: there was one man, however, Aconteus by name, a soldier of Perseus, for whom while he was fighting, on beholding the Gorgon, he grew hard with stone rising upon him. Astyages, thinking him still alive, struck him with his long sword; the sword resounded with a shrill ringing. While Astyages was in amazement, he took on himself the same nature: and the look of one in surprise remained on his marble features. It is a tedious task to recount the names of the men of the lower rank. Two hundred bodies were yet remaining for the fight: two hundred bodies, on beholding the Gorgon, grew stiff.

Now at length Phineus repents of this unjust warfare. But what can he do? He sees statues varying in form, and he recognizes his friends, and demands help of them each, called by name; and not yet persuaded, he touches the bodies next him; they are marble. He turns away his eyes; and thus suppliant, and stretching forth his hands, that confessed his fault, and his arms obliquely extended, he says, "Perseus, thou hast conquered; remove the direful monster, and take away that stone-making face of thy Medusa, whatever she may be; take it away, I pray. It is not hatred, or the desire of a kingdom, that has urged me to war: for a wife I wielded arms. Thy cause was the better in point of merit, mine in point of time. I am not sorry to yield. Grant me nothing, most valiant man, beyond this life; the rest be thine." Upon his saying such things, and not daring to look upon him, whom he is entreating with his voice, Perseus says, "What am I able to give thee, most cowardly Phineus, and, a great boon to a craven, that will I give; lay aside thy fears; thou shalt be hurt by no weapon. Moreover, I will give thee a monument to last forever, and in the house of my father-in-law thou shalt always be seen, that my wife may comfort herself with the form of her betrothed." Thus he said, and he turned the daughter of Phorcys to that side, towards which Phineus had turned himself with trembling face. Then, even as he endeavored to turn away his eyes, his neck grew stiff, and the moisture of his eyes hardened in stone. But yet his timid features, and his suppliant countenance, and his hands hanging down, and his guilty attitude, still remained.

The descendant of Abas, together with his wife, enters the walls of his native city; and as the defender and avenger of his innocent mother, he attacks Prœtus.[22] For, his brother being expelled by force of arms, Prœtus had taken possession of the citadel of Acrisius; but neither by the help of arms, nor the citadel which he had unjustly seized, did he prevail against the stern eyes of the snake-bearing monster.

[Footnote 1: Phineus.—Ver. 8. He was the brother of Cepheus, to whom Andromeda had been betrothed. There was another person of the same name, who entertained the Argonauts, and who is also mentioned in the Metamorphoses.]

[Footnote 2: In the cushion.—Ver. 34. This was probably the mattress or covering of the couch on which the ancients reclined during meals. It was frequently stuffed with wool; but among the poorer classes, with straw and dried weeds.]

[Footnote 3: An altar.—Ver. 36. This was either the altar devoted to the worship of the Penates; or, more probably, perhaps, in this instance, that erected for sacrifice to the Gods on the occasion of the nuptials of Perseus and Andromeda.]

[Footnote 4: Gods of hospitality.—Ver. 45. Jupiter was especially considered to be the avenger of a violation of the laws of hospitality.]

[Footnote 5: Athis by name.—Ver. 47. Athis, or Atys, is here described as of Indian birth, to distinguish him from the Phrygian youth of the same name, beloved by Cybele, whose story is told by Ovid in the Fasti.]

[Footnote 6: His falchion.—Ver. 69. The "Harpe" was a short, crooked sword, or falchion: such as we call a "scimitar."]

[Footnote 7: Syene.—Ver. 74. This was a city on the confines of Æthiopia, bordering upon Egypt. Ovid tells us in the Pontic Epistles (Book i. Ep. 5, l. 79), that "there, at the time of the summer solstice, bodies as they stand, have no shadow."]

[Footnote 8: A huge bowl.—Ver. 82. Clarke calls "ingentem cratera" "a swingeing bowl."]

[Footnote 9: Sperchius.—Ver. 86. This was probably a person, and not the river of Thessaly, flowing into the Malian Gulf.]

[Footnote 10: Has declined the warfare.—Ver. 91. This is an illustration of the danger of neutrality, when the necessity of the times requires a man to adopt the side which he deems to be in the right.]

[Footnote 11: Clings to the altars.—Ver. 103. In cases of extreme danger, it was usual to fly to the temples of the Deities, and to take refuge behind the altar or statue of the God, and even to cling to it, if necessity required.]

[Footnote 12: A mournful dirge.—Ver. 118. Clarke translates 'Casuque canit miserabile carmen;' 'and in his fall plays but a dismal ditty.']

[Footnote 13: Cinyphian.—Ver. 124. Cinyps, or Cinyphus, was the name of a river situate in the north of Africa.]

[Footnote 14: Nasamonian land.—Ver. 129. The Nasamones were a people of Libya, near the Syrtes, or quicksands, who subsisted by plundering the numerous wrecks on their coasts.]

[Footnote 15: Bactrian.—Ver. 135. Bactris was the chief city of Bactria, a region bordering on the western confines of India.]

[Footnote 16: The Mendesian.—Ver. 144. Mendes was a city of Egypt, near the mouth of the Nile, where Pan was worshipped, according to Pliny. Celadon was a native of either this place, or of the city of Myndes, in Syria.]

[Footnote 17: Now deceived.—Ver. 147. Because he had not foreseen his own approaching fate.]

[Footnote 18: Bellona.—Ver. 155. She was the sister of Mars, and was the Goddess of War.]

[Footnote 19: Chaonian.—Ver. 163. Chaonia was a mountainous part of Epirus, so called from Chaon, who was accidentally killed, while hunting, by Helenus, the son of Priam. It has been, however, suggested that the reading ought to be 'Choanius;' as the Choanii were a people bordering on Arabia; and very justly, for how should the Chaonians and Nabathæans, or Epirotes, and Arabians become united in the same sentence, as meeting in a region so distant as Æthiopia?]

[Footnote 20: Cyllenian.—Ver. 176. His falchion had been given to him by Mercury, who was born on Mount Cyllene, in Arcadia.]

[Footnote 21: Eryx rebuked them.—Ver. 195. 'Increpat hos Eryx' is translated by Clarke, 'Eryx rattles these blades.']

[Footnote 22: Prœtus.—Ver. 238. He was the brother of Acrisius, the grandfather of Perseus.]

EXPLANATION

The scene of this story is supposed by some to have been in Æthiopia, but it is more probably on the coast of Africa. Josephus and Strabo assert that this event happened near the city of Joppa, or Jaffa: indeed, Josephus says that the marks of the chains with which Andromeda was fastened, were remaining on the rock in his time. Pomponius Mela says, that Cepheus, the father of Andromeda, was king of Joppa, and that the memory of that prince and of his brother Phineus was honored there with religious services. He says, too, that the inhabitants used to show the bones of the monster which was to have devoured Andromeda. Pliny tells us the same, and that Scaurus carried these bones with him to Rome. He calls the monster 'a Goddess,' 'Dea Cete.' Vossius believes that he means the God Dagon, worshipped among the Syrians under the figure of a fish, or sea-monster. Some authors have suggested that the story of the creature which was to have devoured Andromeda, was a confused version of that of the prophet Jonah.

The alleged power of Perseus, to turn his enemies into stone, was probably, a metaphorical mode of describing his heroism, and the terror which everywhere followed the fame of his victory over the Gorgons. This probably caused such consternation, that it was reported that he petrified his enemies by showing them the head of Medusa. Bochart supposes that the rocky nature of the island of Seriphus, where Polydectes reigned, was the ground of the various stories of the alleged metamorphoses into stone, effected by means of the Gorgon's head.

FABLE II [V.243-340]

Polydectes continues his hatred against Perseus, and treats his victories and triumphs over Medusa as mere fictions, on which Perseus turns him into stone. Minerva leaves her brother, and goes to Mount Helicon to visit the Muses, who show the Goddess the beauties of their habitation, and entertain her with their adventure at the court of Pyreneus, and the death of that prince. They also repeat to her the song of the Pierides, who challenged them to sing.

Yet, O Polydectes,[23] the ruler of little Seriphus, neither the valor of the youth proved by so many toils, nor his sorrows have softened thee; but thou obstinately dost exert an inexorable hatred, nor is there any limit to thy unjust resentment. Thou also detractest from his praises, and dost allege that the death of Medusa is but a fiction. "We will give thee a proof of the truth," says Perseus; "have a regard for your eyes, all besides;" and he makes the face of the king become stone, without blood, by means of the face of Medusa.

Hitherto Tritonia had presented herself as a companion to her brother,[24] begotten in the golden shower. Now, enwrapped in an encircling cloud, she abandons Seriphus, Cythnus and Gyarus[25] being left on the right. And where the way seems the shortest over the sea, she makes for Thebes and Helicon, frequented by the virgin Muses; having reached which mountain she stops, and thus addresses the learned sisters: "The fame of the new fountain[26] has reached my ears, which the hard hoof of the winged steed sprung from the blood of Medusa has opened. That is the cause of my coming. I wished to see this wondrous prodigy; I saw him spring from the blood of his mother." Urania[27] replies, "Whatever, Goddess, is the cause of thy visiting these abodes, thou art most acceptable to our feelings. However, the report is true, and Pegasus is the originator of this spring;" and then she conducts Pallas to the sacred streams. She, long admiring the waters produced by the stroke of his foot, looks around upon the groves of the ancient wood, and the caves and the grass studded with flowers innumerable; and she pronounces the Mnemonian[28] maids happy both in their pursuits and in their retreat; when one of the sisters thus addresses her:

"O Tritonia, thou who wouldst have come to make one of our number, had not thy valor inclined thee to greater deeds, thou sayest the truth, and with justice thou dost approve both our pursuits and our retreat; and if we are but safe, happy do we reckon our lot. But (to such a degree is no denial borne by villany) all things affright our virgin minds, and the dreadful Pyreneus is placed before our eyes; and not yet have I wholly recovered my presence of mind. He, in his insolence, had taken the Daulian and Phocean[29] land with his Thracian troops, and unjustly held the government. We were making for the temple of Parnassus; he beheld us going, and adoring our Divinities[30] in a feigned worship he said (for he had recognized us), 'O Mnemonian maids, stop, and do not scruple, I pray, under my roof to avoid the bad weather and the showers (for it was raining); oft have the Gods above entered more humble cottages.' Moved by his invitation and the weather, we assented to the man, and entered the front part of his house. The rain had now ceased, and the South Wind now subdued by the North, the black clouds were flying from the cleared sky. It was our wish to depart. Pyreneus closed his house, and prepared for violence, which we escaped by taking wing. He himself stood aloft on the top of his abode, as though about to follow us, and said 'Wherever there is a way for you, by the same road there will be one for me.' And then, in his insanity, he threw himself from the height of the summit of the tower, and fell upon his face, and with the bones of his skull thus broken, he struck the ground stained with his accursed blood."

Thus spoke the Muse. Wings resounded through the air, and a voice of some saluting them[31] came from the lofty boughs. The daughter of Jupiter looked up, and asked whence tongues that speak so distinctly made that noise, and thought that a human being had spoken. They were birds; and magpies that imitate everything, lamenting their fate, they stood perched on the boughs, nine in number. As the Goddess wondered, thus did the Goddess Urania commence: "Lately, too, did these being overcome in a dispute, increase the number of the birds. Pierus, rich in the lands of Pella,[32] begot them; the Pæonian[33] Evippe[34] was their mother. Nine times did she invoke the powerful Lucina, being nine times in labor. This set of foolish sisters were proud of their number, and came hither through so many cities of Hæmonia, and through so many of Achaia,[35] and engaged in a contest in words such as these: "Cease imposing upon the vulgar with your empty melody. If you have any confidence in your skill, ye Thespian Goddesses, contend with us; we will not be outdone in voice or skill; and we are as many in number. Either, if vanquished, withdraw from the spring formed by the steed of Medusa, and the Hyantean Aganippe,[36] or we will retire from the Emathian plains, as far as the snowy Pæonians. Let the Nymphs decide the contest." It was, indeed, disgraceful to engage, but to yield seemed even more disgraceful. The Nymphs that are chosen swear by the rivers, and they sit on seats made out of the natural rock. Then, without casting lots, she who had been the first to propose the contest, sings the wars of the Gods above, and gives the Giants honor not their due, and detracts from the actions of the great Divinities; and sings how that Typhœus, sent forth from the lowest realms of the earth, had struck terror into the inhabitants of Heaven; and how they had all turned their backs in flight, until the land of Egypt had received them in their weariness, and the Nile, divided into its seven mouths. She tells, how that Typhœus had come there, too, and the Gods above had concealed themselves under assumed shapes; and 'Jupiter,' she says, 'becomes the leader of the flock, whence, even at the present day, the Libyan Ammon is figured with horns. Apollo, the Delian God, lies concealed as a crow, the son of Semele as a he-goat, the sister of Phœbus as a cat, Juno, the daughter of Saturn, as a snow-white cow, Venus as a fish,[37] Mercury, the Cyllenian God, beneath the wings of an Ibis.'[38]

"Thus far she had exerted her noisy mouth to the sound of the lyre; we of Aonia[39] were then called upon; but perhaps thou hast not the leisure, nor the time to lend an ear to our strains." Pallas says, "Do not hesitate, and repeat your song to me in its order;" and she takes her seat under the pleasant shade of the grove. The Muse then tells her story. "We assigned the management of the contest to one of our number. Calliope rises, and, having her long hair gathered up with ivy, tunes with her thumb the sounding chords; and then sings these lines in concert with the strings when struck."

[Footnote 23: Polydectes.—Ver. 242. Polydectes was king of the little island of Seriphus, one of the Cyclades. His brother Dictys had removed Perseus, with his mother Danaë, to the kingdom of Polydectes. The latter became smitten with love for Danaë, though he was about to marry Hippodamia. On this occasion he exacted a promise from Perseus, of the head of the Gorgon Medusa. When Perseus returned victorious, he found that his mother, with her protector Dictys, had taken refuge at the altars of the Deities, against the violence of Polydectes; on which Perseus changed him into stone. The story of Perseus afforded abundant materials to the ancient poets. Æschylus wrote a Tragedy called Polydectes,

Sophocles one called Danaë, while Euripides composed two, called respectively Danaë and Dictys. Pherecydes also wrote on this subject, and his work seems to have been a text book for succeeding poets. Polygnotus painted the return of Perseus with the head of Medusa, to the island of Seriphus.]

[Footnote 24: To her brother.—Ver. 250. As both Tritonia, or Minerva, and Perseus had Jupiter for their father.]

[Footnote 25: Gyarus.—Ver. 252. Cythnus and Gyarus were two islands of the Cyclades.]

[Footnote 26: The new fountain.—Ver. 256. This was Helicon, which was produced by a blow from the hoof of Pegasus.]

[Footnote 27: Urania.—Ver. 260. One of the Muses, who presided over Astronomy.]

[Footnote 28: Mnemonian.—Ver. 268. The Muses are called 'Mnemonides,' from the Greek word μνήμων 'remembering,' or 'mindful,' because they were said to be the daughters, by Jupiter, of Mnemosyne, or Memory.]

[Footnote 29: Phocean.—Ver. 276. Daulis was a city of Phocis; a district between Bœotia and Ætolia, in which the city of Delphi and Mount Parnassus were situate.]

[Footnote 30: Our Divinities.—Ver. 279. 'Nostra veneratus numina,' is translated by Clarke, 'and worshipping our Goddessships.']

[Footnote 31: Some saluting them.—Ver. 295. That is, crying out χαῖρε, χαῖρε, the usual salutation among the Greeks, equivalent to our 'How d'ye do?' From two lines of Persius, it seems to have been a common thing to teach parrots and magpies to repeat these words.]

[Footnote 32: Lands of Pella.—Ver. 302. Pella was a city of Macedonia, in that part of it which was called Emathia. It was famed for being the birthplace of Philip, and Alexander the Great.]

[Footnote 33: Pæonian.—Ver. 303. Pæonia was a mountainous region of Macedonia, adjacent to Emathia.]

[Footnote 34: Evippe.—Ver. 303. Evippe was the wife of Pierus, and the mother of the Pierides.]

[Footnote 35: Achaia.—Ver. 306. The Achaia here mentioned was the Hæmonian, or Thessalian Achaia. The other parts of Thessaly were Phthiotis and Pelasgiotis.]

[Footnote 36: Aganippe.—Ver. 312. Aganippe was the name of a fountain in Bœotia, near Helicon, sacred to the Muses. It is called Hyantean, from the ancient name of the inhabitants of the country.]

[Footnote 37: Venus as a fish.—Ver. 331. The story of the transformation of Venus into a fish, to escape the fury of the Giants, is told, at length, in the second Book of the Fasti.]

[Footnote 38: Wings of an Ibis.—Ver. 331. The Ibis was a bird of Egypt, much resembling a crane, or stork. It was said to be of peculiarly unclean habits, and to subsist upon serpents.]

EXPLANATION

According to Plutarch, the adventure of the Muses with Pyreneus, and of their asking wings of the Gods to save themselves, is a metaphor, which shows that he, when reigning in Phocis, was no friend to learning. As he had caused all the institutions in which it was taught to be destroyed, it was currently reported, that he had offered violence to the Muses, and that he lost his life in pursuing them. Ovid is the only writer that mentions him by name.

The challenge given by the Pierides to the Muses is not mentioned by any writer before the time of Ovid. By way of explaining it, it is said, that Pierus was a very bad poet, whose works were full of stories injurious to the credit of the Gods. Hence, in time, it became circulated, that his daughters, otherwise his works, were changed into magpies, thereby meaning that they were full of idle narratives, tiresome and unmeaning. It is not improbable that the story of Typhœus, who forces the Gods to conceal themselves in Egypt, under the forms of various animals, was a poem which Pierus composed on the war of the Gods with the Giants.

FABLE III [V.341-384]

One of the Muses repeats to Minerva the song of Calliope, in answer to the Pierides; in which she describes the defeat of the Giant Typhœus, and Pluto viewing the mountains of Sicily, where Venus persuades her son Cupid to pierce his heart with one of his arrows.

"Ceres was the first to turn up the clods with the crooked plough; she first gave corn and wholesome food to the earth; she first gave laws; everything is the gift of Ceres. She is to be sung by me; I only wish that I could utter verses worthy of the Goddess, for doubtless she is a Goddess worthy of my song. The vast island of Trinacria[40] is heaped up on the limbs of the Giant, and keeps down Typhœus, that dared to hope for the abodes of Heaven, placed beneath its heavy mass. He, indeed, struggles, and attempts often to rise, but his right hand is placed beneath the Ausonian Pelorus,[41] his left under thee, Pachynus;[42] his legs are pressed down by Lilybœum;[43] Ætna bears down his head; under it Typhœus, on his back, casts forth sand, and vomits flame from his raging mouth; often does he struggle to throw off the load of earth, and to roll away cities and huge mountains from his body. Then does the earth tremble, and the King of the shades himself is in dread, lest it may open, and the ground be parted with a wide chasm, and, the day being let in, may affright the trembling ghosts.

"Fearing this ruin, the Ruler had gone out from his dark abode; and, carried in his chariot by black horses, he cautiously surveyed the foundations of the Sicilian land. After it was sufficiently ascertained that no place was insecure, and fear was laid aside, Erycina,[44] sitting down upon her mountain, saw him wandering; and, embracing her winged son, she said, Cupid, my son, my arms, my hands, and my might, take up those darts by which thou conquerest all, and direct the swift arrows against the breast of the God, to whom fell the last lot of the triple kingdom.[45] Thou subduest the Gods above, and Jupiter himself; thou subduest the conquered Deities of the deep, and him who rules over the Deities of the deep. Why is Tartarus exempt? Why dost thou not extend the Empire of thy mother and thine own? A third part of the world is now at stake. And yet so great power is despised even in our own heaven, and, together with myself, the influence of Love becomes but a trifling matter. Dost thou not see how that Pallas, and Diana, who throws the javelin, have renounced me? The daughter of Ceres, too, will be a virgin, if we shall permit it, for she inclines to similar hopes. But do thou join the Goddess to her uncle, if I have any interest with thee in favor of our joint sway.

"Venus thus spoke. He opened his quiver, and, by the direction of his mother, set apart one out of his thousand arrows; but one, than which there is not any more sharp or less unerring, or which is more true to the bow. And he bent the flexible horn, by pressing his knee against it, and struck Pluto in the breast with the barbed arrow."

[Footnote 40: Trinacria.—Ver. 347. Sicily was called Trinacris, or Trinacria, from its three corners or promontories, which are here named by the Poet.]

[Footnote 41: Pelorus.—Ver. 350. This cape, or promontory, now called Capo di Faro, is on the east of Sicily, looking towards Italy, whence its present epithet, 'Ausonian.' It was so named from Pelorus, the pilot of Hannibal, who, suspecting him of treachery, had put him to death, and buried him on that spot.]

[Footnote 42: Pachynus.—Ver. 351. This Cape, now Capo Passaro, looks towards Greece, from the south of Sicily.]

[Footnote 43: Lilybæum.—Ver. 351. Now called Capo Marsala. It is on the west of Sicily, looking towards the African coast.]

[Footnote 44: Erycina.—Ver. 363. Venus is so called from Eryx, the mountain of Sicily, on which her son Eryx, one of the early Sicilian kings, erected a magnificent temple in her honor.]

[Footnote 45: The triple kingdom.—Ver. 368. In the partition of the dominion of the universe the heavens fell to the lot of Jupiter, the seas to that of Neptune; while the infernal regions, or, as some say, the earth, were awarded to Pluto.]

EXPLANATION

The ancients frequently accounted for natural phænomena on fabulous grounds: and whatever they found difficult to explain, from their ignorance of the principles of natural philosophy, they immediately attributed to the agency of a supernatural cause. Ætna was often seen to emit flames, and the earth was subjected to violent shocks from the forces of its internal fires when struggling for a vent. Instead of looking for the source of these eruptions in the sulphur and bituminous matter in which the mountain abounds, they fabled, that the Gods, having vanquished the Giant Typhœus, or, according to some authors, Enceladus, threw Mount Ætna on his body; and that the attempts he made to free himself from the superincumbent weight were the cause of those fires and earthquakes.

FABLE IV [V.385-461]

Pluto surprises Proserpina in the fields of Henna, and carries her away by force. The Nymph Cyane endeavors, in vain, to stop him in his passage, and through grief and anguish, dissolves into a fountain. Ceres goes everywhere in search of her daughter, and, in her journey, turns the boy Stellio into a newt.

"Not far from the walls of Henna[46] there is a lake of deep water, Pergus by name; Cayster does not hear more songs of swans, in his running streams, than that. A wood skirts the lake, surrounding it on every side, and with its foliage, as though with an awning, keeps out the rays of the sun. The boughs produce a coolness, the moist ground flowers of Tyrian hue. There the spring is perpetual. In this grove, while Proserpina is amusing herself, and is plucking either violets or white lilies, and while, with childlike eagerness, she is filling her baskets and her bosom, and is striving to outdo her companions of the same age in gathering, almost at the same instant she is beheld, beloved, and seized by Pluto;[47] in such great haste is love. The Goddess, affrighted, with lamenting lips calls both her mother and her companions,[48] but more frequently her mother;[49] and as she has torn her garment from the upper edge, the collected flowers fall from her loosened robes. So great, too, is the innocence of her childish years, this loss excites the maiden's grief as well. The ravisher drives on his chariot, and encourages his horses, called, each by his name, along whose necks and manes he shakes the reins, dyed with swarthy rust. He is borne through deep lakes, and the pools of the Palici,[50] smelling strong of sulphur, and boiling fresh from out of the burst earth; and where the Bacchiadæ,[51] a race sprung from Corinth, with its two seas,[52] built a city[53] between unequal harbors.

"There is a stream in the middle, between Cyane and the Pisæan Arethusa, which is confined within itself, being enclosed by mountain ridges at a short distance from each other. Here was Cyane,[54] the most celebrated among the Sicilian Nymphs, from whose name the pool also was called, who stood up from out of the midst of the water, as far as the higher part of her stomach, and recognized the God, and said, 'No further shall you go. Thou mayst not be the son-in-law of Ceres against her will. The girl should have been asked of her mother, not carried away. But if I may be allowed to compare little matters with great ones, Anapis[55] also loved me. Yet I married him, courted, and not frightened into it, like her.' She thus said, and stretching her arms on different sides, she stood in his way. The son of Saturn no longer restrained his rage; and encouraging his terrible steeds, he threw his royal sceptre, hurled with a strong arm, into the lowest depths of the stream. The earth, thus struck, made a way down to Tartarus, and received the descending chariot in the middle of the yawning space. But Cyane, lamenting both the ravished Goddess, and the slighted privileges of her spring, carries in her silent mind an inconsolable wound, and is entirely dissolved into tears, and melts away into those waters, of which she had been but lately the great guardian Divinity. You might see her limbs soften, her bones become subjected to bending, her nails lay aside their hardness: each, too, of the smaller extremities of the whole of her body melts away; both her azure hair, her fingers, her legs, and her feet; for easy is the change of those small members into a cold stream. After that, her back, her shoulders, her side, and her breast dissolve, vanishing into thin rivulets. Lastly, pure water, instead of live blood, enters her corrupted veins, and nothing remains which you can grasp in your hand.

"In the mean time, throughout all lands and in every sea, the daughter is sought in vain by her anxious mother. Aurora, coming with her ruddy locks does not behold her taking any rest, neither does Hesperus. She, with her two hands, sets light to some pines at the flaming Ætna, and giving herself no rest, bears them through the frosty darkness. Again, when the genial day has dulled the light of the stars, she seeks her daughter from the rising of the sun to the setting thereof. Fatigued by the labor, she has now contracted thirst, and no streams have washed her mouth, when by chance she beholds a cottage covered with thatch, and knocks at its humble door, upon which an old woman[56] comes out and sees the Goddess, and gives her, asking for water, a sweet drink which she has lately distilled[57] from parched pearled barley. While she is drinking it thus presented, a boy[58] of impudent countenance and bold, stands before the Goddess, and laughs, and calls her greedy. She is offended; and a part being not yet quaffed, the Goddess sprinkles him, as he is thus talking, with the barley mixed with the liquor.

"His face contracts the stains, and he bears legs where just now he was bearing arms; a tail is added to his changed limbs; and he is contracted into a diminutive form, that no great power of doing injury may exist; his size is less than that of a small lizard. He flies from the old woman, astounded and weeping, and trying to touch the monstrosity; and he seeks a lurking place, and has a name suited to his color, having his body speckled with various spots."

[Footnote 46: Henna.—Ver. 385. Henna, or Enna, was a city so exactly situated in the middle of Sicily that it was called the navel of that island. The worship of Ceres there was so highly esteemed, that ancient writers remarked, that you might easily take the whole place for one vast temple of that Goddess, and all the inhabitants for her priests. Proserpine is said by many authors, besides Ovid, to have been carried away by Pluto in the vicinity of Henna; though some writers say that it took place in Attica, and others again in Asia, while the Hymn of Orpheus mentions the western coast of Spain. Cicero describes this spot in his Oration against Verres: his words are, 'It is said that Libera, who is the Deity that we call Proserpine, was carried away from the Grove of Enna. Enna, where these events took place to which I now refer, is in a lofty and exposed situation; but on the summit the ground presents a level surface, and there are springs of everflowing water. The spot is entirely cut off and separated from all [ordinary] means of approach. Around it are many lakes and groves, and flowers in bloom at all seasons of the year; so that the very spot seems to portray the rape of the damsel, with which story, from our very infancy, we have been familiar. Close by, there is a cavern with its face towards the north, of an immense depth, from which they say that father Pluto, in his chariot, suddenly emerged, and carrying off the maiden, bore her away from that spot, and then, not far from Syracuse, descended into the earth, from which place a lake suddenly arose; where, at the present day, the inhabitants of Syracuse celebrate a yearly festival.']

[Footnote 47: Seized by Pluto.—Ver. 395. Pluto is here called 'Dis.' This name was given to him as the God of the Earth, from the bowels of which riches are dug up.]

[Footnote 48: Her companions.—Ver. 397. Pausanias, in his Messeniaca, has preserved the names of the companions of Ceres, having copied them from the works of Homer.]

[Footnote 49: Her mother.—Ver. 397. Homer, in his poem on the subject, represents that Ceres heard the cries of her daughter, when calling upon her mother for assistance. Ovid recounts this tale much more at length in the fourth Book of the Fasti.]

[Footnote 50: The Palici.—Ver. 406. The Palici were two brothers, sons of Jupiter and the Nymph Thalea, and, according to some, received their name from the Greek words πάλιν ἱκέσθαι, 'to come again [to life].' Their mother, when pregnant, prayed the earth to open, and to hide her from the vengeful wrath of Juno. This was done; and when they had arrived at maturity, the Palici burst from the ground in the island of Sicily. They were Deities much venerated there, but their worship did not extend to any other countries. We learn from Macrobius that the natives of Sicily pointed out two small lakes, from which the brothers were said to have emerged, and that the veneration attached to them was such, that by their means they decided disputes, as they imagined that perjurers would meet their death in these waters, *while the guiltless would be able to come forth from them unharmed. They were fetid, sulphureous pools of water, probably affected by the volcanic action of Mount Ætna.]*

[Footnote 51: The Bacchiadæ.—Ver. 407. Archias, one of the race of the Bacchiadæ, a powerful Corinthian family, being expelled from Corinth, was said to have founded Syracuse, the capital of Sicily. The family sprang either from Bacchius, a son of Dionysus, or Bacchus, or from the fifth king of Corinth, who was named Bacchis. The family was expelled from Corinth by Cypselus, either on account of their luxury and extravagant mode of life, or because they were supposed to aim at the sovereignty.]

[Footnote 52: With its two seas.—Ver. 407. Corinth is called 'Bimaris' by the Latin poets, from its having the Ægean sea on one side of it, and the Ionian sea on the other.]

[Footnote 53: Built a city.—Ver. 408. Syracuse had two harbors, one of which was much larger than the other.]

[Footnote 54: Cyane.—Ver. 412. According to Claudian, Cyane was one of the companions of Proserpine, when she was carried off by Pluto.]

[Footnote 55: Anapis.—Ver. 417. This was a river of Sicily, which, mingling with the waters of the fountain Cyane, falls into the sea at Syracuse, opposite to the island of Ortygia. This island, in which the fountain of Arethusa was situate, was separated from the isle of Sicily by a narrow strait of the sea, and communicating with the city of Syracuse by a bridge, was considered as part of it.]

[Footnote 56: An old woman.—Ver. 449. Arnobius calls this old woman here mentioned by the name of Baubo. Nicander, in his Theriaca, calls her Metaneira. Antoninus Liberalis calls her Misma, and Ovid, in the fourth Book of the Fasti, Melanina.]

[Footnote 57: Lately distilled.—Ver. 450. Orpheus, in his Hymn, calls the drink given by the old woman to Ceres κυκεών. According to Arnobius, it was a mixed liquor, called by the Romans 'cinnus;' made of parched pearled barley, honey, and wine, with flowers and various herbs floating in it. Antoninus Liberalis says, that Ceres drank it off, ἀθρόως, 'at one draught.']

[Footnote 58: A boy.—Ver. 451. According to Nicander, the boy was the son of the old woman. If so, the Goddess made her but a poor return for her hospitality.]

EXPLANATION

The story of the rape of Proserpine has caused much inquiry among writers, both ancient and modern, as to the facts on which it was founded. Some have grounded it on principles of natural philosophy; while others have supposed it to contain some portion of ancient history, defaced and blemished in lapse of time.

The antiquarian Pezeron is of opinion, that in the partition of the world among the Titan kings, Pluto had the west for his share; and that he carried a colony to the further end of Spain, where he caused the gold and silver mines of that region to be worked. The situation of his kingdom, which lay very low, comparatively with Greece, and which the ancients believed to be covered with eternal darkness, gave rise to the fable, that Pluto had got Hell for his share; and this notion was much encouraged by the subterranean nature of the mines which he caused to be worked. He thinks that the river Tartarus, so famed in the realms of Pluto, was no other than the Tartessa, or Guadalquivir of the present day, which runs through the centre of Spain. Lethe, too, he thinks to have been the Guadalaviar, in the same country. Pluto, he suggests, had heard of the beauty of Proserpine, the daughter of Ceres, queen of Sicily, and carried her thence, which gave rise to the tradition that she had been carried to the Infernal Regions.

Le Clerc, on the other hand, thinks that it was not Pluto that carried away Proserpine, but Aidoneus, king of Epirus, or Orcus king of the Molossians. Aidoneus is supposed to have wrought mines in his kingdom, and, as the entrance into it was over a river called Acheron, that prince has often been confounded with Pluto; Epirus too, which was situate very low, may have been figuratively described as the Infernal Regions; for which reason, the journeys of Theseus and Hercules into Epirus may have been spoken of as descents into the Stygian abodes. Le Clerc supposes that Ceres was reigning in Sicily at the time when Aidoneus was king of Epirus, and that she took great care to instruct her subjects in the art of tilling the ground and sowing corn, and established laws for regulating civil government and the preservation of private property; for which reasons she was afterward deemed to be the Goddess of the Earth, and of Corn. Cicero and Diodorus Siculus tell us that Ceres made her residence at Enna, or Henna, in Sicily, which name, according to Bochart, signifies 'agreeable fountain.' Cicero and Strabo agree with Ovid in telling us that Proserpine, the only daughter of Ceres, whom other writers name Pherephata, was walking in the adjacent meadows, and gathering flowers with her companions; upon which, certain pirates seized her, and, placing her in a chariot, carried her to the seaside, whence they embarked for Epirus. As Pausanias tells us, it was immediately spread abroad, that Aidoneus, or Pluto, as he was called, had done it, the act having been really committed by others, according to his orders. As those who carried her off concealed themselves in the caverns of Mount Ætna, awaiting their opportunity to escape, it was afterwards fabled that Pluto came out of the Infernal Regions at that place; as that mountain, from its nature, was always deemed one of the outlets of Hell. Upon this, Ceres went to Greece, in search of her daughter; and, resting at Eleusis, in Attica, she heard that the ship in which her daughter was carried away had sailed westward. On this, she complained to Jupiter, one of the Titan kings, but could obtain no further satisfaction than that her daughter should be permitted to visit her occasionally, whereby, at length, her grief was mitigated.

Banier does not agree with these suggestions of Pezeron and Le Clerc, and thinks that Ceres is no other personage than the Isis of the Egyptians, supposing that the story is founded on the following circumstance:—Greece, he says, was afflicted with famine in the reign of Erectheus, who was obliged to send to Egypt for corn, when those who went for it brought back the worship of the Deity who presided over agriculture. The evils which the Athenians had suffered by the famine, and the dread of again incurring the same calamity, made them willingly embrace the rites of a Goddess whom they believed able to protect them from it. Triptolemus established her worship in Eleusis, and there instituted the mysteries which he had brought over from Egypt. These had been previously introduced into Sicily, which was the reason why it was said that Ceres came from Sicily to Athens. Her daughter was said to have been taken away, because corn and fruit had not been produced in sufficient quantities, for some time, to furnish food for the people. Pluto was said to have carried her to the Infernal regions, because the grain and seeds at that time remained buried, as it were, at the very center of the earth. Jupiter was said to have decided the difference between Ceres and Pluto, because the earth again became covered with crops.

This appears to be an ingenious allegorical explanation of the story; but it is not at all improbable that it may have been founded upon actual facts, and that, having lost her daughter, and going to Attica to seek her, Ceres taught Triptolemus the mysteries of Isis; and that, in process of time, Ceres, having become enrolled among the Divinities of Greece, her worship became confounded with that of Isis.

It is very possible that the story of the transformation of Stellio into a newt may have had no other foundation than the Poet's fancy.

FABLE V [V. 462-563]

Ceres proceeds in a fruitless search for her daughter over the whole earth, until the Nymph Arethusa acquaints her with the place of her ravisher's abode. The Goddess makes her complaint to Jupiter, and obtains his consent for her daughter's return to the upper world, provided she has not eaten anything since her arrival in Pluto's dominions. Ascalaphus, however, having informed that she has eaten some seeds of a pomegranate, Ceres is disappointed, and Proserpine, in her wrath, metamorphoses the informer into an owl. The Sirens have wings given them by the Gods, to enable them to be more expeditious in seeking for Proserpine. Jupiter, to console Ceres for her loss, decides that her daughter shall remain six months each year with her mother upon earth, and the other six with her husband, in the Infernal Regions.

"It were a tedious task[59] to relate through what lands and what seas the Goddess wandered; for her search the world was too limited. She returns to Sicily; and while, in her passage, she views all places, she comes, too, to Cyane; she, had she not been transformed, would have told her everything. But both mouth and tongue were wanting to her, thus desirous to tell, and she had no means whereby to speak. Still, she gave unmistakable tokens, and pointed out, on the top of the water, the girdle[60] of Proserpine, well known to her parent, which by chance had fallen off in that place into the sacred stream.

"Soon as she recognized this, as if then, at last, she fully understood that her daughter had been carried away[61] the Goddess tore her unadorned hair, and struck her breast again and again with her hands. Not as yet does she know where she is, yet she exclaims against all countries, and calls them ungrateful, and not worthy of the gifts of corn; and Trinacria before all others, in which she has found the proofs of her loss. Wherefore, with vengeful hand, she there broke the ploughs that were turning up the clods, and, in her anger, consigned to a similar death both the husbandmen and the oxen that cultivated the fields, and ordered the land to deny a return of what had been deposited therein, and rendered the seed corrupted. The fertility of the soil, famed over the wide world, lies in ruin, the corn dies in the early blade, and sometimes excessive heat of the sun, sometimes excessive showers, spoil it. Both the Constellations and the winds injure it, and the greedy birds pick up the seed as it is sown; darnel, and thistles, and unconquerable weeds, choke the crops of wheat.

"Then the Alpheian Nymph[62] raised her head from out of the Elean waters, and drew back her dripping hair from her forehead to her ears, and said, "O thou mother of the virgin sought over the whole world, and of the crops as well, cease at length thy boundless toil, and in thy wrath be not angered with a region that is faithful to thee. This land does not deserve it; and against its will it gave a path for the commission of the outrage. Nor am I now a suppliant for my own country; a stranger I am come hither. Pisa is my native place, and from Elis do I derive my birth. As a stranger do I inhabit Sicily, but this land is more pleasing to me than any other soil. I, Arethusa, now have this for my abode, this for my habitation; which, do thou, most kindly Goddess, preserve. Why I have been removed from my native place, and have been carried to Ortygia, through the waters of seas so spacious, a seasonable time will come for my telling thee, when thou shalt be eased of thy cares, and wilt be of more cheerful aspect. The pervious earth affords me a passage, and, carried beneath its lowest caverns, here I lift my head again, and behold the stars which I have not been used to see. While, then, I was running under the earth, along the Stygian stream, thy Proserpine was there beheld by my eyes.[63] She indeed was sad, and not as yet without alarm in her countenance, but still she is a queen, and the most ennobled female in the world of darkness; still, too, is she the powerful spouse of the Infernal King."

"The mother, on hearing these words, stood amazed, as though she had been made of stone, and for a long time was like one stupefied; and when her intense bewilderment was dispelled by the weight of her grief, she departed in her chariot into the ætherial air, and there, with her countenance all clouded, she stood before Jupiter, much to his discredit, with her hair dishevelled; and she said, "I have come, Jupiter, as a suppliant to thee, both for my own offspring and for thine. If thou hast no respect for the mother, still let the daughter move her father; and I pray thee not to have the less regard for her, because she was brought forth by my travail. Lo! my daughter, so long sought for, has been found by me at last; if you call it finding[64] to be more certain of one's loss; or if you call it finding, to know where she is. I will endure the fact, that she has been carried off, if he will only restore her. For, indeed, a daughter of thine is not deserving of a ravisher for a husband, if now my own daughter is." Jupiter replied, "Thy daughter is a pledge and charge, in common to me and thee; but, should it please thee only to give right names to things, this deed is not an injury, but it is a mark of affection, nor will he, as a son-in-law, be any disgrace to us, if thou only, Goddess, shouldst give thy consent. Although other recommendations were wanting, how great a thing is it to be the brother of Jupiter! and besides, is it not because other points are not wanting, and because he is not my inferior, except by the accident of his allotment of the Stygian abodes? But if thy eagerness is so great for their separation, let Proserpine return to heaven; still upon this fixed condition, if she has touched no food there with her lips; for thus has it been provided by the law of the Destinies."

"Thus he spoke; still Ceres is now resolved to fetch away her daughter; but not so do the Fates permit. For the damsel had broke her fast; and, while in her innocence she was walking about the finely-cultivated garden, she had plucked a pomegranate[65] from the bending tree, and had chewed in her mouth seven grains[66] taken from the pale rind. Ascalaphus[67] alone, of all persons, had seen this, whom Orphne, by no means the most obscure among the Nymphs of Avernus,[68] is said once to have borne to her own Acheron within his dusky caves. He beheld this, and cruelly prevented her return by his discovery. The Queen of Erebus grieved, and changed the informer into an accursed bird, and turned his head, sprinkled with the waters of Phlegethon,[69] into a beak, and feathers, and great eyes. He, thus robbed of his own shape, is clothed with tawny wings, his head becomes larger, his long nails bend inwards, and with difficulty can he move the wings that spring through his sluggish arms. He becomes an obscene bird, the foreboder of approaching woe, a lazy owl, a direful omen to mortals.

"But he, by his discovery, and his talkativeness, may seem to have merited punishment. Whence have you, daughters of Acheloüs,[70] feathers and the feet of birds, since you have the faces of maidens? Is it because, when Proserpine was gathering the flowers of spring, you were mingled in the number of her companions? After you had sought her in vain throughout the whole world, immediately, that the waters might be sensible of your concern, you wished to be able, on the support of your wings, to hover over the waves, and you found the Gods propitious, and saw your limbs grow yellow with feathers suddenly formed. But lest the sweetness of your voice, formed for charming the ear, and so great endowments of speech, should lose the gift of a tongue, your virgin countenance and your human voice still remained."

[Footnote 59: A tedious task.—Ver. 463. 'Dicere longa mora est,' is rendered by Clarke, 'It is a tedious business to tell.']

[Footnote 60: The girdle.—Ver. 470. The zone, or girdle, a fastening round the loins, was much worn by both sexes among the ancients. It was sometimes made of netted work, and the chief use of it was for holding up the tunic, and keeping it from dragging on the ground. Among the Romans, the Magister Equitum, or 'Master of the Horse,' wore a girdle of red leather, embroidered by the needle, and having its extremities joined by a gold buckle. It also formed part of the cuirass of the warrior. The girdle was used sometimes by men to hold money instead of a purse; and the 'pera,' 'wallet,' or 'purse,' was generally fastened to the girdle. As this article of dress was used to hold up the garments for the sake of expedition, it was loosened when people were supposed to be abstracted from the cares of the world, as in performing sacrifice or attending at funeral rites. A girdle was also worn by the young women, even when the tunic was not girt up; and it was only discontinued by them on the day of marriage. To that circumstance, allusion is made in the present instance, as a proof of the violence that had been committed on Proserpine.]

[Footnote 61: Had been carried away.—Ver. 471. Clarke translates 'tunc denique raptam Scisset,' 'knew that she had been kidnapped.']

[Footnote 62: Alpheian Nymph.—Ver. 487. Alpheus was a river of Elis, in the northwestern part of Peloponnesus. Its present name is 'Carbon.']

[Footnote 63: Beheld by my eyes.—Ver. 505. Ovid here makes Arethusa the discoverer to Ceres of the fate of her daughter. In the Fourth Book of the Fasti, he represents the Sun as giving her that information, in which he follows the account given by Homer. Apollodorus describes the descent of Pluto as taking place at Hermione, a town of Argolis, in Peloponnesus, and the people of that place as informing Ceres of what had happened to her daughter.]

[Footnote 64: If you call it finding.—Ver. 520. This remark of the Goddess is very like that of the Irish sailor, who vowed that a thing could not be said to be lost when one knows where it is; and that his master's kettle was quite safe, for he knew it to be at the bottom of the sea.]

[Footnote 65: Plucked a pomegranate.—Ver. 535. It was for this reason that the Thesmophoriazusæ, in the performance of the rites of Ceres, were especially careful not to taste the pomegranate. This fruit was most probably called 'malum,' or 'pomum punicum,' or 'puniceum,' from the deep red or purple color of the inside, and not as having been first introduced from Phœnicia.]

[Footnote 66: Seven grains.—Ver. 537. He says here 'seven,' but in the Fourth Book of the Fasti, only 'three' grains.]

[Footnote 67: Ascalaphus.—Ver. 539. He was the son of Acheron, by the Nymph Orphne, or Gorgyra, according to Apollodorus. The latter author says, that for his unseasonable discovery, Ceres placed a rock upon him; but that, having been liberated by Hercules, she changed him into an owl, called ὦτον. The Greek name of a lizard being ἀσκάλαβος, Mellman thinks that the transformation of the boy into a newt, or kind of lizard, which has just been related by the Poet, may have possibly originated in a confused version of the story of Ascalaphus.]

[Footnote 68: Avernus.—Ver. 540. Avernus was a lake of Campania, near Baiæ, of a fetid smell and gloomy aspect. Being feigned to be the mouth, or threshold, of the Infernal Regions, its name became generally used to signify Tartarus, or the Infernal Regions. The name is said to have been derived from the Greek word ἄορνος, 'without birds,' or 'unfrequented by birds,' as they could not endure the exhalations that were emitted by it.]

[Footnote 69: Phlegethon.—Ver. 544. This was a burning river of the Infernal Regions; which received its name from the Greek word φλέγω, 'to burn.']

[Footnote 70: Acheloüs.—Ver. 552. The Sirens were said to be the daughters of the river Acheloüs and of one of the Muses, either Calliope, Melpomene, or Terpsichore.]

EXPLANATION

Apollodorus says, that the terms of the treaty respecting Proserpine were, that she should stay on earth nine months with Ceres, and three with Pluto, in the Infernal Regions. Other writers divide the time equally; six months to Ceres, and six to Pluto. They also tell us that the story of Ascalaphus is founded on the fact, that he was one of the courtiers of Pluto, who, having advised his master to carry away Proserpine, did all that lay in his power to obstruct the endeavors of Ceres, and hinder the restoration of her daughter, on which Proserpine had him privately destroyed; to screen which deed the Fable was invented; the pernicious counsels which he gave his master being signified by the seeds of the pomegranate. It has also been suggested that the story of his change into an owl was based on the circumstance that he was the overseer of the mines of Pluto, in which he perished, removed from the light of day. Perhaps he was there crushed to death by the fall of a rock, which caused the poets to say that Proserpine had covered him with a large stone, as Apollodorus informs us, who also says that it was Ceres who inflicted the punishment upon him. The name 'Ascalaphus' signifies, 'one that breaks stones,' and, very probably, that name was only given him to denote his employment. Some writers state that he was changed into a lizard, which the Greeks call 'Ascalabos,' and, probably, the resemblance between the names gave rise to this version of the story.

Probably, the story of the Nymph Cyane reproaching Pluto with his treatment of Proserpine, and being thereupon changed by him into a fountain, has no other foundation than the propinquity of the place where Pluto's emissaries embarked to a stream of that name near the city of Syracuse; which was, perhaps, overflowing at that time, and may have impeded their passage.

Ovid, probably, feigned that the Sirens begged the Gods to change them into birds, that they might seek for Proserpine, on the ground of some existing tradition, that living on the coast of Italy, near the island of Sicily, and having heard of the misfortune that had befallen her, they ordered a ship with sails to be equipped to go in search of her. Further reference to the Sirens will be made, on treating of the adventures of Ulysses.

The Muse continues her song, in which Ceres, being satisfied with the decision of Jupiter relative to her daughter, returns to Arethusa, to learn the history of her adventures. The Nymph entertains the Goddess with the Story of the passion of Alpheus, and his pursuit of her; to avoid which, she implores the assistance of Diana, who changes her into a fountain.

"But Jupiter being the mediator between his brother and his disconsolate sister, divides the rolling year equally between them. For now, the Goddess, a common Divinity of two kingdoms, is so many months with her mother, and just as many with her husband. Immediately the appearance of both her mind and her countenance is changed; for the brow of the Goddess, which, of late, might appear sad, even to Pluto, himself, is full of gladness; as the Sun, which has lately been covered with watery clouds, when he comes forth from the clouds, now dispersed. The genial Ceres, now at ease on the recovery of her daughter, thus asks, 'What was the cause of thy wanderings? Why art thou, Arethusa, a sacred spring?' The waters are silent, and, the Goddess raises her head from the deep fountain; and, having dried her green tresses with her hand, she relates the old amours of the stream of Elis.[71]

"'I was,' says she, 'one of the Nymphs which exist in Achaia, nor did any one more eagerly skim along the glades than myself, nor with more industry set the nets. But though the reputation for beauty was never sought by me, although, too, I was of robust make, still I had the name of being beautiful. But my appearance, when so much commended, did not please me; and I, like a country lass, blushed at those endowments of person in which other females are wont to take a pride, and I deemed it a crime to please. I remember, I was returning weary from the Stymphalian[72] wood; the weather was hot, and my toil had redoubled the intense heat. I found a stream gliding on without any eddies, without any noise, and clear to the bottom; through which every pebble, at so great a depth, might be counted, and which you could hardly suppose to be in motion. The hoary willows[73] and poplars, nourished by the water, furnished a shade, spontaneously produced, along the shelving banks. I approached, and, at first, I dipped the soles of my feet, and then, as far as the knee. Not content with that, I undressed, and I laid my soft garments upon a bending willow; and, naked, I plunged into the waters.

"'While I was striking them, and drawing them towards me, moving in a thousand ways, and was sending forth my extended arms, I perceived a most unusual murmuring noise beneath the middle of the stream; and, alarmed, I stood on the edge of the nearer bank. 'Whither dost thou hasten, Arethusa?' said Alpheus from his waves. 'Whither dost thou hasten?' again he said to me, in a hollow tone. Just as I was, I fled without my clothes; for the other side had my garments. So much the more swiftly did he pursue, and become inflamed; and, because I was naked, the more tempting to him did I appear. Thus was I running; thus unrelentingly was he pursuing me; as the doves are wont to fly from the hawk with trembling wings, and as the hawk is wont to pursue the trembling doves, I held out in my course even as far as Orchomenus,[74] and Psophis,[75] and Cyllene, and the Mænalian valleys, and cold Erymanthus and Elis. Nor was he swifter than I, but unequal to him in strength, I was unable, any longer, to keep up the chase; for he was able to endure prolonged fatigue. However, I ran over fields and over mountains covered with trees, rocks too, and crags, and where there was no path. The sun was upon my back; I saw a long shadow advancing before my feet, unless, perhaps, it was my fear that saw it. But, at all events, I was alarmed at the sound of his feet, and his increased hardness of breathing was now fanning the fillets of my hair. Wearied with the exertion of my flight, I said, 'Give aid, Dictynna, to thy armor-bearer, or I am overtaken; I, to whom thou hast so often given thy bow to carry, and thy darts enclosed in a quiver.' The Goddess was moved, and, taking one of the dense clouds, she threw it over me. The river looked about for me, concealed in the darkness, and, in his ignorance sought about the encircling cloud and twice, unconsciously did he go around the place where the Goddess had concealed me, and twice did he cry, 'Ho, Arethusa![76] Ho, Arethusa!' What, then, were my feelings in my wretchedness? Were they not just those of the lamb, as it hears the wolves howling around the high sheep-folds? Or of the hare, which, lurking in the bush, beholds the hostile noses of the dogs, and dares not make a single movement with her body? Yet he does not depart; for no further does he trace any prints of my feet. He watches the cloud and the spot. A cold perspiration takes possession of my limbs thus besieged, and azure colored drops distil from all my body. Wherever I move my foot, there flows a lake; drops trickle from my hair, and, in less time than I take in acquainting thee with my fate, I was changed into a stream. But still the river recognized the waters, the objects of his love; and, having laid aside the shape of a mortal, which he had assumed, he was changed into his own waters, that he might mingle with me. Thereupon, the Delian Goddess cleaved the ground. Sinking, I was carried through dark caverns to Ortygia,[77] which, being dear to me, from the surname of my own Goddess, was the first to introduce me to the upper air.'"

[Footnote 71: Stream of Elis.—Ver. 576. The Alpheus really rose in Arcadia; but, as it ran through the territory of the Eleans, and discharged itself into the sea, near Cyllene, the seaport of that people, they worshipped it with divine honors.]

[Footnote 72: Stymphalian.—Ver. 585. Stymphalus was the name of a city, mountain, and river of Arcadia, near the territory of Elis.]

[Footnote 73: Hoary willows.—Ver. 590. The leaf of the willow has a whitish hue, especially on one side of it.]

[Footnote 74: Orchomenus.—Ver. 607. This was a city of Arcadia, in a marshy district, near to Mantinea. There was another place of the same name, in Bœotia, between Elatea and Coronea, famous for a splendid temple to the Graces, there erected.]

[Footnote 75: Psophis.—Ver. 607. This was a city of Arcadia also, adjoining to the Elean territory, which received its name from Psophis, the daughter of Lycaon, or of Eryx, according to some writers. There were several other towns of the same name. The other places here mentioned, with the exception of Elis, were mountains of Arcadia.]

[Footnote 76: Ho, Arethusa!—Ver. 625-6. Clarke thus translates these lines:—'And twice called out Soho, Arethusa! Soho, Arethusa! What thought had I then, poor soul!']

[Footnote 77: To Ortygia.—Ver. 640. From the similarity of its name to that of the Goddess Diana, who was called Ortygia, from the Isle of Delos, where she was born.]

EXPLANATION

Bochart tells us that the story of the fountain Arethusa and the river Alpheus, her lover, who traversed so many countries in pursuit of her, has no other foundation than an equivocal expression in the language of the first inhabitants of Sicily. The Phœnicians, who went to settle in that island, finding the fountain surrounded with willows, gave it the name of 'Alphaga,' or 'the fountain of the willows.' Others, again, gave it the name of 'Arith,' signifying 'a stream.' The Greeks, arriving there in after ages, not understanding the signification of these words, and remembering their own river Alpheus, in Elis, imagined that since the river and the fountain had nearly the same name, Alpheus had crossed the sea, to arrive in Sicily.

This notion appearing, probably, to the poets not devoid of ingenuity, they accordingly founded on it the romantic story of the passion of the river God Alpheus for the Nymph Arethusa. Some of the ancient historians appear, however, in their credulity, really to have believed, at least, a part of the story, as they seriously tell us, that the river Alpheus passes under the bed of the sea, and rises again in Sicily, near the fountain of Arethusa. Even among the more learned, this fable gained credit; for we find the oracle of Delphi ordering Archias to conduct a colony of Corinthians to Syracuse, and the priestess giving the following directions:—'Go into that island where the river Alpheus mixes his waters with the fair Arethusa.'

Pausanias avows, that he regards the story of Alpheus and Arethusa as a mere fable; but, not daring to dispute a fact established by the response of an oracle, he does not contradict the fact of the river running through the sea, though he is at a loss to understand how it can happen.

FABLE VII [V.642-678]

Ceres entrusts her chariot to Triptolemus, and orders him to go everywhere, and cultivate the earth. He obeys her, and, at length, arrives in Scythia, where Lyncus, designing to kill him, is changed into a lynx. The Muse then finishes her song, on which the daughters of Pierus are changed into magpies.

"Thus far Arethusa. The fertile Goddess yoked[78] two dragons to her chariot, and curbed their mouths with bridles; and was borne through the mid air of heaven and of earth, and guided her light chariot to the Tritonian citadel, to Triptolemus; and she ordered him to scatter the seeds that were entrusted to him partly in the fallow ground, and partly in the ground restored to cultivation after so long a time. Now had the youth been borne on high over Europe and the lands of Asia,[79] and he arrived at the coast of Scythia: Lyncus was the king there. He entered the house of the king. Being asked whence he came, and the occasion of his coming, and his name, and his country, he said, 'My country is the famous Athens, my name is Triptolemus. I came neither in a ship through the waves, nor on foot by land; the pervious sky made a way for me. I bring the gifts of Ceres, which, scattered over the wide fields, are to yield you the fruitful harvests, and wholesome food.' The barbarian envies him; and that he himself may be deemed the author of so great a benefit, he receives him with hospitality, and, when overpowered with sleep, he attacks him with the sword. But, while attempting to pierce his breast, Ceres made him a lynx; and again sent the Mopsopian[80] youth to drive the sacred drawers of her chariot through the air.

"The greatest of us[81] had now finished her learned song. But the Nymphs, with unanimous voice, pronounced that the Goddesses who inhabit Helicon had proved the conquerors. Then the others, thus vanquished, began to scatter their abuse: 'Since,' said she, 'it is a trifling matter for you to have merited punishment by this contest, you add abuse, too, to your fault, and endurance is not permitted us: we shall proceed to punishment, and whither our resentment calls, we shall follow.' The Emathian sisters smiled, and despised our threatening language; and endeavoring to speak, and to menace with their insolent hands amid great clamor, they beheld quills growing out of their nails, and their arms covered with feathers. And they each see the face of the other shooting out into a hard beak, and new birds being added to the woods. And while they strive to beat their breasts elevated by the motion of their arms, they hang poised in the air, as magpies, the scandal of the groves. Even then their original talkativeness remains in them as birds, and their jarring garrulity, and their enormous love of chattering."

[Footnote 78: Goddess yoked.—Ver. 642. Clarke renders 'geminos Dea fertilis angues curribus admovit,' 'the fertile Goddess clapped two snakes to her chariot.']

[Footnote 79: Lands of Asia.—Ver. 648. Asia Minor is here meant; the other parts of Asia being included under the term 'Scythicas oras.']

[Footnote 80: Mopsopian.—Ver. 661. This very uneuphonious name is derived from Mopsopus, one of the ancient kings of Attica. It here means 'Athenian.']

[Footnote 81: The greatest of us.—Ver. 662. Namely, Calliope, who had commenced her song as the representative of the Muses, at line 341.]

EXPLANATION

Triptolemus reigned at Eleusis at the time when the mysteries of Ceres were established there. As we are told by Philochorus, he went with a ship, to carry corn into different countries, and introduced there the worship of Ceres, whose priest he was. This is, doubtless, the key for the explanation of the story, that Ceres nursed him on her own milk, and purified him by fire. Some have supposed that the fable refers to the epoch when agriculture was introduced into Greece: but it is much more probable that it relates simply to the introduction there of the mysterious worship of Ceres, which was probably imported from Egypt. It is possible that, at the same period, the Greeks may have learned some improved method of tilling the ground, acquired by their intercourse with Egypt.

Probably, the dangers which Triptolemus experienced in his voyages and travels, gave rise to the story of Lyncus, whose cruelty caused him to be changed into a lynx. Bochart and Le Clerc think that the fable of Triptolemus being drawn by winged dragons, is based upon the equivocal meaning of a Phœnician word, which signified either 'a winged dragon,' or 'a ship fastened with iron nails or bolts.' Philochorus, however, as cited by Eusebius, says that his ship was called a flying dragon, from its carrying the figure of a dragon on its prow. We learn from a fragment of Stobæus, that Erectheus, when engaged in a war against the Eleusinians, was told by the oracle that he would be victorious, if he sacrificed his daughter Proserpine. This, perhaps, may have given rise, or added somewhat, to the story of the rape of Proserpine by Pluto.

According to a fragment of Homer, cited by Pausanias, the names of the first Greeks, who were initiated into the mysteries of Ceres, were,—Celeus, Triptolemus, Eumolpus, and Diocles. Clement of Alexandria calls them Baubon, Dysaulus, Eubuleüs, Eumolpus, and Triptolemus. Eumolpus being the Hierophant, or explainer of the mysteries of Eleusis, made war against Erectheus, king of Athens. They were both killed in battle, and it was thereupon agreed that the posterity of Erectheus should be kings of Athens, and the descendants of Eumolpus should, in future, retain the office of Hierophant.

FABLE I [VI.1-145]

Arachne, vain-glorious of her ingenuity, challenges Minerva to a contest of skill in her art. The Goddess accepts the challenge, and, being enraged to see herself outdone, strikes her rival with her shuttle; upon which, Arachne, in her distress, hangs herself. Minerva, touched with compassion, transforms her into a spider.

Tritonia had meanwhile lent an ear to such recitals as these, and she approved of the songs of the Aonian maids, and their just resentment. Then thus she says to herself: "To commend is but a trifling matter; let us, too, deserve commendation, and let us not permit our divine majesty to be slighted without due punishment." And then she turns her mind to the fate of the Mæonian Arachne; who, as she had heard, did not yield to her in the praises of the art of working in wool. She was renowned not for the place of her birth, nor for the origin of her family, but for her skill alone. Idmon, of Colophon,[1] her father, used to dye the soaking wool in Phocæan[2] purple.[3] Her mother was dead; but she, too, was of the lower rank, and of the same condition with her husband. Yet Arachne, by her skill, had acquired a memorable name throughout the cities of Lydia; although, born of a humble family, she used to live in the little town of Hypæpæ.[4] Often did the Nymphs desert the vineyards of their own Tymolus, that they might look at her admirable workmanship; often did the Nymphs of the river Pactolus[5] forsake their streams. And not only did it give them pleasure to look at the garments when made, but even, too, while they were being made, so much grace was there in her working. Whether it was that she was rolling the rough wool into its first balls, or whether she was unravelling the work with her fingers, and was softening the fleeces worked over again with long drawings out, equalling the mists in their fineness; or whether she was moving the smooth round spindle with her nimble thumb, or was embroidering with the needle, you might perceive that she had been instructed by Pallas.

This, however, she used to deny; and, being displeased with a mistress so famed, she said, "Let her contend with me. There is nothing which, if conquered, I should refuse to endure." Pallas personates an old woman; she both places false gray hair on her temples, and supports as well her infirm limbs by a staff. Then thus she begins to speak: "Old age has not everything which we should avoid; experience comes from lengthened years. Do not despise my advice; let the greatest fame for working wool be sought by thee among mortals. But yield to the Goddess, and, rash woman, ask pardon for thy speeches with suppliant voice. She will grant pardon at my entreaty." The other beholds her with scowling eyes, and leaves the threads she has begun; and scarcely restraining her hand, and discovering her anger by her looks, with such words as these does she reply to the disguised Pallas: "Thou comest here bereft of thy understanding, and worn out with prolonged old age; and it is thy misfortune to have lived too long. If thou hast any daughter-in-law, if thou hast any daughter of thy own, let her listen to these remarks. I have sufficient knowledge for myself in myself, and do not imagine that thou hast availed anything by thy advice; my opinion is still the same. Why does not she come herself? why does she decline this contest?"

Then the Goddess says, "Lo! she is come;" and she casts aside the figure of an old woman, and shows herself as Pallas. The Nymphs and the Mygdonian[6] matrons venerate the Goddess. The virgin alone is not daunted. But still she blushes, and a sudden flush marks her reluctant features, and again it vanishes; just as the sky is wont to become tinted with purple, when Aurora is first stirring, and after a short time to grow white from the influence of the Sun. She persists in her determination, and, from a desire for a foolish victory, she rushes upon her own destruction. Nor, indeed, does the daughter of

Jupiter decline it, or advise her any further, nor does she now put off the contest. There is no delay; they both take their stand in different places, and stretch out two webs on the loom with a fine warp. The web is tied around the beam; the sley separates the warp; the woof is inserted in the middle with sharp shuttles, which the fingers hurry along, and being drawn within the warp, the teeth notched in the moving sley strike it. Both hasten on, and girding up their garments to their breasts, they move their skilful arms, their eagerness beguiling their fatigue. There both the purple is being woven, which is subjected to the Tyrian brazen vessel,[7] and fine shades of minute difference; just as the rainbow, with its mighty arch, is wont to tint a long tract of the sky by means of the rays reflected by the shower: in which, though a thousand different colors are shining, yet the very transition eludes the eyes that look upon it; to such a degree is that which is adjacent the same; and yet the extremes are different. There, too, the pliant gold is mixed with the threads, and ancient subjects are represented on the webs.

Pallas embroiders the rock of Mars[8] in Athens, the citadel of Cecrops, and the old dispute about the name of the country. Twice six[9] celestial Gods are sitting on lofty seats in august state, with Jupiter in the midst. His own proper likeness distinguishes each of the Gods. The form of Jupiter is that of a monarch. She makes the God of the sea to be standing there, and to be striking the rugged rocks with his long trident, and a wild horse to be springing forth[10] out of the midst of the opening of the rock; by which pledge of his favor he lays claim to the city. But to herself she gives the shield, she gives the lance with its sharp point; she gives the helmet to her head, and her breast is protected by the Ægis. She there represents, too, the earth struck by her spear, producing a shoot of pale olive with its berries, and the Gods admiring it. Victory is the end of her work. But that the rival of her fame may learn from precedents what reward to expect for an attempt so mad, she adds, in four different parts, four contests bright in their coloring, and distinguished by diminutive figures. One corner contains Thracian Rhodope and Hæmus, now cold mountains, formerly human bodies, who assumed to themselves the names of the supreme Gods. Another part contains the wretched fate of the Pygmæan matron.[11] Her, overcome in a contest, Juno commanded to be a crane, and to wage war against her own people. She depicts, too, Antigone,[12] who once dared to contend with the wife of the great Jupiter; and whom the royal Juno changed into a bird; nor did Ilion protect her, or her father Laomedon, from assuming wings, and as a white crane, from commending herself with her chattering beak. The only corner that remains, represents the bereft Cinyras;[13] and he, embracing the steps of a temple, once the limbs of his own daughters, and lying upon the stone, appears to be weeping. She surrounds the exterior borders with peaceful olive. That is the close; and with her own tree she puts an end to the work.

The Mæonian Nymph delineates Europa, deceived by the form of the bull; and you would think it a real bull, and real sea. She herself seems to be looking upon the land which she has left, and to be crying out to her companions, and to be in dread of the touch of the dashing waters, and to be drawing up her timid feet. She drew also Asterie,[14] seized by the struggling eagle; and made Leda, reclining beneath the wings of the swan. She added, how Jupiter, concealed under the form of a Satyr, impregnated Antiope,[15] the beauteous daughter of Nycteus, with a twin offspring; how he was Amphitryon, when he beguiled thee, Tirynthian[16] dame; how, turned to gold, he deceived Danaë; how, changed into fire, the daughter of Asopus;[17] how, as a shepherd, Mnemosyne;[18] and as a speckled serpent, Deois.[19] She depicted thee too, Neptune, changed into a fierce bull, with the virgin daughter[20] of Æolus. Thou, seeming to be Enipeus,[21] didst beget the Aloïdæ; as a ram, thou didst delude Theophane, the daughter of Bisaltis.[22] Thee too the most bounteous mother of corn, with her yellow hair, experienced[23] as a steed; thee, the mother[24] of the winged horse, with her snaky locks, received as a bird; Melantho,[25] as a dolphin. To all these did she give their own likeness, and the real appearance of the various localities. There was Phœbus, under the form of a rustic; and how, besides, he was wearing the wings of a hawk at one time, at another the skin of a lion; how, too, as a shepherd, he deceived Isse,[26] the daughter of Macareus. How Liber deceived Erigone,[27] in a fictitious bunch of grapes; and how Saturn[28] begot the two-formed Chiron, in the form of a horse. The extreme part of the web, being enclosed in a fine border, had flowers interwoven with the twining ivy.

Pallas could not blame that work, nor could Envy censure it. The yellow-haired Virgin grieved at her success, and tore the web embroidered with the criminal acts of the Gods of heaven. And as she was holding her shuttle made of boxwood from Mount Cytorus, three or four times did she strike the forehead of Arachne, the daughter of Idmon. The unhappy creature could not endure it; and being of a high spirit, she tied up her throat in a halter. Pallas, taking compassion, bore her up as she hung; and thus she said: "Live on indeed, wicked one,[29] but still hang; and let the same decree of punishment be pronounced against thy race, and against thy latest posterity, that thou mayst not be free from care in time to come." After that, as she departed, she sprinkled her with the juices of an Hecatean herb;[30] and immediately her hair, touched by the noxious drug, fell off, and together with it her nose and ears. The head of herself, now small as well throughout her whole body, becomes very small. Her slender fingers cleave to her sides as legs; her belly takes possession of the rest of her; but out of this she gives forth a thread; and as a spider, she works at her web as formerly.

[Footnote 1: Colophon.—Ver. 8. Colophon was an opulent city of Lydia, famous for an oracle of Apollo there.]

[Footnote 2: Phocæan.—Ver. 9. Phocæa was a city of Æolia, in Ionia, on the shores of the Mediterranean, famous for its purple dye.]

[Footnote 3: Purple.—Ver. 9. 'Murex' was a shell-fish, now called 'the purple,' the juices of which were much used by the ancients for dyeing a deep purple color. The most valuable kinds were found near Tyre and Phocæa, mentioned in the text.]

[Footnote 4: Hypæpæ.—Ver. 13. This was a little town of Lydia, near the banks of the river Cayster. It was situate on the descent of Mount Tymolus, or Tmolus, famed for its wines and saffron.]

[Footnote 5: Pactolus.—Ver. 16. This was a river of Lydia, which was said to have sands of gold.]

[Footnote 6: Mygdonian.—Ver. 45. Mygdonia was a small territory of Phrygia, bordering upon Lydia, and colonized by a people from Thrace. Probably these persons had come from the neighboring country, to see the exquisite works of Arachne. As the Poet tells us, many were present when the Goddess discovered herself, and professed their respect and veneration, while Arachne alone remained unmoved.]

[Footnote 7: Brazen vessel.—Ver. 60. It seems that brazen cauldrons were used for the purposes of dyeing, in preference to those of iron.]

[Footnote 8: Rock of Mars.—Ver. 70. This was the spot called Areiopagus, which was said to have received its name from the trial there of Mars, when he was accused by Neptune of having slain his son Halirrothius.]

[Footnote 9: Twice six.—Ver. 72. These were the 'Dii consentes,' mentioned before, in the note to Book i., l. 172. They are thus enumerated in an Elegiac couplet, more consistent with the rules of prosody than the two lines there quoted:—

'Vulcanus, Mars, Sol, Neptunus, Jupiter, Hermes, Vesta, Diana, Ceres, Juno, Minerva, Venus.']

[Footnote 10: To be springing forth.—Ver. 76-7. Clarke renders 'facit—e vulnere saxi Exsiluisse ferum,' 'she makes a wild horse bounce out of the opening in the rock.']

[Footnote 11: Pygmæan matron.—Ver. 90. According to Ælian, the name of this queen of the Pigmies was Gerane, while other writers call her Pygas. She was worshipped by her subjects as a Goddess, which raised her to such a degree of conceit, that she despised the worship of the Deities, especially of Juno and Diana, on which in their indignation, they changed her into a crane, the most active enemy of the Pygmies. These people were dwarfs, living either in India, Arabia, or Thrace, and they were said not to exceed a cubit in height.]

[Footnote 12: Antigone.—Ver. 93. She was the daughter of Laomedon, king of Troy, and was remarkable for the extreme beauty of her hair. Proud of this, she used to boast that she resembled Juno; on which the Goddess, offended at her presumption, changed her hair into serpents. In compassion, the Deities afterwards transformed her into a stork.]

[Footnote 13: Cinyras.—Ver. 98. Cinyras had several daughters (besides Myrrha), remarkable for their extreme beauty. Growing insolent upon the strength of their good looks, and pretending to surpass even Juno herself in beauty, they incurred the resentment of that Goddess, who changed them into the steps of a temple, and transformed their father into a stone, as he was embracing the steps.]

[Footnote 14: Asterie.—Ver. 108. She was the daughter of Cæus, the Titan, and of Phœbe, and was ravished by Jupiter under the form of an eagle. She was the wife of Perses, and the mother of Hecate. Flying from the wrath of Jupiter, she was first changed by him into a quail; and afterwards into a stone.]

[Footnote 15: Antiope.—Ver. 110. Antiope was the daughter of Nycteus, a king of Bœotia. Being seduced by Jupiter under the form of a Satyr, she bore two sons, Zethus and Amphion. On being insulted by Dirce, she was seized with madness, and was cured by Phocus, whom she is said to have afterwards married.]

[Footnote 16: Tirynthian.—Ver. 112. Tirynthus was a city near Argos, where Hercules was born and educated, and from which place his mother, Alcmene, derived her present appellation.]

[Footnote 17: Daughter of Asopus.—Ver. 113. Jupiter changed himself into fire, or, according to some, into an eagle, to seduce Ægina, the daughter of Asopus, king of Bœotia. By her he was the father of Æacus.]

[Footnote 18: Mnemosyne.—Ver. 114. This Nymph, as already mentioned, became the mother of the Nine Muses, having been seduced by Jupiter.]

[Footnote 19: Deois.—Ver. 114. Proserpine was called Deois, or Dêous Δηοῦς κόρη, from her mother Ceres, who was called Δηὼ by the Greeks, from the verb δήω, 'to find;' because as it was said, when seeking for her daughter, the universal answer of those who wished her success in her search, was, δήεις, 'You will find her.']

[Footnote 20: Virgin daughter.—Ver. 116. This was Canace, or Arne, the daughter of Æolus, whom Neptune seduced under the form of a bull.]

[Footnote 21: Enipeus.—Ver. 116. Under the form of Enipeus, a river of Thessaly, Neptune committed violence upon Iphimedeia, the wife of the giant Aloëus, and by her was the father of the giants Otus and Ephialtes.]

[Footnote 22: Bisaltis.—Ver. 117. Theophane was the daughter of Bisaltis. Changing her into a sheep, and himself into a ram, Neptune begot the Ram with the golden fleece, that bore Phryxus to Colchis.]

[Footnote 23: Experienced.—Ver. 119. 'Te sensit,' repeated twice in this line, Clarke translates, not in a very elegant manner, 'had a bout with thee,' and 'had a touch from thee.' By Neptune, Ceres became the mother of the horse Arion; or, according to some, of a daughter, whose name it was not deemed lawful to mention.]

[Footnote 24: Thee the mother.—Ver. 119. This was Medusa, who, according to some, was the mother of the horse Pegasus, by Neptune, though it is more generally said that it sprang from her blood, when she was slain by Perseus.]

[Footnote 25: Melantho.—Ver. 120. Melantho was the daughter either of Proteus, or of Deucalion, and was the mother of Delphus, by Neptune.]

[Footnote 26: Isse.—Ver. 124. She was a native of either Lesbos, or Eubœa. Her father, Macareus, was the son of Jupiter and Cyrene.]

[Footnote 27: Erigone.—Ver. 125. She was the daughter of Icarus, and was placed among the Constellations.]

[Footnote 28: How Saturn.—Ver. 126. By Phillyra, Saturn was the father of the Centaur Chiron. We may here remark, that Arachne was not very complimentary to the Gods, in the choice of her subjects; probably it was not her intention or wish to be so.]

[Footnote 29: Wicked one.—Ver. 136. Clarke translates 'improba,' 'thou wicked jade.']

[Footnote 30: An Hecatean Herb.—Ver. 139. This was aconite, or wolfsbane, said to have been discovered by Hecate, the mother of Medea. She was the first who sought after, and taught the properties of poisonous herbs. Some accounts say, that the aconite was produced from the foam of Cerberus, when dragged by Hercules from the infernal regions.]

EXPLANATION

The story of Arachne is most probably based upon the simple fact, that she was the most skilful artist of her time, at working in silk and wool. Pliny the Elder tells us, that Arachne, the daughter of Idmon, a Lydian by birth, and of low extraction, invented the art of making linen cloths and nets; which invention was also by some attributed to Minerva. This competition, then, for the merit of the invention, is the foundation of the challenge here described by the Poet. As, however, Arachne is said to have hanged herself in despair, she probably fell a prey to some cause of grief or discontent, the particulars of which, in their simple form, have not come down to us. Perhaps the similarity of her name and employment with those of the spider, as known among the Greeks, gave rise to the story of her alleged transformation; unless we should prefer to attribute the story to the fact of the Hebrew word "arag," signifying to spin, and, in some degree, resembling her name.

In this story, Ovid takes the opportunity of touching upon several fables, the subjects whereof he states to have been represented in the works of Minerva and Arachne. He alludes, among other matters, to the dispute between Neptune and Minerva, about giving a name to the city of Athens. St. Augustine, on the authority of Varro, says, that Cecrops, in building that city, found an olive tree and a fountain, and that the oracle at Delphi, on being consulted, stating that both Minerva and Neptune had a right to name the city, the Senate decided in favor of the Goddess; and this circumstance, he says, gave rise to the story. According to some writers, it was based on the fact, that Cranaüs changed the name of the city from Poseidonius, which it was called after Neptune, to Athenæ, after his own daughter Athena: and as the Areiopagus sanctioned this change, it was fabled that Neptune had been overcome by the judgment of the Gods.

The Jesuit Tournemine suggests the following explanation of the story:—He says, that the aborigines of Attica, being conquered by the Pelasgians, learned from them the art of navigation, which they turned to account by becoming pirates. Cecrops, bringing a colony from Saïs, in Egypt, tried to abolish this barbarous custom, and taught them a more civilized mode of life; and, among other things, he showed them how to till the earth, and to raise the olive, for the cultivation of which he found the soil very favorable. He also introduced the worship of Minerva, or Athena, as she was called, a Goddess highly honored at Saïs, and to whom the olive tree was dedicated. Her the Athenians afterwards regarded as the patroness of their city, which they called after her name. Athens becoming famous for its olives, and, considerable profit arising from their cultivation, the new settlers attempted to wean the natives from piracy, by calling their attention to agricultural pursuits. To succeed in this, they composed a fable, in which Neptune was said to be overcome by Minerva; who, even in the judgment of the twelve greater deities, had found out something of more utility than he. This fable Tournemine supposes to have been composed in the ancient language of the country, which was the Phrygian, mingled with many Phœnician words; and, as in those languages the same word signifies either a ship or a horse, those who afterwards interpreted the fable, took the word in the latter signification, and spoke of a horse instead of a ship, which was really the original emblem employed in the fiction.

Vossius thinks that the fable originated in a dispute between the sailors of Athens, who acknowledged Neptune for their chief, and the people, who followed the Senate, governed by Minerva. The people prevailed, and a life of civilization, marked by attention to the pursuits of agriculture, was substituted for one of piracy; which gave occasion for the saying, that Minerva had overcome Neptune.

With reference to the intrigues and lustful actions attributed to the various Deities by Arachne in the delineations on her embroidery, we may here remark, by way of elucidating the origin of these stories in general, that, in early times, when the earth was sunk in ignorance and superstition, and might formed the only right in the heathen world, where a king or petty chieftain demanded the daughter of a neighbor in marriage, and met with a refusal, he immediately had recourse to arms, to obtain her by force. Their standards and ships, on these expeditions, carrying their ensigns, consisting of birds, beasts, or fabulous monsters, gave occasion to those who described their feats of prowess to say, that the ravisher had changed himself into a bull, an eagle, or a lion, for the purpose of effecting his object. The kings and potentates of those days, being frequently called Jupiter, Apollo, Neptune, etc., and the priests of the Gods so named often obtaining their ends by assuming the names of the Divinities they served, we can account the more easily for the number of intrigues and abominable actions, attended by changes and transformations, which the poets and mythologists attribute to many of the Deities.

Palæphatus suggests a very ingenious method of accounting for these stories; founded, however, it must be owned, on a very low estimate of female virtue in those times. He says, that these fabulous narratives originate in the figures of different animals which were engraved on the coins of those times; and that, when money was given to buy over or to procure the seduction of a female, it was afterward said that the lover had himself taken the figure which was represented on the coin, by means of which his object had been effected.

Ovid, in common with many of the ancient historians, geographers, and naturalists, mentions the Pygmies, of which, from the time of Homer downwards, a nation was supposed to exist, in a state of continual warfare with the Cranes. Aristotle, who believed in their existence, placed them in Æthiopia; Pliny, Solinus, and Philostratus in India, near the source of the Ganges; others again, in Scythia, on the banks of the Danube. Some of the moderns have attempted to explain the origin of this prevalent notion. Olaüs Magnus thinks the Samoeids and Laplanders to have been the Pygmies of Homer. Gesner and others fancy that they have found their originals in Thuringia; while Albertus Magnus supposed that the Pygmies were the monkeys, which are so numerous in the interior of Africa, and which were taken for human beings of diminutive stature. Vander Hart, who has written a most ingenious treatise on the subject, suggests that the fable originated in a war between two cities in Greece, Pagæ and Gerania, the similarity of whose names to those of the Pygmies and the Cranes, gave occasion to their neighbors, the Corinthians, to confer on them those nicknames. It is most probable, however, that the story was founded upon the diminutive stature of some of the native tribes of the interior of Africa.

As to the fable of Pygas being changed into a crane, Banier suggests, that the origin of it may be found in the work of Antoninus Liberalis, quoting from the Theogony of Bœus. That poet, whose works are lost, says, that among the Pygmies there was a very beautiful princess, named Œnoë, who greatly oppressed her subjects. Having married Nicodamas, she had by him a son, named Mopsus, whom her subjects seized upon, to educate him in their own way. She accordingly raised levies against her own subjects; and that circumstance, together with the name of Gerane, which, according to Ælian, she also bore, gave rise to the fable, which said that she was changed into a crane; the resemblance which it bore to 'geranos,' the Greek for 'a crane,' suggesting the foundation of the story.

FABLE II [VI.146-312]

The Theban matrons, forming a solemn procession in honor of Latona, Niobe esteems herself superior to the Goddess, and treats her and her offspring with contempt; on which, Apollo and Diana, to avenge the affront offered to their mother, destroy all the children of Niobe; and she, herself, is changed into a statue.

All Lydia is in an uproar, and the rumor of the fact goes through the town of Phrygia, and fills the wide world with discourse thereon. Before her own marriage Niobe had known her,[31] at the time, when still single, she was inhabiting Mæonia and Sipylus.[32] And yet by the punishment of her countrywoman, Arachne, she was not warned to yield to the inhabitants of Heaven, and to use less boastful words. Many things augmented her pride; but yet, neither the skill of her husband, nor the descent of them both, nor the sovereignty of a mighty kingdom, pleased her so much (although all of them did please her) as her own progeny; and Niobe might have been pronounced the happiest of mothers, if she had not so seemed to herself.

For Manto, the daughter of Tiresias, foreknowing the future, urged by a divine impulse, had proclaimed through the middle of the streets, "Ye women of Ismenus, go all of you,[33] and give to Latona, and the two children of Latona, the pious frankincense, together with prayers, and wreathe your hair with laurel; by my mouth does Latona command this." Obedience is paid; and all the Theban women adorn their temples with leaves of laurel, as commanded, and offer frankincense on the sacred fires, and words of supplication. Lo! Niobe comes, surrounded with a crowd of attendants, conspicuous for the gold interwoven in her Phrygian garments, and beautiful, so far as anger will allow; and tossing her hair, hanging down on both shoulders, with her graceful head, she stands still; and as she loftily casts around her haughty eyes, she says, "What madness is this to prefer the inhabitants of Heaven, that you have only heard of, to those who are seen? or why is Latona worshipped at the altars, and my Godhead is still without its due frankincense? Tantalus was my father, who alone was allowed to approach the tables of the Gods above. The sister of the Pleiades[34] is my mother; the most mighty Atlas is my grandsire, who bears the æthereal skies upon his neck. Jupiter is my other grandsire; of him, too, I boast as my father-in-law.[35] The Phrygian nations dread me; the palace of Cadmus is subject to me as its mistress; and the walls that were formed by the strings of my husband's lyre, together with their people, are governed by me and my husband; to whatever part of the house I turn my eyes, immense wealth is seen. To this is added a face worthy of a Goddess. Add to this my seven daughters,[36] and as many sons, and, at a future day, sons-in-law and daughters-in-law. Now inquire what ground my pride has for its existence; and presume to prefer Latona the Titaness, the daughter of some obscure Cæus, to whom, when in travail,[37] the great earth once refused a little spot, to myself. Neither by heaven, nor by earth, nor by water, was your Goddess received; she was banished the world, till Delos, pitying the wanderer, said, "Thou dost roam a stranger on the land, I in the waves;" and gave her an unstable place of rest. She was made the mother of two children, that is but the seventh part of my issue. I am fortunate, and who shall deny it? and fortunate I shall remain; who, too, can doubt of that? Plenty has made me secure; I am too great for Fortune possibly to hurt; and, though she should take away many things from me, even then much more will she leave me: my many blessings have now risen superior to apprehensions. Suppose it possible for some part of this multitude of my children to be taken away from me; still, thus stripped, I shall not be reduced to two, the number of Latona; an amount, by the number of which, how far, I pray, is she removed from one that is childless? Go from the sacrifice; hasten away from the sacrifice, and remove the laurel from your hair!"

They remove it, and the sacrifice they leave unperformed; and what they can do, they adore the Divinity in gentle murmurs. The Goddess was indignant; and on the highest top of Mount Cynthus, she spoke to her two children in such words as these: "Behold! I, your mother, proud of having borne you, and who shall yield to no one of the Goddesses, except to Juno alone, am called in question whether I am a Goddess, and, for all future ages, I am driven from the altars devoted to me, unless you give me aid. Nor is this my only grief; the daughter of Tantalus has added abusive language to her shocking deeds, and has dared to postpone you to her own children, and (what I wish may fall upon herself), she has called me childless; and the profane wretch has discovered a tongue like her father's."[38] To this relation Latona was going to add entreaties, when Phœbus said, "Cease thy complaints, 'tis prolonging the delay of her punishment." Phœbe said the same; and, by a speedy descent through the air, they arrived, covered with clouds, at the citadel of Cadmus.

There was near the walls a plain, level, and extending far and wide, trampled continually by horses, where multitudes of wheels and hard hoofs had softened the clods placed beneath them. There, part of the seven sons of Amphion are mounting upon their spirited steeds, and press their backs, red with the Tyrian dye, and wield the reins heavy with gold; of these, Ismenus, who had formerly been the first burden of his mother, while he is guiding the steps of the horses in a perfect circle, and is curbing their foaming mouths, cries aloud, "Ah, wretched me!" and, pierced through the middle of his breast, bears a dart therein; and the reins dropping from his dying hand, by degrees he falls on his side, over the horse's shoulder. The next to him, Sipylus, on hearing the sound of a quiver in the air, gives rein[39] to his horse; as when the pilot, sensible of the storm approaching, flies on seeing a cloud, and unfurls the hanging sails on every side, that the light breeze may by no means escape them. He gives rein, I said; while thus giving it, the unerring dart overtakes him, and an arrow sticks quivering in the top of his neck, and the bare steel protrudes from his throat. He, as he is bending forward, rolls over the neck, now let loose, and over the mane, and stains the ground with his warm blood. The unhappy Phædimus, and Tantalus, the heir to the name of his grandsire, when they had put an end to their wonted exercise of riding, had turned to the youthful exercises of the palæstra, glowing with oil;[40] and now had they brought[41] breast to breast, struggling in a close grapple, when an arrow, sped onward from the stretched bow, pierced them both, just as they were united together. At the same instant they groaned aloud, and together they laid their limbs on the ground, writhing with pain; together as they lay, for the last time, they rolled their eyeballs, and together they breathed forth their life.

Alphenor sees this, and, beating his torn breast, flies to them, to lift up their cold limbs in his embrace, and falls in this affectionate duty. For the Delian God pierces the inner part of his midriff with the fatal steel. Soon as it is pulled out, a part of his lungs is dragged forth on the barbs, and his blood is poured forth, with his life, into the air; but no single wound reaches the unshaven Damasicthon. He is struck where the leg commences, and where the sinewy ham makes the space between the joints soft; and while he is trying with his hand to draw out the fatal weapon, another arrow is driven through his neck, up to the feathers. The blood drives this out, and itself starting forth, springs up on high, and, piercing the air, spouts forth afar. The last of them, Ilioneus, had raised his unavailing arms in prayer, and had said, "O, all ye Gods, in common, (not knowing that all were not to be addressed) spare me!" The God, the bearer of the bow, was moved, when now his arrow could not be recalled; yet he died with the slightest wound of all, his heart not being struck deep by the arrow.

The report of this calamity, and the grief of the people, and the tears of her family, made the mother acquainted with a calamity so sudden, wondering that it could have happened, and enraged that the Gods above had dared this, and that they enjoyed a privilege so great. For Amphion the father, thrusting his sword through his breast, dying, had ended his grief together with his life. Alas! how different is this Niobe from that Niobe who had lately driven the people from the altars of Latona, and, with lofty head, had directed her steps through the midst of the city, envied by her own people, but now to be pitied even by an enemy! She falls down upon the cold bodies, and with no distinction she distributes her last kisses among all her sons. Raising her livid arms from these towards heaven, she says, "Glut thyself, cruel Latona, with my sorrow; glut thyself, and satiate thy breast with my mourning; satiate, too, thy relentless heart with seven deaths. I have received my death-blow;[42] exult and triumph, my victorious enemy. But why victorious? More remains to me, in my misery, than to thee, in thy happiness. Even after so many deaths, I am the conqueror." Thus she spoke; when the string twanged from the bent bow, which affrighted all but Niobe alone; she became bold by her misfortunes.

The sisters were standing in black array, with their hair dishevelled, before the biers[43] of their brothers. One of these, drawing out the weapon sticking in her entrails, about to die, swooned away, with her face placed upon her brother. Another, endeavoring to console her wretched parent, was suddenly silent, and was doubled together with an invisible wound; and did not close her mouth, until after the breath had departed. Another, vainly flying, falls down; another dies upon her sister; another lies hid; another you might see trembling. And now six being put to death, and having received different wounds, the last only remains; her mother covering her with all her body, and with all her garments, cries, "Leave me but one, and that the youngest; the youngest only do I ask out of so many, and that but one." And while she was entreating, she, for whom she was entreating, was slain. Childless, she sat down among her dead sons and daughters and husband, and became hardened by her woes. The breeze moves no hair of hers; in her features is a color without blood; her eyes stand unmoved in her sad cheeks; in her form there is no appearance of life. Her tongue itself, too, congeals within, together with her hardened palate, and the veins cease to be able to be moved. Her neck can neither be bent, nor can her arms give any motion, nor her feet move. Within her entrails, too, it is stone.

Still did she weep on; and, enveloped in a hurricane of mighty wind, she was borne away to her native land. There, fixed on the top of a mountain,[44] she dissolves; and even yet does the marble distil tears.

[Footnote 31: Had known her.—Ver. 148. This was the more likely, as Tantalus, the father of Niobe, was king of both Phrygia and Lydia.]

[Footnote 32: Sipylus.—Ver. 149. This was the name of both a city and a mountain of Lydia.]

[Footnote 33: Go all of you.—Ver. 159. Clarke renders the words 'Ismenides, ite frequentes,' 'Go, ye Theban ladies in general.']

[Footnote 34: Sister of the Pleiades.—Ver. 174. Taygete, one of the Pleiades, was the mother of Niobe.]

[Footnote 35: As my father-in-law.—Ver. 176. Because Jupiter was the father of her husband, Amphion.]

[Footnote 36: Seven daughters.—Ver. 182. Tzetzes enumerates fourteen daughters of Niobe, and gives their names.]

[Footnote 37: When in travail.—Ver. 187. She alludes to the occasion on which Latona fled from the serpent Python, which Juno, in her jealousy, had sent against her; and when Delos, which had hitherto been a floating island, became immovable, for the convenience of Latona, in labor with Apollo and Diana. That island was said to have received its name from the Greek, δῆλος, 'manifest,' or 'appearing,' from having risen to the surface of the sea on that occasion.]

[Footnote 38: Like her father's.—Ver. 213. Latona alludes to one of the crimes of Tantalus, the father of Niobe, who was accused of having indiscreetly divulged the secrets of the Gods.]

[Footnote 39: Gives rein.—Ver. 230. This was done with the intention of making his escape.]

[Footnote 40: Glowing with oil.—Ver. 241. Clarke renders this line, 'Were gone to the juvenile work of neat wrestling.' It would be hard to say what 'neat' wrestling is. He seems not to have known, that the 'Palæstra' was called 'nitida,' as shining with the oil which the wrestlers used for making their limbs supple, and the more difficult for their antagonist to grasp. Juvenal gives the epithet 'ceromaticum' to the neck of the athlete, or wrestler, which word means 'rubbed with wrestler's oil.']

[Footnote 41: Now had they brought.—Ver. 243-4. Clarke thus translates 'Et jam contulerant arcto luctantia nexu Pectora pectoribus;' 'And now they had clapped breast to breast, struggling in a close hug.']

[Footnote 42: I have received my death-blow.—Ver. 283. 'Efferor' literally means, 'I am carried out.' 'Effero' was the term used to signify the carrying of the body out of the city walls, for the purposes of burial.]

[Footnote 43: Before the biers.—Ver. 289. The body of the deceased person was in ancient times laid out on a bed of the ordinary kind, with a pillow for supporting the head and back; among the Romans, it was placed in the vestibule of the house, with its feet towards the door, and was dressed in the best robe which the deceased had worn when alive. Among the better classes, the body was borne to the place of burial, or the funeral pile, on a couch, which was called 'feretrum,' or 'capulus.' This was sometimes made of ivory, and covered with gold and purple.]

[Footnote 44: Top of a mountain.—Ver. 311. This was Mount Sipylus, in Bœotia, which, as we learn from Pausanias, had on its summit a rock, which, at a distance, strongly resembled a female in an attitude of sorrow. This resemblance is said to exist even at the present day.]

EXPLANATION

All the ancient historians agree with Diodorus Siculus and Apollodorus, that Niobe was the daughter of Tantalus, and the sister of Pelops; but she must not be confounded with a second Niobe, who was the daughter of Phoroneus, and the first mortal (Homer tells us) with whom Jupiter fell in love. Homer says that she was the mother of twelve children, six sons and six daughters. Herodotus says, that she had but two sons and three daughters. Diodorus Siculus makes her the mother of fourteen children, seven of each sex. Apollodorus, on the authority of Hesiod, says, that she had ten sons and as many daughters; but gives the names of fourteen only. The story of the destruction of her children is most likely based upon truth, and bears reference to a historical fact. The plague, which ravaged the city of Thebes, destroyed all the children of Niobe; and contagious distempers being attributed to the excessive heat of the sun, it was fabled that Apollo had killed them with his arrows; while women, who died of the plague, were said to owe their death to the anger of Diana. Thus, Homer says, that Laodamia and the mother of Andromache were killed by Diana. Valerius Flaccus relates the sorrow of Clytie, the wife of Cyzicus, on the death of her mother, killed by the same Goddess; so the Scholiast on Pindar (Pythia, ode iii.) says, on the authority of Pherecydes, that Apollo sent Diana to kill Coronis and several other women. Eustathius distinctly asserts, that the poets attributed the deaths of men, who died of the plague, to Apollo; and those of women, dying a similar death, to Diana.

This supposition is based upon rational and just grounds; since many contagious distempers may be clearly traced to the exhalations of the earth, acted on by the intense heat of the sun. Homer, most probably, means this, when he says that the plague came upon the Grecian camp, on the God, in his anger, discharging his arrows against it; or, in other words, when the extreme heat of his rays had caused a corruption of the atmosphere. It may be here observed, that arrows were the symbol of Apollo, when angry, and the harp when he was propitious. Diogenes Laertius tells us, that, during the prevalence of the plague, it was the custom to place branches of laurel on the doors of the houses, in the hope that the God, being reminded of Daphne, would spare the places which thereby claimed his protection.

Ovid says, that the sons of Niobe were killed while managing their horses; but Pausanias tells us that they died on Mount Cithæron, while engaged in hunting, and that her daughters died at Thebes. Homer says, that her children remained nine days without burial, because the Gods changed the Thebans into stones, and that the offended Divinities themselves performed the funeral rites on the tenth day; the meaning probably, is, that, they dying of the plague, no one ventured to bury them, and all seemed insensible to the sorrows of Niobe, as each consulted his own safety. Ismenus, her eldest son, not being able to endure the pain of his malady, is said to have thrown himself into a river of Bœotia, which, from that circumstance, received his name. After the death of her husband and children, Niobe is said to have retired to Mount Sipylus, in Lydia, where she died. Here, as Pausanias informs us, was a rock, resembling, at a distance, a woman overwhelmed with grief; though according to the same author, who had visited it, the resemblance could not be traced on approaching it. On this ground, Ovid relates, that she was borne on a whirlwind to the top of a Lydian mountain, where she was changed into a rock.

Pausanias tells us, that Melibœa, or Chloris, and Amycle, two of her daughters, appeased Diana, who preserved their lives; or that, in other words, they recovered from the plague; though he inclines to credit the version of Homer, who says that all of her children died by the hands of Apollo and Diana. Melibœa received the surname of Chloris, from the paleness which ensued on her alarm at the sudden death of her sisters.

FABLE III [VI.313-381]

Latona, fatigued with the burden of her two children, during a long journey, and parched with thirst, goes to drink at a pond, near which some countrymen are at work. These clowns, in a brutal manner, not only hinder her from drinking, but trouble the water to make it muddy; on which, the Goddess, to punish their brutality, transforms them into frogs.

But then, all, both women and men, dread the wrath of the divinity, thus manifested, and with more zeal than ever all venerate with divine worship the great godhead of the Deity who produced the twins; and, as commonly happens, from a recent fact they recur to the narration of former events.

One of them says, "Some countrymen of old, in the fields of fertile Lycia, once insulted the Goddess, but not with impunity. The thing, indeed, is but little known, through the obscure station of the individuals, still it is wonderful. I have seen upon the spot, the pool and the lake noted for the miracle. For my father being now advanced in years, and incapable of travel, ordered me to bring thence some choice oxen, and on my setting out, had given me a guide of that nation: with whom, while I was traversing the pastures, behold! an ancient altar, black with the ashes of sacrifices, was standing in the middle of a lake, surrounded with quivering reeds. My guide stood still, and said in a timid whisper, 'Be propitious to me;' and with a like whisper, I said, 'Be propitious.' However, I asked him whether it was an altar of the Naiads, or of Faunus, or of some native God; when the stranger answered me in such words; 'Young man, there is no mountain Divinity for this altar. She calls this her own, whom once the royal Juno banished from the world; whom the wandering Delos, at the time when it was swimming as a light island, hardly received at her entreaties. There Latona, leaning against a palm, together with the tree of Pallas, brought forth twins, in spite of their stepmother Juno. Hence, too, the newly delivered Goddess is said to have fled from Juno, and in her bosom to have carried the two divinities, her children. And now the Goddess, wearied with her prolonged toil, being parched with the heat of the season, contracted thirst in the country of Lycia, which bred the Chimæra[45] when the intense sun was scorching the fields; the craving children, too, had exhausted her suckling breasts. By chance she beheld a lake[46] of fine water, in the bottom of a valley; some countrymen were there, gathering bushy osiers, together with bulrushes, and sedge natural to fenny spots. The Titaness approached, and bending her knee, she pressed the ground, that she might take up the cool water to drink; the company of rustics forbade it. The Goddess thus addressed them, as they forbade her: 'Why do you deny me water? The use of water is common to all. Nature has made neither sun, nor air, nor the running stream, the property of any one. To her public bounty have I come, which yet I humbly beg of you to grant me. I was not intending to bathe my limbs here, and my wearied joints, but to relieve my thirst. My mouth, as I speak, lacks moisture, and my jaws are parched, and scarce is there a passage for my voice therein; a draught of water will be nectar to me, and I shall own, that, together with it, I have received my life at your hands. In that water you will be giving me life. Let these, too, move you, who hold out their little arms from my bosom'; and by chance the children were holding out their arms.

"What person might not these kindly words of the Goddess have been able to influence? Still, they persist in hindering the Goddess thus entreating them; and moreover add threats and abusive language, if she does not retire to a distance. Nor is this enough. They likewise muddy the lake itself with their feet and hands; and they raise the soft mud from the very bottom of the water, by spitefully jumping to and fro. Resentment removes her thirst. For now no longer does the daughter of Cæus supplicate the unworthy wretches, nor does she any longer endure to utter words below the majesty of a Goddess; and raising her hands to heaven, she says, 'For ever may you live in that pool.' The wish of the Goddess comes to pass. They delight to go beneath the water, and sometimes to plunge the whole of their limbs in the deep pool; now to raise their heads, and now to swim on the top of the water; oft to sit on the bank of the pool, and often to leap back again into the cold stream. And even now do they exercise their offensive tongues in strife: and banishing all shame, although they are beneath the water, still beneath the water,[47] do they try to keep up their abuse. Their voice, too, is now hoarse, and their bloated necks swell out; and their very abuse dilates their extended jaws. Their backs are united to their heads: their necks seem as though cut off; their backbone is green; their belly, the greatest part of their body, is white; and as new-made frogs, they leap about in the muddy stream."

[Footnote 45: The Chimæra.—Ver. 339. The Chimæra, according to the poets, was a monster having the head of a lion, the body of a goat, and the tail of a dragon. It seems, however, that it was nothing more than a volcanic mountain of Lycia, in Asia Minor, whence there were occasional eruptions of flame. The top of it was frequented by lions; the middle afforded plentiful pasture for goats; and towards the bottom, being rocky, and full of caverns, it was infested by vast numbers of serpents, that harbored there.]

[Footnote 46: Beheld a lake.—Ver. 343. Probus, in his Commentary on the Second Book of the Georgics, says that the name of the spring was Mela, and that of the shepherd who so churlishly repulsed Latona, was Neocles. Antoninus Liberalis says, that the name of the stream was Melites, and that Latona required the water for the purpose of bathing her children. He further tells us, that on being repulsed, she carried her children to the river Xanthus, and returning thence, hurled stones at the peasants, and changed them into frogs.]

[Footnote 47: Beneath the water.—Ver. 376. Some commentators are so fanciful as to say, that the repetition of the words 'sub aqua,' in the line 'Quamvis sint sub aquâ, sub aquâ, maledicere tentant,' not inelegantly [non ineleganter] expresses the croaking noise of the frogs. A man's fancy must, indeed, be exuberant to find any such resemblance; more so, indeed, than that of Aristophanes, who makes his frogs say, by way of chorus, 'brekekekekex koäx koäx.' Possibly, however, that might have been the Attic dialect among frogs.]

This story may possibly be based upon some current tradition of Latona having been subjected to such cruel treatment from some country clowns; or, which is more probable, it may have been originally invented as a satire on the rude manners and uncouth conduct of the peasantry of ancient times. The story may also have been framed, to account, in a poetical manner, for the origin of frogs.

FABLE IV [VI.382-411]

The Satyr Marsyas, having challenged Apollo to a trial of skill on the flute, the God overcomes him, and then flays him alive for his presumption. The tears that are shed on the occasion of his death produce the river that bears his name.

When thus one, who, it is uncertain, had related the destruction of these men of the Lycian race, another remembers that of the Satyr;[48] whom, overcome in playing on the Tritonian reed, the son of Latona visited with punishment. "Why," said he, "art thou tearing me from myself? Alas! I now repent; alas," cried he, "the flute is not of so much value!" As he shrieked aloud, his skin was stript[49] off from the surface of his limbs, nor was he aught but one entire wound. Blood is flowing on every side; the nerves, exposed, appear, and the quivering veins throb without any skin. You might have numbered his palpitating bowels, and the transparent lungs within his breast. The inhabitants of the country, the Fauns, Deities of the woods, and his brothers the Satyrs, and Olympus,[50] even then renowned, and the Nymphs lamented him; and whoever besides on those mountains was feeding the wool-bearing flocks, and the horned herds.

The fruitful earth was moistened, and being moistened received the falling tears, and drank them up in her lowest veins, which, when she had turned into a stream, she sent forth into the vacant air. And then, as the clearest river in Phrygia, running towards the rapid sea within steep banks, it bears the name of Marsyas.

From narratives such as these the people return at once to the present events, and mourn Amphion extinct together with all his race. The mother is an object of hatred. Yet her brother Pelops is said alone to have mourned for her as well; and after he had drawn his clothes from his shoulder towards his breast, he discovered the ivory on his left shoulder. This shoulder, at the time of his birth, was of the same color with the right one, and was formed of flesh. They say that the Gods afterwards joined his limbs cut asunder by the hands of his father; and the rest of them being found, that part which is midway between the throat and the top of the arm, was wanting. Ivory was inserted there, in the place of the part that did not appear; and so by that means Pelops was made entire.

[Footnote 48: The Satyr.—Ver. 382. Herodotus tells this story of the Satyr Marsyas, under the name of Silenus. Fulgentius informs us, that in paintings, Marsyas was represented with the tail of a pig.]

[Footnote 49: His skin was stript.—Ver. 387. Apollo fastened him to a pine-tree, or, according to Pliny the Elder, a plane-tree, which was to be seen even in his day. The skin was afterwards suspended by Apollo in the city of Celenæ. Hyginus says, that Apollo hewed Marsyas to pieces. The description here of the *flaying is, perhaps, very natural; but it is all the more disgusting for being so. A commentator justly says, that it might suit a Roman, whose eyes were familiar with bloodshed, much better than the taste of the reader of modern times.]*

[Footnote 50: Olympus.—Ver. 393. He was a Satyr, the brother and pupil of Marsyas. Pausanias describes a picture, painted by Polygnotus, in which Olympus was represented as sitting by Marsyas, clad as a youth, and learning to play on the flute. Euripides, in the Iphigenia in Aulis (l. 576) says that Olympus discovered some new measures for the 'tibia,' or flute. From Hyginus we learn, that Apollo delivered to him the body of Marsyas for burial.]

EXPLANATION

Marsyas was the son of Hyagnis, the inventor of a peculiar kind of flute, and of the Phrygian measure. Livy and Quintus Curtius tell us, that the story of Apollo and Marsyas is an allegory; and that the river Marsyas gave rise to it. They say that the river, falling from a precipice, in the neighborhood of the town of Celenæ, in Phrygia, made a very stunning and unpleasant noise; but that the smoothness of its course afterwards gave occasion for the saying, that the vengeance of Apollo had rendered it more tractable.

It is, however, not improbable that the story may have been based on historical facts. Having learned from his father, Hyagnis, the art of playing on the flute, and, proud of his skill, at a time when the musical art was yet in its infancy, Marsyas may have been rash enough to challenge either a priest of Apollo, or some prince who bore that name, and, for his presumption, to have received the punishment described by Ovid. Herodotus certainly credited the story; for he says that the skin of the unfortunate musician was to be seen, in his time, in the town of Celenæ. Strabo, Pausanias, and Aulus Gellius also believe its truth. Suidas tells us, that Marsyas, mortified at his defeat, threw himself into the river that runs near Celenæ, which, from that time, bore his name. Strabo says, that Marsyas had stolen the flute from Minerva, which proved so fatal to him, and had thereby drawn upon himself the indignation of that Divinity. Ovid, in the Sixth Book of the Fasti, and Pausanias, quoting from Apollodorus, tell us, that Minerva, having observed, by seeing herself in the river Meander, that, when she played on the flute, her cheeks were swelled out in an unseemly manner, threw aside the flute in her disgust, and Marsyas finding it, learned to play on it so skilfully, that he challenged Apollo to a trial of proficiency. Hyginus, in his 165th Fable, says that Marsyas was the son of Œagrius, and not Hyagnis; perhaps, however, this is a corrupt reading.

FABLE V [VI.412-586]

Tereus, king of Thrace, having married Progne, the daughter of Pandion, king of Athens, falls in love with her sister Philomela, whom he ravishes, and then, having cut out her tongue, he shuts her up in a strong place in a forest, to prevent a discovery. The unfortunate Philomela finds means to acquaint her sister with her misfortunes; for, weaving her story on a piece of cloth, she sends it to Progne by the hands of one of her keepers.

The neighboring princes met together; and the cities that were near, entreated their kings to go to console Pelops, namely, Argos and Sparta, and the Pelopean Mycenæ, and Calydon,[51] not yet odious to the stern Diana, and fierce Orchomeneus, and Corinth famous for its brass,[52] and fertile Messene, and Patræ, and humble Cleonæ,[53] and the Neleian Pylos, and Trœzen not yet named from Pittheus;[54] and other cities which are enclosed by the Isthmus between the two seas, and those which, situated beyond, are seen from the Isthmus between the two seas. Who could have believed it? You, Athens, alone omitted it. A war prevented this act of humanity; and barbarous troops[55] brought thither by sea, were alarming the Mopsopian walls. The Thracian Tereus had routed these by his auxiliary forces, and by his conquest had acquired an illustrious name. Him, powerful both in riches and men, and, as it happened, deriving his descent from the mighty Gradivus, Pandion united to himself, by the marriage of his daughter Progne.

Neither Juno, the guardian of marriage rites, nor yet Hymeneus, nor the Graces,[56] attended those nuptials. On that occasion, the Furies brandished torches, snatched from the funeral pile. The Furies prepared the nuptial couch, and the ill-boding owl hovered over the abode, and sat on the roof of the bridal chamber. With these omens were Progne and Tereus wedded; with these omens were they made parents. Thrace, indeed, congratulated them, and they themselves returned thanks to the Gods, and they commanded the day, upon which the daughter of Pandion was given to the renowned prince, and that upon which Itys was born, to be considered as festivals. So much does our true interest lie concealed from us. Now Titan had drawn the seasons of the repeated year through five autumns, when Progne, in gentle accents, said to her husband, "If I have any influence with thee, either send me to see my sister, or let my sister come hither. Thou shalt promise thy father-in-law that she shall return in a short time. As good as a mighty God wilt thou be to me, if thou shalt allow me to see my sister."

He thereupon ordered ships to be launched;[57] and with sails and oars he entered the Cecropian harbor, and landed upon the shores of the Piræus.[58] As soon as ever an opportunity was given of addressing his father-in-law, and right hand was joined to right hand, with evil omen their discourse began. He had commenced to relate the occasion of his coming, and the request of his wife, and to promise a speedy return for Philomela, if sent. When lo! Philomela comes, richly adorned in costly apparel; richer by far in her charms; such as we hear of the Naiads and Dryads as they haunt the middle of the forests, if you were only to give them the like ornaments and dress. Tereus was inflamed upon seeing the virgin, no otherwise than if one were to put fire beneath the whitening ears of corn, or were to burn leaves and dry grass laid up in stacks. Her beauty, indeed, is worthy of love; but inbred lust, as well, urges him on, and the people in those regions are naturally much inclined to lustfulness. He burns, both by his own frailty and that of his nation. He has a desire to corrupt the care of her attendants, and the fidelity of her nurse, and besides, to tempt herself with large presents, and to spend his whole kingdom in so doing; or else, to seize her, and, when seized, to secure her by a cruel war. And there is nothing which, being seized by an unbridled passion, he may not dare; nor does his breast contain the internal flame. And now he ill bears with delay; and with eager mouth returns to urge the request of Progne, and under it he pleads his own wishes; passion makes him eloquent. As oft as he presses beyond what is becoming, he pretends that Progne has thus desired. He adds tears as well, as though she had enjoined them too. O ye Gods above, how much of dark night do the breasts of mortals contain! Through his very attempt at villany, Tereus is thought to be affectionate, and from his crime does he gather praise.

And how is it, too, that Philomela desires the same thing? and fondly embracing the shoulders of her father with her arms, she begs, even by her own safety (and against it too), that she may visit her sister. Tereus views her, and, while viewing her, is embracing her beforehand in imagination; and, as he beholds her kisses, and her arms around her father's neck, he receives them all as incentives, and fuel, and the food of his furious passion; and, as often as she embraces her father, he could wish to be that father, and, even then, he would have been not the less impious. The father is overcome by the entreaties of them both. She rejoices, and returns thanks to her parent, and, to her misfortune, deems that the success of both, which will be the cause of sorrow to them both. Now but little of his toil was remaining for Phœbus, and his steeds were beating with their feet the descending track of Olympus; a regal banquet was set on the tables, and wine in golden vessels; after this, their bodies were given up to gentle sleep. But the Odrysian king,[59] though he was withdrawn, still burned for her; and, recalling her form, her movements, her hands, fancies that which he has not yet seen, to be such as he wishes; and he himself feeds his own flames, his anxiety preventing sleep.

It was now day; and Pandion, grasping the right hand of his son-in-law, about to depart, with tears bursting forth, recommended his companion to his care. "I commit her, my dear son-in-law, to thee, because reasons, grounded on affection, have compelled me, and both my daughters have desired it, and thou as well, Tereus, hast wished it; and I entreat thee, begging by thy honor, by thy breast thus allied to us, and by the Gods above, to protect her with the love of a father; and do send back to me, as soon as possible, this sweet comfort of my anxious old age, for all delay will be tedious to me, and do thou, too, Philomela, if thou hast any affection for me, return as soon as possible: 'tis enough that thy sister is so far away." Thus did he enjoin, and at the same time he gave kisses to his daughter, and his affectionate tears fell amid his instructions. He then demanded the right hands of them both, as a pledge of their fidelity, and joined them together when given, and bade them, with mindful lips, to salute for him his absent daughter and grandson, and with difficulty[60] uttered the last farewell, his mouth being filled with sobs; and he shuddered at the presages of his own mind. But as soon as Philomela was put on board of the painted ship, and the sea was urged by the oars, and the land was left behind, he exclaimed, "I have gained my point; the object of my desires is borne along with me." The barbarian exults, too, and with difficulty defers his joy in his intention, and turns not his eyes anywhere away from her. No otherwise than when the ravenous bird of Jupiter, with crooked talons, has placed a hare in his lofty nest; there is no escape for the captive; the plunderer keeps his eye on his prey. And now the voyage is ended, and now they have gone forth from the wearied ship, upon his own shore; when the king drags the daughter of Pandion into a lofty dwelling, concealed in an ancient wood, and there he shuts her up, pale and trembling, and dreading everything, and now with tears inquiring where her sister is; and confessing his baseness, he masters by force her a maiden, and but one, while she often vainly calls on her father, often on her sister, and on the great Gods above all. She trembles like a frightened lamb, which, wounded, being snatched from the mouth of a hoary wolf, does not as yet seem to itself in safety; and as a dove, its feathers soaked with its own blood, still trembles, and dreads the ravening talons wherein it has been lately held. But soon, when consciousness returned, tearing her dishevelled hair like one mourning, and beating her arms in lamentation, stretching out her hands, she said, "Oh, barbarous wretch, for thy dreadful deeds; oh, cruel monster! have neither the requests of my father, with his affectionate tears, moved thee, nor a regard for my sister, nor my virgin state, nor the laws of marriage? Thou hast confounded all. I am become the supplanter of my sister; thou, the husband of both of us. This punishment was not my due. Why dost thou not take away this life, that no villany, perfidious wretch, may remain unperpetrated by thee? and would that thou hadst done it before thy criminal embraces! then I might have had a shade void of all crime. Yet, if the Gods above behold these things, if the majesty of the Gods be anything; if, with myself, all things are not come to ruin; one time or other thou shalt give me satisfaction. I myself, having cast shame aside, will declare thy deeds. If opportunity is granted me, I will come among the people; if I shall be kept imprisoned in the woods, I will fill the woods, and will move the conscious rocks. Let Heaven hear these things, and the Gods, if there are any in it."

After the wrath of the cruel tyrant was aroused by such words, and his fear was not less than it, urged on by either cause, he drew the sword, with which he was girt, from the sheath, and seizing her by the hair, her arms being bent behind her back, he compelled her to submit to chains. Philomela was preparing her throat, and, on seeing the sword, had conceived hopes of her death. He cut away, with his cruel weapon, her tongue seized with pincers, while giving vent to her indignation, and constantly calling on the name of her father, and struggling to speak. The extreme root of the tongue still quivers. The tongue itself lies, and faintly murmurs, quivering upon the black earth; and as the tail of a mangled snake is wont to writhe about, so does it throb, and, as it dies, seeks the feet of its owner. It is said, too, that often after this crime (I could hardly dare believe it) he satisfied his lust upon her mutilated body.

He has the effrontery, after such deeds, to return to Progne, who, on seeing her husband, inquires for her sister; but he heaves feigned sighs, and tells a fictitious story of her death; and his tears procure him credit. Progne tears from her shoulders her robes, shining with broad gold, and puts on black garments, and erects an honorary sepulchre, and offers expiation to an imaginary shade; and laments the death of a sister not thus to be lamented.

The God Apollo, the year being completed, had run through the twice six signs of the Zodiac. What can Philomela do? A guard prevents her flight; the walls of the house are hard, built of solid stone: her speechless mouth is deprived of the means of discovering the crime. But in grief there is extreme ingenuity, and inventive skill arises in misfortunes. She skilfully suspends the warp in a web of Barbarian design,[61] and interweaves purple marks with white, as a mode of discovering the villany of Tereus; and delivers it, when finished, to one of her attendants, and begs her, by signs, to carry it to her mistress. As desired, she carries it to Progne, and does not know what she is delivering in it. The wife of the savage tyrant unfolds the web, and reads the mournful tale[62] of her sister, and (wondrous that she can be so!) she is silent. 'Tis grief that stops her utterance, and words sufficiently indignant fail her tongue, in want of them; nor is there room for weeping. But she rushes onward, about to confound both right and wrong, and is wholly occupied in the contrivance of revenge.

[Footnote 51: Calydon.—Ver. 415. This was a city of Ætolia, which derived its name from Calydon, the son of Endymion. Diana, being incensed against Œneus, its king, because he omitted her when offering the first fruits to the other Deities, sent an immense boar to ravage its fields, which was slain by Meleager. Ovid recounts these circumstances in the eighth book of the Metamorphoses. Argos, Sparta, and Mycenæ, are also included in one line, by Homer, as having been under the particular tutelage of Juno.]

[Footnote 52: Famous for its brass.—Ver. 416. According to some writers, the Corinthian brass became famous after the fall of Corinth, when it was taken and burnt by the Consul Mummius. On that occasion, they say, that from the immense number of statues melted in the conflagration, a stream of metal poured through the streets, consisting of melted gold, silver, and copper; in which, of course, the latter would be predominant. If that was the ground on which the Corinthian brass was so much commended, Ovid is here guilty of an anachronism.]

[Footnote 53: Cleonæ.—Ver. 417. This was a little town, situate between Argos and Corinth. It is called 'humilis,' not from its situation, but from the small number of its inhabitants. Patræ was a city of Achaia.]

[Footnote 54: Pittheus.—Ver. 418. He was the uncle of Theseus; and was (after the time here mentioned) the king of Trœzen, in Peloponnesus.]

[Footnote 55: Barbarous troops.—Ver. 423. Some suggest that it is here meant that Attica was invaded by the Amazons at this time; and they rely on a passage of Justin in support of the position. The story is, however, very improbable.]

[Footnote 56: The Graces.—Ver. 429. The Graces, who were the attendants of Venus, were three in number, Aglaia, Thalia, and Euphrosyne.]

[Footnote 57: To be launched.—Ver. 445. The ships were launched into the sea by means of rollers placed beneath them, from which circumstance they were said 'deduci,' 'to be led down.']

[Footnote 58: Shores of the Piræus.—Ver. 446. The Piræus was the arsenal and the harbor of the Athenians, and owed its magnificence to the vast conceptions of Themistocles.]

[Footnote 59: The Odrysian king.—Ver. 490. Tereus is thus called, from the Odrysæ, a people of Thrace.]

[Footnote 60: With difficulty.—Ver. 510. Clarke translates 'vix,' 'with much ado.']

[Footnote 61: Barbarian design.—Ver. 576. Probably of a Phrygian design.]

[Footnote 62: The mournful tale.—Ver. 582. This line is translated by Clarke, 'And reads the miserable ditty of her sister.']

EXPLANATION

The gravest authors among the ancients, such as Strabo and Pausanias, speaking of this tragical story, agree that the narrative, divested of its poetical ornaments, is strictly conformable to truth; though, of course, the sequel bears evident marks of embellishment either by the fancy of the Poet, or the superstition of the vulgar.

FABLE VI [VI.587-676]

Progne delivers her sister Philomela from captivity, and brings her to the court of Tereus, where she revolves in her mind her different projects of revenge. Her son Itys, in the meantime, comes into her apartment, and is murdered by his mother and aunt. Progne afterwards serves him up at a feast, which she prepares for her husband; on which, being obliged to fly from the fury of the enraged king, she is changed into a swallow, Philomela into a nightingale, and Tereus himself into a lapwing.

It is now the time[63] when the Sithonian[64] matrons are wont to celebrate the triennial festival of Bacchus. Night is conscious of their rites; by night Rhodope resounds with the tinklings of the shrill cymbal. By night the queen goes out of her house, and is arrayed according to the rites of the God, and carries the arms of the frantic solemnity. Her head is covered with vine leaves; from her left side hang down the skins of a deer;[65] upon her shoulder rests a light spear. Then the terrible Progne rushing through the woods, a multitude of her followers attending her, and agitated by the fury of her resentment, pretends, Bacchus, that it is inspired by thee.

She comes at length to the lonely dwelling, and howls aloud, and cries "Evoë!" and breaks open the gates, and seizes her sister, and puts upon her, so seized, the badges of Bacchus, and conceals her countenance under the foliage of ivy; and dragging her along, full of amazement, leads her within her threshold. When Philomela perceives that she has arrived at that accursed house,[66] the wretched woman shudders, and paleness spreads over her whole face. Progne having now got a fitting place for so doing, takes away the symbols of the rites,[67] and unveils the blushing face of her wretched sister; and holds her in her embraces. But she, on the other hand, cannot endure to lift up her eyes; seeming to herself the supplanter of her sister, and fixing her looks on the ground, her hand is in the place of voice to her, as she desires to swear and to call the Gods to witness that this disgrace has been brought upon her by violence. Progne burns with rage, and contains not her anger; and checking the grief of her sister, she says, "We must not act in this matter with tears, but with the sword, and even with anything, if such thou hast, that can possibly outdo the sword. I have, sister, prepared myself for every crime! Either, when I shall have set fire to the royal palace with torches, I will throw the artful Tereus into the midst of the flames, or with the steel will I cut away his tongue or his eyes, or the members that have deprived thee of thy chastity, or by a thousand wounds will I expel his guilty soul from his body. Something tremendous am I prepared for; what it is, I am still in doubt."

While Progne was uttering such expressions, Itys came to his mother. By him she was put in mind of what she might do; and looking at him with vengeful eyes, she said, "Ah! how like thou art to thy father!" And saying no more, she prepared for a horrible deed, and burned with silent rage. Yet when her son came to her, and saluted his mother and drew her neck towards him with his little arms, and added kisses mingled with childish endearments, the mother, in truth, was moved, and her anger abated, and her eyes, in spite of her, became wet with tears thus forced from her. But soon as she found the mother in her shrinking from excess of affection, from him again did she turn towards the features of her sister; and looking at them both by turns, she said, "Why does the one employ endearments, while the other is silent with her tongue torn from her? Why does she not call her sister, whom he calls mother? Consider to what kind of husband thou art married, daughter of Pandion. Thou dost grow degenerate. Tenderness in the wife of Tereus is criminality." No more delay is there; she drags Itys along, just as the tigress of the banks of the Ganges does the suckling offspring of the hind, through the shady forests. And when they are come to a remote part of the lofty house, Progne strikes[68] him with the sword, extending his hands, and as he beholds his fate, crying now "Alas!" and now "My mother!" and clinging to her neck, where his breast joins his side; nor does she turn away her face. Even one wound alone is sufficient for his death; Philomela cuts his throat with the sword; and they mangle his limbs, still quivering and retaining somewhat of life. Part of them boils,[69] in the hollow cauldrons; part hisses on spits; the inmost recesses stream with gore. His wife sets Tereus, in his unconsciousness, before this banquet; and falsely pretending rites after the manner of her country, at which it is allowed one man only to be present, she removes his attendants and servants. Tereus himself, sitting aloft on the throne of his forefathers, eats and heaps his own entrails into his own stomach. And so great is the blindness of his mind, that he says, "Send for Itys." Progne is unable to conceal her cruel joy; and now, desirous to be the discoverer of her having murdered him, she says, "Thou hast within thee, that for which thou art asking." He looks around, and inquires where he is; as he inquires, and calls him again, Philomela springs forth, just as she is, with her hair disordered by the infernal murder, and throws the bloody head of Itys in the face of his father; nor at any time has she more longed to be able to speak, and to testify her joy by words such as are deserved.

The Thracian pushes from him the table with a loud cry, and summons the Viperous sisters[70] from the Stygian valley; and at one moment he desires, if he only can, by opening his breast to discharge thence the horrid repast, and the half-digested entrails. And then he weeps, and pronounces himself the wretched sepulchre of his own son; and then he follows the daughters of Pandion with his drawn sword. You would have thought the bodies of the Cecropian[71] Nymphs were supported by wings; and they were supported by wings. The one of them makes for the woods, the other takes her place beneath the roofs of houses. Nor even as yet have the marks of murder withdrawn from her breast; and her feathers are still stained with blood. He, made swift by his grief, and his desire for revenge, is turned into a bird, upon whose head stands a crested plume; a prolonged bill projects in place of the long spear. The name of the bird is 'epops' [lapwing]; its face appears to be armed. This affliction dispatched Pandion to the shades of Tartarus before his day, and the late period of protracted old age.

[Footnote 63: Now the time.—Ver. 587. This was the festival of Bacchus, before mentioned as being celebrated every three years, in memory of his Indian expedition.]

[Footnote 64: Sithonian.—Ver. 588. Sithonia was a region of Thrace, which lay between Mount Hæmus and the Euxine sea. The word, however, is often used to signify the whole of Thrace.]

[Footnote 65: Skins of a deer.—Ver. 593. These were the 'nebrides,' or skins of fawns and deer, which the Bacchanals wore when celebrating the orgies. The lance mentioned here was, no doubt, the thyrsus.]

[Footnote 66: That accursed house.—Ver. 601. Clarke translates this line, 'As soon as Philomela perceived she had got into the wicked rogue's house.']

[Footnote 67: Symbols of the rites.—Ver. 603. These were the ivy, the deer-skins, and the thyrsus.]

[Footnote 68: Progne strikes.—Ver. 641. 'Ense ferit Progne' is translated by Clarke, 'Progne strikes with the sword poor Itys.']

[Footnote 69: Part of them boils.—Ver. 645-6. Clarke gives this comical translation: 'Then part of them bounces about in hollow kettles; part hisses upon spits; the parlor runs down with gore.']

[Footnote 70: Viperous sisters.—Ver. 662. Tereus invokes the Furies, who are thus called from having their hair wreathed with serpents. Clarke translates, 'ingenti clamore,' in line 661, 'with a huge cry.']

[Footnote 71: Cecropian.—Ver. 667. The Cecropian or Athenian Nymphs are Progne and Philomela, the daughters of Pandion, king of Athens.]

EXPLANATION

By the symbolical changes of Philomela, Progne, and Tereus, those who framed this termination of the story intended to depict the different characters of the persons whose actions are there represented. As the lapwing delights in filth and impurity, the ancients thereby portrayed the unscrupulous character of Tereus; and, as the flight of that bird is but slow, it shows that he was not able to overtake his wife and her sister. The nightingale, concealed in the woods and thickets, seems there to be concealing her misfortunes and sorrows; and the swallow, which frequents the abodes of man, shows the restlessness of Progne, who seeks in vain for her son, whom, in her frantic fit, she has so barbarously murdered.

Anacreon and Apollodorus, however, reverse the story, saying that Philomela was changed into a swallow, and Progne into a nightingale. This event is said by some writers to have happened not in Thrace, but at Daulis, a town of Phocis, where Tereus is supposed to have gone to settle. Pausanias tells us, that the tomb of Tereus was to be seen near Athens, so that it is probable that he died at a distance from Thrace, his native country. Homer alludes to the story of Philomela in somewhat different terms; speaking of the grounds of the grief of Penelope, he says, that 'she made her complaints to be heard like the inconsolable Philomela, the daughter of Pandarus, always hidden among the leaves and branches of trees. When the Spring arrives, she makes her voice echo through the woods, and laments her dear Itylus, whom she killed by an unhappy mistake; varying, in her continued plaints, the mournful melody of her notes.' By this, Homer seems to have known nothing of Tereus or of Progne, and to have followed a tradition, which was to the following effect:—Pandarus had three daughters, Ædon, Mecrope, and Cleothera. Ædon, the eldest, was married to Zethus, the brother of Amphion, by whom she had one son, who was named Itylus. Envying the more numerous family of Niobe, her sister-in-law, she resolved to despatch the eldest of her nephews; and, as her son was brought up with his cousin, and was his bedfellow, she bade him change his place in the bed, on the night on which she intended to commit the crime. Itylus forgot her commands, and consequently his mother killed him by mistake for her nephew.

FABLE VII [VI.677-721]

Boreas, not obtaining the consent of Erectheus, king of Athens, for the marriage of his daughter, Orithyïa, takes that princess in his arms, and carries her away into Thrace. By her he has two sons, Calaïs and Zethes, who have wings, like their father, and afterwards embark with Jason in search of the Golden Fleece.

Erectheus[72] received the sceptre of that country, and the government of the state; it is a matter of doubt whether he was more powerful through his justice, or by his mighty arms. He had, indeed, begotten four sons, and as many of the female sex: but the beauty of two of them was equal. Of these, Cephalus,[73] the son of Æolus, was blessed with thee, Procris, for his wife; Tereus and the Thracians were an obstacle to Boreas; and long was that God without his much-loved Orithyïa, while he was entreating, and choosing rather to use prayers than force. But when nothing was effected by blandishments, terrible with that rage which is his wont, and but too natural with that wind, he said, "And this is deservedly done; for why did I relinquish my own weapons, my violence, my strength, my anger, and my threatening spirit, and turn to prayers, the employment of which ill becomes me? Violence is suitable for me; by violence do I dispel the lowering clouds, by violence do I arouse the seas, and overthrow the knotted oaks, and harden the snow, and beat the earth with hail. I too, when I have met with my brothers in the open air (for that is peculiarly my field), struggle with efforts so great, that the intermediate sky thunders again with our onset, and fires flash, struck forth from the hollow clouds. I too, when I have descended into the hollow recesses of the earth, and in my rage have placed my back against its lowest depths, disturb the shades below, and the whole globe with earthquakes. By these means should I have sought this alliance; and Erectheus ought not to have been entreated to be my father-in-law, but made so by force."

Boreas, having said these words, or some not less high-sounding than these, shakes his wings, by the motion of which all the earth is fanned, and the wide sea becomes ruffled; and the lover, drawing his dusty mantle over the high tops of mountains, sweeps the ground, and, wrapt in darkness, embraces with his tawny wings Orithyïa, as she trembles with fear. As she flies, his flame, being agitated, burns more fiercely. Nor does the ravisher check the reins of his airy course, before he reaches the people and the walls of the Ciconians.[74] There, too, is the Actæan damsel made the wife of the cold sovereign, and afterwards a mother, bringing forth twins at a birth, who have the wings of their father, the rest like their mother. Yet they say that these wings were not produced together with their bodies; and while their long beard, with its yellow hair, was away, the boys Calaïs and Zethes were without feathers. But soon after, at once wings began to enclose both their sides, after the manner of birds, and at once their cheeks began to grow yellow with down. When, therefore, the boyish season of youth was passed, they sought,[75] with the Minyæ, along the sea before unmoved,[76] in the first ship that existed, the fleece that glittered with shining hair of gold.

[Footnote 72: Erectheus.—Ver. 677. This personage really was king of Athens before Pandion, the father of Progne and Philomela, and not after him, as Ovid here states; at least, such is the account given by Pausanias and Eusebius: the order of succession being Actæus, Cecrops, Cranaüs, Amphictyon, Erecthonius, Pandion, Erectheus, Cecrops II., Pandion II., Ægeus, Theseus.]

[Footnote 73: Cephalus.—Ver. 681. He was the son of Deioneus, and the grandson of Æolus. According to some writers, he was the son of Mercury; in and the Art of Love (Book iii. l. 725) he is called 'Cyllenia proles.' Strabo says that he was the son-in-law of Deioneus. His story is related at length in the next Book.]

[Footnote 74: The Ciconians.—Ver. 710. The Cicones were a people of Thrace, living near Mount Ismarus, and the Bistonian lake.]

[Footnote 75: They sought.—Ver. 720. This was the fleece of the ram that carried Phryxus along the Hellespont to Colchis, which is mentioned again in the next Book.]

[Footnote 76: Before unmoved.—Ver. 721. This passage may mean that that part of the sea had not been navigated before; though many of the poets assert that the Argo was the first ship that was ever built. It is more probable that it was the first vessel that was ever fitted out as a ship of war.]

EXPLANATION

Plato tells us that the story of the rape of Orithyïa is but an allegory, which signifies that, by accident, she was blown by the wind into the sea, where she was drowned. Apollodorus and Pausanias, however, assert that this story is based on historical facts, and that Boreas, king of Thrace, seized Orithyïa, the daughter of Erectheus, king of Athens, and sister of Procris, as she was passing the river Ilissus, and carried her into his dominions, where she became the mother of twins, Calaïs and Zethes. In the Argonautic expedition, these chiefs delivered Phineus, the king of Bithynia, from the persecution of the Harpies, which were in the habit of snatching away the victuals served up at his table.

FABLE I [VII.1-158]

Jason, after having met with various adventures, arrives with the Argonauts in Colchis, and demands the Golden Fleece. Medea falls in love with Jason, and by the power of her enchantments preserves him from the dangers he has to encounter in obtaining it. He obtains the prize, and carrying off Medea, returns in triumph to Thessaly.

And now the Minyæ[1] were ploughing the sea in the Pagasæan ship;[2] and Phineus prolonging a needy old age under perpetual night, had been visited, and the youthful sons of the North wind had driven the birds with the faces of virgins from before the mouth of the distressed old man;[3] and having suffered many things under the famous Jason, had reached at length the rapid waters of the muddy Phasis.

And while they go to the king, and ask the fleece that once belonged to Phryxus, and conditions are offered them, dreadful for the number of mighty labors; in the meantime, the daughter of Æetes[4] conceives a violent flame; and having long struggled against it, after she is unable to conquer her frenzy by reason, she says: "In vain, Medea, dost thou resist; some God, who, I know not, is opposing thee. It is a wonder too, if it is not this, or at least something like this, which is called 'love.' For why do the commands of my father appear too rigid for me? and yet too rigid they are. Why am I in dread, lest he whom I have seen but so lately, should perish? What is the cause of alarm so great? Banish the flames conceived in thy virgin breast, if thou canst, unhappy creature. If I could, I would be more rational. But a new power draws me on, against my will; and Cupid persuades one thing, reason another. I see which is the more proper course, and I approve of it, while I follow the wrong one. Why, royal maiden, art thou burning for a stranger, and why coveting the nuptial ties of a strange country? This land, too, may give thee something which thou mayst love. Whether he shall live, or whether die, is in the disposal of the Gods. Yet he may survive; and that I may pray for, even without love. For what fault has Jason committed? Whom, but one of hard heart, would not the youthful age of Jason affect? his descent too, and his valor? Whom, though these other points were wanting, would not his beauty move? at least, he has moved my breast. But unless I shall give him aid, he will be breathed upon by the mouths of the bulls; and will engage with his own kindred crops, an enemy sprung from the earth; or he will be given as a cruel prey to the ravenous dragon. If I allow this, then I will confess that I was born of a tigress; then, too, that I carry steel and stone in my heart. Why do I not as well behold him perish? Why not, too, profane my eyes by seeing it? Why do I not stimulate the bulls against him, and the fierce sons of the earth, and the never-sleeping dragon? May the Gods award better things. And yet these things are not to be prayed for, but must be effected by myself. Shall I then betray the kingdom of my father? and by my aid shall some stranger, I know not who, be saved; that being delivered by my means, he may spread his sails to the winds without me, and be the husband of another; and I, Medea, be left for punishment? If he can do this, and if he is capable of preferring another to me, let him perish in his ingratitude. But not such is his countenance, not such that nobleness of soul, that gracefulness of person, that I should fear treachery, and forgetfulness of what I deserve. Besides, he shall first pledge his faith, and I will oblige the Gods to be witnesses of our compact. What then dost thou dread, thus secure? Haste then,[5] and banish all delay. Jason will ever be indebted to thee for his preservation; thee will he unite to himself in the rites of marriage, and throughout the Pelasgian cities[6] thou wilt be celebrated by crowds of matrons, as the preserver of their sons. And shall I then, borne away by the winds, leave my sister[7] and my brother,[8] and my father, and my Gods, and my native soil? My father is cruel, forsooth; my country, too, is barbarous;[9] my brother is still but an infant; the wishes of my sister are in my favor. The greatest of the Gods is in possession of me. I shall not be relinquishing anything great; I shall be pursuing what is great; the credit of saving the youth of Greece,[10] acquaintance with a better country, and cities, whose fame is flourishing even here, and the politeness and the arts of their inhabitants; and the son of Æson, whom I could be ready to take in exchange for all the things that the whole world contains; with whom for my husband I shall both be deemed dear to the Gods, and shall reach the stars with my head. Why say that I know not what mountains[11] are reported to arise in the midst of the waves, and that Charybdis, an enemy to ships, one while sucks in the sea, at another discharges it; and how that Scylla, begirt with furious dogs, is said to bark in the Sicilian deep? Yet holding him whom I love, and clinging to the bosom of Jason, I shall be borne over the wide seas; embracing him, naught will I dread; or if I fear anything, for my husband alone will I fear. And dost thou, Medea, call this a marriage, and dost thou give a plausible name to thy criminality? Do but consider how great an offence thou art meditating, and, while still thou mayst, fly from guilt."

Thus she said, and before her eyes stood Virtue, Affection, and Modesty; and now Cupid turned his vanquished back. She was going to the ancient altars of Hecate,[12] the daughter of Perses, which a shady grove and the recesses of a wood concealed. And now she was resolved, and her passion being checked, had subsided; when she beheld the son of Æson, and the extinguished flame revived. Her cheeks were covered with blushes, and her whole face was suffused with a glow. As a spark is wont to derive nourishment from the winds, which, but small when it lay concealed beneath the ashes cast over it, is wont to increase, and aroused, to rise again to its original strength, so her love, now declining, which you would suppose was now growing languid, when she beheld the youth, was rekindled with the appearance of him before her eyes. And by chance, on that day, the son of Æson was more beauteous than usual. You might forgive her loving him. She gazes; and keeps her eyes fixed upon his countenance, as though but now seen for the first time; and in her frenzy she thinks she does not behold the face of a mortal; nor does she turn away from him. But when the stranger began to speak, and seized her right hand, and begged her assistance with a humble voice, and promised her marriage; she said, with tears running down, "I see what I ought to do; and it will not be ignorance of the truth, but love that beguiles me. By my agency thou shalt be saved; when saved, grant what thou hast promised."

He swears by the rites of the Goddess of the triple form, and the Deity which is in that grove, and by the sire[13] of his future father-in-law, who beholds all things, and by his own adventures, and by dangers so great. Being believed by her, he immediately received some enchanted herbs, and thoroughly learned the use of them, and went away rejoicing to his abode. The next morning had now dispersed the twinkling stars, when the people repaired to the sacred field of Mavors, and ranged themselves on the hills. In the midst of the assembly sat the king himself, arrayed in purple, and distinguished by a sceptre of ivory. Behold! the brazen-footed bulls breathe forth flames[14] from their adamantine nostrils; and the grass touched by the vapors is on fire. And as the forges filled with fire are wont to roar, or when flints[15] dissolved in an earthen furnace receive intense heat by the sprinkling of flowing water; so do their breasts rolling forth the flames enclosed within, and their scorched throats, resound. Yet the son of Æson goes forth to meet them. The fierce bulls turn their terrible features, and their horns pointed with iron, towards his face as he advances, and with cloven hoofs they spurn the dusty ground, and fill the place with lowings, that send forth clouds of smoke. The Minyæ are frozen with horror. He comes up, and feels not the flames breathed forth by them, so great is the power of the incantations. He even strokes their hanging dewlaps with a bold right hand, and, subjected to the yoke, he obliges them to draw the heavy weight of a plough, and to turn up with the share the plain till now unused to it.[16]

The Colchians are astonished; the Minyæ fill the air with their shouts, and give him fresh courage. Then in a brazen helmet he takes the dragon's teeth,[17] and strews them over the ploughed up fields. The ground, impregnated beforehand with a potent drug, softens the seed; and the teeth that were sown grow up, and become new bodies. And as the infant receives the human form in the womb of the mother, and is there formed in all its parts, and comes not forth into the common air until at maturity, so when the figure of man is ripened in the bowels of the pregnant earth, it arises in the fruitful plain; and, what is still more surprising, it brandishes arms produced at the same time. When the Pelasgians saw them preparing to hurl their spears with sharp points at the head of the Hæmonian youth, they lowered their countenances and their courage, quailing with fear. She, too, became alarmed, who had rendered him secure; and when she saw the youth, being but one, attacked by so many enemies, she turned pale, and suddenly chilled with fear, sat down without blood in her cheeks. And, lest the herbs that had been given by her, should avail him but little, she repeats an auxiliary charm, and summons to her aid her secret arts. He, hurling a heavy stone into the midst of his enemies, turns the warfare, now averted from himself, upon themselves. The Earth-born brothers perish by mutual wounds, and fall in civil fight. The Greeks congratulate him, and caress the conqueror, and cling to him in hearty embraces. And thou too, barbarian maiden, wouldst fain have embraced him; 'twas modesty that opposed the design; otherwise thou wouldst have embraced him; but regard for thy reputation restrained thee from doing so. What thou mayst do, thou dost do; thou rejoicest with a silent affection, and thou givest thanks to thy charms, and to the Gods, the authors of them.

It still remains to lay asleep with herbs the watchful dragon, who, distinguished by his crest and his three tongues, and terrible with his hooked teeth, is the keeper of the Golden Fleece. After he has sprinkled him with herbs of Lethæan juice,[18] and has thrice repeated words that cause placid slumbers, which would even calm the boisterous ocean, and which would stop the rapid rivers, sleep creeps upon the eyes that were strangers to it, and the hero, the son of Æson, gains the gold; and proud of the spoil and bearing with him the giver of the prize as a second spoil, he arrives victorious, with his wife, at the port of Iolcos.[19]

[Footnote 1: The Minyæ.—Ver. 1. The Argonauts. The Minyæ were a people of Thessaly, so called from Minyas, the son of Orchomenus.]

[Footnote 2: Pagasæan ship.—Ver. 1. Pagasæ was a seaport of Thessaly, at the foot of Mount Pelion, where the ship Argo was built.]

[Footnote 3: Distressed old man.—Ver. 4. Clarke translates 'miseri senis ore,' 'from the mouth of the miserable old fellow.']

[Footnote 4: Daughter of Æetes.—Ver. 9. Medea was the daughter of Æetes, the king of Colchis. Juno, favoring Jason, had persuaded Venus to inspire Medea with love for him.]

[Footnote 5: Haste then.—Ver. 47. Clarke translates 'accingere,' more literally than elegantly, 'buckle to.']

[Footnote 6: Pelasgian cities.—Ver. 49. Pelasgia was properly that part of Greece which was afterwards called Thessaly. The province of Pelasgiotis, in Thessaly, afterwards retained its name, which was derived from the Pelasgi, an early people of Greece. Pliny informs us that Peloponnesus at first had the names of 'Apia' and 'Pelasgia.' Some suppose that the Pelasgi derived their name from Pelasgus, the son of Jupiter; while other writers assert that they were so called from πελαργοὶ, 'storks,' from their wandering habits. The name is frequently used, as in the present instance, to signify the whole of the Greeks.]

[Footnote 7: My sister.—Ver. 51. Her sister was Chalciope, who had married Phryxus, after his arrival in Colchis. Her children being found by Jason, in the isle of Dia, they came with him to Colchis, and presented him to their mother, who afterwards commended him to the care of Medea.]

[Footnote 8: And my brother.—Ver. 51. Her brother was Absyrtus, whose tragical death is afterwards mentioned.]

[Footnote 9: Is barbarous.—Ver. 53. It was certainly 'barbara' in the eyes of a Greek; but the argument sounds rather oddly in the mouth of Medea, herself a native of the country.]

[Footnote 10: The youth of Greece.—Ver. 56. These were the Argonauts, who were selected from the most noble youths of Greece.]

[Footnote 11: What mountains.—Ver. 63. These were the Cyanean rocks, or Symplegades, at the mouth of the Euxine sea.]

[Footnote 12: Hecate.—Ver. 74. Ancient writers seem to have been much divided in opinion who Hecate was. Ovid here follows the account which made her to be the daughter of Perses, who, according to Diodorus Siculus, was the son of Phœbus, and the brother of Æetes. Marrying her uncle Æetes, she is said to have been the mother of Circe, Medea, and Absyrtus. By some writers she is confounded with the Moon and with Proserpine; as identical with the Moon, she has the epithets 'Triceps' and 'Triformis,' often given to her by the poets, because the Moon sometimes is full, sometimes disappears, and often shows but part of her disk.]

[Footnote 13: And by the sire.—Ver. 96. Allusion is made to the Sun, who was said to be the father of Æetes, the destined father-in-law of Jason.]

[Footnote 14: Breathe forth flames.—Ver. 104. The name of the God of fire is here used to signify that element. Apollodorus says, that Medea gave Jason a drug (φάρμακον) to rub over himself and his armor.]

[Footnote 15: Or when flints.—Ver. 107. It is difficult to determine whether 'silices' here means 'flint-stones,' or 'lime-stone;' probably the latter, from the mention of water sprinkled over them. If the meaning is 'flint-stones,' the passage may refer to the manufacture of glass, with the art of making which the ancients were perfectly acquainted.]

[Footnote 16: Unused to it.—Ver. 119. Because, being sacred to Mars, it was not permitted to be ploughed.]

[Footnote 17: Dragon's teeth.—Ver. 122. These were a portion of the teeth of the dragon slain by Cadmus, which Mars and Minerva had sent to Æetes.]

[Footnote 18: Lethæan juice.—Ver. 152. Lethe was a river of the infernal regions, whose waters were said to produce sleep and forgetfulness.]

[Footnote 19: Port of Iolcos.—Ver. 158. Iolcos was a city of Thessaly, of which country Jason was a native.]

To understand this story, one of the most famous in the early history of Greece, we must go back to the origin of it, and examine the fictions which the poets have mingled with the history of the expedition of the Argonauts, one of the most remarkable events of the fabulous ages.

Athamas, the son of Æolus, grandson of Hellen, and great-grandson of Deucalion, having married Ino, the daughter of Cadmus, was obliged to divorce her, on account of the madness with which she was attacked. He afterwards married Nephele, by whom he had a son and daughter, Phryxus and Helle; but on his taking his first wife again, she brought him two sons, Learchus and Melicerta. Ino, hating the children of Nephele, sought to destroy them. Phryxus being informed thereof, ordered a ship to be privately prepared; and taking his father's treasures, sailed with his sister Helle, to seek a retreat in the court of Æetes, his kinsman. Helle died on the voyage, but Phryxus arrived in Colchis, where he dedicated the prow of his ship to Neptune, or Jupiter. He there married Chalciope, by whom he had four sons, Argos, Phrontes, Molas, and Cylindus. Some years after, Æetes caused him to be assassinated; and his sons fleeing to the court of their grandfather, Athamas, were shipwrecked on an island, where they remained until found there by Jason, who took them back to their mother. Having mourned them as dead, she was transported with joy on finding them, and used every exertion to aid Jason in promoting his addresses to Medea. Æetes having seized the treasures of Athamas on the death of Phryxus, the Greeks prepared an expedition to recover them, and to avenge his death. Pelias, who had driven his brother Æson from the throne of Iolcos, desiring to procure the absence of his son Jason, took this opportunity of engaging him in an enterprise, which promised both glory, profit, and a large amount of personal exertion. The uneasiness which Pelias felt was caused by the prediction of an oracle, that he should be killed by a prince of the family of Æolus, and which warned him to beware of a person who should have but one shoe. Just at that period, Jason, returning from the school of Chiron, lost one of his shoes in crossing a river. On this, his uncle was desirous to destroy him; but not daring to do so publicly, he induced him to embark with the Argonauts, expecting that he would perish in an undertaking of so perilous a nature. Many young nobles of Greece repaired to the court of Iolcos, and joined in the undertaking, when they chose Jason for their leader, and embarked in a ship, the name of which was Argo, and from which the adventurers received the name of Argonauts.

Diodorus Siculus says, that the ship was so named from its swiftness; while others say, that it was so called from Argus, the name of its builder, or from the Argives, or Greeks, on board of it. Bochart, however, supposes, that the name is derived from the Phœnician word 'arco,' which signifies 'long,' and suggests, that before that time the Greeks sailed in vessels of a rounder form, Jason being the first who sailed in a ship built in the form of a galley. After many adventures, on arriving at the Isle of Lemnos, they found that the women had killed their husbands in a fit of jealousy, on which the Argonauts took wives from their number, and Jason received for his companion Hypsipyle, the daughter of Thoas. Putting to sea again, they were driven on the coast of Bithynia, where they delivered Phineus, its king, from the persecution of the Harpies, who were in the habit of snatching away the victuals from his table. These monsters, of hideous form, with crooked beaks and talons, huge wings, and the faces of women, the Argonauts, and especially Calais and Zethes, pursued as far as the islands called Strophades, in the Ionian sea, where Iris appearing to them, enjoined them to pursue the Harpies no further, promising that Phineus should no longer be persecuted by them. To explain this story, some suppose that the Harpies were the daughters of Phineus, who by their dissipation and extravagance, had ruined him in his old age, which occasioned the saying, that they snatched the victuals out of his mouth. Le Clerc thinks, that the Harpies were vast swarms of grasshoppers, which ravaged all Paphlagonia, and caused a famine in the dominions of Phineus; the word 'arbati,' whence the term 'Harpy' is derived, signifying 'a grasshopper;' and that the North wind blowing them into the Ionian sea, it gave rise to the saying, that the sons of Boreas pursued them so far. Diodorus Siculus does not mention the Harpies, though he speaks of the arrival of the Argonauts at the court of Phineus.

After some other adventures, the Argonauts arrived at Colchis. Æetes, or Æeta, the king, having been forewarned by an oracle, that a stranger should deprive him of his crown and life, had established a custom of sacrificing all strangers found in his dominions. His daughter Medea, falling in love with Jason, promised him her assistance in preserving them from the dangers to which they were exposed, on the condition of his marrying her. Having engaged to do so, she conducted him by night to the royal palace, and gave him a false key, by means whereof he found the royal treasures, and carrying them off, embarked with Medea and his companions. By way of explaining the miraculous portion of the story, we may, perhaps, not err in supposing, that the account of it was originally written in the Phœnician language; and through not understanding it, the Greeks invented the fiction of the Fleece, the Dragon, and the Fiery Bulls. Bochart and Le Clerc have observed, that the Syriac word 'gaza,' signifies either 'a treasure,' or 'a fleece.' 'Saur,' which means 'a wall,' also means 'a bull;' and in the same language the same word, 'nachas,' signifies both 'brass,' 'iron,' and 'a dragon.' Hence, instead of the simple narrative, that Jason, by the aid of Medea, carried away the treasures which Æetes kept within walls, with bolts, or locks of metal, and which Phryxus had carried to Colchis in a ship with the figure of a ram at the prow, it was published, and circulated by the ignorant, that the Gods, to save Phryxus from his stepmother, sent him a sheep with a golden fleece, which bore him to Colchis; that its fleece became the object of the ambition of the leading men of Greece; and that whoever wished to bear it away was obliged to contend with bulls and dragons. Some historians, by way of interpreting the story, affirm, that the keeper of the treasures was named 'Draco,' or 'Dragon,' and that the garrison of the stronghold of Æetes was brought from the 'Tauric' Chersonesus. They say also, that the fleece was the skin of the sheep which Phryxus had sacrificed to Neptune, which he had caused to be gilt. It is not, however, very likely, that an object so trifling could have excited the avarice of the Greeks, and caused them to undertake an expedition accompanied with so many dangers. The dragon's teeth most probably bear reference to some foreign troops which Jason, in the same way as Cadmus had done, found means to alienate from Æetes, and to bring over to his own side. Homer makes but very slight allusion to the adventures of the Argonauts.

FABLE II [VII.159-349]

Jason, after his return home, requests Medea to restore his father Æson to youth, which she performs; then, going to the court of Pelias, she avenges the injuries which he had done to the family of Jason, by making him the victim of the credulity of his own daughters, who, in compliance with her pretended regard for them, stab him to death. Medea, having executed her design, makes her escape in her chariot.

The Hæmonian mothers and aged fathers bring presents, for receiving their sons safe home; and frankincense dissolves, piled on the flames, and the devoted victim falls, having its horns gilded. But Æson is not among those congratulating, being now near death, and worn out with the years of old age; when thus the son of Æson addresses Medea: "O wife, to whom I confess that I owe my safety, although thou hast granted me everything, and the sum of thy favors exceeds all belief; still, if thy enchantments can effect this (and what can enchantments not effect?), take away from my own years, and, when taken, add them to those of my father."

And thus saying, he could not check his tears. She was moved with the affection of the petitioner; and her father, Æetes, left behind, recurred to her mind, unlike that of Jason; yet she did not confess any such feelings. "What a piece of wickedness, husband," said she, "has escaped thy affectionate lips! Can I, then, seem capable of transferring to any one a portion of thy life? May Hecate not allow of this; nor dost thou ask what is reasonable; but, Jason, I will endeavor to grant thee a favor still greater than that which thou art asking. By my arts we will endeavor to bring back the long years of my father-in-law, and not by means of thy years; if the Goddess of the triple form[20] do but assist, and propitiously aid so vast an undertaking." Three nights were now wanting that the horns of the Moon might meet entirely, and might form a perfect orb. After the Moon shone in her full, and looked down upon the Earth, with her disk complete, Medea went forth from the house, clothed in garments flowing loose, with bare feet,[21] and having her unadorned hair hanging over her shoulders, and unattended, directed her wandering steps through the still silence of midnight. Sound sleep has now relaxed the nerves of both men, and birds, and beasts; the hedges and the motionless foliage are still, without any noise, the dewy air is still; the stars alone are twinkling; towards which, holding up her arms, three times she turns herself about, three times she besprinkles her hair with water taken from the stream; with three yells she opens her mouth, and, her knee bending upon the hard ground, she says, "O Night, most faithful to these my mysteries, and ye golden Stars, who, with the Moon, succeed the fires of the day, and thou, three-faced Hecate,[22] who comest conscious of my design, and ye charms and arts of the enchanters, and thou, too, Earth, that dost furnish the enchanters with powerful herbs; ye breezes, too, and winds, mountains, rivers, and lakes, and all ye Deities of the groves, and all ye Gods of night, attend here; through whose aid, whenever I will, the rivers run back from their astonished banks to their sources, and by my charms I calm the troubled sea, and rouse it when calm; I disperse the clouds, and I bring clouds upon the Earth; I both allay the winds, and I raise them; and I break the jaws of serpents with my words and my spells; I move, too, the solid rocks, and the oaks torn up with their own native earth, and the forests as well. I command the mountains, too, to quake, and the Earth to groan, and the ghosts to come forth from their tombs. Thee, too, O Moon, do I draw down, although the Temesæan[23] brass relieves thy pangs. By my spells, also, the chariot of my grandsire is rendered pale; Aurora, too, is pale through my enchantments. For me did ye blunt the flames of the bulls, and with the curving plough you pressed the necks that never before bore the yoke. You raised a cruel warfare for those born of the dragon among themselves, and you lulled to sleep the keeper of the golden fleece, that had never known sleep; and thus, deceiving the guardian, you sent the treasure into the Grecian cities. Now there is need of juices, by means of which, old age, being renewed, may return to the bloom of life, and may receive back again its early years; and this ye will give me; for not in vain did the stars just now sparkle; nor yet in vain is the chariot come, drawn by the necks of winged dragons."

A chariot sent down from heaven was come; which, soon as she had mounted, and had stroked the harnessed necks of the dragons, and had shaken the light reins with her hands, she was borne aloft, and looked down upon Thessalian Tempe below her, and guided her dragons towards the chalky regions;[24] and observed the herbs which Ossa, and which the lofty Pelion bore, Othrys, too, and Pindus, and Olympus still greater than Pindus; and part she tore up by the root gently worked, part she cut down with the bend of a brazen sickle.[25] Many a herb, too, that grew on the banks of Apidanus[26] pleased her; many, too, on the banks of Amphrysus; nor, Enipeus, didst thou escape. The Peneian waters, and the Spercheian as well, contributed something, and the rushy shores of Bœbe.[27] She plucks, too, enlivening herbs by the Eubœan Anthedon,[28] not yet commonly known by the change of the body of Glaucus.[29] And now the ninth day,[30] and the ninth night had seen her visiting all the fields in her chariot, and upon the wings of the dragons, when she returned; nor had the dragons been fed, but with the odors of the plants: and yet they cast the skin of old age full of years. On her arrival she stood without the threshold and the gates, and was canopied by the heavens alone, and avoided the contact of her husband, and erected two altars of turf; on the right hand, one to Hecate, but on the left side one to Youth.[31] After she had hung them round with vervain and forest boughs, throwing up the earth from two trenches not far off, she performed the rites, and plunged a knife into the throat of a black ram, and besprinkled the wide trenches with blood. Then pouring thereon goblets[32] of flowing wine, and pouring brazen goblets of warm milk; she at the same time utters words, and calls upon the Deities of the earth, and entreats the king of the shades[33] below, together with his ravished wife, that they will not hasten to deprive the aged limbs of life. When she had rendered them propitious both by prayers and prolonged mutterings, she commanded the exhausted body of Æson to be brought out to the altars, and stretched it cast into a deep sleep by her charms, and resembling one dead, upon the herbs laid beneath him.

She orders the son of Æson to go far thence, and the attendants, too, to go afar; and warns them to withdraw their profane eyes from her mysteries. At her order, they retire. Medea, with dishevelled hair, goes round the blazing altars like a worshipper of Bacchus, and dips her torches, split into many parts, in the trench, black with blood, and lights them, thus dipt, at the two altars. And thrice does she[34] purify the aged man with flames, thrice with water, and thrice with sulphur. In the meantime the potent mixture[35] is boiling and heaving in the brazen cauldron, placed on the flames, and whitens with swelling froth. There she boils roots cut up in the Hæmonian valleys, and seeds and flowers and acrid juices. She adds stones fetched from the most distant East, and sand, which the ebbing tide of the ocean has washed. She adds, too, hoar-frost gathered at night by the light of the moon, and the ill-boding wings of a screech owl,[36] together with its flesh; and the entrails of an ambiguous wolf, that was wont to change its appearance of a wild beast into that of a man. Nor is there wanting there the thin scaly slough of the Cinyphian water-snake,[37] and the liver of the long-lived stag;[38] to which, besides, she adds the bill and head of a crow that had sustained an existence of nine ages. When, with these and a thousand other things without a name, the barbarian princess has completed the medicine prepared for the mortal body, with a branch of the peaceful olive long since dried up, she stirs them all up, and blends the lowest ingredients with the highest. Behold! the old branch, turned about in the heated cauldron, at first becomes green; and after no long time assumes foliage, and is suddenly loaded with heavy olives. Besides, wherever the fire throws the froth from out of the hollow cauldron, and the boiling drops fall upon the earth, the ground becomes green, and flowers and soft grass spring up.

Soon as Medea sees this, she opens the throat[39] of the old man with a drawn sword; and allowing the former blood to escape, replenishes his veins with juices. Soon as Æson has drunk them in, either received in his mouth or in his wound, his beard and his hair[40] laying aside their hoariness, assume a black hue. His leanness flies, being expelled; his paleness and squalor are gone. His hollow veins are supplied with additional blood, and his limbs become instinct with vigor. Æson is astonished, and calls to recollection that he was such four times ten years before.

Liber had beheld from on high the miraculous operations of so great a prodigy; and taught thereby that youthful years can be restored to his nurses,[41] he requests this present from the daughter of Æetes.[42]

And that her arts[43] may not cease, the Phasian feigns a counterfeited quarrel with her husband, and flies as a suppliant to the threshold of Pelias[44] and (as he himself is oppressed with old age) his daughters receive her; whom, after a short time, the crafty Colchian engages to herself by the appearance of a pretended friendship. And while among the greatest of her merits, she relates that the infirmities of Æson have been removed, and is dwelling upon that part of the story, a hope is suggested to the damsels, the daughters of Pelias, that by the like art their parent may become young again; and this they request of her, and repeatedly entreat her to name her own price. For a short time she is silent, and appears to be hesitating, and keeps their mind in suspense, as they ask, with an affected gravity.

Afterwards, when she has promised them, she says, "That there may be the greater confidence in this my skill, the leader of the flock among your sheep, which is the most advanced in age, shall become a lamb by this preparation." Immediately, a fleecy ram, enfeebled by innumerable years, is brought, with his horns bending around his hollow temples; whose withered throat, when she has cut with the Hæmonian knife, and stained the steel with its scanty blood, the enchantress plunges the limbs of the sheep, and her potent juices together, into the hollow copper. The limbs of his body are lessened, and he puts off his horns, and his years together with his horns; and in the midst of the kettle a low bleating is heard. And without any delay, while they are wondering at the bleating, a lamb springs forth, and gambols in its course, and seeks the suckling dugs. The daughters of Pelias are amazed; and after her promises have obtained her credit, then, indeed, they urge her still more strongly. Phœbus had thrice taken the yoke off his horses sinking in the Iberian sea;[45] and upon the fourth night the radiant stars were twinkling, when the deceitful daughter of Æetes set pure water upon a blazing fire, and herbs without any virtue. And now sleep like to death, their bodies being relaxed, had seized the king, and the guards together with their king, which her charms and the influence of her enchanting tongue had caused. The daughters of the king, as ordered, had entered the threshold, together with the Colchian, and had surrounded the bed; "Why do you hesitate now, in your indolence? Unsheathe your swords," says she, "and exhaust the ancient gore, that I may replenish his empty veins with youthful blood. The life and the age of your father is now in your power. If you have any affection and cherish not vain hopes, perform your duty to your father, and drive away old age with your weapons, and, thrusting in the steel, let out his corrupted blood."

Upon this exhortation, as each of them is affectionate, she becomes especially undutiful, and that she may not be wicked, she commits wickedness. Yet not one is able to look upon her own blow; and they turn away their eyes, and turning away their faces, they deal chance blows with their cruel right hands. He, streaming with gore, yet raises his limbs on his elbows, and, half-mangled, attempts to rise from the couch; and in the midst of so many swords stretching forth his pale arms, he says, "What are you doing, my daughters? What arms you against the life of your parent?" Their courage and their hands fail them. As he is about to say more, the Colchian severs his throat, together with his words, and plunges him, thus mangled, in the boiling cauldron.

[Footnote 20: Of the triple form.—Ver. 177. Hecate, the Goddess of enchantment.]

[Footnote 21: With bare feet.—Ver. 183. To have the feet bare was esteemed requisite for the due performance of magic rites, though sometimes on such occasions, and probably in the present instance, only one foot was left unshod. In times of drought, according to Tertullian, a procession and ceremonial, called 'nudipedalia,' were resorted to, with a view to propitiate the Gods by this token of grief and humiliation.]

[Footnote 22: Three-faced Hecate.—Ver. 194. Though Hecate and the Moon are here mentioned as distinct, they are frequently considered to have been the same Deity, with different attributes. The three heads with which Hecate was represented were those of a horse, a dog, and a pig, or sometimes, in the place of the latter, a human head.]

[Footnote 23: Temesæan.—Ver. 207. Temesa was a town of the Brutii, on the coast of Etruria, famous for its copper mines. It was also sometimes called Tempsa. There was also another Temesa, a city of Cyprus, also famous for its copper.]

[Footnote 24: Chalky regions.—Ver. 223. Such was the characteristic of the mountainous country of Thessaly, where she now alighted.]

[Footnote 25: Brazen sickle.—Ver. 227. We learn from Macrobius and Cælius Rhodiginus that copper was preferred to iron in cutting herbs for the purposes of enchantment, in exorcising spirits, and in aiding the moon in eclipses against the supposed charms of the witches, because it was supposed to be a purer metal.]

[Footnote 26: Apidanus.—Ver. 228. This and Amphrysus were rivers of Thessaly.]

[Footnote 27: Shores of Bœbe.—Ver. 231. Strabo makes mention of lake Bœbeis, near the town of Bœbe, in Thessaly. It was not far from the mouth of the river Peneus.]

[Footnote 28: Anthedon.—Ver. 232. This was a town of Bœotia, opposite to Eubœa, being situated on the Euripus, now called the straits of Negropont.]

[Footnote 29: Glaucus.—Ver. 233. He was a fisherman, who was changed into a sea God, on tasting a certain herb. His story is related at the end of the 13th Book.]

[Footnote 30: Ninth day.—Ver. 234. The numbers three and nine seem to have been deemed of especial virtue in incantations.]

[Footnote 31: One to youth.—Ver. 241. This goddess was also called Hebe, from the Greek word signifying youth. She was the daughter of Juno, and the wife of Hercules. She was also the cup-bearer of the Gods, until she was supplanted by Ganymede.]

[Footnote 32: Goblets.—Ver. 246. 'Carchesia.' The 'carchesium' was a kind of drinking cup, used by the Greeks from very early times. It was slightly contracted in the middle, and its two handles extended from the top to the bottom. It was employed in the worship of the Deities, and was used for libations of blood, wine, milk, and honey. Macrobius says that it was only used by the Greeks. Virgil makes mention of it as used to hold wine.]

[Footnote 33: King of the shades.—Ver. 249. Pluto and Proserpine. Clarke translates this line and the next, 'And prays to the king of shades with his kidnapped wife, that they would not be too forward to deprive the limbs of the old gentleman of life.']

[Footnote 34: Thrice does she.—Ver. 261. Clarke thus renders this and the two following lines: 'And purifies the old gentleman three times with flame, three times with water, and three times with sulphur. In the meantime the strong medicine boils, and bounces about in a brazen kettle set on the fire.']

[Footnote 35: The potent mixture.—Ver. 262. This reminds us of the line of Shakespeare in Macbeth, 'Make the hell-broth thick and slab.']

[Footnote 36: A screech owl.—Ver. 269. 'Strigis.' The 'strix' is supposed to have been the screech owl, and was a favorite bird with the enchanters, who were supposed to have the power of assuming that form. From the description given of the 'striges' in the Sixth Book of the Fasti, it would almost appear that the qualities of the vampyre bat were attributed to them.]

[Footnote 37: Water snake.—Ver. 272. The 'chelydrus' was a venomous water-snake of a powerful and offensive smell. The Delphin Commentator seems to think that a kind of turtle is here meant.]

[Footnote 38: Long-lived stag.—Ver. 273. The stag was said to live four times, and the crow nine times, as long as man.]

[Footnote 39: Opened the throat.—Ver. 285-6. Clarke translates the words 'quod simul ac vidit, stricto Medea recludit Ense senis jugulum,' 'which as soon as Medea saw, she opens the throat of the old gentleman with a drawn sword.']

[Footnote 40: And his hair.—Ver. 288. Medea is thought by some writers not only to have discovered a dye for giving a dark color to grey hair, but to have found out the invigorating properties of the warm bath.]

[Footnote 41: To his nurses.—Ver. 295. These (in Book iii. l. 314.) he calls by the name of Nyseïdes; but in the Fifth Book of the Fasti they are styled Hyades, and are placed in the number of the Constellations. A commentator on Homer, quoting from Pherecydes, calls them 'Dodonides.']

[Footnote 42: Daughter of Æetes.—Ver. 296. The reading in most of the MSS. here is Tetheiâ, or 'Thetide;' but Burmann has replaced it by Æetide, 'the daughter of Æetes.' It has been justly remarked, why should Bacchus apply to Tethys to have the age of the Nymphs, who had nursed him, renewed, when he had just beheld Medea, and not Tethys, do it in favor of Æson?]

[Footnote 43: That her arts.—Ver. 297. 'Neve doli cessent' is translated by Clarke, 'and that her tricks might not cease.']

[Footnote 44: Pelias.—Ver. 298. He was the brother of Æson, and had dethroned him, and usurped his kingdom.]

[Footnote 45: The Iberian sea.—Ver. 324. The Atlantic, or Western Ocean, is thus called from Iberia, the ancient name of Spain; which country, perhaps, was so called from the river Iberus, or Ebro, flowing through it.]

EXPLANATION

The authors who have endeavored to explain the true meaning and origin of the story of the restitution of Æson to youth, are much divided in their opinions concerning it. Some think it refers to the mystery of reviving the decrepit and aged by the transfusion of youthful blood. It is, however, not improbable, that

Medea obtained the reputation of being a sorceress, only because she had been taught by her mother the virtues of various plants: and that she administered a potion to Æson, which furnished him with new spirits and strength.

The daughters of Pelias being desirous to obtain the same favor of Medea for their father, she, to revenge the evils which he had brought upon her husband and his family, may possibly have mixed some venomous herbs in his drink, which immediately killed him.

FABLE III [VII.350-401]

Medea, after having killed Pelias, goes through several countries to Corinth, where, finding that Jason, in her absence, has married the daughter of king Creon, she sets fire to the palace, whereby the princess and her father are consumed. She then murders the two children which she had by Jason, before his face, and takes to flight.

And unless she had mounted into the air with winged dragons, she would not have been exempt from punishment; she flies aloft, over both shady Pelion, the lofty habitation[46] of the son of Phillyra, and over Othrys, and the places noted for the fate of the ancient Cerambus.[47] He, by the aid of Nymphs, being lifted on wings into the air, when the ponderous earth was covered by the sea pouring over it, not being overwhelmed, escaped the flood of Deucalion. On the left side, she leaves the Æolian Pitane,[48] and the image of the long Dragon[49] made out of stone, and the wood of Ida,[50] in which Bacchus hid a stolen bullock beneath the appearance of a fictitious stag; the spot too, where the father of Corythus[51] lies buried beneath a little sand, and the fields which Mæra[52] alarmed by her unusual barking.

The city, too, of Eurypylus,[53] in which the Coan matrons[54] wore horns, at the time when the herd of Hercules[55] departed thence; Phœbean Rhodes[56] also, and the Ialysian Telchines,[57] whose eyes[58] corrupting all things by the very looking upon them, Jupiter utterly hating, thrust beneath the waves of his brother. She passed, too, over the Cartheian walls of ancient Cea,[59] where her father Alcidamas[60] was destined to wonder that a gentle dove could arise from the body of his daughter.

After that, she beholds the lakes of Hyrie,[61] and Cycneian Tempe,[62] which the swan that had suddenly become such, frequented. For there Phyllius, at the request of the boy, had given him birds, and a fierce lion tamed; being ordered, too, to subdue a bull, he had subdued him; and being angry at his despising his love so often, he denied him, when begging the bull as his last reward. The other, indignant, said, "Thou shalt wish that thou hadst given it;" and then leaped from a high rock. All imagined he had fallen; but, transformed into a swan, he hovered in the air on snow-white wings. But his mother, Hyrie, not knowing that he was saved, dissolved in tears, and formed a lake called after her own name.

Adjacent to these places is Pleuron;[63] in which Combe,[64] the daughter of Ophis, escaped the wounds of her sons with trembling wings. After that, she sees the fields of Calaurea,[65] sacred to Latona, conscious of the transformation of their king, together with his wife, into birds. Cyllene is on the right hand, on which Menephron[66] was one day to lie with his mother, after the manner of savage beasts. Far hence she beholds Cephisus,[67] lamenting the fate of his grandson, changed by Apollo into a bloated sea-calf; and the house of Eumelus,[68] lamenting his son in the air.

At length, borne on the wings of her dragons, she reached the Pirenian Ephyre.[69] Here, those of ancient times promulgated that in the early ages mortal bodies were produced from mushrooms springing from rain. But after the new-made bride was consumed, through the Colchian drugs, and both seas beheld the king's house on fire, her wicked sword was bathed in the blood of her sons; and the mother, having thus barbarously revenged herself, fled from the arms of Jason. Being borne hence by her Titanian dragons,[70] she entered the city of Pallas, which saw thee, most righteous Phineus,[71] and thee, aged Periphas,[72] flying together, and the granddaughter of Polypemon[73] resting upon new-formed wings.

[Footnote 46: Lofty habitation.—Ver. 352. The mountains of Thessaly are so called, because Chiron, the son of the Nymph Phillyra, lived there.]

[Footnote 47: Cerambus.—Ver. 353. Antoninus Liberalis, quoting from Nicander, calls him Terambus, and says that he lived at the foot of Mount Pelion; he incurred the resentment of the Nymphs, who changed him into a scarabæus, or winged beetle. Flying to the heights of Parnassus, at the time of the flood of Deucalion, he thereby made his escape. Some writers say that he was changed into a bird.]

[Footnote 48: Pitane.—Ver. 357. This was a town of Ætolia, in Asia Minor, near the mouth of the river Caicus.]

[Footnote 49: The long dragon.—Ver. 358. He alludes, most probably, to the story of the Lesbian changed into a dragon or serpent, which is mentioned in the Eleventh book, line 58.]

[Footnote 50: Wood of Ida.—Ver. 359. This was the grove of Ida, in Phrygia. It is supposed that he refers to the story of Thyoneus, the son of Bacchus, who, having stolen an ox from some Phrygian shepherds, was pursued by them; on which Bacchus, to screen his son, changed the ox into a stag, and invested Thyoneus with the garb of a hunter.]

[Footnote 51: Father of Corythus.—Ver. 361. Paris was the father of Corythus, by Œnone. He was said to have been buried at Cebrena, a little town of Phrygia, near Troy.]

[Footnote 52: Mæra.—Ver. 362. This was the name of the dog of Icarius, the father of Erigone, who discovered the murder of his master by the shepherds of Attica, and was made a Constellation, under the name of the Dog-star. As, however, the flight of Medea was now far distant from Attica, it is more likely that the Poet refers to the transformation of some female, named Mæra, into a dog, whose story has not come down to us; indeed, Lactantius expresses this as his opinion. Burmann thinks that it refers to the transformation of Hecuba, mentioned in the 13th book, line 406; and that 'Mæra' is a corruption for some other name of Hecuba.]

[Footnote 53: Eurypylus.—Ver. 363. He was a former king of the Isle of Cos, in the Ægean Sea, and was much famed for his skill as an augur.]

[Footnote 54: The Coan matrons.—Ver. 363. Lactantius says that the women of Cos, extolling their own beauty as superior to that of Venus, incurred the resentment of that Goddess, and were changed by her into cows. Another version of the story is, that these women, being offended at Hercules for driving the oxen of Ægeon through their island, were very abusive, on which Juno transformed them into cows: to this latter version reference is made in the present passage.]

[Footnote 55: Hercules.—Ver. 364. He besieged and took the chief city of the island, which was also called Cos; and having slain Eurypylus, carried off his daughter Chalciope.]

[Footnote 56: Phœbean Rhodes.—Ver. 365. The island of Rhodes, in the Mediterranean, off the coast of Asia Minor, was sacred to the Sun, and was said never to be deserted by his rays.]

[Footnote 57: Ialysian Telchines.—Ver. 365. Ialysus was one of the three most ancient cities of Rhodes, and was said to have been founded by Ialysus, whose parent was the Sun. The Telchines, or Thelchines, were a race supposed to have migrated thither from Crete. They were persons of great artistic skill, on which account they may, possibly, have obtained the character of being magicians; such was the belief of Strabo.]

[Footnote 58: Whose eyes.—Ver. 366. The evil eye was supposed by the ancients not only to have certain fascinating powers, but to be able to destroy the beauty of any object on which it was turned.]

[Footnote 59: Cea.—Ver. 368. This island, now Zia, is in the Ægean sea, near Eubœa. Carthæa was a city there, the ruins of which are still in existence.]

[Footnote 60: Alcidamas.—Ver. 369. Antoninus Liberalis says, that Alcidamas lived not at Carthæa, but at Iülis, another city in the Isle of Cea.]

[Footnote 61: Lakes of Hyrie.—Ver. 371. Hyrie was the mother of Cycnus; and pining away with grief on the transformation of her son, she was changed into a lake, called by her name.]

[Footnote 62: Cycneian Tempe.—Ver. 371. This was not Thessalian Tempe, but a valley of Teumesia, or Teumesus, a mountain of Bœotia.]

[Footnote 63: Pleuron.—Ver. 382. This was a city of Ætolia, near Mount Curius. It was far distant from Bœotia and Lake Hyrie. Some commentators, therefore, suggest that the reading should be Brauron, a village of Attica, near the confines of Bœotia.]

[Footnote 64: Combe.—Ver. 383. She was the mother of the Curetes of Ætolia, who, perhaps, received that name from Mount Curius. There was another Combe, the daughter of Asopus, who discovered the use of brazen arms, and was called Chalcis, from that circumstance. She was said to have borne a hundred daughters to her husband.]

[Footnote 65: Calaurea.—Ver. 384. This was an island between Crete and the Peloponnesus, in the Saronic gulf, which was sacred to Apollo. Latona resided there, having given Delos to Neptune in exchange for it. Demosthenes died there.]

[Footnote 66: Menephron.—Ver. 386. Hyginus says, that he committed incest both with his mother Blias, and with Cyllene, his daughter.]

[Footnote 67: Cephisus.—Ver. 388. The river Cephisus, in Bœotia, had a daughter, Praxithea. She was the wife of Erectheus, and bore him eight sons, the fate of one of whom is perhaps here referred to.]

[Footnote 68: Eumelus.—Ver. 390. He was the king of Patræ, on the sea-coast of Achaia. Triptolemus visited him with his winged chariot; on which, Antheas, the son of Eumelus, ascended it while his father was sleeping, and falling from it, he was killed. He is, probably, here referred to; and the reading should be 'natum,' and not 'natam.' Some writers, however, suppose that his daughter was changed into a bird.]

[Footnote 69: Pirenian Ephyre.—Ver. 391. Corinth was so called from Ephyre, the daughter of Neptune, who was said to have lived there. Its inhabitants were fabled to have sprung from mushrooms.]

[Footnote 70: Titanian dragons.—Ver. 398. Her dragons are so called, either because, as Pindar says, they had sprung from the blood of the Titans, or because, according to the Greek tradition, the chariot and winged dragons had been sent to Medea by the Sun, one of whose names was Titan.]

[Footnote 71: Phineus.—Ver. 399. Any further particulars of the person here named are unknown. Some commentators suggest 'Phini,' and that some female of the name of Phinis is alluded to, making the adjective 'justissime' of the feminine gender.]

[Footnote 72: Periphas.—Ver. 400. He was a very ancient king of Attica, before the time of Cecrops, and was said to have been changed into an eagle by Jupiter, while his wife was transformed into an osprey.]

[Footnote 73: Polypemon.—Ver. 401. This was a name of the robber Procrustes, who was slain by Theseus. Halcyone, the daughter of his son Scyron, having been guilty of incontinence, was thrown into the sea by her father, on which she was changed into a kingfisher, which bore her name.]

EXPLANATION

Jason being reconciled to the children of Pelias, gave the crown to his son Acastus. Becoming tired of Medea, he married Glauce, or Creüsa, the daughter of Creon, king of Corinth. Medea, hastening to that place, left her two sons in the temple of Juno, and set fire to Creon's palace, where he and his daughter were consumed to ashes, after which she killed her own children. Euripides, in his tragedy of Medea, makes a chorus of Corinthian women say, that the Corinthians themselves committed the murder, and that the Gods sent a plague on the city, as a punishment for the deed. Pausanias also says, that the tomb of Medea's children, whom the Corinthians stoned to death, was still to be seen in his time; and that the Corinthians offered sacrifices there every year, to appease their ghosts, as the oracle had commanded them.

Apollodorus relates this story in a different manner. He says, that Medea sent her rival a crown, dipped in a sort of gum of a combustible nature; and that when Glauce had put it on her head, it began to burn so furiously, that the young princess perished in the greatest misery. Medea afterwards retired to Thebes, where Hercules engaged to give her assistance against Jason, which promise, however, he failed to perform. Going thence to Athens, she married Ægeus.

The story of her winged dragons may, perhaps, be based on the fact, that her ship was called 'the Dragon.' In recounting the particulars of her flight, Ovid makes allusion to several stories by the way, the most of which are entirely unknown to us. With regard to these fictions, it may not be out of place to remark here, as affording a key to many of them, that where a person escaped from any imminent danger, it was published that he had been changed into a bird. If, to avoid pursuit, a person hid himself in a cave, he was said to be transformed into a serpent; and if he burst into tears, from excess of grief, he was reported to have changed into a fountain; while, if a damsel lost herself in a wood, she became a Nymph, or a Dryad. The resemblance of names, also, gave rise to several fictions: thus, Alopis was changed into a fox; Cygnus into a swan; Coronis into a crow; and Cerambus into a horned beetle. As some few of the stories here alluded to by Ovid, refer to historical events, it may be remarked, that the account of the women of Cos being changed into cows, is thought by some to have been founded on the cruel act of the companions of Hercules, who sacrificed some of them to the Gods of the country. The inhabitants of the Isle of Rhodes were said to have been changed into rocks, because they perished in an inundation, which laid a part of that island under water, and particularly the town of Ialysus. The fruitfulness of the daughter of Alcidamas occasioned it to be said, that she was changed into a dove. The rage of Mæra is shown by her transformation into a bitch; and Arne was changed into a daw, because, having sold her country, her avarice was well depicted under the symbol of that bird, which, according to the popular opinion, is fond of money. Phillyra, the mother of the Centaur Chiron, was said to be changed into a linden-tree, probably because she happened to bear the name of that tree, which in the Greek language is called φιλύρα.

FABLE IV [VII.402-468]

Hercules chains the dog Cerberus, the guardian of the gates of the Infernal Regions. Theseus, after his exploits at Corinth, arrives at Athens, where Medea prepares a cup of poison for him. The king, however, recognizing his son, just as he is about to drink, snatches away the cup from him, while Medea flies in her chariot. Ægeus then makes a festival, to celebrate the arrival and preservation of Theseus. In the mean time, Minos, the king of Crete, solicits several princes to assist him in a war against Athens, to revenge the death of his son Androgeus, who had been murdered there.

Ægeus, to be blamed for this deed alone, shelters her; and hospitality is not enough, he also joins her to himself by the ties of marriage. And now was Theseus, his son, arrived, unknown to his father, who, by his valor, had established peace in the Isthmus between the two seas. For his destruction Medea mingles the wolfsbane, which she once brought with her from the shores of Scythia. This, they say, sprang from the teeth of the Echidnean dog. There is a gloomy cave,[74] with a dark entrance, wherein there is a descending path, along which the Tirynthian hero dragged away Cerberus resisting, and turning his eyes sideways from the day and the shining rays of the Sun, in chains formed of adamant; he, filled with furious rage, filled the air with triple barkings at the same moment, and sprinkled the verdant fields with white foam. This, they suppose, grew solid, and, receiving the nourishment of a fruitful and productive soil, acquired the power of being noxious. Because, full of life, it springs up on the hard rock, the rustics call it aconite.[75]

This, by the contrivance of his wife, the father Ægeus himself presented to his son,[76] as though to an enemy. Theseus had received the presented cup with unsuspecting right hand, when his father perceived upon the ivory hilt of his sword the tokens of his race,[77] and struck the guilty draught from his mouth. She escaped death, having raised clouds by her enchantments.

But the father, although he rejoices at his son's being safe, astonished that so great a wickedness can be committed with so narrow an escape from death, heats the altars with fires, and loads the Gods with gifts; and the axes strike the muscular necks of the oxen having their horns bound with wreaths. No day is said ever to have shone upon the people of Erectheus more famous than that—the senators and the common people keep up the festivity; songs, too, they sing, wine inspiring wit. "Thee, greatest Theseus," said they, "Marathon[78] admired for shedding the blood of the Cretan bull; and that the husbandman ploughs Cromyon[79] in safety from the boar, is thy procurement and thy work. By thy means the country of Epidaurus saw the club-bearing son of Vulcan[80] fall; and the banks of the river Cephisus[81] saw the cruel Procrustes fall by thee. Eleusis, sacred to Ceres, beheld the death of Cercyon.[82] Sinnis[83] fell too, who barbarously used his great powers; who was able to bend huge beams, and used to pull pine trees from aloft to the earth, destined to scatter human bodies far and wide. The road to Alcathoë,[84] the Lelegeïan city, is now open in safety, Scyron[85] being laid low in death: and the earth denies a resting-place, the water, too, denies a resting-place to the bones of the robber scattered piecemeal; these, long tossed about, length of time is reported to have hardened into rocks. To these rocks the name of Scyron adheres. If we should reckon up thy glorious deeds, and thy years, thy actions would exceed thy years in number. For thee, bravest hero, we make public vows: in thy honor do we quaff the draughts of wine." The palace rings with the acclamations of the populace, and the prayers of those applauding; and there is no place sorrowing throughout the whole city.

And yet (so surely is the pleasure of no one unalloyed, and some anxiety is ever interposing amid joyous circumstances), Ægeus does not have his joy undisturbed, on receiving back his son. Minos prepares for war; who, though he is strong in soldiers, strong in shipping, is still strongest of all in the resentment of a parent, and, with retributive arms, avenges the death of his son Androgeus. Yet, before the war, he obtains auxiliary forces, and crosses the sea with a swift fleet, in which he is accounted strong. On the one side, he joins Anaphe[86] to himself; and the realms of Astypale; Anaphe by treaty, the realms of Astypale by conquest; on the other side, the low Myconos, and the chalky lands of Cimolus,[87] and the flourishing Cythnos, Scyros, and the level Seriphos;[88] Paros, too, abounding in marble, and the island wherein the treacherous Sithonian[89] betrayed the citadel, on receiving the gold, which, in her covetousness, she had demanded. She was changed into a bird, which even now has a passion for gold, the jackdaw namely, black-footed, and covered with black feathers.

[Footnote 74: A gloomy cave.—Ver. 409. This cavern was called Acherusia. It was situate in the country of the Mariandyni, near the city of Heraclea, in Pontus, and was said to be the entrance of the Infernal Regions. Cerberus was said to have been dragged from Tartarus by Hercules, through this cave, which circumstance was supposed to account for the quantity of aconite, or wolfsbane, that grew there.]

[Footnote 75: Call it aconite.—Ver. 419. From the Greek ακόνη, 'a whetstone.']

[Footnote 76: Presented to his son.—Ver. 420. Medea was anxious to secure the succession to the throne of Athens to her son Medus, and was therefore desirous to remove Theseus out of the way.]

[Footnote 77: Tokens of his race.—Ver. 423. Ægeus, leaving Æthra at Trœzen, in a state of pregnancy, charged her, if she bore a son, to rear him, but to tell no one whose son he was. He placed his own sword and shoes under a large stone, and directed her to send his son to him when he was able to lift the stone, and to take them from under it; and he then returned to Athens, where he married Medea. When Theseus had grown to the proper age, his mother led him to the stone under which his father had deposited his sword and shoes, which he raised with ease, and took them out. It was, probably, by means of this sword that Ægeus recognized his son in the manner mentioned in the text.]

[Footnote 78: Marathon.—Ver. 434. This was a town of Attica, adjoining a plain of the same name, where the Athenians, under the command of Miltiades, overthrew the Persians with immense slaughter.]

The bull which Theseus slew there was presented by Neptune to Minos. Being brought into Attica by Hercules, it laid waste that territory until it was slain by Theseus.]

[Footnote 79: Cromyon.—Ver. 435. This was a village of the Corinthian territory, which was infested by a wild boar of enormous size, that slew both men and animals. It was put to death by Theseus.]

[Footnote 80: Vulcan.—Ver. 437. By Antilia, Vulcan was the father of Periphetes, a robber who infested Epidaurus, in the Peloponnesus. He was so formidable with his club, that he was called Corynetas, from κορύνη, the Greek for 'a club.']

[Footnote 81: Cephisus.—Ver. 438. Procrustes was a robber of such extreme cruelty that he used to stretch out, or lop off, the extremities of his captives, according as they were shorter or longer than his bedstead. He infested the neighborhood of Eleusis, in Attica, which was watered by the Cephisus. He was put to death by Theseus.]

[Footnote 82: Cercyon.—Ver. 439. It was his custom to challenge travellers to wrestle, and to kill them, if they declined the contest, or were beaten in it. Theseus accepted his challenge; and having overcome him, put him to death. Eleusis was especially dedicated to Ceres; there the famous Eleusinian mysteries of that Goddess were held.]

[Footnote 83: Sinnis.—Ver. 440. He was a robber of Attica, to whom reference is made in the Ibis, line 409.]

[Footnote 84: Alcathoë.—Ver. 443. Megara, or Alcathoë, which was founded by Lelex, was almost destroyed by Minos, and was rebuilt by Alcathoüs, the son of Pelops. He, flying from his father, on being accused of the murder of his brother Chrysippus, retired to the city of Megara, where, having slain a lion which was then laying waste that territory, he was held in the highest veneration by the inhabitants.]

[Footnote 85: Scyron.—Ver. 443. This robber haunted the rocks in the neighborhood of Megara, and used to insist on those who became his guests washing his feet. This being done upon the rocks, Scyron used to kick the strangers into the sea while so occupied, where a tortoise lay ready to devour the bodies. Theseus killed him, and threw his body down the same rocks, which derived their name of Saronic, or Scyronic, from this robber.]

[Footnote 86: Anaphe.—Ver. 461. This, and the other islands here named, were near the isle of Crete, and perhaps in those times were subject to the sway of Minos.]

[Footnote 87: Cimolus.—Ver. 463. Pliny the Elder tells us, that this island was famous for producing a clay which seems to have had much the properties of soap. It was of a grayish white color, and was also employed for medicinal purposes.]

[Footnote 88: Seriphos.—Ver. 464. Commentators are at a loss to know why Seriphos should here have the epithet 'plana,' 'level,' inasmuch as it was a very craggy island. It is probably a corrupt reading.]

[Footnote 89: Sithonian.—Ver. 466. This was Arne, whose story is referred to in the Explanation, p. 242 / p. 270.]

EXPLANATION

If it is the fact, as many antiquarians suppose, that much of the Grecian mythology was derived from that of the Egyptians, there can be but little doubt that their system of the Elysian Fields and the Infernal Regions was derived from the Egyptian notions on the future state of man. The story too, of Cerberus is, perhaps, based upon the custom of the Egyptians, who kept dogs to guard the fields or caverns in which they kept their mummies.

It is, however, very possible that the story of Cerberus may have been founded upon a fact, or what was believed to be such. There was a serpent which haunted the cavern of Tænarus, in Laconia, and ravaged the districts adjacent to that promontory. This cave, being generally considered to be one of the avenues to the kingdom of Pluto, the poets thence derived the notion that this serpent was the guardian of its portals. Pausanias observes, that Homer was the first who said that Cerberus was a dog; though, in reality, he was a serpent, whose name in the Greek language signified 'one that devours flesh.' The story that Cerberus, with his foam, poisoned the herbs that grew in Thessaly, and that the aconite and other poisonous plants were ever after common there, is probably based on the simple fact, that those herbs were found in great quantities in that region.

Women, using these herbs in their pretended enchantments, gave ground for the stories of the witches of Thessaly, and of their ability to bring the moon down to the earth by their spells and incantations; which latter notion was probably based on the circumstance, that these women used to invoke the Night and the Moon as witnesses of their magical operations.

FABLE V [VII.469-613]

Minos, having engaged several powers in his interest, and having been refused by others, goes to the island of Ægina, where Æacus reigns, to endeavor to secure an alliance with that prince; but without success. Upon his departure, Cephalus arrives, as ambassador, from Athens, and obtains succors from the king; who gives him an account of the desolation which a pestilence had formerly made in his country, and of the surprising manner in which it had been re-peopled.

But Oliaros,[90] and Didyme, and Tenos,[91] and Andros,[92] and Gyaros,[93] and Peparethos, fruitful in the smooth olive,[94] do not aid the Gnossian ships. Then Minos makes for Œnopia,[95] the kingdom of Æacus, lying to the left. The ancients called it Œnopia, but Æacus himself called it Ægina, from the name of his mother. The multitude rushes forth, and desires greatly to know a man of so great celebrity. Both Telamon,[96] and Peleus, younger than Telamon, and Phocus, the king's third son, go to meet him. Æacus himself, too, though slow through the infirmity of old age, goes forth, and asks him what is the reason of his coming? The ruler of a hundred cities, being put in mind of his fatherly sorrow for his son, sighs, and gives him this answer: "I beg thee to assist arms taken up on account of my son; and be a party in a war of affection. For his shades do I demand satisfaction." To him the grandson of Asopus says, "Thou askest in vain, and for a thing not to be done by my city; for, indeed, there is no land more closely allied to the people of Cecropia. Such are the terms of our compact." Minos goes away in sadness, and says, "This compact of thine will cost thee a dear price;" and he thinks it more expedient to threaten war than to wage it, and to waste his forces there prematurely.

Even yet may the Lyctian[97] fleet be beheld from the Œnopian walls, when an Attic ship, speeding onward with full sail, appears, and enters the friendly harbor, which is carrying Cephalus, and together with him the request of his native country. The youthful sons of Æacus recognize Cephalus, although seen but after a long period, and give their right hands, and lead him into the house of their father. The graceful hero, even still retaining some traces of his former beauty, enters; and, holding a branch of his country's olive, being the elder, he has on his right and left hand the two younger in age, Clytus and Butes, the sons of Pallas.[98] After their first meeting has had words suitable thereto, Cephalus relates the request of the people of Cecrops, and begs assistance, and recounts the treaties and alliances of their forefathers; and he adds, that the subjection of the whole of Achaia is aimed at. After the eloquence of Cephalus has thus promoted the cause entrusted to him, Æacus, leaning with his left hand on the handle of his sceptre, says—

"Ask not for assistance, O Athens, but take it, and consider, beyond doubt, the resources which this island possesses, as thy own, and let all the forces of my kingdom go along with thee. Strength is not wanting. I have soldiers enough both for my defence, and for opposing the enemy. Thanks to the Gods; this is a prosperous time, and one that can excuse no refusal of mine." "Yes, and be it so," says Cephalus:[99] "and I pray that thy power may increase along with thy citizens. Indeed, as I came along just now, I received much pleasure, when a number of youths, so comely and so equal in their ages, came forward to meet me. Yet I miss many from among them, whom I once saw when I was formerly entertained in this city." Æacus heaves a sigh, and thus he says, with mournful voice: "A better fortune will be following a lamentable beginning; I only wish I could relate this to you. I will now tell it you without any order, that I may not be detaining you by any long preamble.[100] They are now lying as bones and ashes, for whom thou art inquiring with tenacious memory. And how great a part were they of my resources that perished! A dreadful pestilence fell upon my people, through the anger of the vengeful Juno, who hated a country named[101] from her rival. While the calamity seemed natural, and the baneful cause of so great destruction was unknown, it was opposed by the resources of medicine. But the havoc exceeded all help, which now lay baffled. At first the heaven encompassed the earth with a thick darkness, and enclosed within its clouds a drowsy heat. And while the Moon was four times filling her orb by joining her horns, and, four times decreasing, was diminishing her full orb, the hot South winds were blowing with their deadly blasts. It is known for a fact that the infection came even into fountains and lakes, and that many thousands of serpents were wandering over the uncultivated fields, and were tainting the rivers with their venom. The violence of this sudden distemper was first discovered by the destruction of dogs, and birds, and sheep, and oxen, and among the wild beasts. The unfortunate ploughman wonders that strong oxen fall down at their work, and lie stretched in the middle of the furrow. And while the wool-bearing flocks utter weakly bleatings, both their wool falls off spontaneously, and their bodies pine away. The horse, once of high mettle, and of great fame on the course, degenerates for the purposes of victory; and, forgetting his ancient honors, he groans at the manger, doomed to perish by an inglorious distemper. The boar remembers not to be angry, nor the hind to trust to her speed, nor the bears to rush upon the powerful herds.

"A faintness seizes all animals; both in the woods, in the fields, and in the roads, loathsome carcases lie strewed. The air is corrupted with the smell of them. I am relating strange events. The dogs, and the ravenous birds, and the hoary wolves, touch them not; falling away, they rot, and, by their exhalations, produce baneful effects, and spread the contagion far and wide. With more dreadful destruction the pestilence reaches the wretched husbandmen, and riots within the walls of the extensive city. At first, the bowels are scorched,[102] and a redness, and the breath drawn with difficulty, is a sign of the latent flame. The tongue, grown rough, swells; and the parched mouth gapes, with its throbbing veins; the noxious air, too, is inhaled by the breathing. The infected cannot endure a bed, or any coverings; but they lay their hardened breasts upon the earth, and their bodies are not made cool by the ground, but the ground is made hot by their bodies. There is no physician at hand; the cruel malady breaks out upon even those who administer remedies; and their own arts become an injury to their owners. The nearer at hand any one is, and the more faithfully he attends on the sick, the sooner does he come in for his share of the fatality. And when the hope of recovery is departed, and they see the end of their malady only in death, they indulge their humors, and there is no concern as to what is to their advantage; for, indeed, nothing is to their advantage. All sense, too, of shame being banished, they lie promiscuously close to the fountains and rivers, and deep wells; and their thirst is not extinguished by drinking, before their life is. Many, overpowered with the disease, are unable to arise thence, and die amid the very water; and yet another even drinks that water. So great, too, is the irksomeness for the wretched creatures of their hated beds, that they leap out, or, if their strength forbids them standing, they roll their bodies upon the ground, and every man flies from his own dwelling; each one's house seems fatal to him: and since the cause of the calamity is unknown, the place that is known is blamed. You might see persons, half dead, wandering about the roads, as long as they were able to stand; others, weeping and lying about on the ground, and rolling their wearied eyes with the dying movement. They stretch, too, their limbs towards the stars of the overhanging heavens, breathing forth their lives here and there, where death has overtaken them.

"What were my feelings then? Were they not such as they ought to be, to hate life, and to desire to be a sharer with my people? On whichever side my eyes were turned, there was the multitude strewed on the earth, just as when rotten apples fall from the moved branches, and acorns from the shaken holm-oak. Thou seest[103] a lofty temple, opposite thee, raised on high with long steps: Jupiter has it as his own. Who did not offer incense at those altars in vain? how often did the husband, while he was uttering words of entreaty for his wife, or the father for his son, end his life at the altars without prevailing? in his hand, too, was part of the frankincense found unconsumed! How often did the bulls, when brought to the temples, while the priest was making his supplications, and pouring the pure wine between their horns, fall without waiting for the wound! While I myself was offering sacrifice to Jupiter, for myself, and my country, and my three sons, the victim sent forth dismal lowings, and suddenly falling down without any blow, stained the knives thrust into it, with its scanty blood; the diseased entrails, too, had lost all marks of truth, and the warnings of the Gods. The baneful malady penetrated to the entrails. I have seen the carcases lying, thrown out before the sacred doors; before the very altars, too, that death might become more odious[104] to the Gods. Some finish their lives with the halter, and by death dispel the apprehension of death, and voluntarily invite approaching fate. The bodies of the dead are not borne out with any funeral rites, according to the custom; for the city gates cannot receive the multitude of the processions. Either unburied they lie upon the ground, or they are laid on the lofty pyres without the usual honors. And now there is no distinction, and they struggle for the piles; and they are burnt on fires that belong to others. They who should weep are wanting; and the souls of sons, and of husbands, of old and of young, wander about unlamented: there is not room sufficient for the tombs, nor trees for the fires."

[Footnote 90: Oliaros.—Ver. 469. This was one of the Cyclades, in the Ægean sea; it was colonized by the Sidonians.]

[Footnote 91: Tenos.—Ver. 469. This island was famous for a temple there, sacred to Neptune.]

[Footnote 92: Andros.—Ver. 469. This was an island in the Ægean Sea, near Eubœa. It received its name from Andros, the son of Anius. The Andrian slave, who gives his name to one of the comedies of Terence, was supposed to be a native of this island.]

[Footnote 93: Gyaros.—Ver. 470. This was a sterile island among the Cyclades; in later times, the Romans made it a penal settlement for their criminals. The mice of this island were said to be able to gnaw iron; perhaps, because they were starved by reason of its unfruitfulness.]

[Footnote 94: Smooth olive.—Ver. 470. Clarke translates 'nitidæ olivæ' 'the neat olive.' 'Nitidus' here means 'smooth and shining.']

[Footnote 95: Œnopia.—Ver. 473. This was the ancient name of the isle of Ægina, in the Saronic Gulf, famous as being the native place of the family of the Æacidæ. It obtained its later name from Ægina, the daughter of Asopus, and the mother of Æacus, whom Jupiter carried thither.]

[Footnote 96: Telamon.—Ver. 476. Telamon, Peleus, and Phocus, were the three sons of Æacus.]

[Footnote 97: Lyctian.—Ver. 490. Lyctus was the name of one of the cities of Crete.]

[Footnote 98: Pallas.—Ver. 500. This was either Pallas the son of Pandion, king of Athens, or of Neleus, the brother of Theseus. This Pallas, together with his sons, was afterwards slain by Theseus.]

[Footnote 99: Cephalus.—Ver. 512. He was the son of Deioneus, or according to some writers, of Mercury and Herse, the daughter of Cecrops.]

[Footnote 100: Long preamble.—Ver. 520. Clarke translates 'neu longâ ambage morer vos,' 'that I may not detain you with a long-winded detail of it.']

[Footnote 101: Country named.—Ver. 524. This was the island of Ægina, so called from the Nymph who was carried thither by Jupiter.]

[Footnote 102: Bowels are scorched.—Ver. 554. Clarke quaintly renders the words 'viscera torrentur primo.' 'first people's bowels are searched;' perhaps, however, the latter word is a misprint for 'scorched.']

[Footnote 103: Thou seest.—Ver. 587. As Æacus says this, he must be supposed to point with his finger towards the temple.]

[Footnote 104: More odious.—Ver. 603. Dead bodies were supposed to be particularly offensive to the Gods.]

EXPLANATION

Minos (most probably the second prince that bore that name), upon his accession to the throne, after the death of his father, Lycastus, made several conquests in the islands adjoining Crete, where he reigned, and, at last, became master of those seas. The strength of his fleet is particularly remarked by Thucydides, Apollodorus, and Diodorus Siculus.

The Feast of the Panathenæa being celebrated at Athens, Minos sent his son Androgeus to it, who joined as a combatant in the games, and was sufficiently skilful to win all the prizes. The glory which he thereby acquired, combined with his polished manners, obtained him the friendship of the sons of Pallas, the brother of Ægeus. This circumstance caused Ægeus to entertain jealous feelings, the more especially as he knew that his nephews were conspiring against him. Being informed that Androgeus was about to take a journey to Thebes, he caused him to be assassinated near Œnoë, a town on the confines of Attica. Apollodorus, indeed, says that he was killed by the Bull of Marathon, which was then making great ravages in Greece; but it is very possible that the Athenians encouraged this belief, with the view of screening their king from the infamy of an action so inhuman and unjust. Diodorus Siculus and Plutarch agree in stating that Ægeus himself caused Androgeus to be murdered.

On hearing the news of his son's death, Minos resolved on revenge. He ordered a strong fleet to be fitted out, and went in person to several courts, to contract alliances, and engage other powers to assist him; and this, with the history of the plague at Ægina, forms the subject of the present narrative.

FABLE VI [VII.614-660]

Jupiter, at the prayer of his son Æacus, transforms the ants that are in the hollow of an old oak into men; these, from the Greek name of those insects, are called Myrmidons.

"Stupefied by so great an outburst of misery, I said, 'O Jupiter! if stories do not falsely say that thou didst come into the embraces of Ægina, the daughter of Asopus, and thou art not ashamed, great Father, to be the parent of myself; either restore my people to me, or else bury me, as well, in the sepulchre.' He gave a signal by lightnings, and by propitious thunders. I accepted the omen, and I said, 'I pray that these may be happy signs of thy intentions: the omen which thou givest me, I accept as a pledge.' By chance there was close by, an oak sacred to Jupiter, of seed from Dodona,[105] but thinly covered with wide-spreading boughs. Here we beheld some ants, the gatherers of corn, in a long train, carrying a heavy burden in their little mouths, and keeping their track in the wrinkled bark. While I was wondering at their numbers, I said, 'Do thou, most gracious Father, give me citizens as many in number, and replenish my empty walls.' The lofty oak trembled, and made a noise in its boughs, moving without a breeze. My limbs quivered, with trembling fear, and my hair stood on an end; yet I gave kisses to the earth and to the oak, nor did I confess that I had any hopes; and yet I did hope, and I cherished my own wishes in my mind. Night came on, and sleep seized my body wearied with anxiety. Before my eyes the same oak seemed to be present, and to bear as many branches, and as many animals in its branches, and to be trembling with a similar motion, and to be scattering the grain-bearing troop on the fields below. These suddenly grew, and seemed greater and greater, and raised themselves from the ground, and stood with their bodies upright; and laid aside their leanness, and the former number of their feet, and their sable hue, and assumed in their limbs the human shape.

"Sleep departs. When now awake, I censured the vision, and complained that there was no help for me from the Gods above. But within my palace there was a great murmur, and I seemed to be hearing the voices of men, to which I had now become unaccustomed. While I was supposing that these, too, were a part of my dream, lo! Telamon came in haste, and, opening the door, said, 'Father, thou wilt see things beyond thy hopes or expectations. Do come out.' I did go out, and I beheld and recognized such men, each in his turn, as I had seemed to behold in the vision of my sleep. They approached, and saluted me as their king. I offered up vows to Jupiter, and divided the city and the lands void of their former tillers, among this new-made people, and I called them Myrmidons,[106] and did not deprive their name of the marks of their origin. Thou hast beheld their persons. Even still do they retain the manners which they formerly had; and they are a thrifty race, patient of toil, tenacious of what they get, and what they get they lay up. These, alike in years and in courage, will attend thee to the war, as soon as the East wind, which brought thee prosperously hither (for the East wind had brought him), shall have changed to the South."

[Footnote 105: From Dodona.—Ver. 623. Dodona was a town of Chaonia, in Epirus, so called from Dodone, the daughter of Jupiter and Europa. Near it was a temple and a wood sacred to Jupiter, which was famous for the number and magnitude of its oaks. Doves were said to give oracular responses there, probably from the circumstance that the female soothsayers of Thessaly were called πελειαδαι. Some writers, however, say that the oaks had the gift of speech, combined with that of prophesying.]

[Footnote 106: Myrmidons.—Ver. 654. From the Greek word μύρμηξ, 'an ant;' according to this version of the story.]

EXPLANATION

This fable, perhaps, has no other foundation than the retreat of the subjects of Æacus into woods and caverns, whence they returned, when the contagion had ceased with which their country had been afflicted, and when he had nearly lost all hopes of seeing them again. It is probable that the old men were carried off by the plague, while the young, who had more strength, resisted its power, which circumstance would fully account for the active habits of the remaining subjects of Æacus. Some writers, however, suppose that the Myrmidons were a barbarous, but industrious people of Thessaly, who usually dwelt in caves, and who were brought thence by Æacus to people his island, which had been made desolate by a pestilence. The similarity of their name to the Greek word μύρμηξ, signifying 'an ant,' most probably gave occasion to the report that Jupiter had changed ants into men.

FABLE VII [VII.661-793]

Cephalus, having resisted the advances of Aurora, who has become enamoured of him while hunting, returns in disguise to his wife, Procris, to try if her affection for him is sincere. She, discovering his suspicions, flies to the woods, and becomes a huntress, with the determination not to see him again. Afterwards, on becoming reconciled to him, she bestows on him a dog and a dart, which Diana had once given her. The dog is turned into stone, while hunting a wild beast, which Themis has sent to ravage the territories of Thebes, after the interpretation of the riddle of the Sphinx, by Œdipus.

In these and other narratives they passed the day. The last part of the day was spent in feasting, and the night in sleep. The golden Sun had now shed his beams, when the East wind was still blowing, and detained the sails about to return. The sons of Pallas repair to Cephalus, who was stricken in years. Cephalus and the sons of Pallas, together with him, come to the king; but a sound sleep still possessed the monarch. Phocus, the son of Æacus, received them at the threshold; for Telamon and his brother were levying men for the war. Phocus conducted the citizens of Cecrops into an inner room, and a handsome apartment. Soon as he had sat down with them, he observed that the grandson of Æolus[107] was holding in his hand a javelin made of an unknown wood, the point of which was of gold.

Having first spoken a few words in promiscuous conversation, he said, "I am fond of the forests, and of the chase of wild beasts; still, from what wood the shaft of the javelin, which thou art holding, is cut, I have been for some time in doubt; certainly, if it were of wild ash, it would be of brown color; if of cornel-wood, there would be knots in it. Whence it comes I am ignorant, but my eyes have not looked upon a weapon used for a javelin, more beautiful than this." One of the Athenian brothers replied, and said, "In it, thou wilt admire its utility, even more than its beauty. Whatever it is aimed at, it strikes; chance does not guide it when thrown, and it flies back stained with blood, no one returning it." Then, indeed, does the Nereian youth[108] inquire into all particulars, why it was given, and whence it came? who was the author of a present of so great value? What he asks, Cephalus tells him; but as to what he is ashamed to tell, and on what condition he received it, he is silent; and, being touched with sorrow for the loss of his wife, he thus speaks, with tears bursting forth: "Son of a Goddess, this weapon (who could have believed it?) makes me weep, and long will make me do so, if the Fates shall grant me long to live. 'Twas this that proved the destruction of me and of my dear wife. Would that I had ever been without this present! Procris was (if perchance the fame of Orithyïa[109] may have more probably reached thy ears) the sister of Orithyïa, the victim of violence. If you should choose to compare the face and the manners of the two, she was the more worthy to be carried off. Her father Erectheus united her to me; love, too, united her to me. I was pronounced happy, and so I was. Not thus did it seem good to the Gods; or even now, perhaps, I should be so. The second month was now passing, after the marriage rites, when the saffron-colored Aurora, dispelling the darkness in the morn, beheld me, as I was planting nets for the horned deer, from the highest summit of the ever-blooming Hymettus,[110] and carried me off against my will. By the permission of the Goddess, let me relate what is true; though she is comely with her rosy face, and though she possesses the confines of light, and possesses the confines of darkness, though she is nourished with the draughts of nectar, still I loved Procris; Procris was ever in my thoughts, Procris was ever on my lips. I alleged the sacred ties of marriage, our late embraces, and our recent union, and the prior engagements of my forsaken bed. The Goddess was provoked, and said, 'Cease thy complaints, ungrateful man; keep thy Procris; but, if my mind is gifted with foresight, thou wilt wish that thou hadst not had her;'" and thus, in anger, she sent me back to her.

"While I was returning, and was revolving the sayings of the Goddess within myself, there began to be apprehensions that my wife had not duly observed the laws of wedlock. Both her beauty and her age bade me be apprehensive of her infidelity; yet her virtue forbade me to believe it. But yet, I had been absent; and besides, she, from whom I was just returning, was an example of such criminality: but we that are in love, apprehend all mishaps. I then endeavored to discover that, by reason of which I must feel anguish, and by bribes to make attempts[111] upon her chaste constancy. Aurora encouraged this apprehension, and changed my shape, as I seemed then to perceive. I entered Athens, the city of Pallas, unknown to any one, and I went into my own house. The house itself was without fault, and gave indications of chastity, and was in concern for the carrying off of its master.

"Having, with difficulty, made my way to the daughter of Erectheus by means of a thousand artifices, soon as I beheld her, I was amazed, and was nearly abandoning my projected trial of her constancy; with difficulty did I restrain myself from telling the truth, with difficulty from giving her the kisses which I ought. She was in sorrow; but yet no one could be more beautiful than she, even in her sadness; and she was consuming with regret for her husband, torn from her. Only think, Phocus, how great was the beauty of her, whom even sorrow did so much become. Why should I tell how often her chaste manners repulsed all my attempts? How often she said, 'I am reserved for but one, wherever he is; for that one do I reserve my joys.' For whom, in his senses, would not that trial of her fidelity have been sufficiently great? Yet I was not content; and I strove to wound myself, while I was promising to give vast sums for but one night, and forced her at last to waver, by increasing the reward. On this I cried out, 'Lo! I, the gallant in disguise, to my sorrow, and lavish in promises, to my misery, am thy real husband; thou treacherous woman! thou art caught, and I the witness.' She said nothing: only, overwhelmed with silent shame, she fled from the house of treachery, together with her wicked husband; and from her resentment against me, abhorring the whole race of men, she used to wander[112] on the mountains, employed in the pursuits of Diana. Then, a more violent flame penetrated to my bones, thus deserted. I begged forgiveness, and owned myself in fault; and that I too might have yielded to a similar fault, on presents being made; if presents so large had been offered. Upon my confessing this, having first revenged her offended modesty, she was restored to me, and passed the pleasant years in harmony with me. She gave me, besides, as though in herself she had given me but a small present, a dog as a gift, which when her own Cynthia had presented to her, she had said, 'He will excel all dogs in running.' She gave her, too, a javelin, which, as thou seest, I am carrying in my hand.

"Dost thou inquire what was the fortune of the other present—hear then. Thou wilt be astonished at the novelty of the wondrous fact. The son of Laius[113] had solved the verses not understood by the wit of others before him; and the mysterious propounder lay precipitated, forgetful of her riddle. But the genial Themis,[114] forsooth, did not leave such things unrevenged. Immediately another plague was sent forth against Aonian Thebes; and many of the peasants fed the savage monster, both by the destruction of their cattle, and their own as well. We, the neighboring youth, came together, and enclosed the extensive fields with toils. With a light bound it leaped over the nets, and passed over the topmost barriers of the toils that were set. The couples were taken off the dogs, from which, as they followed, it fled, and eluded them, no otherwise than as a winged bird. I myself, too, was requested, with eager demands, for my dog Lælaps [Tempest]; that was the name of my wife's present. For some time already had he been struggling to get free from the couples, and strained them with his neck, as they detained him. Scarce was he well let loose; and yet we could not now tell where he was; the warm dust had the prints of his feet, but he himself was snatched from our eyes. A spear does not fly swifter than he did, nor pellets whirled from the twisted sling, nor the light arrow from the Gortynian bow.[115] The top of a hill, standing in the middle, looks down upon the plains below. Thither I mount, and I enjoy the sight of an unusual chase; wherein the wild beast[116] one while seemed to be caught, at another to elude his very bite; and it does not fly in a direct course, and straight onward, but deceives his mouth, as he pursues it, and returns in circles, that its enemy may not have his full career against it. He keeps close to it, and pursues it, a match for him; and though like as if he has caught it, still he fails to catch it, and vainly snaps at the air. I was now turning to the resources of my javelin; while my right hand was poising it, and while I was attempting to insert my fingers in the thongs of it, I turned away my eyes; and again I had directed them, recalled to the same spot, when, most wondrous, I beheld two marble statues in the middle of the plain; you would think the one was flying, the other barking in pursuit. Some God undoubtedly, if any God really did attend to them, desired them both to remain unconquered in this contest of speed."

[Footnote 107: Æolus.—Ver. 672. Apollodorus reckons Deioneus, the parent of Cephalus, among the children of Apollo.]

[Footnote 108: Nereian youth.—Ver. 685. Phocus, who was the son of Æacus, by Psamathe, the daughter of Nereus.]

[Footnote 109: Orithyïa.—Ver. 695. She was the daughter of Erectheus, king of Athens, and was carried off by Boreas, as already stated.]

[Footnote 110: Hymettus.—Ver. 702. This was a mountain of Attica, famous for its honey and its marble.]

[Footnote 111: To make attempts.—Ver. 721. Tzetzes informs us that she was found by her husband in company with a young man named Pteleon, who had made her a present of a golden wreath. Antoninus Liberalis says, that her husband tried her fidelity by offering her a bribe, through the medium of a slave.]

[Footnote 112: Used to wander.—Ver. 746. Some writers say that she fled to Crete, on which, Diana, who was aware of the attachment of Aurora for her husband, made her a present of a javelin, which no person could escape; and gave her the dog Lælaps, which no wild beast could outrun. Such is the version given by Hyginus. But Apollodorus and Antoninus Liberalis say, that she fled to Minos, who, prevailing over her virtue, made her a present of the dog and the javelin. Afterwards, presenting herself before her husband, disguised as a huntress, she gave him proofs of the efficacy of them; and upon his requesting her to give them to him, she exacted, as a condition, what must, apparently, have resulted in a breach of the laws of conjugal fidelity. On his assenting to the proposal, she discovered herself, and afterwards made him the presents which he desired.]

[Footnote 113: The son of Laius.—Ver. 759. Œdipus was the son of Laius, king of Thebes. The Sphinx was a monster, the offspring of Typhon and Echidna, which haunted a mountain near Thebes. Œdipus solved the riddle which it proposed for solution, on which the monster precipitated itself from a rock. It had the face of a woman, the wings of a bird, and the extremities of a lion.]

[Footnote 114: Genial Themis.—Ver. 762. Themis had a very ancient oracle in Bœotia.]

[Footnote 115: Gortynian bow.—Ver. 778. Crete was called Gortynian, from Gortys or Gortyna, one of its cities, which was famous for the skill of its inhabitants in archery.]

[Footnote 116: The wild beast.—Ver. 782. Antoninus Liberalis and Apollodorus say that this was a fox, which was called 'the Teumesian,' from Teumesus, a mountain of Bœotia, and that the Thebans, to appease its voracity, were wont to give it a child to devour every month. Palæphatus says that it was not a wild beast, but a man called Alopis.]

EXPLANATION

There were two princes of the name of Cephalus; one, the son of Mercury and Herse, the daughter of Cecrops; the other, the son of Deïoneus, king of Phocis, and Diomeda, the daughter of Xuthus. The first was carried off by Aurora, and went to live with her in Syria; the second married Procris, the daughter of Erectheus, king of Athens. Though Apollodorus seems, in the first instance, to follow this genealogy, in his third book he confounds the actions of those two princes. Ovid and other writers have spoken only of the son of Deïoneus, who was carried off by Aurora, and having left her, according to them, returned to Procris.

FABLE VIII [VII.794-865]

Procris, jealous of Cephalus, in her turn, goes to the forest, which she supposes to be the scene of his infidelity, to surprise him. Hearing the rustling noise which she makes in the thicket, where she lies concealed, he imagines it is a wild beast, and, hurling the javelin, which she has formerly given to him, he kills her.

Thus far did he speak; and then he was silent. "But," said Phocus, "what fault is there in that javelin?" whereupon he thus informed him of the demerits of the javelin. "Let my joys, Phocus, be the first portion of my sorrowful story. These will I first relate. O son of Æacus, I delight to remember the happy time, during which, for the first years after my marriage, I was completely blessed in my wife, and she was happy in her husband. A mutual kindness and social love possessed us both. Neither would she have preferred the bed of Jupiter before my love; nor was there any woman that could have captivated me, not even if Venus herself had come. Equal flames fired the breasts of us both. The Sun striking the tops of the mountains with his early rays, I was wont generally to go with youthful ardor into the woods, to hunt; but I neither suffered my servants, nor my horses, nor my quick-scented hounds to go with me, nor the knotty nets to attend me; I was safe with my javelin. But when my right hand was satiated with the slaughter of wild beasts, I betook myself to the cool spots and the shade, and the breeze which was breathing forth from the cool valleys. The gentle breeze was sought by me, in the midst of the heat. For the breeze was I awaiting; that was a refreshment after my toils: 'Come, breeze,' I was wont to sing, for I remember it full well, 'and, most grateful, refresh me, and enter my breast; and, as thou art wont, be willing to assuage the heat with which I am parched.' Perhaps I may have added (for so my destiny prompted me) many words of endearment, and I may have been accustomed to say, 'Thou art my great delight; thou dost refresh and cherish me; thou makest me to love the woods and lonely haunts, and thy breath is ever courted by my face.' I was not aware that some one was giving an ear, deceived by these ambiguous words; and thinking the name of the breeze, so often called upon by me, to be that of a Nymph, he believed some Nymph was beloved by me.

"The rash informer of an imaginary crime immediately went to Procris, and with his whispering tongue related what he had heard. Love is a credulous thing. When it was told her, she fell down fainting, with sudden grief; and coming to, after a long time, she declared that she was wretched, and born to a cruel destiny; and she complained about my constancy. Excited by a groundless charge,[117] she dreads that which, indeed, is nothing; and fears a name without a body; and, in her wretchedness, grieves as though about a real rival. Yet she is often in doubt, and, in her extreme wretchedness, hopes she may be deceived, and denies credit to the information; and unless she beholds it herself, will not pass sentence upon the criminality of her husband. The following light of the morning had banished the night, when I sallied forth, and sought the woods; and being victorious in the fields, I said, 'Come, breeze, and relieve my pain;' and suddenly I seemed to hear I know not what groans in the midst of my words; yet I said, 'Come hither, most delightful breeze.' Again, the falling leaves making a gentle noise, I thought it was a wild beast, and I discharged my flying weapon. It was Procris; and receiving the wound in the middle of her breast, she cried out, 'Ah, wretched me!' When the voice of my attached wife was heard, headlong and distracted, I ran towards that voice. I found her dying, and staining her scattered vestments with blood, and drawing her own present (ah, wretched me!) from out of her wound; I lifted up her body, dearer to me than my own, in my guilty arms, and I bound up her cruel wounds with the garments torn from my bosom; and I endeavored to stanch the blood, and besought her that she would not forsake me, thus criminal, by her death. She, wanting strength, and now expiring, forced herself to utter these few words:

"'I suppliantly beseech thee, by the ties of our marriage, and by the Gods above, and my own Gods, and if I have deserved anything well of thee, by that as well, and by the cause of my death, my love even now enduring, while I am perishing, do not allow the Nymph Aura [breeze] to share with thee my marriage ties.' She thus spoke; and then, at last, I perceived the mistake of the name, and informed her of it. But what avails informing her? She sinks; and her little strength flies, together with her blood. And so long as she can look on anything, she gazes on me, and breathes out upon me, on my face,[118] her unhappy life; but she seems to die free from care, and with a more contented look."

In tears, the hero is relating these things to them, as they weep, and, lo! Æacus enters, with his two sons,[119] and his soldiers newly levied; which Cephalus received, furnished with valorous arms.

[Footnote 117: Groundless charge.—Ver. 829. Possibly, Ovid may intend to imply that her jealousy received an additional stimulus from the similarity of the name 'Aura' to that of her former rival, Aurora.]

[Footnote 118: On my face.—Ver. 861. He alludes to the prevalent custom of catching the breath of the dying person in the mouth.]

[Footnote 119: His two sons.—Ver. 864. These were Telamon and Peleus, who had levied these troops.]

EXPLANATION

The love which Cephalus, the son of Deïoneus, bore for the chase, causing him to rise early in the morning for the enjoyment of his sport, was the origin of the story of his love for Aurora. His wife, Procris, as Apollodorus tells us, carried on an amour with Pteleon, and, probably, caused that report to be spread abroad, to divert attention from her own intrigue. Cephalus, suspecting his wife's infidelity, she fled to the court of the second Minos, king of Crete, who fell in love with her. Having, thereby, incurred the resentment of Pasiphaë, who adopted several methods to destroy her rival, and, among others, spread poison in her bed, she left Crete, and returned to Thoricus, the place of her former residence, where she was reconciled to Cephalus, and gave him the celebrated dog and javelin mentioned by Ovid.

The poets tell us, that this dog was made by Vulcan, and presented by him to Jupiter, who gave him to Europa; and that coming to the hands of her son Minos, he presented it to Procris. The wild beast, which ravaged the country, and was pursued by the dog of Procris, and which some writers tell us was a monstrous fox, was probably a pirate or sea robber; and being, perhaps, pursued by some Cretan officer of Minos, who escorted Procris back to her country, on their vessels being shipwrecked near some rocks, it gave occasion to the story that the dog and the monster had been changed into stone. Indeed, Tzetzes says distinctly, that the dog was called Cyon, and the monster, or fox, Alopis; and he also says that Cyon was the captain who brought Procris back from Crete. It being believed that resentment had some share in causing the death of Procris, the court of the Areiopagus condemned Cephalus to perpetual banishment. The island of Cephalenia, which received its name from him, having been given to him by Amphitryon, he retired to it, where his son Celeus afterwards succeeded him.

Henry Thomas Riley (Translator)

Riley was born in June 1816, the only son of Henry Riley of Southwark, an ironmonger.

He was educated at Chatham House, Ramsgate, and at Charterhouse School. University was at Trinity College, Cambridge, but at the end of his first term he moved to Clare College where he was admitted on 17th December 1834 and elected a scholar on 24th January 1835.

He graduated B.A. in 1840.

Riley was called to the bar at the Inner Temple on 23rd November 1847, but early in life he worked for booksellers, editing and translating. These skills were to bring him perhaps the real jewels of his legacy with his translations of Terence, Ovid, Plautus and Lucan during the 1850's.

When the Royal Charter of April 1869 set up the Historical Manuscripts Commission he was engaged as an inspector and tasked with examining the archives of various municipal corporations, the muniments of the colleges at Oxford and Cambridge, and the documents in the registries of various bishops and chapters.

Henry Thomas Riley died at Hainault House, the Crescent, Selhurst, Croydon, on 14th April 1878, aged 61.

www.ingramcontent.com/pod-product-compliance
Lightning Source LLC
LaVergne TN
LVHW041154080426
835511LV00006B/590